IRISH AMERICAN CIVIL WAR SONGS

CONFLICTING WORLDS

New Dimensions of the American Civil War

T. Michael Parrish, Series Editor

IRISH AMERICAN

CIVIL WAR SONGS

Identity, Loyalty, and Nationhood

CATHERINE V. BATESON

LOUISIANA STATE UNIVERSITY PRESS

BATON ROUGE

Published by Louisiana State University Press
lsupress.org

DESIGNER: Michelle A. Neustrom
TYPEFACE: Adobe Caslon Pro

COVER PHOTOGRAPH: Federal prisoners of war from the 69th New York Infantry,
in front of Musical Hall. Library of Congress, Prints and Photographs Division.

LIBRARY OF CONGRESS CATALOGING-IN-PUBLICATION DATA

Names: Bateson, Catherine V., author.
Title: Irish American Civil War songs : identity, loyalty, and nationhood /
  Catherine V. Bateson.
Description: Baton Rouge : Louisiana State University Press, 2022. | Series:
  Conflicting worlds: new dimensions of the American Civil War | Includes
  bibliographical references and index.
Identifiers: LCCN 2022014266 (print) | LCCN 2022014267 (ebook) |
  ISBN 978-0-8071-7793-8 (cloth) | ISBN 978-0-8071-7839-3 (pdf) |
  ISBN 978-0-8071-7838-6 (epub)
Subjects: LCSH: Irish Americans—Music—19th century—History and
  criticism. | United States—History—Civil War, 1861–1865—Music and the
  War. | United States—History—Civil War, 1861–1865—Participation, Irish
  American. | Irish American soldiers—History—19th century.
Classification: LCC ML3554 .B37 2022 (print) | LCC ML3554 (ebook) |
  DDC 781.62/9162073—dc23/eng/20220324
LC record available at https://lccn.loc.gov/2022014266
LC ebook record available at https://lccn.loc.gov/2022014267

For my grandmothers, Audrey Jackson and Betty Bateson

CONTENTS

❖-❖-❖-❖-❖

Photographs follow page 104.

ACKNOWLEDGMENTS

❖⟶❖⟶❖⟶❖⟶❖

Just as Robert E. Lee observed how you could not "have an army without music," it is also true that you cannot do any research project without a wealth of support. I could write a thesis of thanks to all those who have helped and shared in this work along the way. First and foremost, unending gratitude goes to my supervisors at the University of Edinburgh for championing this study from its infancy. Enda Delaney and David Silkenat have provided many helpful suggestions and advice on Irish migrant transnational history and the American Civil War, respectively, and I am forever appreciative of their generous supervision over this project's formative years.

This research would not have been possible without grant support from the United Kingdom's Arts and Humanities Research Council (AHRC) and the Scottish Graduate School for Arts and Humanities (SGSAH), which not only allowed me to pursue a doctorate on this book's topic in the first place but also gave me the ability to travel to archives across the United States, Ireland, and the United Kingdom. Thanks also go to the Royal Historical Society and the Research Society for American Periodicals for further grants that led to transformative research to aid this project (and future ones). I am likewise very grateful to SGSAH for all their training workshops on handling delicate archive material, which proved particularly useful for dealing with wafer-thin songsheets! I am further indebted to the British Library, the Eccles Centre for American Studies, and Boston Athenaeum Library for awarding fellowships that funded trips to study songster and songsheet collections in their incredible special collection holdings. This book first began as an idea while I worked as an intern at the British Library during my master's study at King's College London in 2013, and I am continually thankful for the support from the Americas Collection and Eccles Centre staff past and present for their ongoing interest in my work. My thanks also to special collections archivists at institutions across the United Kingdom, Ireland, and the United States, with particular mention to the wonderful staff at the Boston Athenaeum, New York Public Library, New York University, and the Massachusetts State House. The passionate curators, librarians, and staff at these libraries have helped with primary source discoveries—including finding handwritten song pages in Confederate songsters, conservation notes about Irish American Civil War battle flags, and a wealth of miscellaneous printed ephemera boxes that widened the political and social context of song lyric references. Moreover, gratitude goes to those working behind the screens to maintain countless digital collections that make American Civil War song sources available for transnational researchers. This work owes a great debt to the digital availability of songsheets and interest in the world of wartime song publications.

This study would not have been possible without the enthusiastic support from Louisiana State University Press throughout the process of it becoming the book now in your hands. In particular, I am very grateful for the encouragement, guidance, and editing suggestions made by Rand Dotson, Catherine L. Kadair, Kathryn Kraynik, James Wilson, and the entire LSU Press team, and to the anonymous reviewer who helped me balance the sentiment expressions and music culture atmosphere into which Irish American Civil War songs flourished. A word of eternal thankfulness also goes to my school English teachers, particularly Judith Wakeham, Andrea Mackay, and the late great Rebecca Robertson—the flair for historical storytelling and writing owes as much (if not more) to their classes at Badminton School over a decade ago. Further thanks must go to all those who have offered feedback and comments on aspects of this book at numerous conferences, symposia, and workshops over the past few years. I am especially indebted to the scholarly fervor exhibited on a regular basis by friends and members of the British American Nineteenth Century Historians (BrANCH), the British and European American Studies associations, and to my fellow colleagues and members of the greatest organization in the world—the Scottish Association for the Study of America (SASA). I am also very thankful to guidance from Wendy Ugolini, whose comments helped expand some of the context behind aspects of identity articulations. Thanks also go to Adam Smith and Uta Balbier, whose encouragement led me to expand my lifelong academic interest in Civil War history and historical investigation. A great level of appreciation goes to fellow Irish American scholars, especially David Gleeson and David Sim, for their support and suggestions along the way. Additionally, heartfelt gratitude goes to Damian Shiels and Christian McWhirter, who have responded to every question and have been willing to talk about all aspects of Irish American Civil War history and Civil War song studies. This book owes much to their conversations, source sharing, groundbreaking studies, and the enthusiasm with which Damian and Christian have discussed the subjects in this book.

The journey of this research has led to meeting the most talented and supportive people along the way. I am thankful to the friends and history sisters gained during four years at the University of Edinburgh, alongside my SGSAH buddies. Thanks also to the collective climate of Edinburgh's Modern Irish History group and to my fellow Americanists in the School of History—it was a great joy to be part of such a passionate environment. I am also pleased to have been part of other wonderful departments and American history and American studies communities over the past five years, including at the universities of Gloucestershire, Wolverhampton, Sussex, Durham, and Kent. In addition, I remain a proud cofounder of the War Through Other Stuff Society (WTOS)—the brilliant work of Laura Harrison, Lucie Whitmore, Hanna Smyth, Matilda Grieg, Mark Butterfield, and our organization's followers have generated new questions about approaching the culture of conflict. This book is written with the WTOS ethos in mind.

The encouragement and positive energy of friends and family has helped considerably during the research and writing process, from thesis project to full monograph manuscript. The friendships of Victoria Baker, Hannah Roberts, and Jessica Vas, among others, have been constant since undergraduate history days. The memory of Rachel Jardine is forever cherished. The fellow American Civil War and Irish American transnational history community have always been welcoming, but particular credit goes to my good friends Amanda Bellows, Skye Montgomery, Andrew Phemister, Cathal Smith, David Thomson, and Kevin Waite for their support, being fellow soundingboards, and for countless conference catch-ups, corridor conversations, and championing of new scholarship. A particular big hug of thanks goes to Laura Rattray and Gyorgy Toth, who have never ceased to be encouraging over the last few years and who have a habit of knowing just the right, hopeful things to say at the right moments to aid progress in all things.

No words can fully do justice to the level of friendship Krysten Blackstone has shown, going beyond the call of sisterly support and providing the right tonics on every occasion. She is the best friend anyone can have. Our research trip to old Irish American haunts in New York City added an extra level of understanding of the migrant community in the 1860s thanks to her planning. I also have to thank Krysten for indulging my obvious interest in Michael Corcoran and for all the conversations about soldier experience and modern military history scholarship. I hope I can repay the same amount of support to her own brilliant work and career over the years!

Both Krysten and my wonderful fiancé Tim Galsworthy have gone out of their ways to obtain pieces of Irish American Civil War era and song culture ephemera, bringing the archives quite literally to my desk, and I cannot begin to say what this generosity means to me. An unending amount of thanks goes to Tim for championing this book's transition from a collection of chapters to a much wider research project in hundreds of ways. Aside from being plied with obligatory research/writing cups of tea, Tim has been with me through the last few formative years for this book and has listened to me expand my thoughts on countless walks and trips around Dublin and the United Kingdom (especially around the stunning countryside of East Sussex through COVID-19 lockdowns) while also pursuing his own research. As a scholar of Civil War memory in another era from mine, I have greatly appreciated the different takes Tim has on this work, and his eagerness has massively aided the reediting and writing process above all. I love you very, very much, my fellow nerd.

Finally, a whole world of thanks goes to my family, who encouraged me throughout everything. To my grandfather Barrie Bateson, thank you for listening to tales about the people behind the ballads and for the military knowledge. To my mum and dad, Caroline and David, and my grandfather Peter Jackson, historians all, who ignited the flames of teaching and learning lessons about the past from a young age. I cannot fully express my appreciation for your constant support. Additional thanks go to my parents for being such excellent research companions around Civil War battlefields and for the many memorable trips around the United States (and the rest of the world) that have only furthered my interest in American history. My parents are, indeed, directly responsible for germinating my enduring interest in the Civil War after giving me a children's book about Abraham Lincoln while visiting Washington, DC, in the late 1990s. Photographic proof shows little me reading this rather than looking at the Washington Monument—my head has been buried in exploring Civil War topics ever since! Many, many thanks Mum and Dad. I dedicate this book to your much-missed, inspirational mothers, Audrey Jackson and Betty Bateson. They never heard this history, but their singing spirits have been with me every step of the way while writing it.

IRISH AMERICAN CIVIL WAR SONGS

Introduction

The night before battle, in close-quartered groups, the soldiers of the Irish Brigade gathered to listen to "a dashing young blade" sing ballads. "It was honest Pat Murphy," and it was the last time they heard his dulcet tones. "A hole through his head from rifleman's shot" ended his life the next day. The brigade lamented his loss: "no more in the camp will his laughter be heard, or his voice singing ditties so gaily."[1] Pat's tragic story was not recounted by a fellow soldier writing home to his family. Nor was it published in subsequent wartime memoirs. It was depicted through the medium Murphy himself used. The tale runs through the verses of "Pat Murphy of Meagher's Brigade," written in the middle of the American Civil War. Pat Murphy was a fictional embodiment of Irish-born and descended soldiers who fought for the Union and Confederacy. While the song placed him in the service of the Union Army's Irish Brigade, his imagined tale reflected the real experience of all of those serving in the conflict. The song captured the spirit of front-line singing culture and Irish wartime ballad performance.

"Pat Murphy of Meagher's Brigade" was one of approximately 11,000 songs written during the American Civil War between 1861 and 1865, and one of over 150 ballads composed specifically about the Irish during the conflict. These songs detailed the sentiments, opinions, encounters, and actions of an estimated 200,000 Irish-born, and an even greater number of second-, third-, and subsequent-generation descended men, who fought during the conflict—of which an estimated 180,000 fought for the Union and 20,000 for the Confederacy.[2] They also reflected the expressions of the sizable Irish diaspora in the 1860s. By the Civil War era, over 1.5 million Irish-born immigrants resided in the United States, constituting a little over 5 percent of the nation's population.[3] Although a minority relative to the overall population, their cultural impact and influence was significant. Irish musical tunes and songs shaped many American balladry traditions, laying the foundation of the Civil War's musical soundscape. The songs Pat Murphy sung would have been a mixture of familiar traditional pieces from Ireland, Scotland, Europe, and the United States, alongside newer compositions that sang about the Irish contribution to the war effort.

This book analyzes the songs produced by and about the Irish during the American Civil War and the diaspora's conflict experience as told through lyrical sentiments. Interdisciplinary in its approach, it focuses on the content of song ballads written by, and related to, those of Irish-birth and descent who lived and fought through the conflict. It is not a musicological study; fundamentally, its central investigation examines the lyrics and the songs rather than the music of these songs. While the culture of music-making and the ballad airs these songs were sung to will be discussed, this is first and foremost a study about Irish American Civil War lyrics. It explores their use as sources, their important revelations about contemporary attitudes toward various wartime subjects (including where they differ from historical studies about nineteenth century anti-Irish sentiment in the United States of America), and reveals how song culture provided its own specific expressions of ethnic Irish American community identity in the period.

The Irish involved in the war used balladry to aid their adoption of a collective patriotic character that echoed from the conflict itself through to postbellum memories of service, and to future global hostilities discussions at the time of World War I's outbreak. Indeed, those who had fought in the 1860s had already become American and thus, between 1861 and 1865, sang about their national identity associations with regular occurrence. Assessing song lyrics alongside the discussion of material culture, transnational wartime experiences and views, and identity expressions about loyalty to the United States above all else, demonstrates how the history of the Civil War and its musical productions mattered enormously to the way communities shaped their understanding of America's bloodiest conflict.

The overwhelming majority of songs produced about the Irish wartime experience were specifically about the war itself, making the Irish the most sung about group of any in the period. This is a disproportionate amount in relation to the numbers who served but is evidence of the place Irish-related song subjects had in American culture by the 1860s. Not included in those figures are the countless other songs produced during the antebellum period set to Irish traditional tunes. These had been circulating the country for decades prior to the conflict. A crucial distinction is made in this investigation between songs/ballads—meaning the lyrics/words of compositions—and music/tunes—meaning the melody airs that lyrics were sung to. The reason for separating the two is that they often had very different historical origins. Music tends to be far older and "traditional"; tunes were often composed in the eighteenth or early nineteenth centuries (and earlier in some cases). Songs and lyrics, by comparison, were written at the time of the war itself. The book's main focus is on the latter—the songs and lyrical sentiments—but discussion of musical culture in relation to how music itself is an expression of meaning will also be examined. Several of the songs under analysis contain a myriad of expressions and, therefore, appear throughout the study. Some songs are more relevant and detailed in their lyrical focus, hence their repetition as different sentiments are assessed in relation to the themes and history of Irish American wartime service.

Every song in this study was printed and circulated during the Civil War era, with multiple copies of some examples highlighting the prevalent level of Irish American Civil War song publication in society beyond the diaspora. For example, at least eight different songsheet versions of the ballad "What Irish Boys Can Do" have survived, with various separate productions made in New York and Philadelphia's publishing houses. Most examples in this book come predominately from songsheets, which contained only the lyrics and sometimes (though not always) their musical air. They were also published in specific printed collections of ballads produced during the war, known as songbooks or songsters. Some examples appeared in newspaper publications of ballad verse, and a handful were further printed in music book collections. These latter publications, referred to in this study as scorebooks on account of the inclusion of the musical scores, were collections of sheet music for parlor performances and individual use (either with pianoforte playing, singing, or most likely both). They contained musical notes and the ballad tune's score alongside the lyrics to each verse and chorus. All original spellings and phrases from songs are quoted verbatim.

The songwriters discussed—particularly Harry Macarthy, Charles Graham Halpine, and Tony Pastor—are known figures within American Civil War musicology. The proliferation of their writings and lyrical productions, alongside music hall and theater performances, made them household names in mid-nineteenth-century United States society. Even so, unknown and anonymous authors wrote most of the songs quoted in this study. Soldiers, sailors, professional songwriters, stage performers, journalists, publishers, and home-front civilians all wrote ballad verse and lyrical poetry during the conflict. Tracking these authors is not easy; songsheets often provided more detail about publishers, dedications, and the performance of these songs rather than biographical information about their authorship. Lyricists such as F. Collins, M. Fay, Michael O'Riely, Hugh F. McDermott, and Kate C. M. remain relatively obscure figures.[4] In addition, not all songs were composed by Irish-born writers. Like the ballads themselves, Irish American Civil War songwriters were not exclusively Irish.

Moreover, the majority of songs in this study come from American publishers, but some Irish-produced ballads appear for contrast. These examples also indicate how wartime songs not only spread through the divided nation but also went beyond, and into, a network of transnational dissemination between the United States and Ireland, and vice versa. The older tradition of Celtic and Gaelic oral bardic ballad culture—whereby information and memory was presented through song and speech more so than by writing—is very much evident in these mid-nineteenth-century examples. While arguably ballads sometimes present false memories and specific interpretation of Irish American Civil War experiences, these sentiments are in need of analysis because they provide comparison to other contemporary expressions and historical interpretations. They add to existing understandings about the Irish contribution to, and remembrance of, the conflict.

IRISH AMERICAN CIVIL WAR SONGS AND MUSIC

At the end of the nineteenth century, Alfred M. Williams conveyed the importance of music and songs in his overview of wartime folk ballads. In his brief reference to ethnic groups' contributions to the overall scope of songwriting production, he noted that even thirty years after the conflict, the "immense amount of . . . uncollected and unedited verse" needed historical exploration. Songs produced from 1861 to 1865 had scholarly value and provided another source of opinions to explore. This study advocates that argument. Williams believed ballads illustrated "the sentiments and condition of the people, the waves of popular feeling during the various phases of the war, the impressions of notable incidents and the estimates of prominent personage." These themes are apparent throughout Irish examples. Williams also argued that unlike other Civil War print culture, songs written quickly in the aftermath of events presented particular expressions which were "oftentimes more" revealing about contemporary Union and Confederate society "than the leading articles in the newspapers." They reflected and sung about "how the common people were affected by the tremendous struggle."[5]

Synopsis studies about the main themes and types of Civil War music have contextualized songs, but the specific role and contribution of Irish balladry has been limited within this focus.[6] More recent histories have built on earlier attempts to gather together, analyze, and curate areas of wartime musicology. This process was started by Willard A. Heaps and Porter W. Heaps in *The Singing Sixties*, which presented an overview of the broad themes of general American Civil War songs.[7] E. Lawrence Abel attempted a similar framework in *Singing the New Nation*, which assessed how music and song was part of an effort to create a sense of Confederate nationalism.[8] This scholarship demonstrated that attention has tended to shift to the musical meanings behind ballads since Williams produced his initial Civil War song assessment. Apart from a few works detailing the history of particular songs, studies have looked mostly, and more broadly, at the role ballads and music played.[9] There has been little specific analysis of song lyrics or close reading of lyrical expressions relating to particular groups' ballad outputs.

Alongside the push for exploring lyrical meanings, the study of Civil War ballads has included other observations concerning the intrinsic value of wartime music and song. James H. Stone offered a meaningful attempt to assess the psychological impact music had on soldiers' experiences, showing how both music and song were inherent parts of military lives. They were engrained in the everyday lived experience of the war. The United States was very musically literate in the nineteenth century; the practice and habit of singing and performing around campfires, in intimate settings, in music halls, at military concerts, and in home-front parlors was so commonplace it often went unrecorded in contemporary accounts, letters, reports, or later postbellum memoirs. This lack of reference to everyday song and musical culture exhibits how integral such practices were to society. It was so unremarkable that comment was not necessary. Only specific moments of song singing, lyric writing, and musical performance survive in records, especially in relation to Irish American Civil War songs and music. Stone argued, "it is unnecessary to attempt to list the traditional songs which formed a part of the soldier's musical life, for they may be taken for granted." Traditional songs from older cultures—particularly Irish and Scottish—and contemporary wartime productions "came so naturally to the soldier's lips that he mentions them specifically on too few occasions for their titles to be compiled statistically."[10]

The estimated (and likely underexaggerated) 11,000 songs produced during the Civil War are drawn from records left largely by publishing houses and production copyright offices. The written and printed records of songsheets and songsters are all that remain, but it must be highlighted that music and song were forever adapted and rewritten in the Union and Confederacy. Many more oral and written records of wartime singing culture no longer survive. This has led to ascribing meaning to wartime music and song culture, especially of the soldiers themselves. As Christian McWhirter has stressed, "music was a major rallying point for the soldiers. The songs they heard and performed," as well as wrote, did "everything from boosting morale to shaping political opinions." Enhancing Stone's argument, McWhirter states song and "music became intrinsically linked to the soldiers' Civil War experiences."[11]

This was an argument likewise observed by James A. Davis in his detailed case study about the role of music during Union and Confederate Virginian encampments over the winter of 1863 and 1864. There, the playing and performing of ballads and tunes were an innate part of the "social experience" as "performers and listeners actively participated in bringing music to life and granting it meaning." Although sentiments sometimes differed, there was no sectional difference when it came to the general wartime practice of singing. Union and Confederate camps reflected contemporary American musical practice. "Ultimately the music heard around the firesides and in the tents was neither Northern nor Southern; it spoke to, and of, all soldiers." It was the very habit of song singing and music playing that mattered as it "permeated every Civil War camp and directly impacted every enlisted man, officer, and nearby civilian."[12]

Davis's overall argument that "the importance of music for the troops cannot be overestimated, especially given the vast quantity (of a surprisingly wide variety) that was consumed" echoes a view heard within wartime music culture itself.[13] The editor of the 1862 Confederate songster *War Songs of the South* included an account about song production in the collection's preface that explained why the songbook contained the ballads it did: "Many of the songs have been composed by soldiers in camp, and nearly all have particular reference to some event of the war, some battle, or individual act of heroism . . . They possess all the vitality and force of the testimony of eye-witnesses to a glorious combat, or even of actors in it."[14] This explanatory note supports arguments about the power songs had in shaping lyrical sentiments and culture. All "patriotic songs, songs related to soldiering, songs about home, novelty or humorous songs, and more" connected to front-line experience to one extent or another.[15] Indeed, soldiering songs were one of the main types and lyrical forms of Civil War music.[16]

In addition, McWhirter observed soldiers' wartime song output had immense cultural power in shaping understanding of the conflict. Songs written "for a civilian audience" fostered "cultural connections with the home front" when they were published and performed at music halls. They would also enhance the sense of military community identity and fighting spirit felt by those who served. While some regiments only had marching tunes and pieces without lyrics played by bands, others penned their own regimental ballads with dedicated words to sing. Indeed, "many units had had their own songs. Most of these pieces had some connection with an event from the history of the regiment."[17] Irish units, regiments, and brigades in the Union and Confederacy armies engaged in this cultural production practice to a significant extent.

When it comes to assessing the role and sentiments of Irish American Civil War songs, this subject has only been touched upon briefly in existing scholarship. Davis has contended, "the ethnic identity of particular regiments (especially Irish and German) was celebrated through their musical choices"; "cultural gaps" between Irish, German, and American "music tended to diminish, not amplify" during the war. While true, this forgets the former had shaped much of American musical and song tradition by the 1860s. It is, however, correct to perceive how "music had the ability to bring together disparate individuals into communal groups centered on specific repertories."[18] The argument can go further in relation to the role and meaning behind the significant output of Irish American Civil War songs between 1861 and 1865 and their relationship to articulating wartime sentiments and American identities.

Overall, however, Irish wartime songs have received little analysis. Robert L. Wright's significant collection *Irish Emigrant Ballads and Songs* included many of the songs that appear in this study, but very few have been used as evidence of the diaspora's experience and sentiments during the conflict. In addition, Wright himself merely published the ballads with no discussion of their lyrical sentiments.[19] Studies on the Irish population and traditional music in the United States do not, for instance, discuss the 1860s to any great extent.[20] Likewise, William H. A. Williams skims the surface of Irish American Civil War ballad lyrics in his wide-ranging study on "the image of Ireland and the Irish" in American song from 1800 to the early 1900s. His attention was on popular reproductions and musical hall entertainment instead of soldiers' output.[21] More recently, Dan Milner has explored songs published about the Irish in New York over a 100-year period from 1783 to 1883. Civil War cultural outputs do feature here, although this analysis reinforces prevailing focus on the New York Irish. For the most part, Milner's approach also takes the songs in whole rather than assessing how lyrics correspond to different strands and themes.[22] Yet his work, along with this study, points the way to utilizing lyrical source study within wider Irish American diaspora studies and histories, alongside more traditional primary print culture material.

Michael Saffle's discussion of Irish American music in the period has made an important contribution to determining what made a song and music "Irish" in the Civil War: "There is no uniquely 'Irish' effect, just as there is nothing unmistakably 'Irish' in a great many Irish American dances, marches, and parlor songs. Nevertheless, 'Irishness' often seems to be present in Irish American music. Occasionally this is linked with high spirits, as in jigs and reels."[23] This definition, while useful, mostly pertains to the general musical culture of Irish American productions and assessment of Irish musicians—like the Irish-born bandmaster Patrick Gilmore—not the songwriting element or the lyrical sentiments of songs themselves.[24] William H. A. Williams, by comparison, offered an eight-point methodological framework for what qualified "an 'Irish song.'" It had to have "at least two of the following criteria" relating to the title, reference to Ireland, appearance of Irish or Irish-descended persons (real or fictional), Irish lyrics, Irish performers, Irish melodies, Irish illustrations on songsheets, or "became accepted by Irish Americans as part of their culture."[25]

This study uses Williams's framework, adopting all of its eight points. It also expands this framework to add a ninth factor: it includes all songs written by, about, or related to the Irish experience of the American Civil War.

This includes more general wartime songs where the Irish in the Union (and very occasionally in the Confederacy) were mentioned. By combining Irish American, Civil War, material and musical culture strands, this book will demonstrate how the use and study of Irish American wartime ballads and songs—and some of the music their lyrics were set to—widen exploration of the diaspora's experiences and sentiments regarding fighting and living through the tumultuous 1860s. As Georges-Denis Zimmerman observed in his study of Irish political street ballads, "a song is more than a text and a melody which can be recorded or printed, examined and criticized."[26]

The lack of song sources in Irish American Civil War scholarship complicates some arguments put forward in historiographical studies. One dominant narrative centers on the impression that the Irish were disillusioned by the middle of the war. In reaction to a culmination of factors and events, including high casualty numbers and military draft policies, "native-born Americans stopped celebrating Irish military traditions, fighting abilities, and other examples of ethnic pride." Nonetheless, songs about all of these themes continued to be written, performed and heard throughout American society. Irish immigrant "heritage shaped how [the diaspora] viewed the war and how they responded to it."[27] A fundamental part of that heritage was the culture of articulating views through broadside balladry.

Songs were the primary shapers of reporting and establishing the combative character of Irish-born and descended soldiers. They provide supportive evidence to claims of how established "the fighting reputation of the Irish Brigade in the Army of the Potomac" was in wartime society, along with the repute of other Irish-dominated regiments and martial units. That reputation, and that the diaspora's soldiers continued to enlist and serve throughout the war knowing what their brethren had done before, "should give one . . . pause" for thought before assuming the Irish were co-opted, drafted and forced into service, and came to see the war in a negative light.[28] Extending Robert R. Grimes's thesis about Irish music and song in the antebellum United States, both the war and postbellum periods did not see "a distinctive Irish-American musical culture develop" that drew on "ideas and attitudes which formed this culture" in the years before the conflict.[29] Distinctive Irish American heritage, which included extolling foreign military histories, was *already* in existence since the turn of the nineteenth century.

The absence of song sources in historical studies fails to appreciate how critical these lyrical productions were in articulating attitudes right in the heart of the conflict. This goes beyond simply drawing meaning from the ballad words themselves. It relates to a greater appreciation of how intrinsic song singing and music was to broader culture and to personal lived experiences. Wartime musical and balladry importance can be viewed in arguments about their provision of emotional sustenance for soldiers and, by extension, for home-front communities. Those on both Union and Confederate sides "relied on music for support . . . [and] grasped for whatever music they could find and drew from it the emotional sustenance needed to cope with the trauma that governed their lives" during the war. Music was "important to the emotional stability of the men" and "helped them to relate to those around them and to provide structure to their tumultuous world."[30] Lyrical sentiment's context of greater themes, therefore, must be added to our understanding of the Irish American Civil War experience, specifically, and of Civil War history more broadly.

One critical development helping to shed new archival evidence in Irish American Civil War and transnational studies is the advent of digitization. Combined with "the material turn" in cultural history, this has led to "substantial scholarship on the value of material objects for historical research."[31] It has also allowed for a plethora of Civil War print culture to become available during and after the conflict's sesquicentennial. The digitization of songsheets, books, and musical scores with lyrics and harmony notation has allowed for greater availability of printed ephemera sources. Recent methodological arguments about print culture society, and the power of material culture's role to "help the discipline of history . . . change, develop and ask new questions about the past," can bridge the gap between primary source analysis and use of nontraditional print material. "Material culture," after all, "frames all of our actions and experiences and is constitutive of them." The role of songs and their dissemination was a fundamental aspect of American Union and Confederate "production and consumption of goods . . . power relations, social bonds and networks, gender interactions, identities, cultural affiliations and beliefs."[32] Irish American Civil War examples are part of this framework and need to be analyzed with these themes in mind.

Using this approach to Irish American Civil War material culture, wartime songwriting, production, and singing corresponds with assertions by Benedict Anderson in relation to "the central importance of print-capitalism" to disseminate and establish community identity articulations and expressions. This is a factor often missing in Civil War song and music scholarship. Ballad production supports arguments about how the conflict articulated "the birth of the imagined community of the nation," namely, the nation of Irish America. The "ephemeral popularity" of the print-capitalism marketplace—to which Irish American Civil War songs contributed and expanded—meant that the Irish were able "to think about themselves, and to relate themselves to others, in profoundly new ways" in the 1860s.[33] This book will demonstrate how the diaspora did this through singing their wartime sentiments into American culture.

Nevertheless, there is a question about Civil War material culture and where songsheets and songsters fit within the realm of wartime printed ephemera. Broadside ballad sheets in particular were not meant to survive. Material culture ephemera can be defined as being "things which were created to have a temporary or transient existence, intended by their makers originally to be discarded."[34] Broadsides and songsheets—single pieces of paper like posters and notices pasted on walls—were meant to be short-lived. Songsters, because they were books, are also material ephemera in part, but these were likely to be kept because of their more durable quality. Between these two products were scrapbooks and private songster collections made up of individual songsheets bound together for personal (and often private) use. These books have been preserved and have their own archival survival story to tell.[35] That someone in the war and over the postbellum period collated such collections is in itself a sentiment of importance that illustrates how Irish songs were disseminated and retained even after the conflict had come to an end.

The "societal value" of material culture—meaning "the way objects are valued by the society in which they were made and by subsequent societies" that preserve and study them—provides a framework for interpreting the Civil War through nontraditional military narratives.[36] Irish American Civil War songs are a good source base to begin exploration of Civil War material culture and the ballads' importance in wartime society because they sing of sentiments and values that correspond with and divert from established scholarship. At the same time, the sources quoted in this book say much *in between* the lyrics as well as *within* them about their identity, transmission, place in social culture, and articulations of the diaspora's experience in the middle of the nineteenth century in the United States. As historical scholarship embraces ephemeral aspects of material and cultural studies more fully, particularly in subjects relating to conflict studies, it will ensure the forgotten voices of the Irish in the American Civil War era are returned to the forefront. In turn, this will further enhance interpretations in Irish American Civil War diaspora and transnational studies.

THE AMERICAN CIVIL WAR IN IRISH AMERICAN STUDIES

Scholarship on the Irish migrant diaspora in the United States has tended to subsume the Civil War into broader periods that focus on the history of Irish migration, settlement, and social and political life in the new immigrant homeland. One of the first of such studies, Thomas Brown's *Irish-American Nationalism,* bypassed the conflict altogether and focused on experiences of alienation and poverty between 1870 and 1890—a view that has pervaded impressions about the diaspora over the nineteenth century.[37] In the last thirty years, studies have generated greater exploration of longer Irish migrant history, led by Kerby Miller's *Emigrants and Exiles,* which centers on the idea that Irish migrants to the United States were exiles from Ireland and thought of themselves as exiles throughout their experiences from the 1600s to the 1920s.[38] While this sentiment was certainly present in balladry, it was heard infrequently during the Civil War. Songs spread around the country during the conflict did not project the image of a lamenting Irish man or woman longing for Ireland. Wartime issues and fighting service took lyrical focus.

Miller also placed the Irish who lived through the Civil War within a *post-*Famine generation of settlers, those who arrived and settled in the aftermath of the Great Irish Famine of the 1840s and early 1850s.[39] By comparison, Kevin Kenny's studies of Irish American history placed the Irish of 1860s America *within* the Famine generation umbrella.[40] Following in Brown and Miller's footsteps, Kenny established the assessment of pre-Famine, Famine, and post-Famine generations. The pre-Famine generation encompassed all those who migrated to the newly independent United States in the late eighteenth century and the first half of the nineteenth century. This includes several waves of settlement by multiple generations—grandparents, parents, and children born in Ireland. Within this group were both Protestant and Catholic Irish communities across numerous states, building on mostly Protestant colonial migration from the seventeenth and early eighteenth century. These earlier waves of Irish migrants had subsequently assimilated and became American by the time the main nineteenth-century waves of migrants arrived. Within this pre-Famine generation were also Scots-Irish settlers in the Appalachian and Mid-Atlantic regions. They had likewise integrated into American society by the Civil War era. This generation, encompassing several generations of those born in America, also influenced the earliest dissemination and production of Irish musical culture in the country, as will be discussed in chapter 1. The latter post-Famine generation encompassed those already settled in the United States from the 1870s onward and expanded to account for post–Civil War migrations through the end of the nineteenth century. Like their pre-Famine counterparts, these generations spread across the country, going beyond Chicago and further into the Western states and territories away from the Eastern seaboard.

It is Kenny's Famine generation period that is of most interest to the Irish American Civil War experience. This migrant period, ranging from the 1840s to the early 1870s, and encompassing groups in the thirty-year period during and after the Great Famine's impact on Ireland, included the approximately 1.5 million Irish immigrants and their families who came across the Atlantic and resided in the country by the time of the outbreak of conflict in the 1860s. Using Miller and Kenny's frameworks, the Irish American Civil War generations can thus be situated *between* Famine and post-Famine history. That has had an impact on how those who fought in the Civil War have been considered in relation to wider diaspora experiences in the United States. This influx of Irish immigrants brought about one of the largest extensions of the Catholic Irish diaspora in the United States, and the expansion of migrant communities in urban enclaves, including New York, Boston, Philadelphia, and Chicago, and southward to New Orleans and Atlanta. Many of these were the "firstborn" generation—those born in Ireland but who later lived and fought in their new home country across the Atlantic.

Most of the figures who wrote and appeared in ballad lyrics, led Irish American Union and Confederate Army units, and recorded their wartime incidents in memoirs were born in Ireland and, therefore, were part of the Famine generation. However, songs were written, sung to, and disseminated by members of the broader diaspora who encompassed other generations, especially those of second and third generations born in the United States of America with either one or both Irish-born parents (and Irish grandparents).

These American-born members of the diaspora demonstrated simultaneous connections to their Irish heritage and strong association to their American birthplace. Recovering the experience of the second and subsequent generations of soldiers and their families is harder than those of the firstborn generation, mostly because their collective experiences are less readily studied, even though their individual experiences and memoirs reveal perspective shifts in views, material culture productions, and wartime attitudes that differ at times from their first-generation fellows. Intergenerational study is in itself a developing area of Irish American transnational studies, and this book offers some indirect early evaluation of these generations' histories in the 1860s.[41] What is certainly true is that both firstborn and descended generation standpoints are important to wider Irish American Civil War history, especially in relation to cultural outputs. It is through these generations that the influence and adoption of particular ideals, reasons for fighting, and expressions of national pride—be that Irish or American—can be seen and heard. This has implications for understanding the main sentiments in wartime Irish ballads.

Lyrical expression about Irish loyalty to America is best understood in the context of the fact that many Famine migrants resided in the country for a good decade before the outbreak of the Civil War. The main Irish Famine migrations between 1845 and 1852 brought with it more than one age range of generations. While migrants may have been born in Ireland, grandparents, parents, and children formed their own generational subgroups within the population. For instance, many of the soldiers who fought in the war migrated as children and young adults. Their formative years growing into young adulthood were in the United States—albeit in Irish community settings—with the notions of the nation instilled in the cultural climate in which they lived. Their sentiments chime with those heard by descended generations who were born, lived in, and were already in the country by the time of the war. Thus, this book's focus takes a *multi*generational and *inter*generational approach, taking into account the sentiments and culture of the Irish diaspora from more than one band of migrant experience.

The field of Irish American history, and especially Irish American Civil War studies, needs greater differentiation when it comes to discussing generational differences, particularly in relation to the immigrant, Irish-born population. Acknowledging that this group comprised generations of different ages helps to explain how and why Irish communities sought to maintain and facilitate a cultural heritage identity, as demonstrated within Irish American Civil War songs. In Kenny's work, the diaspora members were an "established community," which implies a sense of Irish American cohesion.[42] This is indicative of a tendency to view the Irish in the nineteenth-century United States as an homogenous collective because "historians more readily ascribe homogeneity to an experience involving millions of people rather than dozens or hundreds. The sheer scale of Irish emigration . . . discourages one from standing back in order to appreciate its complexity and diversity."[43]

Lack of a workable "Irish American" definition has led to additional interpretive difficulties, as evidenced by Christian Samito's assessment of the Civil War's impact on Irish American and African American understandings of nationality and citizenship. He suggests Irish migrants *became* American through their war service and experiences as citizens, mostly in the Union: "many Irish Americans increasingly came to recognize during the Civil War an American identity in addition to an Irish one," caused by undefined "shifts in Irish American identity that took place during the Civil War."[44] Yet, throughout his work Samito refers to the diaspora as "Irish Americans," giving them a separate national identity that implied they had already become Americans before the war. Exploration of the lyrical sentiments heard in Civil War ballads will demonstrate that the Irish articulated a strong association and connection to the ideals of their American homeland by the 1860s and were identifying as being American through balladry productions.

In addition, the Irish-born generations have often been assessed in relation to their specific religious and regional experiences. The sentiments and wartime views discussed in the songs of this study reflect both Roman Catholic and Protestant soldiers and their families. Civil War ballads are relatively silent on religious affiliation and related topics, and while many Irish soldiers were Catholic, no explicit and direct reference to their faith was made in their popular balladry. Moreover, there has been a continued focus on the New York Irish migrant experience. Although problematic as a one-regional historical viewpoint, it is understandable because the city was home to the highest proportion of Irish Catholic immigrants in the nineteenth century. The history of the Irish in New York City also dominates the source and archival evidence. Even during the Civil War, including in the songs throughout this study, the

New York Irish were the foundation of mid-nineteenth-century Irish American society and culture. The New York experience was itself multifaceted, and the city's "Irish community . . . has always been a complex and diverse one."[45]

Despite efforts to move away from a New York Irish-centric study, this book does draw heavily on song dedications and lyrics about the role of New York's Irish soldiering sons and Union Army regiments. References to the city's and state's units, even in songs about the wider Irish Brigade, are inescapable in song productions. This observation is emphasized even more given that of the five main Irish Brigade regiments, three were from New York, reflecting the size of the diaspora in the area. Over the course of the conflict, the Irish Brigade comprised of the 63rd, 69th, and 88th New York infantries, along with the 28th (and briefly 29th) Massachusetts Infantry, and the 116th Pennsylvania Infantry. Its New York units, and the 69th New York in particular, appeared in ballads more than any other group. Despite this, songs and lyrical references about non-Irish Brigade units do appear in this study, including those dominated by Irish soldiers and ethnic connections such as the 9th Massachusetts, 9th Connecticut, and 69th Pennsylvania. Some Confederate units with Irish-born and descended soldiers serving in their ranks appear, too, although their lyrical appearances were considerably limited.

Even with other unit evaluations as points of comparison, the overwhelming focus of this book remains on the lyrics and experiences connected to New York's Irish martial elements. Not only does this follow observations about how intransigent the New York Irish narrative is given the considerable size and dominance of the Irish in New York during this period, but it reveals a wider observation about mid-1800s Irish American culture. In song manifestations, the Irish Brigade stood as representatives for the whole diaspora. Stories of the 69th New York State Militia at the First Battle of Bull Run and their later service as a regiment within the Irish Brigade, along with the Brigade more broadly, captured popular and cultural imagination. This was especially true in ballads. These units had potent symbolic value as representatives for every Irish-born and descended members of military service, even when the vast majority did not serve in specific Irish-dominated regiments, companies, or naval crews. Lyrics about them could be applied to *any* Irish-born and descended soldier's experience. Therefore, while a song on the surface was singing about this one narrative, it could—and sometimes was—interpreted and adapted to other groups of the diaspora's soldiers, sailors, and their families beyond New York's Irish enclave and those directly serving in the Union Army's Irish Brigade.

The majority of Irish American Civil War scholarship has ensured that New York remains central to the history of Irish America even when discussing comparable communities across the country. Susannah Ural, for instance, focused on Irish Catholic Union Army volunteers more broadly, although she also discusses home-front experiences, especially in New York City.[46] Ural's arguments also claim the diaspora's support for the war ended within eighteen months of the start of the conflict; by 1863, high casualty figures, emancipation legislation, and army draft policies led to widespread community disillusionment. Certainly, the Emancipation Proclamation's freeing of enslaved peoples in the Confederate states on 1 January 1863 provoked aggravated reactions from sections of the home front. The introduction of the Union Army draft in the following months exacerbated tensions in some enclaves of the Northern states' diaspora. Both contributed to the growing "animosity between Irish Catholic frustration and disillusionment with the Lincoln administration."[47] A division appears to have developed between views about Irish war service in the first years of conflict (1861–62) and those of the war's latter years (1863–65). The peak of this attitude separation came in 1863, particularly around the summer, two years into the fighting and when wartime policies began to take their toll on home-front attitudes. As will be shown, songs by and about the Irish in Civil War America challenge these arguments about the Irish experience of the conflict and overall views of wartime actions.

By comparison, David Gleeson's work on the Irish who fought and lived in the Confederacy offers a nuanced argument about an admittedly smaller number of inhabitants and fighters. He places the Irish in the Southern states in context with Confederate nationalism and loyalty to the secessionist cause.[48] The overall military contribution by Irish-born and descended soldiers to the Confederate Army was relatively minimal—and this extends to Irish Confederate ballad output. The Confederacy produced significantly fewer songs during the conflict; only a handful of ballads exist in records about the approximately 20,000 Irish-born and subsequent descended soldiers who fought for the seceded Southern states. Confederate songbooks barely refer to Irish fighting service, a stark difference to their prevalence in Union examples. This connected to the diaspora's smaller numbers in the Southern states.

It is also due to a lack of central Irish American Confederate units that the Southern public could focus on, another distinction of the Union's Irish Brigade. Instead of omitting Irish Confederate American Civil War songs completely, they, too, will be analyzed in this study. They provide important comparative examples, even when some sentiments—namely, national identity and fighting service—are less overt than their Union lyrical counterparts. Additionally, many Confederate songs' tunes owed their origins to both traditional Irish and Scottish music and have their own importance beyond just lyrical expressions. These examples, as will be shown in chapter 1, highlight the prevailing influence of Irish music on shaping Confederate ballads.

In the most recent analysis of the Irish in the American Civil War era, there has been some attempt to counter previous historical assessments. Ryan Keating, for instance, has drawn focus away from studies specific to New York and the Irish Brigade with his work on Irish-born and descended soldiers fighting in other Union Army regiments. Taking issue with how "the Irish Brigade has assumed an unmatched place within the memory of Irish service in the Civil War," Keating is right to address the ways "Irish American service was . . . much more complex than is widely realized." The Irish Brigade of the eastern New York, Pennsylvania, and Massachusetts diasporas did not represent the entire wartime experience. Instead, Keating details the service of three other Irish-dominant regiments: the 9th Connecticut, 23rd Illinois, and 17th Wisconsin. Nevertheless, these regiments are still put into context with, and in relation to, the Irish Brigade. This confirms the difficulty of moving away from their dominant wartime narrative. Although Keating argues "there were similarities in experiences across the North," ultimately "there is no simple narrative with which to describe ethnic service in the Civil War."[49]

Such an approach indicates Irish American Civil War studies appear to be heading toward local and individual experiences while acknowledging a homogenized view cannot fit all. In relation to wartime identity developments, this presents the impression of a more fluid identity than the diaspora holding solid (and separate) dual identity loyalties to Ireland and America. Current studies focusing on Irish American Civil War military service and history likewise demonstrate a strong sense of American identity coming to the fore. Damian Shiels has also helped to unlock a rich variety of Irish American Civil War stories through his work on wartime pension files.[50] From the soldiers' perspective, it is possible to see American identity articulations coming to the fore, with implications about how this relates to diaspora home-front narratives.

Recent Irish transnational studies have shifted focus from grand diaspora narratives toward microhistorical accounts, regional histories, and personal stories of Irish American Civil War era experiences while contributing to larger Civil War transnational studies.[51] The rich depth of transnational history brings promising areas of expansion into our understanding of the global Civil War in the United States and abroad while also complicating overall conclusions. Where Irish America Civil War songs fit within this approach regarding the diaspora's cultural expressions creates further issues because while they retained a sense of Irish cultural heritage, they were simultaneously American outputs that sang of an American identity. Far from being muted by the sounds of war, Irish culture's adoption of American tropes and identities were all enhanced by the conflict in the 1860s.

THEMES

The first part of this book focuses on the wider context of Irish American song and music dissemination by the time of the Civil War. Chapter 1 analyses the context of Irish music and song culture influence in the United States up to the 1860s before discussing how Irish songs written during the Civil War itself were circulated through society from the front line to the home front in chapter 2. The remainder of the book then analyzes the sentiments and main themes of Irish American Civil War songs. Chapter 3 explores how songs were used to recount and spread stories of Irish-born and descended soldiers' war service and fighting experience as well as being the means for creating lyrical heroes out of Irish-born officers such as General Michael Corcoran, who originally came from County Sligo, and General Thomas Francis Meagher, originally from County Waterford. These two figures will feature throughout this book. A lyrical biography of their wartime service and notable influence within ballad outputs will be assessed across multiple topics of analysis. Corcoran especially provides an interesting case study as his own personal sentiments and ballad appearances speak to a number of different themes discussed.

Chapter 4 expands on this martial theme in relation to the diaspora's lyrical recollection of Irish foreign fighting service and expression of ethnic cultural heritage within the warring country. Chapter 5 continues an Irish focus by discussing the appearance of Irish nationalist views and sympathies within

American Civil War balladry alongside the publication of contemporary songs supporting Irish Fenian aspirations for Ireland's eventual freedom from British rule. This chapter explores the way these sentiments combined with wartime expressions and views about American support for Irish independence and what song lyrics from the 1860s reveal about the state of Irish nationalism and nationalist identity in the United States.

Throughout this study, a division appears between the lyrical soldiering experience and home-front views of the conflict. Chapter 6 furthers this point by discussing the way contemporary political opinions were sung about in Irish American wartime balladry. Some themes were not discussed to any great extent. For example, topics relating to emancipation and army service drafts are relatively muted, but throughout 1863 and 1864 lyrical expressions relating to midwar policies appeared that have not been explored previously in broader histories. Chapter 7 brings together the underlying theme running throughout this book in relation to identity expressions in Irish American Civil War songs, namely, one that centers articulation on Americanness. This last chapter argues that an apparent American national identity sentiment appears within lyrical articulations and needs to be considered within broader Irish American transnational studies. Although the diaspora retained Irish cultural heritage aspects during the conflict, the songs discussed here were sung with an American spirit. What pervades throughout is an established sense of Irish American identity whereby the focus was placed on the *American* side first and foremost.

Of course, while this book focuses on the Irish American diasporic experience of the Civil War, they were not the only ethnic group to sing of their military service. The Scottish-dominated 79th New York "Highlanders" Regiment adopted the 1861 ballad "War Song for the 79th Regiment" as their martial air before fighting began. It sang of the "Sons of Freedom" who arose to fight the Confederacy. Set to the Scottish tune "Scots Wha Hae Wi' Wallace Bled," its lyrical focus about fighting "for Liberty and right" applied to all Union Army units, including the Irish.[52] By comparison, German Americans penned many of their own ballads during the Civil War, such as "Our German Volunteers" (1862). With over five verses, it details how "German volunteers" of the 8th New York Infantry Regiment "fought well."[53] These Scottish and German examples raised the same dominant sentiments heard in Irish American Civil War songs. They all shared expressions about ethnic communities' commitment to fight, serve, and defend the American Union and the nation's ideals of freedom and liberty against Confederate secession. One exemplary Irish American Civil War verse from 1861 set the scene for the singing sentiments heard throughout this history:

> The war trump has sounded, our rights are in danger;
> Shall the brave sons of Erin be deaf to the call,
> When freedom demands of both native and stranger,
> Their aid, lest the greatest of nations should fall?[54]

1

Irish Music and Songs in Mid-Nineteenth-Century America

Songs produced by and about the Irish American Civil War experience entered a cultural marketplace suffused with Irish tunes and ballads that sang of immigrant and diasporic sentiments and themes. The fundamental reason why there were so many specific Irish-related wartime ballads was because the genre of Irish music and song was already popular in the mid-nineteenth century. Established Irish music and lyric themes had circulated from the earliest waves of seventeenth- and eighteenth-century migrations and were part of a broader foundation developed through the continual use and fusion of many different British, Irish, and European balladry traditions.

The growth of printing and press culture helped create a firm Irish music and song presence in the United States by the 1860s. This was in keeping with E. P. Thompson's assertion that "oral tradition [was] supplemented by growing literacy" that led to "widely circulated printed products," including songsheets and broadsides.[1] Such practice cemented traditional folk lyrics and tunes via the publication of printed materials that spread easily through society. They constructed one common cultural platform onto which musical variations and lyrical adaptations could be built.

Most American Civil War songs and music can thus be traced to ballads and tunes produced decades, sometimes even centuries, before. The musical tunes behind many Irish and more general American wartime song lyrics also presented their own sentiments as tunes carried meanings that emphasized the subject matters being sung about. For example, ballads dedicated to the Union Army's Irish Brigade used airs considered to be fundamentally American—that is tunes written in the United States and not originating from former migrant homelands. This served to strengthen the lyrical message of American loyalty and identity affiliation while revealing the simultaneous Americanization of traditional Irish tunes.

EARLY IRISH MUSIC AND SONG DISSEMINATION

Transnational dissemination of Irish traditional music and song had occurred since the early 1700s, when "ballad sheets and songbooks were being carried as goods from Ireland to America."[2] This was alongside song and music transportation by immigrants and travelers through migrants' oral culture practices. By the early 1800s, it is possible to trace the emergence of surviving music and songs that shaped later cultural outputs heard on Civil War battlefields, in home-front parlors, and in music halls. Printed distribution was reinforced by the publication of one predominantly influential Irish songbook: Thomas Moore's *Irish Melodies.*

Moore, the Dublin-born "poet and historian," produced numerous writings and lyrical works in first half of the nineteenth century that became "the text to Ireland's national music."[3] His works inspired subsequent songwriters and composers of Irish balladry and "established the vogue" of transnational Irish song and music appreciation and adoption.[4] The ballads in *Irish Melodies,* along with accompanying musical settings drawn from older traditional folk airs and Moore's own compositions, "influenced the composure of tunes that came after," especially in the United States.[5] The dissemination and "early importation of Thomas Moore's ballads" effectively established the Irish music and song genre as a transnational cultural product. They had a "major impact on popular song" for much of the nineteenth century.[6]

Moore's first published *Irish Melodies* volume appeared in the United States in 1808, a year after its publication in Ireland. The collection's main printing ran to 1837 with several adaptations totaling ten volumes and 124 songs. These editions were met with "an immediate success on both sides of the Atlantic."[7] In particular, *Irish Melodies* spread rapidly through American society. Like other ballad compositions from Ireland and the British Isles, particularly Scottish works by Robert Burns, pirated editions from multiple publishers only furthered the work's dissemination. "As early as 1815," pocket-sized editions of *Irish Melodies* and its composite songs were spreading "widely among the American public."[8]

This practice of spreading songsters would be repeated in the Civil War as collections were sent from the home front to the front line. Moore's work especially turned Irish song as a genre of music into "a commercial product" that all could purchase, perform, and hear.[9] His ballads, and other fellow traditional songs, were adopted beyond diasporic centers, especially in the years prior to mass Irish migration in the 1840s and 1850s. Consequently, the beginning of the process of Irish songs taking on an American identity began with Moore's works. "The relative ease with which Irish traditional material could be received into Anglo-American song" revealed a process of "Anglicized Irish" music-making, to which Moore made a significant contribution.[10]

Moore's songs made frequent appearances during the Civil War in various guises, demonstrating their establishment across Union and Confederate societies. The periodical *Dwight's Journal of Music* printed regular advertisements for *Irish Melodies* collections, an interesting promotion in an antebellum music journal mostly concerned with European classical and operatic airs and not traditional ethnic folk tunes.[11] Inclusion of advertisements for Moore's work indicate the level of importance they received even among an American cultural elite, supporting claims about their Americanization. One advertisement informed *Dwight's* readers that "no library is complete" without a copy of Moore's work. Although by 1861 there were "many editions of these *Melodies* published in this country," the advertisement hoped this particular "very neat, convenient, and durable form [of] the charming ballads" would appeal to buyers.[12] Moore's songs continued to be disseminated during the war itself, often in individual form as part of Union and Confederate songster collections. Numerous Southern songbooks included several reprints of Moore's most famous songs, particularly "The Last Rose of Summer," "The Harp That Once Through Tara's Halls," and "The Minstrel Boy."

The universal appeal of *Irish Melodies,* along with the connection it had to Irish cultural heritage, was appropriated by the diaspora on specific occasions. At the New York Friendly Sons of St. Patrick's dinner held in honor of Ireland's patron saint in March 1861, the diaspora's *Irish-American* newspaper reported how Moore's "The Minstrel Boy" was sung and played among a number of other pieces before declarations of Irish loyalty were articulated to the Union on the eve of conflict.[13] The following year, the newspaper provided more detail on the musical aspects of the society's 1862 St. Patrick's Day event. It reported how "Gustavus Geary, the celebrated Irish tenor" and "an excellent band of music [played] Irish and American National airs through the evening." This included the appropriate "St. Patrick's Day" ballad, followed by "The Star Spangled Banner," and a repeated rendition of "The Minstrel Boy."[14]

The extent to which *Irish Melodies* dominated pre–Civil War Irish traditional music and song makes it hard to separate Moore's cultural output from other traditional Irish productions circulating throughout mid-nineteenth-century America. The "words and music" of *One Hundred Songs of Ireland*, advertised for sale in early 1861, described its anthology as being "a capital collection, including the best sentimental, patriotic, traditional and humorous Songs and Melodies of 'the land of sweet Erin.'" Claiming to be "the most complete compilation of Irish songs, published in connection with Music, obtainable," this songbook contained "amongst the number . . . several of Moore's best songs."[15] Here, the famed Irish ballad lyricist's work was coming to the fore even in a publication containing non-Moore ballad pieces.

Other Irish song collections produced originally in Ireland, and later distributed in the United States, did not always rely on Moore's name for publicity. One example was the 1843 *Spirit of the Nation*. First collated and printed in Dublin, this was a publication of predominately Irish nationalist works championed by the Young Ireland movement, a group of campaigners for Ireland's independence in the 1840s. Young Irelanders such as future Confederate supporter John Mitchel, future Canadian Federation father Thomas D'Arcy McGee, Irish-Welsh writer Thomas Davis, Charles Gavan Duffy, and Thomas Francis Meagher, among others, were all skilled penmen. In 1842, they began the *Nation* newspaper to champion Irish history, memory and use of the past to shape and fight for an independent country.[16] As one of the group's leading voices before his death in 1845, Davis created most of *Spirit of the Nation*'s ballads alongside other nationalist lyric compositions. Like *Irish Melodies*, songs by Davis and the *Spirit of the Nation* collection soon spread across the Atlantic where they gained popularity. Charles Gavan Duffy claimed that once there, "more copies were sold than any other book published in Ireland." The songster reached nearly one hundred different published editions and, comparable to Moore's *Irish Melodies*, continued to be produced in multiple countries into the first decades of the twentieth century.[17]

One hint about *Spirit of the Nation* appeared in Thomas Francis Meagher's account of the Irish-dominant 69th New York State Militia's journey to Manassas in July 1861. Describing the bivouac one evening, the then-Captain Meagher recalled Irish-born and descended voices "more than once gave way to cheerier ones, rudely musical with all the proverbial spirit of the Irish soldier, his pride, recklessness and love. Snatches of songs—mostly those that Davis wrote for us—broke at times through the subdued buzz and hum of those darkened ranks."[18] Given Meagher's own personal association to Davis as a fellow Young Irelander, he was no doubt remembering his friend's lyrical works and was pleased to hear them once again. His description of an early wartime occurrence of Irish soldiers singing traditional Irish ballads remarked upon Davis's sustained influence and that his Irish nationalist ballads were known among American audiences some eighteen years after their initial publication. Moreover, Meagher's nostalgic comment connected Irish cultural heritage to the formation of a new transnational story as the 69th New York State Militia became subjects of their own 1860s ballads. In this manner, they bore similarity to the ways in which Thomas Davis had once penned songs in the 1840s about the long history of Irish foreign military service.

CULTURAL APPROPRIATION OF IRISH AND SCOTTISH MUSIC AND SONGS

The prevalence of Irish songs and airs appearing in wartime songsters reveals how integral Irish productions were to American musical culture. This was especially true of two traditional ballads not associated with Thomas Moore: "Kathleen Mavourneen" and "The Girl I Left Behind." Englishman Frederick Nicholls Crouch composed the former in the 1830s, a sentimental romantic ballad about an Irish immigrant and his sweetheart, with lyrics written by Crouch's wife, Julia Crawford.[19] Although the song had English roots, it was very much an Irish ballad. As Seán O'Boyle has observed, "traditions so overlap" in the eighteenth and nineteenth centuries "that it is impossible to dogmatize about the origins of some songs, either in words or in music." While a song and ballad tune may not necessarily originate from an Irish-born musician like Moore, the poetry in "Kathleen Mavourneen" is "ultimately Irish in origin."[20] It began to be published in the United States around 1840, within a couple of years of its first appearance in England. Crouch himself migrated in 1849 and discovered his ballads, particularly "Kathleen Mavourneen," had "already been pirated by American publishers" and spread through the country.[21] Full and shortened versions of his production appeared frequently in antebellum Southern music collections, and "Kathleen Mavourneen" could be found in numerous Union and Confederate songsters. Such was its prevalence that Crouch would have likely heard and played the song on a regular basis as trumpeter in the Confederate Army.

By comparison, "The Girl I Left Behind," also published as "The Girl I Left Behind Me," had existed in the traditional folk music repertoire since the late eighteenth century as both a song in its own right and as a tune for other ballads. Variations of the piece were "associated with soldiers for at least two hundred years" in the American colonies and later states.[22] Indeed, "it had been played and sung by American soldiers on the march since the Revolutionary War," having become a "long-established import" that was "widely popular both on stage," in music halls, and as a dance tune. It was adopted into the American lyrical songbook, hence its inclusion in numerous publications by the 1860s.[23]

"The Girl I Left Behind" also became associated with other ethnic military communities. German American Union soldiers sang the tune as they performed their own Civil War anthem "I Goes to Fight Mit Sigel." John F. Poole, who penned several Irish wartime songs, wrote this German-English language composition in 1861. He was no stranger to using traditional Irish airs for his compositions, making good use of recognizable tunes to create new productions. Furthermore, the lyrical focus of "I Goes to Fight Mit Sigel" shared similar ethnic pride with Irish wartime ballads, as it discussed enlistment and proud service under German-born Major General Franz Sigel's command.[24]

Additionally, the tune remained connected to Irish soldiering experience through the regular publication of "Songs of the Camp." Set to the variant air "The Girls We Left Behind Us," the lyrics of "Songs of the Camp" sang of broader military service by Irish and British Isles soldiers. It presented four-nations commentary on general warfare, singing about the "brave hearts from Severn and from Clyde, and from the banks of Shannon," relating to Welsh, Scottish, and Irish military service.[25] The American wartime diplomat Bayard Taylor wrote the song in 1854 under the title "A Crimean Episode," using the older Irish tune as his lyrical foundation. Verses sang about the Crimean War (1853–56), which included Irish soldiers who served in the British Army. The song continued to circulate around the start of the Civil War, with *Dwight's Journal of Music* printing Taylor's original Crimean version in September 1861. This provides an interesting comparison to an amended, shorter adaptation seen in *The Camp-Fire Songster* in 1862. Here, "A Crimean Episode" appeared under its new title "Songs of the Camp."[26] Regardless of the alterations, both versions still retained reference to four nations' martial service and continued to be sung to the established "Girl I Left Behind" air.

Other traditional Irish tunes and ballads were heard throughout American antebellum and Civil War society, though none reached the same constant republishing level as Thomas Moore's songs, "Kathleen Mavourneen" or "The Girl I Left Behind." One folk song, "The Irishman's Shanty" (ca. 1859), made a few appearances in wartime collections, suggesting a level of popularity for the piece that led to publishers printing differing versions. This included one 1861 edition of *Hopkins' New-Orleans 5 Cent Song-Book* that contained "The Irishman's Shanty" in its ballad anthology.[27] A different (but similarly named) Hopkins-published songbook contained another general Irish folk song, "Limerick Races" (ca. 1861).[28] The addition of both songs in these two particular Confederate songsters speaks to the fact that they were published in Louisiana, home to the largest Irish diaspora population in the Southern states and would have appealed to those of Irish descent in the region.[29] Their publication again reveals continual wider circulation of general traditional Irish songs across the country.

This cultural appropriation and knowledge of Irish tunes and ballads is counter to dominant narratives that center on how the Irish—especially Irish Catholics who settled in the United States in the 1840s and 1850s—were on the peripheries of American society. Subject to nativist anti-Irish attacks in the decades before the Civil War, mostly in the Eastern Seaboard's urban areas, these Irish migrants were not broadly accepted socially or politically. Anti-Catholic views held by national and regional political administrations sought to keep the Irish Catholics on society's bottom rungs alongside their working-class counterparts. Lyrical expressions related to this aspect of Irish American lives are discussed in greater detail in chapter 6. What is certain is that a different narrative appears when assessing the cultural adoption and influence of Irish ballad and music dissemination, song singing, and songwriting traditions. By the time of the American Civil War, there was a well-engrained cultural acceptance that did not equate to overall political tolerance in the years preceding the conflict's outbreak.

The success of Irish folk songs, and especially their musical airs, points toward a story of Irish cultural dominance in the United States despite nativist feelings. Their strength challenges arguments about how the Irish in America were socially disconnected. Instead, the nation came to subsume Irish song and music culture into its own, with the knowledge of musical airs originating from across the Atlantic being a case in point. Most songster collections published the lyrics only, thus relying on a high level of public musical literacy that assumed readers and performers would know the relevant singing tune. That so many Irish ballads appeared in multiple songsheet, songster book, and musical score publications in the antebellum and wartime periods shows the impact of Irish singing, songwriting, and printing culture in the United States.

The reasons for this cultural success during a period of political and social suspicion in wider nonmigrant America are multifaceted. On an important cultural level, the Irish diaspora was considerably more engrained than the traditional view of Irish Catholic American nineteenth-century history has led many to believe. Famine-era tunes and song productions were readily subsumed and circulated into wider American adoption of migrant culture notwithstanding simultaneous periods of migrant social and political rejection. Even in areas where Irish-born and descended populations were smaller (relative to the diasporic centers of New York, Massachusetts, and Pennsylvania), Irish music and song was prevalent. The fact that fewer specific songs about Irish-born and descended soldiers in the Confederate Army were written is related to the significantly smaller number of Irish residents in the Confederate states by comparison with their Union brethren. Yet, concurrently, Confederate songsters are full of references to traditional Irish music and songs. This indicates again how widespread and adopted those pieces were beyond the diaspora's central enclaves.

Embracing music and song from Irish and traditional folk roots alone is not enough. Their use was divorced from opinions about migrants' social standing, and cultural acceptance did not equate with immediate tolerance of Catholic Irish Famine migrant settlers. Nonetheless, it *is* in keeping with other contemporary comparable cultural practices. Minstrel shows, for instance, saw an obvious appropriation of the music, storytelling customs, and heritage of enslaved peoples and African Americans. Songwriters latched on to this popular entertainment genre with their own creations of minstrel plays and racially loaded comic and sentimental musical pieces. The roots of this began in the mid-1800s as music hall productions and audiences began to grow and extended beyond the Civil War into the eventual establishment of vaude-ville theater culture in the late nineteenth and early twentieth centuries.[30]

Minstrel and music hall shows as areas of cultural performance and displays of societal views—including Irish songs and skits in wartime productions—are beyond the scope of this book. Some of the songsheet publications dis-cussed came from music hall ballad concerts, but their specific performance on stage did not impact their lyrical message. To some extent, the acceptance of Irish musical culture in these music hall stage settings is analogous with the American public's devouring of minstrelsy in the antebellum and war periods. It also runs parallel to displays of unwillingness to accept Black Americans (free and formerly enslaved) into society as equal members.

Use of cultural tropes from African customs, enslaved cultures, and of migrant traditions from their original mother countries were part of the rep-resentation of "exoticism" in theater and music performances in nineteenth-century United States.[31] Irish music and music hall stage stereotype characters were appropriated in similar fashion to African American caricatures, though often with less overtly offensive portrayals. It should also be noted that many Irish music-hall performers and writers (such as Harry Macarthy discussed below) were like their American counterparts: they played-up their own eth-nic stereotypes on occasion and fully embraced minstrelsy's dehumanizing depictions of enslaved figures in their works. Subsuming the practices of other groups was how the nation appeared to expand culturally even while its prog-ress remained deeply racialized.

Use of immigrant customs to increase culture was a particularly crucial part of Confederate American national song and music formation. Debates over the meaning and creation of a separate Confederate national identity are also beyond the capacity of this study, but the attempted creation of a distinct music and song tradition connects to wider dissemination of ethnic folk tunes and ballads. One argument is that "every component of Confederate culture needed to be original" to establish a stronger separate identity that could not be tied to Union culture. "Any hint of foreign intrusion" was guarded against.[32] This echoes the prefatory commentary of the 1864 Confederate *Southern Sol-dier's Prize Songster.* Its publisher W. F. Wisley argued that over the course of the war: "Many songbooks have been issued to supply the great demand for that species of literature in our Army, but they have been almost exclusively collections of European or Yankee lyrics, ill-ly suited, if not adverse, to the spirit and purposes of our people." In an attempt to aid Confederate cultural nationalism, Wisley stated he was "determined to use his efforts to produce a collection of original songs by Southern writers . . . credible to the heart and mind of our country."[33] Nonetheless, the continual presence of European musical tunes made attempts to create a separate Confederate musical culture unsuccessful. Irish traditional melodies and songs, as well as other tunes and ballads from the British Isles and Europe, were too established across North America by the 1860s. They could not be removed fully, even after Confederate secession.

Despite Wisley's bold introductory claim, *The Southern Soldier's Prize Songster* itself betrayed the reality of non-American original music, although by this point in their cultural dissemination these tunes had American identities that did not necessarily acknowledge their transnational origins. This particular Confederate songster contained several adaptations of "Yankee Doodle," which carried a tune originally from England. The popular Confederate song "God Save the South," set to the English anthemic air "God Save the King/Queen," also appeared.[34] Additionally, the collection contained the ballad "Clocknaben," which had been composed during wartime and that drew on another ethnic musical and cultural tradition from across the Atlantic. According to the explanatory song footnote, the title referred to "the gathering cry of one of the clans of Scotland" as depicted by the author Sir Walter Scott.[35] This was one of many Scottish-related outputs that, like their Irish counterparts, shaped American musical culture from the colonial period.

Comparatively, Scottish ballads and tunes in the United States show that the Irish example was by no means unique. "Two important tributaries, Scots and English, flow into the mainstream of Irish song," influencing productions before they had traveled first to the American colonies and then to the later independent nation.[36] This helped the establishment of a wider Celtic musical culture.[37] Arguably, Scottish music and parlor songs "appear . . . about as often as the Irish" examples in the nineteenth century. Prior to Thomas Moore's collections being sold in the United States—which led to Irish music supplanting that of its Scottish cultural cousins—Scottish ballad sharing was far more commonplace.[38] When *Dwight's Journal of Music* advertised *One Hundred Songs of Scotland,* it suggested: "a musical family cannot afford to be without a good edition of the songs of Scotland . . . In a musical library of half a dozen volumes, these songs should be one of the six."[39]

Similar to Moore's *Irish Melodies* songs, "Kathleen Mavourneen" and "The Girl I Left Behind," several particular Scottish ballad tunes and songs reappear throughout Civil War collections. "Annie Laurie," versions of "Auld Lang Syne," and "Bruce's Address to his Army" (also known as "Scots Wha Hae," or "Scots Wha Hae Wi' Wallace Bled"), were especially popular with soldiers and civilians on either side. The latter two were Robert Burns's compositions. Burns—Scotland's perennially popular national bard—wrote some two decades before Moore and received even greater widespread recognition in the early American republic than his later Irish counterpart. Burns continued to be a firm cultural favorite across the nation long after his death in 1796, and his poetical ballad works were recirculated frequently.[40]

One particular Burns ballad verse had continued resonance in both the Northern and Southern states. "Scots Wha Hae" was the air of several Confederate compositions, revealing a similar knowledge of the tune across American society comparable to contemporary Irish music. The "Texan General's Address to His Army" (1864) was one such song. Its Scottish air was used to recall past conflicts of the Scottish Wars of Independence (1296–1357) and fights between Scottish and English kingdoms in the thirteenth and fourteenth centuries. This served to cement a longer heritage of Celtic fighting inspiration for Confederate listeners.[41] The "Scots Wha Hae" tune was further used as the foundation for "War Song for the 79th Regiment," which was dedicated to the Union Army's 79th New York Infantry.[42] Contemporaries of the Irish 69th New York, the unit was named in honor of their Scottish British Army regimental ancestors and carried the same "Highlanders" moniker. In "War Song for the 79th Regiment," Scottish American soldiers used the traditional Scottish melody to create a song about their wartime service. This was similar to the way Irish American regiments appropriated Irish tunes for their own wartime compositions.

Confederate use of Scottish musical tunes is in keeping with theories of Southern-Celtic identity associations. Cultural connections between Scotland and the American South had existed since the seventeenth century: "the same tunes have been played on both instruments" such as bagpipes and fiddles "in much the same style" from that time in the region.[43] The war appears to have strengthened this aspect of Southern identity.[44] The examples of "Scots Wha Hae" and "Clocknaben" support arguments that "Southern patriotic songs are heavy with the rhetoric of chivalry and feudalism" component themes in Irish and Scottish Celtic ballad and oral myth culture. The American popularity of Burns's and Walter Scott's poetical and literary outputs helped both Union and Confederate images of "knighthood and chivalry" echo in wartime songs set to Scottish tunes.[45]

Like antebellum Irish songs and music, Scottish folk songs became "Anglicized-Scottish" songs—meaning Americanized. They sat alongside Irish pieces through a similar pattern of transnational dissemination and assimilation.[46] Moreover, one particular wartime musical and song production, originating in the South and which combined Scottish, Irish, and American elements, was met with a success that placed it above all other examples discussed previously. "The Irish Jaunting Car" had significant impact on Confederate and Union cultures, and the tune's multilayered Irish, American, and Confederate resonance is in need of closer analysis to understand the impact of "The Bonnie Blue Flag" during the Civil War.

HARRY MACARTHY, "THE IRISH JAUNTING CAR," AND "THE BONNIE BLUE FLAG"

By the time Scots-Irish songwriter and entertainer Harry Macarthy arrived in Louisiana in August 1861 to give a series of his "personation" comic impressionist concerts and music hall shows, the *New Orleans Daily Crescent* described him as the "author of the New National Song of the South."[47] The advertisement was referring to "The Bonnie Blue Flag," first written by Macarthy several months earlier to commemorate Mississippi's secession, where the Bonnie Blue Flag—a blue flag with a single white star that harked back to the 1810 Republic of West Florida—was waved at the state's convention. The lyrics sang of Southern heritage, Confederate nationalism, and each seceded state's desire to defend their independence under the Bonnie Blue banner. After "Dixie," the song became a de facto Confederate anthem and spread through the South within weeks of Macarthy's first publication. The song's overwhelming success was not solely due to its passionate Confederate nationalist rhetoric; the upbeat marching-pace tune Macarthy set the lyrics to had existed in American musical culture since the eighteenth century. The dissemination of this Confederate, and later Union, song owed much to the exemplar transnational tune of "The Irish Jaunting Car."

Versions of "The Irish Jaunting Car" can be found in Irish folk music tradition from the late 1700s, but song adaptations that provided its nineteenth-century melody name appeared in Ireland during the mid-1800s. The American use of "The Jaunting Car" can be traced to a version composed by "the great polynational mimic," Irish music hall performer Valentine Vousden. In the early 1850s he produced "The Irish Jaunting Car" to commemorate when Britain's Queen Victoria "came to Ireland, for her health to drive."[48] Originally published in Dublin, copies of the song were soon sold by London and Manchester publishing houses. As is common for this period, tracking an original "Irish Jaunting Car" version is difficult. Adaptations produced in the British Isles contained different lyrics to those printed on songsheets from Dublin but Vousden's composition, however, is the likely foundation piece upon which subsequent variations evolved on both sides of the Irish Sea and across the Atlantic. Similar themes appear in all the different Irish and British 1850s productions, including the main subject matter of a jaunting car carriage ride through Dublin, Victoria's royal visits to Ireland in 1849 and 1853, and—crucially for subsequent connection to Irish involvement in the United States—reference to the Crimean War.

Aside from being a general traditional Irish folk song, "The Irish Jaunting Car" is part of the genre of Irish songs that sang of the nation's relationship to foreign wars and military service. Many versions from around 1854 included verses that provided broadside balladry information about ongoing events in the Crimean conflict. Lyrics sang about how participating countries "are in want of men, both English and French . . . It's all about the Russian war." They encouraged volunteering to fight the "Russian bear," with the song's protagonist carriage driver stating that he would "drive them [volunteer soldiers] all to Russia in my Irish Jaunting car."[49] Within months of appearing in Ireland and Britain, American publishers produced the same ballad copies. One songsheet printed in New York even provided details of how a Crimean War version of the song was disseminated into American musical culture. It revealed that the lyrics had been "sung to tremendous applause by J. B. Smith, the Celebrated Irish Vocalist" in one of the city's music halls.[50] Music and songsheet advertisements traced antebellum circulation of "The Irish Jaunting Car" as one 1857 example highlighted how the composition could be found within a recently published collection printed in Richmond. It was placed alongside six hundred "different kinds" of new songs that were described as "the grave, the gay, the comic."[51] Despite different adaptations, all these songs used the same tune. They helped establish its firm place in the traditional Irish music lexicon, with "The Irish Jaunting Car" fixed as the melody's name.

Macarthy's use of "The Irish Jaunting Car" tune as the foundation for "The Bonnie Blue Flag" came from a number of influences related to the transnational propagation of traditional Irish music. One important factor was that Macarthy himself was second-generation Scots-Irish, born in England, but familiar with Irish and Scottish music given the broader dissemination of both countries' cultures across the British Isles. After migrating to the United States of America in 1849, the young Macarthy was part of Phineas Taylor (P. T.) Barnum's troop of performers working at Barnum's American Museum on Broadway, New York City, where he honed his music hall songwriting and acting talents. He was therefore in the country in the 1850s at the same time printed copies of "The Irish Jaunting Car" were circulating. Well-known within the Irish diaspora and wider society, the traditional music tune of "The Irish Jaunting Car" provided Macarthy with an established popular platform onto which he crafted his Confederate secession lyrics when he wrote "The Bonnie Blue Flag" in 1861.

There was nothing new in this intertextuality and practice. Many songs in America, especially in the Confederacy, had new lyrics grafted onto older Irish, Scottish, and English tunes. Macarthy's lyrical production is comparable to other contemporary Southern musical favorites with European roots. The poem "Maryland, My Maryland," written at the start of the conflict by James Ryder Randall to emphasize pro-Confederate sentiment in the contentious border state, was set to a medieval German tune, "Lauriger Horatius," by Baltimore sisters Jennie and Hetty Cary not long after the poem's initial publication.[52] "Dixie," written by the Irish descended Daniel Decatur Emmett in 1859, could trace its prewar origins to a combination of minstrel show tunes and enslaved people's music traditions. Macarthy's "Bonnie Blue Flag" was merely adding to this convention of borrowing older ethnic musical styles to form new and long-lasting creations, which, in turn, became American songs in their own right.

The majority of the most popular Union and Confederate Civil War songs were based on tunes that had been present in the United States for decades before the conflict. Songwriters played to this musical knowledge when fixing their lyrical compositions to tunes because the fastest way for a performer and audience to learn and spread song words was to set them to familiar melodies. This was a practice developed from early European hymnal composition productions. The fast circulation of "The Bonnie Blue Flag" in the spring and summer of 1861 can be explained because a musically literate American population knew its "Irish Jaunting Car" tune. One 1863 advertisement for an adaptation of "The Bonnie Blue Flag" noted its "air . . . is one familiar and original with our people and certainly enchanting."[53] Other Confederate versions influenced by "The Bonnie Blue Flag" appeared throughout the conflict, furthering the dissemination and familiarity of "The Irish Jaunting Car" and "The Bonnie Blue Flag" melodies.

Macarthy's habit of adding new lyrics to his original version as more Southern states seceded also inspired writers to pen their own extra verses. "An Addition to the Bonnie Blue Flag," published in a London-produced Confederate songster just after the war in 1866, provided two verses that stressed Kentucky's pro-Southern support. They were written as "a tribute to true Kentuckians" loyal to the Confederacy and provided supplementary lyrics that could be added to performances of Macarthy's song.[54] Furthermore, one border state resident produced "additional words to 'The Bonnie Blue Flag' as sung by Missourians during the war." Lyrics again stressed Confederate sentiments, though it is unknown if these particular handwritten verses were ever printed and sold.[55] Nevertheless, such extra stanzas demonstrate how widespread Macarthy's song and its original tune were. His song provided inspiration for other songwriting adaptations.

Noticeably in original and subsequent versions, "The Bonnie Blue Flag" abandoned its Irish associations as it spread around the Confederacy, a transition cemented by Macarthy's arrival in New Orleans in the late summer of 1861. As well as Macarthy's own performance of the song on a regular basis to enthusiastic crowds of Confederate soldiers in the city's music halls and on open air stage displays, distribution of "The Bonnie Blue Flag" throughout the South was aided by the commercial exploits of Armand Edward Blackmar, owner of the Confederacy's most successful music and song publishing company.[56] Blackmar produced multiple songsheet copies, decorative song and music scorebooks with illustrated Bonnie Blue Flag covers, and songster collections, including one first produced in 1862 that was named after Macarthy's Confederate anthem. Through Blackmar's printing house dissemination, this Scots-Irish lyricist became a Confederate writer. References to his ethnicity and that of the original tune were removed. On multiple *Bonnie Blue*

Flag scorebooks containing pianoforte music notations, performers were told to play and sing the song "with spirit," making no reference to the original "Irish Jaunting Car" air.[57]

Likewise, songsheet versions provided no tune description even when Northern publishers reproduced the Confederate song.[58] Knowledge of the air was presumed. In wartime copies printed in Britain, "The Bonnie Blue Flag" was described purely as "a Southern Patriotic Song."[59] When Cheltenham-based "music sellers to the Queen" Edward Hale & Co. printed their musical score edition in 1864, the title cover described it as a "National Confederate Song" with no other associations, even though its Irish melody would have been familiar in Britain.[60] Pianoforte "variations" further adapted the tune, merging it with other musical arrangements to form one composition. These publications certainly helped establish "The Bonnie Blue Flag" in American musical culture. It did so at the cost of dismissing its older traditional Irish musical extraction.[61] By the time Blackmar printed his third edition of *The Bonnie Blue Flag Song Book* in 1863, the song was listed as having "words and music by Harry Macarthy," establishing the lyricist as the tune's composer.[62] Although far from the truth, this example was another indicator of "The Irish Jaunting Car" air adopting a Confederate American identity during the war.

This musical characteristic was strengthened by other ballads produced later in the conflict that also used Macarthy's "Bonnie Blue Flag" melody. The famous Confederate ballad "The Homespun Dress," sometimes published as "The Southern Girl's Song," kept the separate, distinctive chorus refrain of "The Bonnie Blue Flag." It adapted the original's "Hurrah! Hurrah! For Southern rights Hurrah! Hurrah for the Bonnie Blue Flag that bears a single star!" to "Hurrah! Hurrah! For the sunny South so dear; three cheers for the homespun dress the Southern ladies wear!"[63] It too reflected the same sentiments of Southern national pride, focusing particularly on the home-front sacrifice women made in support of the Confederate cause—in this case Southern women making homespun material clothing. "The Homespun Dress" first appeared in 1862, published once again by Armand Blackmar as he extended his New Orleans–based printing house's association with dissem-inating pieces set to the traditional Irish tune. There was a subtle difference in this version's use of the melody, however. "The Homespun Dress" was sung at a more lamenting pace instead of one with upbeat, martial connotations.

This tonal change added to the sense of female secessionist sacrificial gravitas conveyed by the lyrics.

Other wartime songs using "The Irish Jaunting Car" and "The Bonnie Blue Flag" air made similar musical alterations to suit more soporific tones. This included "Mother on the Brain," a somber sentimental ballad about a soldier's dying thoughts.[64] Regardless of claims that "The Homespun Dress" was prevalent in the Confederacy, and arguments that the song tune's use and reappropriation "proved extremely popular with both civilians and soldiers," it never reached the same widespread dissemination as Macarthy's "Bonnie Blue Flag."[65] The ballad is missing in numerous Confederate songster publications, limiting the notion that it was reproduced throughout the South with the same regularity as its song forefather.[66] Likewise, when Macarthy's reappropriated his own song at the end of the Civil War to compose the unifying ballad "Our Country's Flag," he failed to meet the equivalent high level of impact of his earlier wartime anthem.[67] In these examples, lyrical subject matter influenced song popularity more so than did familiarity with the established musical tune for "The Irish Jaunting Car."

At the same time as these Confederate versions, "The Bonnie Blue Flag" developed a comparable Union American identity, which further removed the tune from its traditional Irish roots. In keeping with a common habit of both warring sides adopting and adapting their respective songs to create opposing lyrical replies parodies, Northern writers and publishers produced their own versions with different words. The first of these appeared within months of Macarthy's song spreading through the seceded states. These Union productions again carried "The Irish Jaunting Car" tune, though none stated this musical heritage. One frequently reproduced Union response was "A Reply to the Bonnie Blue Flag" written by a Mrs. C. Sterett in 1862. On the ballad's first songsheet copy, a detailed explanatory note from the *Despatch* newspaper was added to explain the context for a Union lyrical reply to the Confederate version. It described Macarthy's "Bonnie Blue Flag" as a "song published and set to music in New Orleans, and sung and played in every section of Secessia." Yet, while "the music is delightful," it was "well worthy of a better theme." In other words pro-Union lyrics were needed to suit "The Irish Jaunting Car" tune. Sterett's version provided an answer to this.[68]

The story behind this particular Union "Bonnie Blue Flag" dissemination echoes the phrasing of an advertisement in *Dwight's Journal of Music* from the

February issue of the same year that was promoting the sale of "The Bonnie Red, White and Blue" (1862), another Union version of Macarthy's song. The advertisement described "the melody . . . of 'The Bonnie Blue Flag' [is] very popular at the South" but that "it too good to be any longer coupled with a se-cesh [secessionist] song." This particular Union version gave "The Irish Jaunt-ing Car" air a "new and reformed life," and the advertisement hoped it "should be a favorite" in Northern musical culture.[69] Additional Union responses fol-lowed suit throughout 1862, including "Glorious Old Flag—A Reply to the Bonnie Blue Flag," and "The Flag with the Thirty Four Stars." The latter kept the tune but turned the lyrical subject matter into one of American unity not sectional fighting.[70]

The most successful Union response was "The Bonnie Flag with the Stars and Stripes," "written in answer to 'The Bonnie Blue Flag'" by a Colonel J. L. Geddes of the 8th Iowa Infantry. Numerous scorebook copies of this song were printed between 1862 and 1863, indicating how popular it was throughout Northern society. Commemorative covers were issued to mark the thirtieth, fiftieth, one hundredth, and "50th Thousand Edition" of the ballad's publica-tion.[71] All of these versions made no mention of the tune's Irish origins or of Macarthy's initial "Bonnie Blue Flag" authorship. They were fundamentally American in their musical identity. They also helped transform the traditional Irish air into an American melody. In other words, "The Irish Jaunting Car" tune had become American through repeated cultural usage as the foundation to a plethora of Union and Confederate ballads.

On the other hand, the Irish American diaspora did not abandon the original harmony altogether. One of the first Northern replies to Macarthy's song was produced during Union Army mobilization in June 1861. Dedicated to the 13th Massachusetts Volunteer Infantry Regiment, "Hurrah for the Ban-ner of Red, White and Blue," written by Thomas M. Brown, was advertised for sale by *Dwight's Journal of Music*. Like the majority of the state's Union Army regiments, the 13th Massachusetts contained many Irish-born and descended soldiers who would have recognized "The Irish Jaunting Car" tune. Even the advertisement alluded to the melody's connection to the diaspora's cultural heritage: it was "a song for the Irish volunteers of the Union, adapted to a well-known Irish air," though it did not name this air explicitly.[72] Despite this musical recall, the song's subject matter and its title was one centered more on the American Union than the Irish volunteering service. It indicated Irish articulations about identity transition that emphasized American loyalty and nationality through song.

Brown's use of "The Irish Jaunting Car" for his ballad about Irish volunteers in the Union Army harked back to another musical tradition from Ireland familiar within the diaspora. Numerous "Irish Volunteer"–entitled ballads circulated around Ireland from the eighteenth century onward, inspired by late 1700s Irish Patriot political and nationalist groups.[73] These songs reflected Irish martial and political themes carried to the United States through cultural emigration. This included "The Irish Volunteers of 1860," a contemporary song about Irish soldiers in the British Army, local Irish county issues, and Irish national independence sentiment.[74] Though unstated on broadside editions, its verse structure fits "The Irish Jaunting Car" tune. It provides another pre–American Civil War example of the air's dissemination and link to Irish soldiering. Macarthy used it for "The Bonnie Blue Flag" because he either knew "The Irish Jaunting Car" melody or because he knew the air from Irish volunteering songs, or most likely, he knew both. "The Irish Jaunting Car" and volunteering ballads' music avenues are long enough for the origin to be lost, yet both remained connected to Irish cultural heritage and oral folk music traditions in mid-nineteenth century America.[75] The Civil War understandably added to this "Irish Volunteer" genre.

Whether inspired by Brown's local Massachusetts version or from older Irish ballads, several songs appeared in the conflict set to tunes associated with "The Irish Jaunting Car" and the variations of "Irish Volunteer." One such example, by a Michael O'Riely, sang of Irish loyalty to the Union cause and Irish volunteerism in the Union Army's Irish Brigade.[76] Music hall impresario and songwriter Tony Pastor likewise contributed to this genre with "The Irish Volunteer No. 3" (1862), which focused its lyrical attention on Irish-born General Michael Corcoran and mimicked other volunteer songs in its theme and tune.[77] Arthur McFadden's 1861 song "Col. Owens' Gallant Irish Volunteers" about the Irish-dominated 69th Pennsylvania Volunteer Regiment was set to "The Irish Volunteer" and thus, by extension, "The Irish Jaunting Car" melody.[78] These ballad examples reveal further blurring of Irish American identity focus. Here again were songs about Irish wartime service that focused on American loyalty and were set to an old Irish tune that had become part of an American musical tradition.

The wider Union military community appropriated "Irish Volunteer" examples as evidenced by *The Camp-Fire Songster*'s inclusion of "The New York Volunteer" within its collection. This ballad sang of New York's strong spirit of volunteerism, which also involved the Irish-dominated 69th New York. The unit's soldiers received particular mention in the song's penultimate verse about its reorganization into the Irish Brigade.[79] Its lyrics fit that of "The Irish Jaunting Car" and the familiar tune, recognizable to both Irish and American audiences, would have helped the song's popularity. "The New York Volunteer" went from a musical hall performance by Sam Long, to a printing house, and into a songster for sale across the Union in 1862.[80]

The combination of these music and lyrical factors made even Irish-specific appropriations of "The Irish Jaunting Car" universal. Songwriters continued to play on this musical familiarity to aid broader receivership of their compositions and to ensure their lyrics would be memorable. This was especially important if they were carrying a particular message aimed at wider society, hence the tune's continual use for ballads about the loyalty of the Irish American Union Army volunteers. It was also the reason behind "What Irish Boys Can Do," an 1863 lyrical response to lingering anti-Irish nativist critiques about how devoted the diaspora was to the American Union. These criticisms, mostly voiced first by American Party/Know Nothing politicians in the 1850s, were aimed at Catholic immigrant communities and the Irish who resided in Eastern cities.[81] The sentiments of "What Irish Boys Can Do" regarding Irish-born and descended soldiers' service, and the place of the diaspora in home-front society, were directed at the whole country.[82] Instead of setting the lyrics to the tune of antebellum British and American "No Irish Need Apply" ballads, "What Irish Boys Can Do" was set to "The Irish Jaunting Car" melody. This reaffirmed the tune's traditional roots and drew on its success as recognizable American music. In other words, the music's subconscious sentiment stressed the Irish cultural impact on the country as well as social, military, political, and economic contributions.

Conversely, a far more conscious postbellum Irish reappropriation of "The Irish Jaunting Car" melody was influenced directly by "What Irish Boys Can Do." "What Irishmen Have Done" was an American-published ballad written for Irish nationalist Fenian circles by songwriter Eugene T. Johnston. He often wrote mid-nineteenth-century music hall songs related to the Irish American experience, and this was just one example of his repertoire. "What Irish Boys Have Done" continued a similar theme to its wartime counterpart, singing about Irish contributions to American society. One songsheet copy, published in New York by Charles Magnus around 1870, listed the air as "The Irish Jaunting Car."[83] This was a deliberate diasporic reclamation of the song's inherent Irishness.

This musical clarity on a Fenian ballad helped enforce an Irish nationalist sentimental message. It echoed back to an old established Irish tune instead of referring to its newer American identity, thus stressing Irish heritage. It also suggests "The Irish Jaunting Car" has yet to disappear from the musical lexicon, despite the dominance of the tune's name as "The Bonnie Blue Flag" during and after the Civil War. There is some evidence that other Irish songs continued to use the underlying harmony of "The Irish Jaunting Car" as well, even when their subject matters did not directly relate to fighting. "Dublin Jaunting Car," called "a lively Irish song" in one songsheet advertisement, described a carriage tour of Dublin in its verses. By doing so, it recalled the same lyrical themes as original 1850s versions of the "Irish Jaunting Car."[84]

The multiple disseminations within the Irish diaspora, wider American Union and Confederate societies, and the numerous uses and reuses of "Irish Jaunting Car" music during the Civil War are comparable with another popular Irish tune that developed its own American identity in the same period. Much musicological debate exists around the origins of "When Johnny Comes Marching Home," often associated in the mid-nineteenth century with the Irish ballad "Johnny, I Hardly Knew Ye." The tune likely gained its latter (and now well-known) title after 1865, inspired by the former version. Yet, it can be traced back to similar comparable pieces from early 1600s appearances in Irish, Scottish, and English folk music traditions. It evolved into military compositions tied to the British Army's colonial engagements in India, the Crimean War, and the Opium Wars (1839–60).

The specific "When Johnny Comes Marching Home" American Civil War version sings more of general sentiments not explicit to the Irish experience of the conflict.[85] What is parallel to the dissemination of "The Irish Jaunting Car," however, is the way in which Patrick Gilmore—the famed County Galway-born Massachusetts-based Union Army bandmaster and conductor—took a traditional (probable) Irish tune and used it as the foundation of his "When Johnny Comes Marching Home" lyrics in 1863.[86] This echoed Macarthy's "Bonnie Blue Flag" writing process. Both Gilmore and Macarthy had Irish and Scots-Irish cultural heritage associations and used this personal and traditional musical familiarity to construct their ballads written in the United States. In turn, they furthered these respective melodies' American identities.

Many Irish American Civil War songs were set to American music tunes come the 1860s, particularly using airs with origins more recognizable than "The Irish Jaunting Car." This followed a well-established practice of writing songs known as contrafacta (or singular contrafactum), wherein lyricists would keep an older tune for a new piece; the melody remains while the lyrics are altered and are often replaced by entirely new words. For instance, Eugene T. Johnston set his lines for "Corcoran's Irish Legion," a song about Michael Corcoran's Irish New York Union Army regimental command, to the 1850s American-produced melody "The Flag of Our Union."[87] Contrafacta were incredibly prolific in nineteenth-century musical culture, and songwriters would often appropriate preexisting tunes for their new lyrics to ensure a sense of familiarity when learning different compositions. It is far easier to remember new song lyrics when the melody used is one already identifiable. "The Homespun Dress" and "Bonnie Blue Flag" made use of the very well-known "Irish Jaunting Car" air for their respective different lyrics and provide very clear examples of contrafacta.

Songs connected to the Irish went further with their adoption of contrafacta by musically appropriating American tunes. One melody originating in the United States that gained particular use in Irish song creation during the Civil War was "Columbia, Gem of the Ocean," also called "Red, White, and Blue." One of the country's unofficial anthems in the first half of the nineteenth century, "Columbia, Gem of the Ocean" was written in the United States in the 1840s. Unlike many of its patriotic national counterparts, including "The Star Spangled Banner" (the tune of which began as an English drinking song written after the American Revolution), the song had no prior influential musical life in the British Isles, Ireland, or in Europe.

With almost two decades of tune establishment in popular culture, it is no surprise that "Columbia, Gem of the Ocean" became the dominant American-produced tune found on Irish wartime songsheets. It was an intrinsic part of the musical zeitgeist. The air appeared on Irish American Civil War songsheets on several occasions, printed under various ballad titles, including "The Gallant 69th Regiment" and one "Irish Brigade" song from 1862.[88] The former even played on the American version's first line to stress its Irish identity, singing "Oh! Hibernia, green Gem of thee Ocean," instead of "O Columbia, the gem of the ocean." The latter "Irish Brigade" song used the same tune for lyrics that extolled Irish fighting service in the Union Army and devotion to the country.[89] The Fenians made similar use of this American air, as evidenced by copies of "Our Own Flag of Green" (ca. 1865) that noted how the piece was to be sung to "Columbia, Gem of the Ocean." This American tune's use of an Irish nationalist ballad complicated the movement's own dual identity articulations (as discussed in chapter 5).[90]

The use of American patriotic music tunes and contrafacta reinforced clear impressions of the diaspora's American identity articulations. Reverse appropriation and co-optation of American-produced music tunes added another layer of legitimacy and musical authority to the messages Irish American ballads presented. In particular, setting lyrics to established American pieces such as "Columbia, Gem of the Ocean" strengthened the sense that wartime songs about the diaspora's experiences were being sung with an American voice. Music-making identity expression through melody use was a simultaneous sign of the Irish diaspora's own assimilation of American culture. It was part of melding Irish lyrical songwriting with American music creation and popular culture.

In "The Irish Jaunting Car" and "Bonnie Blue Flag" examples above—including those focusing on Irish American Civil War experience—lyrical focus centered on America (Union and Confederate), on themes of fighting and serving the country on the battlefield and in society, on loyalty to the Stars and Stripes or Bonnie Blue/Confederate banners, and discussion of the ideals of republican democracy and freedom. Even though American Civil War "Irish Volunteer" ballads, "What Irish Boys Can Do," and their other adaptations used a tune that recalled an ethnic-Irish identity, the multiple variations of "The Irish Jaunting Car" air—coupled with lyrical sentiments related to the diaspora's Civil War development of an American identity—further diluted the melody's inherent Irishness. Songs became simultaneously American-centered compositions because the Irish tune took on an American character, adding an Irish American singing voice to these lyrical sentiments. This again created a blurred dual identity of Irish American musical culture. It allowed for songs to be read and sung as both Irish and American, with the melody's two national identities suiting whatever message performers and audiences wanted to express and hear.

As "The Bonnie Blue Flag" and its offshoots spread throughout the country during the Civil War, "The Irish Jaunting Car" tune shed its Irish cultural connections as a result of its lyrical and musical Americanization. Direct Irish connections to the song were lost within and beyond the diaspora. This can be seen in the way Irish-related songs that used the melody moved their lyrical focus to one based on an American articulation of ethnic identity. Such traditional cultural loss and evolution was in part thanks to Harry Macarthy himself, his adoption of "The Irish Jaunting Car" tune, and the success of his Confederate "Bonnie Blue Flag." The musical marrying of an established Irish tune with a new harmony for an American Union and Confederate nation was common practice, but this specific example and its subsequent influence on wider musical culture had the most significant impact of an Irish tune becoming American by the mid-nineteenth century. It was into this musical climate of traditional tune appropriation and ballad writing adaptation that songs by and about the Irish fighting and living through the American Civil War circulated.

2

The Production of Irish American Civil War Songs

In June 1864, *Dwight's Journal of Music* advertised a newly composed song dedicated to the Irish 9th Massachusetts Volunteer Infantry. Written by Thomas M. Brown, "Cead Mille Fealthe—A Hundred Thousand Welcomes" gave "a hearty Irish welcome to the returning heroes of the 9th Mass. Regiment" when they arrived back in Boston that summer. One of the few conflict songs about the unit, it was produced for "the officers who went, but did not return with the others."[1] According to the song's scorebook, its lyrics were "written and adapted to a favorite Irish melody"—Thomas Moore's "The Pretty Girl Milking Her Cow."[2] There was a commercial reason behind this advertisement. During the conflict, the prolific Boston-based publisher Oliver Ditson printed *Dwight's Journal of Music*. In addition, Ditson sold a significant number of Irish-related wartime ballads and musical content. *Dwight's* advertising pages not only displayed notices of new music and songs for sale but also helped Ditson publicize other areas of his production line, including "Cead Mille Fealthe."

The song's scorebook—with lyrics and pianoforte music included—was sold by Ditson and advertised in *Dwight's* the day after the 9th Massachusetts mustered out of Union Army service. In keeping with the fast output of Civil War songs, lyricist Brown and publisher Ditson worked quickly to print, advertise, and sell "Cead Mille Fealthe" in time for the regiment's return. The song was performed at celebratory events to mark this occasion. Ditson's publishing and advertising of "Cead Mille Fealthe" presents a traceable, direct publication route of an Irish wartime ballad. This specific example's production, along with its performance, was subsumed into the wartime cultural climate and followed established antebellum practices of traditional

Irish music and song adoption and adaption in the United States, as discussed in the previous chapter.

Music and songs have long been ubiquitous in American culture and society, so much so that many Irish soldiers and officers' accounts did not make regular mention of the plethora of songs written by and about them during the Civil War. That does not mean these pieces had no value. As Christian McWhirter has argued, "Civil War soldiers were highly musical and constituted a huge market for new songs," becoming "enthusiastic consumers [and] . . . most effective distributors" of lyrical and musical outputs.[3] Ballads by and about the Irish wartime experience were part of this wartime development. Moreover, "the onset of the war stimulated music publishing as composers set quickly unfolding events to music," with printing houses profiting from the boom in new lyrical and musical productivity.[4]

It is unsurprising that Irish wartime songs and music spread around soldiering and civilian communities, creating new outputs with connections to previous practice. Crucially though, these outputs spread both within and beyond Irish communities across the Union and Confederacy. Irish wartime songs were part of publishers' commercial interest, and the general popularity of Irish-related musical content helped these songs find a ready market. "The writing and publishing of music was not only an expression of patriotism. It was a business," and one which printers exploited to profitable ends regardless of a song's subject matter and content.[5] This included songs that sang of an Irish-specific experience. It also reached into a wartime society already extremely familiar with general Irish lyrical sentiments and traditional tunes. In the antebellum period, publishers "sought to tap the growing Catholic market" of immigrant communities by publishing Irish music and ballads.[6] Developed interest in these outputs then gained popularity across wider American society.

Oliver Ditson, along with fellow publishers across the country, expanded this market at the start of the Civil War, although they themselves often had no direct personal Irish connections. Profitability, sales, and popularity of song subjects drove commercial interests. By the time Ditson advertised his sale of "Cead Mille Fealthe" in 1864, the ballad was just one of many similar pieces then circulating in American society that sang of Irish wartime experience. The practice of Irish song and music dissemination through publishing houses via songsheets, songsters, and musical scorebooks during the conflict, and through personal letters and newspaper publications, connects to arguments for how American these cultural products had become. Their distribution reveals much about the place of Irish America Civil War music and song in the conflict's cultural climate.

IRISH SOLDIER SONG WRITING AND PERFORMANCE

The diffusion of "The Irish Jaunting Car" was universal on both sides of the sectional divide, but the majority of songs and musical production saw a more local distribution. These compositions were published by Union and Confederate printing houses, appeared in newspapers, and were performed in music halls, but the level of their widespread dissemination is harder to trace. That is not to limit their importance. The creation and sharing of musical and lyrical outputs added to the broader cultural impact and influence of Irish-related music and song production in the mid-nineteenth century. These are the ballads that carried the bulk of Irish American Civil War song sentiments through American society and were a fundamental part of articulating Irish conflict views and experiences.

Most of the songs discussed in this book do not have definite origins beyond the information provided on songsheets, music scorebooks, and in details provided by songster publishers. In addition, documents about the performance, sound, and production of wartime tunes and ballads are rare given the overwhelming everyday practice of these cultural actions in the nineteenth century. Music and songs were so prolific in the American soundscape that their daily aural normality muted them in evidential records. Nonetheless, it is still possible to trace some dissemination of broader wartime musicality and production, including that related to the Irish-born and descended soldiers.

Music and songs were an integral part of the soldiering experience. In his close study of the effect music had on soldiering and civilian communities during the 1863–64 winter encampments along the Rapidan River in Virginia, James A. Davis has emphasized how musical melodies and ballads "permeated every Civil War camp and directly impacted every" person who came in contact with both Union and Confederate armies. Their importance "cannot be overestimated, especially given the vast quantity . . . that was consumed."[7] In the heightened atmosphere of warfare and front-line camps, pastimes such as singing, playing instruments, sharing old ballads, and writing new songs were an important part of military life. "In camp, soldiers played games, told stories, and made music."[8] Those in Irish-dominated army regiments were no strangers to these diversions.

From the beginning of their war service, Irish-born and descended soldiers engaged in the music-making and song composing that was an important aspect of army social life. This was a culture that had existed in the earliest days of Irish military service in the United States more broadly. Militia units originated in diaspora enclaves across the Northern and Southern states from the eighteenth century onward, such as the Irish Volunteers, Hibernian Guards, Emerald Guards, and many other Irish-named units. Most were based in urban centers, particularly in New York, Massachusetts, Pennsylvania, Illinois, Louisiana, Georgia, and Virginia. In the war's early years, many of these militias were subsumed into larger companies and regiments. Those already serving in these militias in 1861 remained for initial volunteer service and joined for longer enlistment periods later in the war. Men enlisted for several reasons, including serving out of loyalty and devotion to their respective Union and Confederate causes, a desire to get fighting experience (especially if part of Irish nationalist groups), and in response to military draft policies. The main reason for volunteer enlistment was "for economic need," with army and naval service providing steady income for themselves and their families.[9]

Exact reasons for enrollment, even in antebellum militia, were not the main topics heard in contemporary ballads. Instead, marching bands and soldiers themselves played and sang their own compositions. In the fall of 1862, Corporal John Dougherty of the Irish Brigade's 63rd New York Infantry gave his mother an account of the general atmosphere of the Union Army's Irish regiments: "The cheerful spirit of the Irish Brigade made the road seem short, the funny joke and merry laugh of the men at all times whether on the battlefield, on the march or in camp makes the Brigade the envy of the rest of the army—they would go along in silence looking sad while the Irish men would be laughing and singing."[10]

This musical joviality manifested itself in countless Irish Brigade lyrics during the war. Dougherty described the environment in which songs about his fellow Irish-born and descended soldiers were given life. Around the same time, Derry-born William McCarter described how the Irish Brigade's 116th Pennsylvania Infantry began their journey to war "accompanied by the voices of the regiment." Military bands "struck up the airs of 'Jonny is Gone for a Soldier,' 'The Star Spangled Banner' and 'John Brown's Body Lies Moldering in the Grave,' 'As We Go Marching On'"—an amalgamation of Irish and American airs and ballads.[11]

As well as singing at "spontaneous gatherings, or in organized groups," and on the march to boost morale, soldiers would perform in "concert-like situations."[12] In his 1863 prison memoir, the 69th New York State Militia's Colonel Michael Corcoran recounted how his fellow First Battle of Bull Run prisoners of war held several "concerts" for their Confederate captors in various holdings in the Southern states to pass the time. He detailed one such October 1861 event: "The audience of several Confederate officers . . . seemed highly delighted with the performance, until, in grand strains, we gave them 'Hail Columbia' . . . Desiring to give them a full does of Union melody, we immediately, upon the conclusion of the song, struck up, 'Columbia, Gem of the Ocean.' This forced one or two of them to excuse themselves very suddenly on important duties, and, by the time we got to the middle verse of 'The Star Spangled Banner,' only a solitary one of them remained . . . A rebel fears the stirring notes of 'The Star Spangled Banner.'"[13] Corcoran's account of using pro-Union songs to tease secessionists was part of the rapid increase in "reverence for them" at the beginning of the conflict as Confederates rejected prewar national songs.[14]

This Union and Confederate American anthem adoption and abandonment was not always clear-cut. Several weeks after the October concert performance above, Corcoran was moved to a prison in Columbia, South Carolina. On the journey there, his fellow officers attempted to goad Southern civilians who watched them pass by. Through the use of American Union anthems, they turned song into a weapon. When they "came in sight of the city . . . the leading spirits struck up the noble air of 'Hail Columbia' . . . Every man lent the aid of his lungs to send it up to as high a pitch as possible." The city's residents did not mind this musical form of fighting that much though, especially as they could claim a song cheering on Columbia was praise for their home place rather than an allegorical description of the whole United States. Corcoran noted, "a large number" of Columbia's observers of the prisoners' singing march saw the point of this lyrical jest and "laughed themselves into a good humor over it."[15]

These Confederate-taunting concerts and singing actions were similar to those recalled in other prisoner-of-war accounts. Non-Irish Missouri Union officer William Rogers recounted how his fellow inmates bonded "together with singing" while incarcerated. They passed the time by "giving concerts every evening. We had several good singers, who made quite enjoyable music." They also performed for their Confederate prison guards who "seemed to like our army songs as well as we did. No matter how hard the words hit them they would applaud and called for the 'Jubilee,' 'Star Spangled Banner,' 'Red, White and Blue,' and we used to sing 'Rally round the flag, boys,' putting unnecessary emphasis on 'Down with the traitor and up with the star.'"[16]

The response to Rogers's concerts may well have been influenced by a particular Irish presence among the prison guards. His account makes fond mention of "a burly Irishman" jailer who, during their 1863 "New Year spree," gave Union soldiers extra food and supplies. Together, they celebrated the festive season and enjoyed a "concocted beverage which we called egg-nog." As a result of this libation, Rogers, his companions, and their guards, "began to dance, sing, and get joyfully drunk."[17]

Rogers's and Corcoran's accounts of prison concerts resemble numerous reports across battlefields of military bands and soldiers sharing their respective songs through musical engagements. Occasionally in times of reduced fighting, or while in winter quarters, military and civilian bands and performance troupes would entertain soldiers to occupy daily camp life, similar to entertainment shows in later twentieth-century engagements, such as those in Vietnam. In March 1863, "the Thespians of the 27th Regiment" performed for the 44th Massachusetts Infantry. The latter regiment's Corporal Zenas T. Haines described how military actors "fitted up a little theater, and furnished it with an act drop, scenery &c, of their own painting." They created a military music hall environment to perform "The Irish Tutor" and "Michael Earle." Both pieces were rooted in Irish folk song and stage traditions; the former reappeared in newspaper advertisements during and after the war promoting performances across the country in local theaters. Its dissemination into popular culture provides yet another example of the Irish influence on American musical theater and song. Haines makes no mention of the performers' nationalities, but there were Irish-born and descended soldiers in both the respective 27th and 44th Massachusetts acting company and audience.[18]

Singing—on marches, in concert-like performances, and in prisoner-of-war environments—was essential to community morale. It was also a very public display of engagement with musical military culture, but the songs were not the only avenues by which soldiers could stretch their vocal cords. Performances could be heard around more private campfire settings as soldiers gathered to sing, share, play, and create Civil War music and ballads. This environment generated intimate connections to lyrical articulations and strengthened soldiering identity and communities, especially in ethnic regiments. Welsh migrant Corporal John Griffith [G.] Jones's letters are a case in point. The 23rd Wisconsin Infantry Regiment volunteer and his fellow Welsh Wisconsin soldiers maintained Celtic bardic tradition by having "a sing-song every night."[19] Jones often mentioned how "there is much singing here with all these Welshmen" in camp.[20] This impression could likewise be applied to his fellow Irish brethren. Such moments revealed the power and importance music and song could have in these quieter settings. In his memoir, Michael Corcoran recounted reflective instances when he and his fellow prisoners "would make the room in which we were confined ring again with our swelling choruses. 'Home, Sweet Home' was our favorite and most frequent song; and I have seen the tears coursing down the cheeks of every man . . . whenever it was sung. These touching moments were soon succeeded by those in which martial airs awoke the sterner qualities of our hearts."[21]

Oftentimes, campfire-singing displays included more than just the voice, as musical instruments found their way to the front line. Irish soldiers were great proponents of this performance aspect, an extension of the engrained role instruments played in traditional Irish and Celtic folk music-making. When the Irish Brigade's wartime historian Captain David Power Conyngham narrated the first Union Army Christmas Eve celebrations of the Brigade's 63rd, 69th, and 88th New York regiments in 1861, he included a passage that painted the singing scene at the end of the day. "Seated near the fire was Johnny Flaherty, discoursing sweet music from his violin. Johnny hailed from Boston; was a musical genius, in his way, and though only fourteen years of age, could play on the bagpipes, piano, and Heaven knows how many other instruments; beside him sat his father, fingering the chanters of a bagpipe in elegant style."[22] The presence of such instruments, although seemingly impractical in theaters of war, was commonplace. "Many enlisted men were talented instrumentalists who brought their instruments with them on campaign," and they "took advantage of extended encampment to purchase instruments and replace parts or to request that instruments be sent from home."[23]

Two specific Irish-born and descended soldiers provide examples of this instrumental presence. In April 1863, Patrick Kinnane, a second-generation soldier in the 155th New York Infantry (which formed part of Corcoran's Legion), wrote to his sister Elizabeth about using some of his army earnings to buy a fiddle. He had paid $10 for it. He implored his sister to understand the necessary expense, hoping she would not "think I am doing wrong in buying the fiddle . . . I am sure it is a good bargain." Kinnane had bought it from a fellow musician—"as honest a man as there is in the Legion"—most likely a fellow Irish New Yorker given the unit's ethnic identity. The sale was sweetened by extras included in the deal: "little things such as tuning forks, two bows" and, in another example of musical dissemination, a "music book" with melody scores to play. Kinnane seemed delighted by the items, which made the sale "worth the money."[24] By comparison, County Galway-born Patrick Kelly asked for music, songs, and instruments to be sent to him on the front line instead of making direct purchases himself. After telling his parents he did not "need much at present" in one letter home, he then made the grand request for "a guitar and some song books if you can get the guitar cheap." Kelly promised to send twenty dollars "if we get paid" to cover the cost.[25]

Sometimes only an instrument was needed to awaken the musical lyricism and singing spirit instilled in the Irish of the Union and Confederate armies. In his postbellum recollections, the Irish Brigade chaplain Reverend William Corby made no reference to the singing culture of soldiers under his religious care, save for passing mention of music at Mass services. Nevertheless, there was one section of his account, describing the twilight scene in camp by Harpers Ferry in late fall of 1862, where a "bugler delighted us by sounding clear notes which reverberated through the gulches of the mountains for miles." In this aural climate, Corby remembered how soldiers "listened, late in the calm evening, seated around our campfires, a pathetic feeling crept over us . . . First came flashing through our minds the poor dead companions we had left behind in their cold graves at Antietam. Then, as the scene of the late terrible conflict faded from our minds, while still under the fascinating charm of the clear bugle notes . . . All the vicissitudes of life passed in review before our minds . . . as the bugle tune died before softly in the distant hollows of the mountains."[26]

Corby's account bears striking similarity to a passage in McCarter's wartime memoirs where he too recalled, in almost identical lyrical rhetoric, the power and impact that simply hearing music had on listeners. He detailed one bugle player's "truly wonderful and grand" performance "echoing from hill to hill for miles around. But my powers to do justice in describing these meetings and their effects upon the troops come far short of what is necessary. I may, however, note that they were a source of much comfort and encouragement to myself and others."[27] Corby's and McCarter's descriptions provide a sense of the climate into which the singing and sharing of songs and songwriting would occur in military settings, thus helping soldiers learn and familiarize themselves with older airs and new wartime ballad productions. When John G. Jones discussed the nightly campfire singsongs in his letters, he informed his parents that such regular practice would mean he and his fellow Welsh Wisconsin soldiers "will have learnt to sing perfectly by the time we come home, if we live till then." Jones's comment implied the ballads learned in the camp would disseminate back to the home front through the soldiers' own oral practice.[28]

Corcoran also observed how individual fireside singing recitals could be opportunities for others to create new songs. In his memoir, he recounted one moment of solo singing by a Lieutenant Isaac Hart of Indiana. The officer was portrayed as "not only a beautiful singer, but also a capital poet." While held as a prisoner of war, he "composed several first-rate songs" that he then taught to his fellow captives. Corcoran explained how they "all used to join in" with Hart's ballad composition creations, with each officer prisoner singing "to the extent of our musical abilities" as they learned these new arrangements.[29]

Corcoran was being modest with this latter comment—the Irishman was actually very musically literate. Indeed, both his memoir and private correspondence are full of song references. He often paraphrased lyrics in his writings to add to his already poetic style of phrase. In one letter to his friend, the New York second-generation Irish American Judge Charles P. Daly, Corcoran began by noting "all is now quiet in this locality" around his camp in Suffolk, Virginia, in May 1863. The line was a paraphrased embellishment of the popular wartime song "All Quiet Along the Potomac Tonight" (1863).[30] Corcoran was not alone in this practice of song lines being added into soldiers' letters. William McCarter engaged in lyrical paraphrasing when relating the 116th Pennsylvania's journey to the Southern states: "after the songs" of patriotism and Union commitment were played and sung, "three rousing cheers were given for Philadelphia and the girls we left behind us."[31] This was a reference to the traditional Irish ballad "The Girl I Left Behind" discussed in chapter 1.

Other Irish soldiers were more direct in relating the songs they knew and sung. Patrick Kelly's letters reveal a keen sense of musical awareness, as demonstrated by his guitar request. He also made reference to songs being performed in camp and used lyrical lines in his writings. In one correspondence, he commented that he would "shoot Jeff Davis on a sour apple tree" if given the chance. This was a direct quote from a version of the universally popular Union song "John Brown's Body," with lyrics aimed at the Confederate president.[32] Kelly certainly showed familiarity with contemporary wartime ballads but his letters revealed a complex relationship to the traditional songs of his Irish past. In one letter, he asked for a specific song: "I want Father the next letter he writes to write of the song called 'Mary Le More.' I want to learn it."[33] This ballad had circulated in British and Irish song culture from the 1840s.[34] Kelly gave no indication as to why he wanted to know this particular piece, but as his correspondence details, regular singing among his fellow Irish soldiers of the 28th Massachusetts likely means he heard them perform it around the campfire. Why these soldiers did not teach the song to him is unclear. Through his request, Kelly revealed a gap in his transnational folk music knowledge that was being expanded during his Civil War experience.

Although but one example, Kelly presents an anomaly with the dissemination of Irish tunes in the diaspora. As Davis has asserted, "all soldiers and civilians carried with them a resonance of their past communities," particularly in relation to immigrant groups whose ethnicity "was celebrated through their musical choices." "Most soldiers sang from memory," and, as already explored in this study, reinforced their traditional songs and airs through emigration and dissemination.[35] Many Irish songs during the antebellum period had "been preserved . . . [by] first or second-generation Irish emigrants." Kelly's specific example challenges this, however, while also supporting a crucial caveat. The preservation of Irish songs and music could have occurred "before or after emigrating," which stresses the assessment that not all traditional ballads were necessarily known in Ireland before migrating.[36] Instead, they were learned through dissemination in the migrant community. Kelly was in his early twenties when he enlisted in the 28th Massachusetts, having immigrated to Boston with his parents as a young boy during the peak of the Great Famine migration.[37] His cultural memory of Irish songs was, for the most part, formed in the United States. It developed through repeated family stories, memories, and shared song dissemination and performances, including around the campfires of the Civil War.

HOME-FRONT CIRCULATION
OF IRISH AMERICAN WARTIME SONGS

While Patrick Kelly asked for songs to be sent to him from the home front, later in the war one of his 28th Massachusetts compatriots reversed this song-sharing process by sending a ballad to those at home. Daniel Crowley, originally from Cork, Ireland, served with the regiment in 1864. During the conflict, he kept regular correspondence with his friend Cornelius Flynn, who remained in their Massachusetts hometown of Marlborough (Marlboro). Crowley never made any reference, even in passing, to the singing spirit of his Massachusetts regiment, but he did engage with an alternative form of ballad dissemination. On 6 December 1864, Crowley's letter to Flynn was written on song stationery. In other words, the paper contained a printed song. It was a four-page elaborate piece of writing material, with a copy of "Disbanded O!" on the first sheet.

The song was a Union ballad about "a band of Volunteers" who would "join in heart and hand, and go down to Dixie's Land" to fight the Confederacy and was set to a variant tune of "Yankee Doodle." Publication details on the song page itself reveal it was produced in Washington, DC, with an added note about "packages sent by mail, paid post, to any part of the Army of United States." This reveals that Crowley's letter paper was made specifically as special illustrated writing material for soldiers and civilians. Indeed, on occasion "some publishers produced stationery with song lyrics on the first or last page," like Crowley's example. Such items provided "a creative means of marketing that ensured some exchange of pieces between front and home."[38] Crowley made no allusion as to why he chose to write on this special paper, save for an unclear comment above the lyrics that said, "A. and W. would you like to be Disbanded O!"[39]

"Disbanded O!" was a specific printed song circulation sent by Crowley. By extension, soldiers sent their own written compositions, creating a two-way form of lyrical distribution between the front line and home front. Many remained on the pages of private correspondence. John G. Jones informed his parents he "sent two songs—the work of a boy from the 18th Wisconsin" in previous letters to his family.[40] Some songs found their way to printing houses, where they were published ultimately on songsheets and in songsters. These compositions then spread through society. One Irish-born soldier took his songwriting dissemination even further. County-Meath native Charles Graham Halpine was the most prolific Irish wartime lyricist and poet in the United States of America, famed for his satirical and comic productions penned by his fictional creation, Private Miles O'Reilly. His cultural outputs reached throughout the diaspora and Union society. Halpine's works originated in military settings, and he made use of his prewar journalist contacts to ensure their publication. O'Reilly's first appearance came in the *New York Herald* in September 1863, and the newspaper would print the rest of Halpine's works for the remainder of the war. When they were collated into *The Life and Adventures of Private Miles O'Reilly* in 1864, the book stated its stories had come "from the authentic records of the *New York Herald*," furthering the myth that O'Reilly was one of their correspondents.[41]

Newspapers and periodicals in both the Union and Confederate states would, at times, print songs among their pages, part of a practice developed in early nineteenth-century British, Irish, and North American print press culture where ballads and poems were included to fill space in column inches. In the Civil War, popular wartime anthems circulated this way after initial publication, as was true for "The Battle Hymn of the Republic" and "The Bonnie Blue Flag," along with more individual compositions sent to editors from soldiers and civilians alike. Newspapers were also a primary way for the Irish diaspora to express their lyrical wartime views. The *Irish-American* (New York), the *Pilot* (Boston), and numerous state and regional newspapers all published news and opinion pieces aimed directly at the diaspora, particularly in urban enclaves. Articles, editorials, and reports of public speeches made by leading diaspora figures presented both pro- and anti-wartime sentiments and politics, reflecting a myriad of changing wartime attitudes. These were similar to broader commentaries, such as those seen in the *New York Times* and *New York Herald* that targeted audiences across the country through syndication. In relation to disseminating Irish American Civil War lyrical sentiments, newspapers often carried sections of poem contributions and ballad verses, occasionally with reference to a musical air to aid readers in singing these pieces. These included compositions sent to the *Irish-American*, the main broadsheet for New York's Irish diaspora, although its reach went beyond the city and the state and was circulated within Irish regiments.

Most works were forms of poetry sent from civilian readers, but those fighting also posted their own ballad verses. Soldier Richard Oulahan forwarded his "Camp Song of the Sixty-Ninth" to the *Irish-American* for publication on 15 June 1861 during the conflict's earliest days. Written as the Irish 69th New York State Militia mobilized, it is not surprising that Oulahan dedicated his piece to the unit.[42] His composition corresponds with pre–First Battle of Bull Run songsheet examples about the diaspora militia group. Five months later in November 1861, a Thomas J. MacEvily submitted "War Song of the Irish Brigade" to commemorate the Irish Brigade's foundation. The verses celebrated New York's three regimental brigade contributions and emphasized their Union Army loyalty. An additional musical comment stated that its words were to be sung to "The Star Spangled Banner" melody.[43] Although Oulahan's and MacEvily's compositions were sent to a specific Irish diaspora newspaper, and were New York-centric in their focus, both examples show more individual contributions to the Irish American wartime songwriting milieu.

Not all Irish-related wartime song submissions made it to print. In April 1864, *Harper's New Monthly Magazine* recounted "the following proposal to purchase" a ballad "which comes from Canada" by an unnamed author, who had given the work to the newspaper via "some friends of the Union." The brief article explained how sections of this lyrical poem "composed on the pedigree, emigration, and Military career of Brigadier General Corcoran" had been sent in the hope that the periodical's editor would buy the full piece for subsequent publication. *Harper's* replied: "we decline; but we take the liberty of publishing the sample." It thereby printed the four "Poetry Being verses" at no cost. The second, seventh, twelfth, and sixteenth stanzas appeared in the article, which sang of Michael Corcoran's leadership in his New York regimental legion. This presents an interesting case of editorial choices halting the publication of Irish American Civil War lyrical writing, especially relating to one centered on a popular figure who traversed both Irish and American society.[44]

Alongside wartime newspaper publication, songs circulated from the front line via oral culture transmission in home-front settings. Within the predominance of music and song in everyday American nineteenth-century life, it is possible to hear Irish-related performances within parlors. Corcoran's friend Judge Daly, and his German-descended wife Maria Lydig Daly, were ardent supporters of the Irish Brigade and New York's Irish diaspora and were themselves no strangers to engaging with contemporary songwriting culture. In 1858, the judge received a two-page, color-illustrated personal song about New York City's Irish American Democratic politics.[45] During the war itself, Dublin-born family friend, former Young Irelander, Fenian, and poet John Savage wrote to the Dalys while serving with the 69th New York. In one letter, Savage "enclose[d] a few copies of 'The Starry Flag,'" which he had written, thus disseminating the ballad to the home front via the couple.[46] Several months previously, Maria Daly recorded in her diary that Savage "sang for us, after dinner" not long after his regiment fought at the First Battle of Bull Run. His performance included what she described as "the war song of the 69th 'The Flag of Our Country Forever,' which [Savage] composed himself and set to the tune of 'Dixieland,'" a variant of "Dixie."[47]

Savage returned to the Dalys in the fall of 1861 and sang again, this time to visiting guests. Maria Daly made no mention about what he performed, other than observing how it "amused [the gathered party] very much . . . we had quite a pleasant evening" of music, songs, and "some ice cream and cake"—a civilized form of wartime entertainment.[48] Savage appeared in Maria Daly's diary throughout the course of war, with the Irish nationalist sending her "a little volume . . . of his poems, dedicated to the Judge" as a New Year's gift for her husband in 1864.[49] These diary entries are exceptional reports of simultaneous Irish American Civil War song dissemination, John Savage's American cultural output, and the intimate nature of ballad sharing.

Maria Daly was immersed in contemporary classical, operatic, religious, and traditional musical culture. Her writings demonstrated a keen knowledge of melodies and ballads emanating from the conflict. In one particular diary passage, she described her morning walk "up Broadway [when] the 56th New York passed me going to the seat of war." She recalled how "the men were singing all the way. It was most inspiring."[50] She was also enthused by New York's Irish regiments, and the Dalys served as patrons of the 69th New York. Through their close acquaintance with Michael Corcoran, Judge Daly was instrumental in helping secure the Irish general's release from Confederate captivity. Over the fall of 1862 in the months following Corcoran's return from prison, and while he gathered soldiers for his renewed Union Army command, the Dalys were invited to his headquarters at Camp Scott on Staten Island.

Maria Daly recorded the visit's events as they "went to Corcoran's house, supped and passed the evening talking and singing songs until long after one" in the morning. There they "sang some comical songs and had a right merry evening in the General's room."[51]

Clearly Corcoran, ever the musical performer, lost none of his singing passion exhibited in his prisoner-of-war days. Now returned from the South, one wonders whether he and the Dalys sang some of the songs written about him in his absence. Corcoran would have been aware of the existence of these lyrical compositions' given their wide distribution and his own personal interest in contemporary musical culture. He was not, however, present for the initial performance of the first song about him produced after his July 1861 captivity. "Corcoran to His Regiment" was written to celebrate the 69th New York State Militia's initial volunteering and fighting service. It also sang of Corcoran's insistence that he would not be paroled to the Union. When publishing wholesaler Horace Partridge produced a songsheet copy of the ballad, a comment was added under the title that recorded how the ballad was "as sung at Jones' Wood, 29 August 1861, for the benefit of the widows and orphans of those of the 69th Regiment who fell at Bull-Run."[52]

This referred to the "festival for the benefit of the widows and orphans of the soldiers" of the Irish 69th New York held at Jones's Wood on the Upper East Side of New York City a month after the fighting around Manassas. The gathering served as a welfare fundraising event for the city's Irish diaspora and as an early recruiting rally for the proposed foundation of the Irish Brigade. The *New York Times* detailed, "there was much music and dancing in all parts of the Garden," although it did not mention "Corcoran to His Regiment."[53] Why precise detail about the song's performance at this occasion was added to its songsheet is unknown, but it is interesting to observe that Partridge was based in Boston, not New York. This indicates how Irish New York-centric songs spread through the American Union and played to older traditional broadside news dissemination practices, where added contextual details provided readers and performers with a more singing-news style approach rather than solely reprinting lyrics.

Publishers were inconsistent in adding performance details to songsheets in much the same way that not all added what melody was meant to be used to accompany the lyrics. In the case of the latter, this presupposed performers' own musical knowledge or ability to provide their own tune. The former performance comments reveal songsheets were printed after the fact, with reference to where the song's initial public displays may have been. In other words, the song was first performed and then set down onto songsheets or printed in music scorebooks rather than being written and then publically performed (although this route of dissemination also happened). While performance references were not commonplace additions, it is possible to see some indication of home-front recitals on songsheets. One copy of "Pat Murphy of Meagher's Brigade" produced by New York-based printer H. De Marsan in 1863 referred to the fact it had been "sung with great success by the Comic Vocalist of the day, Tony Pastor."[54] This detail is absent on Horace Partridge's production of the same song, suggesting that either the latter was produced first, before Pastor sung the song, or there was a printing choice to omit the information. The comment also illustrates the role of musical halls—the stages of which Pastor regularly graced and owned—as a space for Civil War song distribution. It further highlights how Irish songs and music continued to form the basis for entertainment, as mentioned in chapter 1.

Irish tunes and ballads had long been performed in music halls and theaters across the country and thus providing an outlet for their performance and spread. For a few successful writers and performers like Tony Pastor and Harry Macarthy, such entertainment locations provided a ready-made audience for new productions. These venues helped propagate new conflict songs, ranging from big anthemic ballads to more specific thematic pieces, including those, like "Pat Murphy of Meagher's Brigade," about the Irish wartime experience. Pastor himself had no direct Irish roots (his parents were Spanish and American-born) but he had strong connections to New York's Irish community and was familiar with the Irish musical lexicon in the United States. He drew from this in his productions during his career, including those of his postbellum phase later in the nineteenth century when he enjoyed dominance as the nation's chief vaudeville impresario and made use of ethnic songs, music, and dance (including Irish examples) regularly.

Pastor's first theater—or "opera-house" as it was sometimes described—was situated at 201 Bowery, close to the Five Points area of New York City, and thus within communities with a large proportion of Irish-born and descended residents.[55] After the war, he established a theater by Union Square next to the political powerhouse Tammany Hall, which had close ties to the city's Irish population. Among Pastor's troupe of frequent stage acts "were Irish-

American performers" similar to fellow entertainer Harry Pell, who toured America and Europe with Irish musicians during the same period. Pastor wrote and performed wartime and Irish ballads himself, as references on Irish Civil War songsheets show. Throughout the 1860s, "he had a number of Irish songs in his repertory, praising participation in the Civil War and decrying no-Irish-need-apply prejudice."[56]

As much as they appealed to audiences' popular culture music tastes, Pastor's close connections to Irish music and song before, during, and after the war were also born of economic reasons. In this he echoed the way music publishing and printing houses produced and circulated wartime songs about Irish experiences and sentiments across the Union and Confederate states. It was part of an extension of general antebellum and postbellum Irish traditional folk song and music inventories. As Christian McWhirter has highlighted, "most published pieces did not sell many copies but almost any song could find a market somewhere." Furthermore, "sheet music sales did not fully measure a song's popularity."[57] That several Irish American Civil War songs were reprinted on songsheets more than once by the same publisher, or by different publishers, highlights an extensive distribution of sales. Certainly, in relation to the examples in this study from numerous songsheets, songsters, and scorebooks, lyrical productions referring to the Irish in the war were deemed profitable and popular enough for publication.

THE PUBLICATION OF IRISH AMERICAN CIVIL WAR SONGS

The vast majority of Irish American Civil War songs produced in the Union states originated from a core group of publishers in New York, Boston, and (to a lesser extent) Philadelphia—all home to long-established printing businesses. Henry De Marsan (known as H. De Marsan) and James Wrigley in New York City and Oliver Ditson and Horace Partridge in Boston printed the bulk of Irish-related songs referenced in this book. Marsan was "the principal publisher of the penny sheets," with "almost a monopoly of the trade." He printed "almost everything that was singable, old Revolutionary ballads, English naval songs . . . as well as Ethiopian melodies [slave and minstrel songs]." Additionally, Marsan sold Civil War folk music and original ballads, including songs pertaining to the Irish.[58] His contemporary Charles Magnus printed other musical and song ephemera to great success as well. Magnus was "the most prolific . . . in terms of both variety of design and quantity" of songsheets, lithographs, envelopes, and other paper items.[59]

For printers such as Magnus and Wrigley, songsheets were just one of the items they sold; Wrigley was often described as a "Publisher, of Songs, Ballads, and Toy Books."[60] Ditson, as mentioned, had other publishing outputs during the war, such as *Dwight's Journal of Music*. Partridge was an even more extensive "Importer, Wholesaler and Retail Dealer." He sold wartime songs alongside "Fancy Goods, Toys, Watches, Jewelry, Yankee Notions, &c."[61] Among all their products were ballads and sheet music relating to the Irish wartime experience. Publishers, through their own commercial choice to print such lyrics and musical scores, played a substantial role in ensuring dissemination of Irish American Civil War songs. They were the middlemen of the process, with their own roles and symbiotic relationships to wartime ballad publication and propagation. It was through these printing houses and publishers that Irish-related songs found their American voice.

None of the major publishers of Irish American Civil War songs and music had any personal ties to their cities' Irish communities. Ditson, Partridge, Magnus, and Marsan were not part of the Irish American diaspora, although they resided in the ethnic group's two largest demographic areas of New York and Boston.[62] They also had subsidiary printing houses in other cities, as was common practice for Union and Confederate publishers. Magnus, for instance, had offices in Washington, DC, and New York City. Partridge, as a wholesaler, bought much of the printed stock Ditson published less than a mile away in the center of Boston, thus creating a further stream of material culture dissemination within the city.[63] Magnus's and Marsan's offices were both on Chatham Street in New York City (now Park Row, close to the Financial District and City Hall Park area of Manhattan). Chatham Street, dubbed "Newspaper Row" in the 1800s, was home to numerous newspapers, printers, publishers, and stationers. All would have been very aware of mutual business trends in this shared commercial sector and neighborhood. There was a similar situation in Augusta, Georgia, and in Richmond, Virginia, where several Confederate printing houses were based in close proximity. This created centers of wartime song and music output where Irish-related items and material and print culture found a marketplace that tapped into an already popular genre. This aided their circulation into, and through, society.

The archival survival of songsheets from these publishers presents the dissemination of a false record. Of course, not all songs produced during the Civil War were written down, including those relating to the Irish conflict experience. Not all of those that were written were printed, and not all copies were exactly alike. Verses and lyrics could alter between publications and printed songsheets, and different publishers created different productions that included or omitted details. In addition, they had varying border illustrations around the lyrics; some were more ornate with figures and pictorial images, including racial minstrelsy and derogatory Irish simian caricatures. These sat alongside sketches of eagles, musical instruments, and depictions of African American Union soldiers later in the war. A few border designs would even be colored vividly in red, blue, and yellow.

Others were less intricate but still had beautiful artistic line-drawn motifs that framed the words. The latter were often shared by other songsheets from publishers' collections, revealing how songsheets were often printed onto standard templates; the border design appeared on the page first before words were added inside the illustrated frame. Although core lyrical sentiments remained across different versions and publications, songsheet broadsides were essentially ephemeral by nature. The reverse side of dissemination culture was the ultimate fact that songsheets were rarely saved by those who printed them or those who purchased them. Scores with the lyrics and music were often kept because of their use in home settings for voice, pianoforte, and instrumental playing, though they too had a transient quality.[64]

By comparison, both soldiers and civilians kept songsters during the war. These played a final important role in a more sweeping dissemination of Irish-related songs through both Union and Confederate societies. Small, pocket-sized—sometimes barely bigger than a palm-hand—songsters form their own particular contributions to the war's musical culture by engraining lyrics in printed book form. They were valued items for consumers. Both Patrick Kelly and Patrick Kinnane made reference to receiving songster books from the home front and through musical purchases. "Soldiers treasured their song-books," and took particular care of these items as prized wartime mementoes.[65] In one copy of *The Virginian Songster*, a Confederate 3rd Missouri Infantry soldier wrote in pencil on the verso of the title cover, recording his purchase of the publication on 1 August 1863. He added the details: "Bought this Book at Augusta Georgia while on my way to Va. [Virginia]." This soldier adapted his purchase by pasting two songsheets to the insides of the outer cover, expanding his songster's ballad repertoire by adding two extra songs. One of these additions was a copy of "The Irishman's Shanty."[66]

Even though titles such as *The Camp-Fire Songster* implied a military setting for song spreading—a notion reinforced by the book's cover illustration that depicted soldiers gathered around a campfire—publishers were aware of their domestic popularity. They appealed to the idea of bringing war culture into the home. At the start of volunteer mobilization in 1861, *Dwight's Journal of Music* advertised "Camp Songs . . . a collection of all the popular National songs." The songster "serve[d] to enliven the soldier's life." Yet, it would also "prove a source of much enjoyment and recreation to all into whose hands it may fall."[67] This included those on the home front who purchased *Camp Songs*, or received it from soldiers sending the book—and other comparable songsters—to families, along with their own lyrical and musical compositions. Three years into the war, *Dwight's* printed another advertisement that reiterated the universal appeal of songbook collections. Its promotion of *War Songs for Freemen* reported that the work was "just the book for soldiers in their tents, and for everyone who wishes to sing on war topics" from the comfort of their parlors.[68]

Songsters provided a way of ensuring that even fleeting compositions, especially from the soldiers themselves, could be saved for cultural posterity. Dissemination of song lyrics to and from the home front ensured personal and cultural connections were maintained, and new adaptations and lyrical writings expanded an already noisy marketplace. This process can be observed through the way songsters traced the impact of specific Irish-related wartime songs. One *Hopkins's New-Orleans 5 Cent Song-Book* edition contained the ballad "Song for the Irish Brigade" (1861). Its verses sang of Irish-born and descended soldiers fighting in the Confederate Army, their martial emulation of previous Irish service in foreign armies, and provided subtle criticism of their official Union Army Irish Brigade opponents.[69]

The song's presence in a songster published in New Orleans is unsurprising as all publishers included productions with regional connections—such as "New Orleans Song of the Times" (ca. 1861), a local adaptation of the Southern ballad "Song of the Times." Hopkins, whose printing house was based at "No. 823 Tchoupitoulas-street, between First and Second Streets, 4th District," included both ballads alongside "Song for the Irish Brigade."[70] This edition also included traditional Irish ballads like "Limerick Races" and "The Irishman's Shanty," as already mentioned in the previous chapter. Hopkins often incorporated these examples in his publications. Given that many of the Confederacy's Irish-born and descended soldiers resided in the region and served in Louisianan regiments, the inclusion of "Song for the Irish Brigade" provided a dual acknowledgment of their military and cultural contributions. The ballad appealed to Louisiana's Irish fighters and to the wider Confederate society already familiar with Irish tunes and lyrics.

Equally, the eighth edition of *The Southern Flag Song Book,* produced by "bookseller and publisher" H. C. Clarke at his printing houses in Vicksburg, Mississippi, and Augusta, Georgia, included "Erin's Dixie" (1863) among its many pro-Confederate songs. The lyrics, set to the prolific and Southern-associated melody of "Dixie," were dedicated to Louisiana's Madison Light Artillery.[71] The unit was nicknamed the "Madison Tipperary's" (or "Tips") in honor of approximately 164 former "Irish laborers working on the canals and ditches of the Mississippi River" who served in the unit. Originally from County Tipperary (hence the nickname), they joined the war effort as a group.[72] This ballad, pertaining to a specific Irish-related Confederate Army group of soldiers local to Louisiana, was included by Clarke in a collection of forty-six ballads printed and sold across the seceded states. "Erin's Dixie" spread beyond its narrow diasporic confines and became a Confederate song through songster reproduction. The fact that it was set to the main unofficial anthem of the Confederacy only aided this Irish version's impact further.

Union songsters that contained more general wartime sentiments for soldiers and civilians to sing placed songs by and about the Irish in the conflict among more American-focused ballads. One of many Union Army Irish Brigade songs entitled "The Irish Brigade" appeared in *The Continental Songster* in 1863. The songster also contained the ballad "Paddy the Loyal." Both songs expressed Irish views of the conflict from the diaspora's home-front perspective. They were placed beside traditional folk songs and other war-related ballads on a varying number of pertinent themes—such as the anti-Confederate "How Are You Jeffy Davis" and pro-Union "A National Melody."[73] These two Irish-related songs were included in an American collection where audiences read, heard, and performed lyrics of Irish loyalty and devotion to the American Union cause. Other songsters gave Irish wartime sentiments an airing through their publication, as demonstrated by "Pat's Opinion of the Stars and

Stripes." This musical hall ballad, "sung, with great applause, by Fred May," was republished in *The Camp-Fire Songster* in 1862.[74] The collection contained other songs that similarly had lyrics about the fighting Irish.

Printing Irish-related songs in general American songbooks gave them an identity and influence beyond one that sang solely to the diaspora. They articulated to Americans that the Irish shared national loyalty and devotion either to the Union or Confederacy (depending on the songster's focus). Placed among ballads that spoke to audiences across the country, the inclusion of Irish-related wartime songs about fighting service, general home-front experiences, and political views provided a platform onto which Irish opinions about the conflict's issues could spread into the general populace. Their lyrical messages were shared mutually between the home front, which produced the songsters, and the front line, where much of their content came from, and circulated back-and-forth between the two. Printing and placement in such songster collections strengthened the American sentiments and identities of these Irish songs on both sides of the sectional divide. It also connected to the established tradition of Irish folk music and ballads becoming American cultural products in their own right.

The presence of Irish wartime songs in American songster collections reinforces an argument that music, as well as songs, "tended to diminish, not amplify, any cultural gaps" because tunes and lyrics had "the ability to bring together disparate individuals into communal groups centered on specific repertoires."[75] What can be classed as "Irish" must simultaneously be seen as American because they did not belong to one ethnic community or heritage. This enhanced the cultural blending of Irish music and song traditions that began decades before the war. Even when music was reclaimed by the diaspora— as in the case of Irish-related songs using "The Irish Jaunting Car" tune after it had become synonymous with "The Bonnie Blue Flag"—Irish identity was diminished through its diffusion into wider culture. All subsequent versions served to reinforce this Civil War era American identity transformation.

Dilution brought great cultural impact as Irish wartime songs came to shape the conflict's musical and lyrical outputs. This was observable in songster contents that included both traditional and contemporary Irish-related song titles. Moreover, it was present in what *Dwight's* called "combination" songs— a distinct form of ballad where the lyrics were all made up of other song titles and paraphrased lines from other recognizable ballads. According to one advertisement, combination song pieces were "curious medley songs for which many people, just now, are so pleased."[76] One example of these unique productions was "The Father of All Songs," set in 1864 to the air of the early war ballad "The Glorious 69th." The latter was about the Irish-born and descended soldiers of the 69th New York. That "The Father of All Songs" was set to a melody created for a song about a specific Union Army Irish regiment was itself a form of dissemination, as its tune and sentiments were transposed onto the new production. This showed the musical impact of "The Glorious 69th."

There was more to "The Father of All Songs" than that it shared its musical melody with an Irish regiment ballad. Its lyrics were made up of song titles that exhibited the cultural legacy of Irish-related traditional and wartime productions. "Corcoran's Irish Legion" was mentioned alongside "The Irishman's Shanty," many of Moore's ballads, and "The Irish Jaunting Car."[77] The piece's song title lyrics reflected their assured place within the contemporary musical climate, and revealed their reach beyond specific Irish enclaves across the country. Irish songs had become part of mainstream American culture. Their tunes had developed American identities. The question remained whether their lyrical sentiments echoed correspondingly with this cultural propagation during the Civil War.

3

Battlefield Balladry

Of subsequent incidents and events, the world, by this time, has heard enough . . . Columns and volumes have been filled . . . Three times did the 69th launch itself . . . Three times, having plunged head-foremost into its deadliest showers, was it hurdled back. We beat their men—their batteries beat us."[1] When Thomas Francis Meagher ended his brief wartime account of the 69th New York State Militia's journey to the First Battle of Bull Run in July 1861, he skimmed over details about the fighting. In his view, there was no point reiterating a by-then familiar story; "the world . . . [had] heard enough." Published several weeks after the Civil War's first major engagement, Meagher made a salient point. Newspaper stories and first-hand testimonies filled "columns and volumes" in the weeks after the battle. Instead, he chose to recount the ten days leading up to 21 July and the skirmishes and marching incidents encountered by Irish-born and descended 69th New York soldiers. He also wrote about his own band of New York Zouaves attached to the 69th in the war's earliest days; Meagher's Civil War career began as a captain of this unit. *The Last Days of the 69th in Virginia*—Meagher's three-part publication—helped establish a contemporary narrative of overall Irish commitment to the American Union war effort from the very start.

"The story of the day"—and the Irish involvement in it—was known via another form of battlefield reporting dissemination: ballad songs about the 69th New York and the First Battle of Bull Run. Irish wartime songs that focused on military experience and sentiments sang about two predominant themes. The first centered on the gallant bravery of the 69th New York as the foundation of all subsequent Irish army engagement in the conflict. The second eulogized their fighting example at Bull Run as an indicator of their American Union loyalty. Throughout the war, songs by and about the Irish recounted events of the battles themselves, often in vivid detail, and described fighting sacrifices, military engagements, regimental actions, and leadership. Irish-born and descended soldiers and the wider Irish diaspora sang of their own Civil War encounters through such songs. They created this lyrical history from the outset.

The Irish in the Union, and on occasion in the Confederacy, sang about their military service and battlefield experience to help establish their own remembrance of their actions. Ballads reported Irish regiments' actions to the home front and to families in Ireland. Songs and lyrics that focused on fighting aspects followed extremely old patterns of war service and news dissemination first seen in oral tradition and echoed established bardic and Celtic practices of singing about battles. They also mirrored subsequent traditions of distributing news through broadside balladry, a commonplace custom in the British Isles and Ireland during the seventeenth and eighteenth centuries. Despite some lyrics taking sweeping liberties, and instances of lyrical false reporting, battlefield songs about wartime service hailed Irish fighting contributions.

These ballads told their own regimental histories of Irish units and revealed how the 69th New York and the Irish Brigade became the lyrical focal point for wartime songs. Frequently they aimed lyrics and song dedications toward two particular Irish-born leaders in the Union Army—Thomas Meagher and Michael Corcoran. Meagher, and to an even greater extent Corcoran, embodied the Irish American Civil War experience. They represented soldiering figures those of Irish-birth and descent could—and in lyrical insistence should—emulate on the battlefield and in society. The 69th New York, Irish Brigade, Meagher, and Corcoran were all extolled in verse and cultural productions during the war, adding new passages to the long history of Irish foreign military service history. As Meagher had described, "every effort and determination" was made by Irish Union and Confederate soldiers on the conflict's battlefields.[2] By extension, every effort was made to sing of a determined and devoted military history that resounded throughout the warring nation.

THE BATTLE OF BULL RUN AND
THE 69TH NEW YORK SONGS

The first ballads about Irish American Civil War battlefield experience were produced within days of the First Battle of Bull Run on 21 July 1861. One of the earliest was "To the Glorious 69th!" which detailed the "chivalry" of the 69th New York State Militia. Alongside their "brave Commander"—then-Colonel Michael Corcoran—soldiers "faced rebels that were mean" and "stood in the hot battle, where balls like hailstones flew."[3] "The Gallant Sons of Erin," likewise "dedicated to the 69th Regt. N.Y.S.M.," echoed the same lyrical sentiments about the militia's fighting bravery. Their "behavior do excel what pen can write or tongue can tell," the song began, before verse after verse praised the titular "gallant sons of Erin" and "these sporting boys from Paddies' land." The song went into vivid detail about the events of the battle itself, suggesting a slightly later publication than "To the Glorious 69th!" to accommodate more information about the events that took place around Manassas.

The second half of "The Gallant Sons of Erin" then became a lyrical war report, singing about Bull Run as if the ballad was a news bulletin. It explained how the 69th New York stayed on the field "when other troops did quickly fly" as Confederate victory looked certain in the afternoon of the engagement:

[They] stood and did their foes defy . . .
At famed Manassas and Bull-Run, where glorious laurels they had won,
Not at a man being absent from his gun.

Near the song and battle's end, one verse depicted the final heroic charge of the 69th New York against the Confederate batteries, echoing Meagher's subsequent account:

Brave Corcoran, wounded on the plain, called to his men to charge again;
Each Captain boldly did maintain a dauntless soldier's station:
And stood the plain for many an hour, though shot and shell like rain did
    shower,
To prove their valor, tact and power as gallant sons of Erin.[4]

Swift on the publication of "To the Glorious 69th!" and "The Gallant Sons of Erin" were ballads specifically about the incidents of that July day. The similarly titled "Battle of Bull's Run" and "Battle of Bull Run" appeared in the immediate weeks following the encounter, again singing of Irish regimental involvement first and foremost. The latter, "Battle of Bull Run," was "dedicated to the 69th Regt. N.Y.S.M." by F. Collins. Its lyrics extolled: "Our gallant soldiers . . . gone to the battle field of fame." The 69th New York stood against the Confederate opposition as "the terror of Bull Run" on this:

> Field of fame we did maintain against an enemy,
> Conceal'd in woods and ambuscades and their masked batteries
> Till Johnson with his forces and the black Cavalry
> Turned our scale of battle or we'd gain the victory.

Collins adopted a traditional broadside balladry style, using song to report events and disseminate news. He informed listeners about what had happened during the fighting, providing information that could be spread widely. He described the layout of Union and Confederate position and presented a lyrical assessment of why the Union lost. In Collins's lyrical interpretation, no matter the level of brave fighting commitment Irish soldiers displayed, eventually the numerical balance shifted toward Confederate troops. This turned the "scale of battle." Despite this, the final four lines of "Battle of Bull Run" stressed that as the 69th New York had performed so gallantly, their retreat was not a loss. If anything, it was a noble surrender justified by Confederate circumstance:

> Over ten long hours we fought most manfully,
> Against four to one a fearful odds of men we could not see,
> Until amongst our teamsters a panic had begun,
> Then we did retreat but were not beat at the battle of Bull Run.

In addition to this sense of Irish victory in defeat, Collins emphasized the Union loss was just a temporary setback for the 69th New York. Future Irish-born and descended army recruits would "make [Confederates] pay severely for the battle at Bull Run." The idea was repeated at the song's conclusion, with the lyrical voice of Colonel Corcoran telling his men, "We'll make them pay some other day for the battle of Bull Run."[5]

By comparison, Arthur McCann's ballad "Battle of Bull's Run" included descriptions of the fighting in its final two verses, but the tone was less enthusiastic about defeat. Despite "the heroes of Erin" having "strong hearts," the toll of unprecedented combat had a cost. One casualty was "Haggerty [who] bled on the field of the brave." This was a reference to the loss of Captain James Haggerty. Originally born in County Donegal, Ireland, Haggerty was a long-standing member of the 69th New York State Militia and became the first Union Army Irish officer casualty of the war. His death and memory would be lamented in subsequent accounts and songs throughout the remainder of the conflict. McCann's lyrics promised that his sacrifice, along with other Irish soldiers who fell, would be remembered: "Long may their names sound in history pages, / That fell in the contest, that day at Bull's Run."[6]

Haggerty's death made another lyrical appearance over the Atlantic in a broadside that reported the First Battle of Bull Run to those observing the conflict from abroad in 1861. "Our Brave Irish Champions," printed in Cork, Ireland, began:

> You feeling-hearted Christians of high & low degree
> I hope you'll pay attention and listen unto me,
> The great battle in America to you I will explain,
> On the 21st day of July, there was 20,000 slain.

Written by Thomas Walsh, this particular Bull Run ballad mirrored eighteenth-century broadside practices of recounting news through song. It informed the Irish in Ireland about the heroic fighting their countrymen in the warring United States were doing, singing about the 69th New York, the battle, and conflict encounters events more broadly. It also related to wider articulations of past Irish martial history through ballad references to the battles of Fontenoy, Waterloo, and the Crimean War. This aspect of Irish ballad culture will be discussed in further detail in chapter 4, but clearly the earliest songs about the Irish American Civil War experience extolled expressions of Irish heroic history. Figurative discussions about battlefield bravery exhibited by tough fighting men run throughout Irish culture and contemporary songs. James Haggerty's example, along with that of his fellow fighting Irish brethren in the Civil War, followed this tradition.[7]

In "Our Brave Irish Champions," this praise was combined with the adoption of a more factual tone, as the song detailed the engagement's events and consequences:

> By the dawn on Sunday morning, that battle did take place,
> 'Till Six o'Clock that Evening, the firing did not cease . . .
> And many a valiant Irishman lay bleeding on the plain. . . .

A scene of horrid slaughter was the battle field that day,
The 69th brave Irishmen were all near cut away.

On the other hand, Walsh's lyrical reporting was not always accurate. Indeed, this particular ballad example serves as a good source of the pitfalls broadside balladry's recounting of events could bring. While it was correct to sing of how "we need expect no more" from the fallen "gallant Captain Haggerty," other 69th New York officers—such as County Down-born Robert Nugent—were described falsely as having died "all bleeding in . . . gore." The lyric prior to this had described how "Nugent fell dead of his horse," which was possibly a mistaken account relating to Thomas Francis Meagher who *did* fall off his horse (but lived) on the Virginian battlefield.

Interestingly, Walsh's ballad later corrects itself in relation to Meagher. It sang of how the Young Irelander, "who was exiled in '48, far from his native land" due to his rebellious Irish nationalism, had in fact *not* fallen in the battle. Lyrics explained: "the great report of Meagher's death is false we understand."[8] This conflation of actual casualties, rumors and confused identities, and the false lyrical reporting of actual events highlights how fluid and changeable dissemination of war news was back to the home front. In this case, the account had further distance to travel, increasing the chance of error as it journeyed to Ireland. There was little process for ensuring accuracy in contemporary cultural accounts.

Walsh's Bull Run ballad also followed a traditional pattern common in British and Irish broadside print culture. Songs could be used to sing shorter, more embellished versions of real-life accounts. Subsequent wartime ballads used headlines to emphasize balladry's role as forms of intelligence. The full title of Walsh's song made this reporting nature explicitly clear: "Our Brave Irish Champions—A New Song on the GREAT BATTLE FOUGHT IN AMERICA! On Sunday, 21st of July, 1861." In May 1862, the "New Song on the Dreadful Engagement, and Tremendous Loss of the Irish in America" gave its own news-esque account about the Union occupation of New Orleans from a Confederate point of view. It observed how Louisiana's Irish diaspora soldiers attempted to resist opposing forces: "Erin's sons did loudly cry—We'll die before we'll yield."[9]

Headline-grabbing song titles continued to appear in Ireland throughout the war, such as "A New Song on the Last Battle Fought in America," which detailed the fighting around Pittsburg Landing, Tennessee, as part of the Battle of Shiloh in April 1862. Its chorus called for cheers "to toast to those across the weaves [waves] each Irishman and Yankie brave."[10] "A Lamentation on the American War—Awful Battle at Vicksburg" by P. J. Fitzpatrick was printed in the late summer of 1863 after the Union victory at Vicksburg, Mississippi. Similar to "Our Brave Irish Champions," its lyrics informed those in Ireland about the fighting and loss of Irish-born and descended soldiers, focusing on those serving in the Confederate Army as well as in the Union.[11]

Irish American Civil War ballads continued to refer to Bull Run in the aftermath of July 1861. The battle, along with the 69th New York's involvement in it, served as the foundation for subsequent productions. Bull Run and the 69th New York created the cultural beginning for future Irish wartime history told through song. Additionally, lyrical reports about their actions that day matched the praise Irish soldiers received from their commanding officers. In the first part of his wartime account, Michael Corcoran recalled the 69th New York's charges as, "my brave boys threw themselves fiercely against the rebel ranks . . . to a single man, they dashed, with terrific shouts and yells, straight onto the battery." As the battle turned, "no man wavered. All behaved with veteran coolness . . . Right gallantly did the men of the Sixty Ninth maintain their proud distinction."[12] Meagher's own Bull Run publication recalled a similar sentiment, arguing that in his mind, "no soldiers could have rushed to battle with healthier elasticity and daring than did the soldiers of the 69th."[13]

Meagher and Corcoran's recollections, as well as subsequent narratives by officer-historians of the Irish American Civil War experience such as David Power Conyngham and St. Clair Augustine Mulholland, reinforced the mutual connection between the stories recounted in wartime ballads and battlefield reports. When Corcoran's memoir began to circulate in 1863 (before gaining wider publication in 1864), his battle description at the start of the book ensured that the memory of Irish service on the battlefield in Bull Run in 1861 was kept alive in the later years of the conflict. It engrained the fighting commitment songs stressed. From "Long Live the Sixty-Ninth" (1861) hailing "the men now in triumph returning . . . radiant with fame" as the unit came home to New York following the engagement to "We Hill Have the Union Still" (1861) reinforcing the message that "though from Bull Run we retreated," the 69th New York's Irish soldiers fought "ten to one" victoriously.[14] Wartime lyricists ensured the whole Union was informed about this military commitment and personal militia success.

They also ensured the wider society knew these soldiers were ready to repeat this fighting performance. "The Gallant 69th Regiment" (1862) even argued in one lyric that the 69th New York were "our brave Army's foundation," placing the Irish at the center of the whole Union Army. They swore allegiance to the country and would help it "ride the foul storm" which secession had caused.[15] Over the course of late summer 1861, the 69th New York reformed from a militia into a regiment (though a militia unit was retained beyond the conflict). They became the founding regiment of the Union Army's official Irish Brigade, commanded ultimately by Meagher himself. Streams of songsheets were penned in honor of the Brigade's formation. Of all the dominant sentiments and subjects sung about in Irish American wartime ballads, lyrics about the Irish Brigade and their fighting prowess were the most frequent and extensive.

IRISH BRIGADE BALLADS

Irish Brigade ballads built on the lyrical sentiments of 69th New York song productions, extolling battle actions, heroic leadership and sacrifice even when the unit was not always present. So critical was the 69th New York's role as the foundation to the Union Army's official Irish military core that "The Irish Brigade" (1862)—the first of numerous ballads of the same name—recalled how when Irish-born and descended soldiers were:

> Surrounded by carnage and slaughter,
> At Bull Run, and Lexington too . . .
> Although by large forces o'erpowered,
> No soldier or chief was afraid:
> There ne'er was traitor or coward,
> In the ranks of the Irish Brigade.[16]

Written in Woburn, Massachusetts, in January 1862, this local lyrical devotion to the Irish Brigade implied the unit fought at the First Battle of Bull Run *before* it had been officially formed, laying the ground for subsequent lyrical conflation between the 69th New York and the Irish Brigade. Combination of the two appeared in subsequent wartime outputs.

This particular Irish Brigade ballad was also produced before the 28th Massachusetts had even joined the unit's ultimate five-regiment complement. Six months after the start of the war, Irish soldiers mustering for the American Union cause had already gained a praiseworthy reputation across the country, aided by early war lyrical productions. Their brave performances, supported by emulation in contemporary ballads, served to raise Irish soldiers in the eyes of their fellow American countrymen. The legacy of singing battlefield honors presented a form of cultural propaganda that bolstered the diaspora's fighting efforts.

As expressed in "The Irish Brigade," the lyrical sentiment of Irish soldiers being unafraid against opposing Confederate forces shaped the way members of the diaspora learned about Irish Brigade conflict stories. Later in the war, when 28th Massachusetts enlistee Daniel Crowley informed his friend Cornelius Flynn that he had joined the regiment, he explained: "I need not tell you that this Regt is one of Gen Meagher's old Brigade. The old fellows here spin some good ones about their escape from death."[17] Crowley's brief comment indicates much about mutual knowledge of the Irish Brigade's wartime encounters. His phrase "I need not tell you" is key here. Crowley did not need to explain—Flynn would immediately understand who the former was fighting with, and what that meant in the context of Irish Union Army service. Tales circulated the home front, comparable to those heard in disseminated songs and stories by the Brigade's "old fellows." If Crowley sounded a tad disbelieving of Irish Brigade veterans spinning good yarns about their service, he needed only to read and listen to the myriad of Irish Brigade ballads that sang about its honorable contributions. Following the Woburn-written "The Irish Brigade," many similar-titled ballads appeared, such as "The Irish Brigade in America," "The Irish Brigade" by Hugh F. McDermott, and "The Irish Brigade" by Kate C. M.

Such was the prevalence of Irish Brigade ballad titles and songs that P. T. Hade's 1861 "Camp Song of the Irish Chicago Brigade" actually altered its specific association during the war. First written and "respectfully dedicated to the Brigade" established in Chicago by a second-generation Irish American, New York-born Colonel James A. Mulligan, the song was produced initially for his 23rd Illinois Volunteer Infantry Regiment. Affectionately known as "the Irish Brigade" in Illinois, the unit was never an official Union Army brigade; the name was in honor of its Eastern state counterparts. Early music scorebooks of Hade's ballad produced by the prolific music publishers Root & Cady contained lyrics, pianoforte, and voice music printed under the full title that referred to Mulligan's regional regiment.[18] Later in the war, when the song was reproduced elsewhere in the Union, including by the Philadelphian printer A. W. Auner, "Chicago" disappeared from the title, turning the song into "Camp Song of the Irish Brigade."[19] Despite the name, Hade's lyrics were not themselves overtly specific to Mulligan's men. As a result, the song was regularly adapted to extol the official Irish Brigade and its composite soldiers from New York, Pennsylvania, and Massachusetts. This subtle change indicates the dominance of the official Brigade and its regiments over both wartime song culture outputs and other Irish-heavy military groups.

Local and specific ballads drawing on Union Army Irish Brigade references could also be found in the Confederacy. In 1861, "Song for the Irish Brigade" sang about Irish-born and descended soldiers serving in Louisianan regiments at the start of the war. As with Mulligan's Illinois example, the Confederacy did not have a comparative official Irish Brigade. Nonetheless, this Confederate "Irish Brigade" song contained the same lyrical rhetoric about Irish loyalty and fighting service, rousing the Irishmen of Louisiana to fight for their state and secession. They would go to the war's battlefields and: "Let the rifle ring, and the bullet sing to the clash of the flashing saber!"[20]

Yet, for all the variations of Irish Brigade-inspired and response ballads, the vast majority focused on the Union Army's Irish 63rd, 69th, and 88th New York, 28th Massachusetts, and 116th Pennsylvania Regiments—the official Irish Brigade organized in the months following the First Battle of Bull Run and led, in the early years of the war, by Thomas Francis Meagher. After their mobilization, Irish Brigade songs sang of the seven days of fighting around Richmond and the Battle of Fair Oaks (Seven Pines) at the end of May 1862, where Meagher roused his units to charge Confederate lines. "Young Ireland and Ould America" reported these events when it was "sung by Tony Pastor" at his New York music hall in July and August 1862. The song praised "America's Irish Brigade!" repeatedly in its chorus refrain. Sung from the point of view of one Irish soldier in the Brigade, it explained:

In the seven days' fight, sure I stood at my post,
And each pop of my gun made some Rebel a ghost;
And whenever the word came to charge, by me sowl [soul]!
I made in some blackguard a bayonet-hole![21]

Despite the violent phrasing, the song's lyrical report removed some of the battle's realism from its recollections. Its verses differ greatly in tone from a postwar account by Irish Brigade chaplain Father William Corby, who recalled the moment he took "a hasty look over the locality" after the fighting at Fair Oaks ceased: "dead horses, broken muskets . . . and general destruction of life and property" were all he saw.[22] None of this detail made it into song. Instead, the fictional singing soldier in "Young Ireland and Ould America" gave more specific detail about charging against Confederate General Stonewall Jackson's troops, and how Fair Oaks was reminiscent of events at Bull Run ten months before. The song drew on this earlier battle engagement for fighting inspiration and further used it as part of a lyrical pun referring to Irish anti-British views and the fight for Irish independence:

When ould Stone-wall came down like a thousand of brick,
It's meself and the boys drove him back double quick:
For, we thought of Bull-Run, and our bosoms were full,
And we wished we were RUN-ning on ould Johnny Bull.[23]

References to Irish Brigade battles in 1862 appeared in ballads across the year and into 1863, with the notable exception of one. Why the Battle of Antietam was omitted from the popular lyrical lexicon is unclear. The Irish Brigade's "extremely high casualty rates" at the impactful September 1862 engagement spoke to their "courage and steadiness under fire," and they were "a credit to the valor and ability of Irish American soldiers on the field."[24] One suggestion for Antietam's lyrical absence is that the reality of American history's bloodiest single day of combat, where the Irish Brigade fought fiercely along a sunken road that became known as "The Bloody Lane," could simply not be expressed in verse. Sixteen months later in January 1864, Patrick Collins—an Irish-descended solider serving in the 6th Maine Infantry—wrote to his sister on the reverse of some songsheet stationery published by New York's

Charles Magnus. The correspondence was similar to the style of letter paper Daniel Crowley used, assessed in chapter 2. The song on Collins's letter was "The Drummer of Antietam," written by Eugene T. Johnston in 1862 and set to Thomas Moore's air "Last Rose of Summer." Despite this ballad's Irish connections, its lyrics were about the general postbattle mournful atmosphere as "the drummer of Antietam lays dead and alone." There were no specific lyrical ties to the battle's ethnic regimental losses.[25]

The Irish Brigade was exclaimed through song on both sides of the Atlantic throughout the middle of the war. One example was "The Irish Brigade in America," also printed under the title "The Soldier's Letter from America" in Ireland and the British Isles in 1863. It began by suggesting, "it is vain for to describe the undaunted bravery of the Irish brigade . . . in North America," before singing about their courageousness over several verses. Its lyrics reinforced the idea the Irish Brigade "fought right manfully" at the Bull Run (while actually meaning the 69th New York State Militia), before describing engagements:

At Port Royal they faced the enemy;
At Fairoaks, through fire and smoke, they made them for to yield;
And twelve hours' engagement we were masters of the field.
The fearful scene at Richmond was dreadful to behold,
By shot and shell some thousands fell, and spread dismay around.

The rest of the ballad then fixed on one particularly infamous moment in Irish American Civil War history. The December 1862 Battle of Fredericksburg cemented the Irish Brigade's lasting Union Army fame. The final verses of "The Irish Brigade in America" focused attention on the unit's fateful charge on the field at Marye's Heights by the edge of the Virginian town of Fredericksburg on 13 December. For the only time in the war, the full five regimental compliment of the Brigade served alongside each other. The ballad detailed events in traditional lyrical reporting style:

At Mary's Heights near Fredericksburg recorded it shall be,
After three days' battle we gained the victory.
The thirteenth of December began this bloody fray,
The Irish brigade six charges made to die or win the day,
With bayonets fixed they charged the heights, and death soon scattered round,

And thousands of the Southerners lay dead upon the ground.
The 69th and 88th were first upon the field,
Led on by Col. Nugent, determined not to yield:
Their band played sweet Garry Owen likewise St. Patrick's day,
And in six decisive charges they nobly cleared the way.

As with similar song-verse news reports, "The Irish Brigade in America" mixed fact and embellishment to enhance the Irish Brigade. It created a noble image of Irish military service spurred on by regimental bands playing the Irish airs of "Garryowen" and "St. Patrick's Day." It made reference to the Irish-born and descended soldiers of the 69th and 88th New York, commanded by Colonel Robert Nugent, who himself was wounded during the engagement. Moreover, it exaggerated the Irish Brigade's role in the fight; regardless of what the lyrics implied, the Union Army did not gain the victory "after three days' battle."[26]

In reality, the Irish Brigade's involvement in the Union Army's charges up Marye's Heights was catastrophic. The Battle of Fredericksburg resulted in an estimated 45 percent loss for the entire Brigade, reducing regimental numbers significantly.[27] The "brigade was cut to pieces" with "only the remnant of a brigade left" following the clash, according to William Corby. The chaplain "had a very small congregation compared with former ones" when he held postbattle Mass services.[28] Other Union Army regiments suffered a similar fate. Despite suggesting the Irish Brigade were victorious within a larger Confederate success, "The Irish Brigade in America" was more subdued in its closing lines. It acknowledged its praiseworthy tone came at a high cost:

To see the dead and wounded it would grieve the heart full sore,
And the moans of dying soldiers all bleeding in their gore.
Oh, many a sweetheart may lament, and mother for her son,
That fell that day at Mary's Heights, Port Royal, and Bull Run.[29]

The Irish Brigade never recovered from the high toll taken on its numbers and leadership by December 1862, and this aspect of their war history has framed views about the diaspora's overall war support levels. Arguments have suggested enthusiasm within Irish American Union state communities declined rapidly from 1863 onward. The decrease in eagerness for conflict participation was a result of heavy losses at Antietam and Fredericksburg, as 1862 "ended in a dark mood." Newspaper editorials—especially in New York's *Irish-American* and Boston's *Pilot* presses—voiced criticism of Meagher's Irish Brigade leadership and Union Army policies. Communities and Irish Catholic clergy lamented Irish soldiers' deaths, replacing "what had begun so gloriously with the formation of the Irish Brigade" with despondency. News of the battle and Irish casualties led to "re-examining the direction of the war, and [the Irish] place in it."[30]

Close analysis of Irish American Civil War songs challenges this assessment. Even as New York, Boston, and Philadelphia's Irish communities came to terms with casualty reports, lyricists penned verses that continued to exalt Irish wartime service, offering counterpoint views to one of unrest. In the weeks following events at Marye's Heights and throughout early 1863, ballad poetry focused on pride in aiding the Union war effort. Lyric bardic arguments in "The Irish Brigade at Fredericksburg," for instance, did not express a pessimistic attitude.[31] On St. Patrick's Day 1863—three months after the devastating battle—one home-front poet wrote and sent "The Irish Dead on Fredericksburg Heights" to the *Irish-American*. Its dominant sentiments applauded Irish soldiers earning fame fighting for the cause of republican liberty and their American home nation. Describing the fallen and buried dead at Fredericksburg, its author Kate M. Boylan called for reverence:

> They came from Carlow's fertile plains,
> And Wexford's woody vales,
> From Innishowen,
> And green Tyrone,
> And Wicklow's hills and dales.
> They came to seek amid the free,
> Homes to reward their toil,
> In which to see
> That Liberty
> Unknown on Erin's soil.[32]

An understandable impression of honorable sacrifice pervades all Irish wartime ballads about their involvement in Civil War battles. Differing from a sense of diaspora despondency, wartime songs praised the dead and injured.

Lamentations were couched in rhetoric about worthy sacrifice to the American Union cause. Lyrics never suggested directly (or even hinted subtly) that the Irish would not fight. While notions of a "growing sense . . . that they were being asked to sacrifice too much" impacted Irish American Union commitment levels in the middle of the conflict, this does not mean the whole diaspora had "diminishing support for the war."[33] To be sure, a sense of war weariness can be observed in later war ballads. Singing about battles ceased in the final year of the conflict, but this is also a trend that can be observed across the broader spectrum of American Civil War songs produced throughout the Union and Confederacy.[34]

The Irish, certainly in song, were no more or less quiet than their fellow American compatriots when it came to singing about their war service as the conflict continued. When "A Lamentation on the American War" reported the events at Vicksburg to those in Ireland, it did not present a sense of despair and rage against the war itself. Singing about Irish soldier service for the Union and Confederacy together in the same ballad song, most of the piece echoed ballad narrative presentation practices, as seen in earlier war examples. It contained a lyrical depiction of the fighting at Vicksburg, and a stark image of its aftermath:

> Like thunder bolts, the balls do fly from the artillery,
> The fire and smoke ascend the sky most dismal for to see,
> The brother fight the brother and the father fight the son,
> And after all no sign at all of this sad war being done.
> Thro' fields of blood we have waded, where, cannon balls do roar
> And many a brave commander lay bleeding in their gore . . .
> After each and every battle, see the memory of the dead,
> Some wanting legs and arms, and more without their heads,
> In pits some thousands here does lie far from their native clay,
> To take a long and silent sleep until the Judgment day.[35]

In a similar vein, lyricist Hugh F. McDermott used vivid imagery to paint the scenes of Fredericksburg and Marye's Heights in his Irish Brigade ballad ode "The Irish Brigade," published in January 1863, a matter of weeks after the battle. An epic-style broadside, McDermott's song stretched to a lengthy thirteen stanzas. Its sole spotlight was on the Irish Brigade at Fredericksburg, their charges up Marye's Heights, and Thomas Francis Meagher's inspiring leadership before the fight. In relentless iambic meter beating through the lyrics, the middle of the song drew listeners onto the field, creating aural and visual sights and sounds experienced by Irish Brigade soldiers:

> With shout and yell, and stunning peal,
> Their vengeance leapt upon their steel;
> With shock and dash, and plunge and stroke,
> 'Mid roaring seas of fire and smoke,
> Their desperate valor shook the earth,
> When the foes cried out, "Who gave them birth?"
> Each heart was steel, each eye was fire,
> With reeling gash from son and sire,
> The pulse so held the breath with might,
> Each vein was soldier in the fight.
> With rage and wroth, and rushing tread,
> Again they charge the rain of lead,
> And vie with those who went before
> To deck their brows with ribbon-gore;
> When soul to soul they pressed attack,
> The thundering cannon swept them back.
> As more they saw red currents flow;
> More fiercely on they charged the foe;
> And as the dying gasped for life
> Their spirit still impelled the strife—
> Like wounded pinions posing high,
> The first to soar—the last to die.[36]

More than any other ballad focusing on war service and battle events, McDermott's "Irish Brigade" ballad created inspiring rhetoric that elevated the Irish Brigade in the eyes of the diaspora and wider Union society when the song circulated in New York and Boston in January 1863. Although also drawing on images of war horror and death, its tone emphasized the repeated refrain of sacrifice with honor. Noble battlefield endeavors should be remembered with commemoration through lyrical praise.

Irish Brigade exploits were written into song and sung with pride, inspiring serving soldiers across the Union Army. They demonstrated how loyal the Irish in America were to the conflict and cause. As Daniel Crowley knew and revealed in his correspondence, he was in a regiment that had witnessed some of the toughest engagements of the war by 1864. Many of these, such as Fredericksburg, were already commemorated in circulating song lyrics. In Crowley's final letter to Flynn at the end of the conflict, the now battle-hardened young Irish-born soldier depicted how the 28th Massachusetts returned to Alexandria, Virginia, via Fredericksburg. He explained to his friend that he had "passed through where this [Irish] Brigade charged under Meagher on the 13 Dec 1862."[37]

Irish Brigade stories printed in diasporic and national newspapers, along with those about other Irish regiments in the Union and Confederate armies, provided evidential support to broadside ballad tales. They too gave inspiration to Irish soldiers who followed wartime accounts through the presses. This was certainly the case in the spring of 1862 when Michael Corcoran recorded how he followed the actions of his former 69th New York soldiers who were now part of the Irish Brigade. He delighted seeing "scraps of information respecting the doings and movements of the GALLANT SIXTY NINTH," and his "eager eyes devoured each word and each letter of the paragraph which told me that the brave Irish lads were once more baring their manly breasts to the battle storm, and that they were once more nerving their brawny arms to strike." In his own particular lyrical language writing style, Corcoran painted his own imaginings about the 69th New York's war bravery. Such thoughts would not be out of place in song. He even drew on ballad rhetoric to enhance his own personal depictions of his what former command was doing: "In fancy I saw them . . . marshaled to the bugle note . . . In fancy I saw them making ready for the onset; saw them moving forward steadily, quicker and quicker, until, with wild shouts of victory, they burst upon and scattered the foe."[38]

This fighting fantasy came from an imprisoned Corcoran who had only ever seen one battle engagement through his participation at the First Battle of Bull Run. He drew from newspaper accounts and songs he read and heard while in Confederate captivity to fight vicariously with them. He was also likely aware that as he read about the exploits of his 69th New York, he too was making an impression in the verses of Irish American Civil War balladry. Michael Corcoran's and Thomas Francis Meagher's own personal military careers added another layer to inspiring war service song rhetoric.

THE LYRICAL LIVES OF MICHAEL CORCORAN
AND THOMAS FRANCIS MEAGHER

Of all the Irish-born and descended officers, soldiers, and sailors whose wartime service was written into songs, arguably Michael Corcoran stands above all others. The most frequent figure in Irish wartime ballads, Corcoran became a familiar person in wider American song culture from the ballads about his command of the 69th New York State Militia in 1861 through to his death in late 1863. His own military service predated the Civil War itself—he had served with the militia from his earliest migrant days, joining the unit in 1849 not long after settling in the country. He rose steadily through its ranks before becoming its colonel prior to Southern secession.

Ballads about Corcoran's early military service in the United States of America were first printed in the aftermath of a well-documented moment in mid-nineteenth-century Irish American history: Corcoran's refusal to participate in a New York City parade held for the visit of Britain's Prince Edward in October 1860. He also declined to go to the postparade "ball in honor of the Prince of Wales . . . given by the citizens of New York."[39] Debate surrounds the reason why he took this course of inaction: rules about how many parades militias could march during a year or personal illness during the royal visit provide two suggestions. A third explanation is related to the diaspora's view of British rule over Ireland, post-Famine hostility, and Irish nationalist tensions. Publicly, Corcoran suggested this was the underlying cause. He was awaiting court martial for his assumed insubordination when South Carolina seceded two months later. As other Southern states followed, he pledged loyalty to the American Union and offered up his militia to defend the nation's capital. The Irish 69th New York became one of the very first units mustered into Union Army service in May 1861, with Corcoran among them, his punishment rescinded.[40]

Corcoran's refusal to parade, along with the 69th New York Prince of Wales story, were cemented by inclusion in ballads written in the first weeks of the war. The history of Irish American Civil War service began with the opening lines of "Col. Corcoran and the Prince of Wales" (1861), as its initial verses reiterated the Prince of Wales affair by retelling Corcoran's version of events:

On the 11th of October eighteen hundred and sixty,
New York was the city for every good thing;
In peace and in plenty the rich ones in numbers
Did march to the tune of God save the King!
Through the street and the parks the Militia did start,
For to take a part in the Royal parade:
There was one stood alone. . . .
[Corcoran] would not comply for to honor the King.
Court-martial was ordered the jury was paneled,
To try this brave Hero for no other offence;
His naturalization doth say that no allegiance we pay,
So he pleaded straightaway against the English Prince.

Once "the South did combine" to secede from "this once very happy land," the court martial "trial was dismiss'd" and "brave Corcoran again did resume his command."[41] The rest of the song detailed the journey of the 69th New York State Militia to the capital and their encampment within the defensive establishment outside the city around Arlington Heights. Here the unit waited at the appropriately renamed Fort Corcoran.[42]

Corcoran became a notable figure present in many Irish-related wartime ballads produced in the aftermath of the First Battle of Bull Run. His inspiring figurative example as the perfect image of a heroic Irish American Union leader was employed in early conflict ballad productions to enthuse Irish-born and descended soldiers to mobilize. Several songs made particular reference to his capture and thirteen-month imprisonment in various Confederate holdings after July 1861, including more general, non-Irish specific songs, such as "We Will Have the Union Still." Its lyrics expressed how the whole Union Army would "avenge the insult" of Corcoran's battlefield seizure and "bring back" the Irish-commander to serve the nation once again.[43] "Free and Easy of Our Union!" (1861) reflected similar sentiments:

Brave Corcoran now is missing,
And his life hangs on a thread;
Irishmen, rescue him if living,
Or avenge him if he's dead.

"Free and Easy of Our Union!" also likened Corcoran to Colonel Elmer E. Ellsworth, who was killed in a skirmish with Confederates in Alexandria, Virginia, in May 1861, several weeks before the Civil War developed into a full-scale, battle-driven conflict. As the first noteworthy Union officer to die in the war, Ellsworth was the recurring subject of several ballads. He was a prolific martyr for the Union cause, and the incarcerated Corcoran became the deceased Ellsworth's living lyrical Irish counterpart. This ballad example strengthened the connection between the two officers by telling Union society to "avenge" both Corcoran and "brave Ellsworth" simultaneously. Such a message reinforced the former's place as a contemporary wartime hero alongside the latter.[44]

Corcoran's story was recognizable throughout the warring nation thanks to documented exchange efforts, his own adamant refusal to take parole, contemporary accounts about his time in Southern prisons which appeared in Union and Confederate newspapers, and his later captivity memoir published during the conflict. Songs likewise expressed joy at his return to the Union states in August 1862. Irish-born soldier Richard Oulahan, who would later serve under Corcoran in the 164th New York, sent the ballad verse "Corcoran! The Prisoner of War" to the *Irish-American* in September 1863. Its lines celebrated Corcoran as "the PATRIOT PRISONER OF WAR!" who "tendered his sword and his life" to the United States, implying the diaspora should follow suit.[45] Subsequent songsheet ballads celebrated Corcoran's return as something that would bring hope to the Union Army. In lyrical form, this Irish-born officer was seen as would-be a savior for the whole country.

John F. Poole's 1862 "Pat's Opinion of the Stars and Stripes"—"sung, with great applause, by Fred May," one of New York City's leading music hall performers—discussed how Irish soldiers would achieve Union victory because:

Corcoran too, we'll have back in the fray,
With the Star-Spangled banner he raises;
Sure, he'll capture ould Jefferson Davis;
And will wallop the rebels like blazes,
An' will die with the *Stars* and the *Stripes!*[46]

The "Return of Gen. Corcoran, of the Glorious 69th" stressed the same message. It used Corcoran's 1861 Bull Run example to galvanize Irish soldiers in

1862 and argued that their war spirits would be enhanced when Corcoran came back from his captivity:

> 'Twas a the battle of Bull-Run, when first they met the foe,
> They charged the rebels with cold steel, and laid their columns low;
> And while the Northern ranks were broke, mid showers of shot and shell
> The Gallant Sixty Ninth still stood, nor flinched, but nobly fell.
> God bless the noble CORCORAN, who led them on the field,
> Against the odds of two to one he fought, but could not yield,
> For CORCORAN, valiant CORCORAN, the bravest of the brave
> Would fight to death, but ne'er retreat before a rebel knave . . .
> Hurrah! Hurrah! for the Sixty-Ninth how brave they look to-day,
> With gallant Corcoran at their head as if to meet the fray—
> God bless our Irish soldiers, in our hearts we shall entwine,
> The name of Michael Corcoran, and the Gallant Sixty-Ninth![47]

Songs did not exaggerate this overwhelming sense of joy when Corcoran rejoined Union Army service. Other contemporary writings shared the same sentiment. *Harper's New Monthly Magazine* illustrated the scene when Corcoran "returned to New York, where he has been received with the utmost enthusiasm . . . His popularity with his fellow-citizens of Irish birth or descent is unbounded."[48] One *Harper's* editorial made a greater feature of Corcoran's homecoming with its own ballad-like tone. It emphasized how important a role he had played, not only in his own personal exemplary conduct, but through the positive light he shone upon the diaspora:

> If General Washington had arrived . . . at Castle Green a few weeks since, he could not have been received with greater popular enthusiasm that which greeted General Corcoran . . . Who was this young hero, then, and what service had he done? The answer is simple enough. He is a Colonel who fought bravely at the head of his regiment and was taken prisoner . . . Why is this soldier, defeated in his only battle, greeted as the leader who had triumphantly ended the war and restored union and peace to the country? The reasons are many, but the chief is undoubtedly this, that, being an Irishman and a New Yorker, and one of the highest in rank who were taken at Bull Run, he was selected as the typical Union soldier in captivity. He suffered not only for

himself, but the nation looked in his person, upon the sufferings of all our hapless friends.[49]

Corcoran was presented as a selfless hero loyal to the United States, immortalized in song and through his actions on and off the battlefield. He was an example for how others should act. Such was his lasting impact among the Irish American Civil War generation that when Daniel Crowley mentioned the Irish Brigade in November 1864, nearly a year after Corcoran's death, he referred to the unit's founding 69th New York regiment as "the old 69th of Bull Run fame under Corcoran."[50]

Songs made it impossible for Corcoran and the 69th New York to be separated from each other. Even "Return of Gen. Corcoran" quoted above made this point clear. The two were forever "entwined" in American cultural memory. That created problems for the way songs described both the 69th New York and Irish Brigade in ballads, leading to a conflation between the two that suggests there was no inherent difference between them. "The Gallant 69th Regiment" and "The 69th Brigade" emphasized this lyrical military license, with the latter even combining the 69th New York and the Irish Brigade together into a "69th Brigade" unit. Such malleability suggests that for those writing and listening to ballads about Irish American Civil War service, it was the battlefield stories and war sentiments that mattered, not nuanced details about accurate units and command. By the time "The 69th Brigade" was written by F. Collins in 1862, Thomas Francis Meagher had, in the song, risen to the 69th New York State Militia's command, despite not actually having this position. William—the fictional young soldier whose story the song focused on—was praised as a "credited to his country, and the Sixty-Ninth Brigade" for having "[en]'listed with bold Meagher."[51]

When songsheets disseminated "The New York Volunteer" in 1862, and Sam Long performed it on New York's music hall stages, the city's eager willingness to send volunteers southward to battle was expressed across its lyrics. It too combined the 69th New York with the future Irish Brigade and held onto Corcoran for martial inspiration even with Meagher's overall Brigade leadership now in place:

The noble Sixty-Ninth,
Just see what they have done . . .

Now, they are reorganizing
Under Thomas Francis Meagher,
And they'll avenge brave Corcoran,
Like New York Volunteers.[52]

These lines—and general 69th New York and Irish Brigade fusion—drew attention to contemporary complex political wrangling among the diaspora's elite, especially in New York, about the formation of an official Union Army Irish Brigade and the selection of an Irish-born commander. Meagher himself initially pushed for James Shields to take command. Originally from County Tyrone, Ireland, Shields was an already-established army commander, having been resident in the United States since the mid-1820s. He had prior military expertise in his favor, having served with distinction in the 1840s during the Mexican-American War. A long-standing politician and commander, Shields was the grand old man of Irish American military service by the time of the Civil War. He was a natural choice for Irish Brigade commander.

As early as the Jones's Wood relief event at the end of August 1861, Meagher was busy behind the scenes to turn the occasion into a de facto recruiting rally to help establish an official Irish Brigade from the diaspora's main centers with Shields at the head. Six days before the gathering, Meagher wrote to Charles P. Daly to demand a breakfast meeting about "this serious business with regard to Shields," which he saw as "the *utmost* consequence."[53] However, Shields showed no real interest in taking Irish Brigade command, declining the offer of leading "a Military Brigade . . . comprised exclusively of Irishmen." He suggested in strong terms "that all action in his regard be suspended," inferring that was he was too old for a prominent position.[54] Shields did serve for a time in other Union Army regiments during the war but did not oversee an exclusively Irish unit. With his refusal to take it, the role of Irish Brigade commander would likely have been Corcoran's had he not been captured at Bull Run. Meagher, therefore, took charge when it was offered to him instead in the second half of 1861. The role never sat completely easy with New York Irish American elites, some of whom voiced "frustration over Meagher's filling the vacancy left by Michael Corcoran's capture."[55]

That frustration was not heard in wartime ballads. Meagher made numerous appearances in Irish Brigade, 69th New York, and more general songs, often appearing alongside, or in relation to, Corcoran. Indeed, Meagher rarely escaped Corcoran's lyrical shadow. "Battle of Bull's Run" described the former Young Irelander as "Meagher the exile, that death never daunted" who would be remembered "from ages to ages . . . as Ireland's Son."[56] By comparison to his fellow Irish-born commander, Meagher was not the specific subject of many Irish American Civil War songs, but when he did appear it was mostly with praise. All the rumors of his drunkenness and dereliction of duty during battles, including at Bull Run and Fredericksburg, which haunt accounts of Meagher's army leadership, were absent from songs.[57]

Meagher played a leading role in McDermott's lengthy "Irish Brigade" at Fredericksburg ballad. Like his lyrics about the Union charge up Marye's Heights, McDermott portrayed the general in elevated rhetoric, drawing on the image of past Irish chieftains rallying the sons of Erin before battle commenced. Based on stories of Meagher calling the Irish Brigade together on the morning of 13 December 1862 to galvanize its five regiments, "The Irish Brigade" explained how its Irish-born and descended soldiers were "impatient . . . [for] their Chief's command" to charge the Confederate line. Then, in an almost mythical depiction, Meagher appeared before his men:

> A planet of Heaven is hailed in Meagher . . .
> Now cheering with his bugle blast,
> That gallant MEAGHER fleets swiftly past;
> Through teeming groans, and clash and jar,
> His trumpet voice thus sounds afar:
> "Again to the charge, old Erin's sons!
> Again to the charge, and mount their guns!"[58]

Such rousing Meagher sentiments echo his various charismatic Irish Brigade recruitment rally speeches between 1861 and 1863 and repeated rhetoric heard in Irish ballads from the start of the war. In November 1861, Thomas J. MacEvily sent "War Song of the Irish Brigade" to the *Irish-American* to commemorate the Brigade's formation. He penned a verse that praised Meagher's command in glowing terms:

> Our leader is youthful, and manly and brave,
> The pride of our race: and a lover of glory . . .
> Then Meagher lead the way. We're eager for the fray,
> With thy spirit to cheer us we'll soon win the day.[59]

As with Corcoran, songs about Meagher presented him as a defender of the American Union. He was someone Irish Brigade soldiers, the diaspora, and wider society could praise as he gave his sword to defending his American home nation. Michael O'Riely's 1861 ballad about Irish volunteers ended with a toast wishing: "Long life of Colonel Meagher, he is a man of birth and fame, and while our Union does exist applauded be his name."[60]

Another O'Reilly, this time in the form of Charles Graham Halpine's fictional soldier Miles O'Reilly, heaped similar praise on Meagher's Irish Brigade leadership in one of his wartime stories. Halpine recounted a tale about the fictional meeting of his Irish-born protagonist with President Lincoln and Thomas Francis Meagher at the White House in 1863. Miles O'Reilly informed Lincoln that "the poor boys of the Irish Brigade" had experienced "days of its hardest fights under General Meagher." As a result, their leader "ought to have two stars on each shoulder or there could be no such thing as justice to Ireland."[61] The implication was that Meagher should be promoted because his influential leadership had inspired brave battlefield actions. Song lyrics reemphasized this point, adding that this showed yet more loyalty to the United States. "What Irish Boys Can Do" (1863) used both the examples of Meagher and Shields to push back against any latent anti-Irish nativism, reminding society about "Meagher, of the seven days fight, that was in front of Richmond, / With General Shields, who fought so brave for the Flag Red, White and Blue."[62]

Regardless of individual praise, Meagher could never truly escape association with his fellow Irish American Union Army commanders, particularly with reference to Michael Corcoran. In late 1862 and throughout 1863, Corcoran continued to be extolled in ballad verse. Not only did lyrics keep Meagher away from exclusive association with the Irish Brigade, they also ensured that, in cultural wartime song recollections at least, Corcoran was *the* figure of Irish American Civil War service. When the fictional soldiers of Paddy O'Toole and Mister McFinnigan sang about "the bould 69th" New York in the 1863 song "O'Toole & McFinnigan on the War," it was "Bould Corcoran leading us" they focused on, not the 69th New York's overall Irish Brigade commander Thomas Francis Meagher.[63]

Any uneasiness about Meagher's Irish Brigade command, or his resignation from the post in 1863 and subsequent service in other Union Army regiments, rarely reached surviving song lyrics. The idea of Meagher's wartime balladry depiction—and at times lack of depiction—related to more critical

home-front opinions of him is complicated by the fact that his soldiers ev-
idently supported him. Overall though, Meagher continued to play second
fiddle to Corcoran in wartime song culture. This was noticeable as Corcoran
set about establishing his own Irish command after his return from Confederate imprisonment. He recruited members of the diaspora, including some
of his old surviving 69th New Yorkers, for his "new brigade of Irishmen who
would preserve America" in late 1862.[64]

As with the 69th New York and Irish Brigade, lyrics about Corcoran's
ethnic-Irish Legion, comprised of five New York regiments—the 155th, 164th,
170th, and 182nd New York—appeared immediately after its establishment.
Richard Oulahan, who rejoined Corcoran's service from the 69th New York to
the 164th New York as a lieutenant, penned other ballad verses for the *Irish-
American* in November 1863. Entitled "Corcoran's Zouaves," it described the
unit's positive mood.[65] Twelve months before, Corcoran himself had observed
that "the health of the command is very good" over the Thanksgiving period.[66]
The former prisoner of war was content to be back in command, and songs
about his new posting reflected this atmosphere. On the other hand, when
Oulahan produced "Corcoran's Irish Legion" in August 1863, he had observed
with frustration that, given Corcoran's praiseworthy early war service, the Legion could be put to better use. After fighting around Centreville and being
camped at Newport News, Fairfax, and Suffolk, Virginia, Oulahan's ballad
verses described the Legion's seemingly quieter war experiences when compared to their Irish Brigade brethren:

> Our Colonels chafe to see us pine,
> Who know we'd all with them go . . .
> They order us to Limbo.
> So here we're doomed to swear and sweat,
> On Bull Run's bloody borders;
> Awaiting, what we hope to get,
> THE GEN'RAL'S MARCHING ORDERS.[67]

Oulahan presented a mundane Civil War reality that was absent in Eu-
gene T. Johnston's ballad about Corcoran's Legion. Johnston's "Corcoran's Irish
Legion" (1863) focused on familiar lyrics of war glory, praising the fact "brave
Corcoran our Leader is again to take Command." It reiterated how his war

service inspired Irish-born and descended soldiers and volunteers; he was "a patriot . . . loved and honored through the land" they wished to follow. The song's lyrics echoed accounts published when Corcoran returned to the North in August 1862 that drew on his reputation as a soldier who "to a traitor he never shall yield." Back in Union service, he would again be a key element in battlefield fights against the Confederacy:

> With a Legion of Irishmen, he'll bravely lead the van,
> And give old Stone wall Irish thunder;
> He never yet did fail; he is the very man
> To crush the traitors asunder![68]

A similar sentiment could be heard in "Corcoran's Ball!" (1863). The song was a parody of the traditional Irish ballad "Lannigan's Ball," well known in American musical culture by the Civil War. On H. De Marsan's songsheet version of the ballad, the publisher added a line about how the song had been "written expressively" by a John Mahon for the music hall performer Thomas L. Donnelly to sing "with tremendous applause at the New Bowery Theater" in New York City. It encouraged diaspora enlistment to Corcoran's Legion as a reward for the commander after his previous incarceration: "Hark to his music, brave Irishmen all! He spent thirteen months in a Southern prison, Boys." The song drew on Corcoran's past 69th New York leadership, his prisoner-of-war experience, the new Legion, and furthered conflation between his old and new regiments. Mahon's verses depicted the Civil War as if it was a ball, with officers and regiments taking their turn on the conflict's dance floor. Once more Corcoran's:

> Own 69th, who once fought so gloriously
> That even the Rebels their prowess admired,
> Are going again, and they'll surely victorious be;
> For, there be sons with virtue and honor are fired . . .
> Some of them passed many months in captivity,
> Practicing steps for Corcoran's ball.
> Come to the ball, Boys; let us not linger now,
> The music strikes up, choose your partners at once . . .
> Away with you now, Boys! Your presence is needed;

Go with the man who would take no parole.
Irishmen! Let not his call be unheeded;
Make Treason skedaddle at Corcoran's ball.[69]

Even though there was no memorable battle hour of trial for the Legion under Corcoran's leadership in 1863—especially when compared to the Irish Brigade's involvement at the Battle of Chancellorsville and Battle of Gettysburg that year—the Irish-born general and American Union song hero remained committed to the Union cause. Corcoran intended his "course to be the same now as I always desired it to be from the commencement of this war, using my best endeavors to discharge my duty in such manner, as that hereafter I may have the consolation of a thorough conviction of having acted to the fullest extent of my ability."[70] This statement best summarizes Corcoran's mentality as exhibited in his writings and song depictions of his Civil War service. Unfortunately for the Irish in America and wider Union society, this exemplar Irish-born general, who devoted his life to the United States and the fight to restore the Union, sacrificed himself at Bull Run, endured thirteen months in prison, returned, and formed his own corps of soldiers inspired by his example, died in December 1863. Corcoran, who once told the nation through his Confederate captivity memoir that "dying for one's country is glorious when it is accompanied by features that strip it of its terror," never had the chance for a final heroic ending on a battlefield that would have earned him the highest honor of lyrical martyred praise.[71] Suffering a fatal head wound after falling from his horse while riding with Meagher at Fairfax Court House, Virginia, Corcoran's death was bittersweet.

Ballad laments were penned in his honor, but had Corcoran died fighting it is likely even more songs would have been produced. One *Irish-American* contributor sent verses to the newspaper in January 1864 under the title "Written On Hearing the Death of General Corcoran." The unknown composer sent the composition from Montreal, Canada, indicative of how prevalent the general's reputation was and how widespread he was mourned.[72] Subsequently, Corcoran stopped appearing in later war songs. So too did the Irish Brigade and its composite regiments as the toll of three years' war service began to impact the way ballads sang about battlefield actions in general. Sentimental rhetoric and themes replaced heroic front-line depictions across the cultural spectrum, not just in Irish examples. Additionally, the fall in Irish Brigade lyrical appearances owed something to the unit's decline in number after the impact of losses at Fredericksburg, Chancellorsville, and Gettysburg. By the time he was entrenched with the 28th Massachusetts at Petersburg, Daniel Crowley reported how "there is no longer an Irish Brigade . . . Tom Meagher and the remnants of his Irish Brigade [were] buried in oblivion" as the unit became a Brigade in-name-only for part of 1864.[73] Yet, just as another Irish Brigade ballad verse grieved for the famed unit's decline it also continued to praise the wartime memory of its battlefield service, highlighting that this latter aspect at least would not be forgotten:

> Our Brigade exists no longer—they have gone—the good the true;
> Pulseless now, the gallant hearts that a craven feat ne'er knew.
> They fell, midst the crash and carnage of the battle's cruel storm . . .
> While thick and fast, upon their ranks, poured burning shot and shell,
> With their green flag floating o'er them, they proudly fought and fell.[74]

IRISH CONFEDERATE AND NON-IRISH BRIGADE BALLADS

In contrast to Irish Brigade examples, very few Confederate counterpart songs exist in surviving records. Nor did the Confederacy have the same general habit of singing about battles even though they were often victors on the field. That there were relatively few songs about the Irish who fought for the Confederacy chimes with David Gleeson's view that "the Irish did not have a huge military effect on the Confederacy." The estimated 20,000 Irish-born soldiers in grey—and the additional second, third, and subsequent generation descended men—were "not enough to have a major impact on the war."[75] By extension, there were not enough to have major impact on Confederate wartime ballad culture and lyrical representation, despite that traditional Irish tunes formed the foundation of much of the Confederate music output. Nonetheless, a couple of specific examples were printed that emphasized the presence of the diaspora's sons in the Confederate Army. "Erin's Dixie" (1863) praised Irish soldiers serving with Louisiana's Madison "Tips" Artillery, with this specific Confederate Irish version of "Dixie" describing how:

> The Irish blood is high and red,
> It always flowed where Freedom bled,

As now it does, it does in Dixie . . .
Each battle-field in Dixie shows it.[76]

One Irish-born general, whose blood flowed on the field at the 1864 Battle of Franklin, Tennessee, was commemorated in a general wartime song that honored the Confederacy's military leadership. "Our Country's Heroes" (1864) listed prominent generals, including Patrick Cleburne. Born in County Cork, Ireland, Cleburne had a long-established career in the British Army prior to emigrating in 1849 and settling in Helena, Arkansas, in the decade before the Civil War. His lyrical appearance demonstrates how "the Irish in the South recognized how important Cleburne had been to their cause, as well as to the South's."[77] It also revealed how wider white Southern society included Cleburne as part of the Confederate nation. The song offered "three cheers . . . for Cleburne" among a whole host of other military leaders—a brief, but important, lyrical inclusion.[78] Despite this specific reference, Cleburne and his Irish brethren in the seceded states never reached the same comparable lyrical level as their Northern compatriots.

In the Union, a few other non-Irish Brigade regiments and individuals found their way into song, separate from the more dominant 69th New York and Irish Brigade examples. Some would be very personal, such as "The Late Captain E. K. Butler," written in commemoration of Captain Edmond Butler, 182nd New York, part of Corcoran's Legion. The *Irish-American* published the composition after Butler's death at the Battle of Cold Harbor in June 1864.[79] The diaspora's prominent newspaper also published a very long ballad verse about Irish-born and descended soldiers fighting around Fort Donelson, Tennessee, in 1862. "Pat Rooney and His Little Ones" (1862) sung of a fictional Irish soldier's experience as color bearer, waving the regimental standard during battle:

He heads the advance,
With bold tread and glance . . .
In Columbia's fight,
Upon Donelson's height,
In defense of the right . . .
In the height of the fray,
His flag's shot away . . .
Amid carnage and flame.[80]

In addition, songs relating to the 69th New York included passing references to Irish soldiers engaging in battles beyond the main eastern theater of the war. "The New York Volunteer" (ca. 1862) described how Confederates would come to fear all Irish engagement in the conflict: "the rebels soon must yield" because "they cannon [cannot] stand our banding." The grouping together of Irish-born and descended soldiers in Union Army service "in Maryland, and New Orleans, and down to South Carolina" would bring a swift end to secession.[81] This sentiment implied the Irish would win the war for the American Union, a notion enhanced by the title of the ballad "Save the Constitution." Written and "dedicated to the 9th Connecticut Volunteers" in 1862, this specific Irish regiment was depicted as "the gallant Ninth, brave and defiant, now organized in splendor." As with fellow Union Army regimental sons of Erin, this particular unit took pride in their commitment, combating the enemy to the very last. One lyric expressed in ardent terms that when the 9th Connecticut were "in the field, they would not yield, in the ranks of dead you'll find them."[82]

The only other dominant Irish Union Army group to have widespread published wartime songs penned in their honor was the 69th Pennsylvania Volunteer Regiment, described by Meagher as "a stubborn Irish regiment, with its hearts as big as its muscle—proud as a true chief of some old Celtic clan."[83] Like their comparable New York regiment companions, the 69th Pennsylvania had their first ballad "respectfully dedicated to them" after their initial muster in August 1861. Written by Arthur McFadden, who served in Company B of the volunteer unit, "Col. Owens' Gallant Irish Volunteers" (1861) sang about yet another "Gallant 69th" who would "make the foe stand clear." Its soldiers were "men [who] are strong and hearty, no danger do they fear." McFadden devoted several lyrics to his Welsh-born commander, Joshua T. Owen, who was to be given "three cheers" alongside "his Irish Volunteers."[84] Originally from Carmarthen, like many of his Welsh countrymen Owen had migrated to Pennsylvania before the war. In command of the state's second most notable Irish regiment after the Irish Brigade's 116th Pennsylvania, Owen's 69th Pennsylvania soldiers obtained praise for their service at Fredericksburg, Chancellorsville, and Gettysburg. Owen himself, by comparison, faced rumors of cowardice at the battles of Chancellorsville, The Wilderness, Spotsylvania, and Cold Harbor. He was awaiting misconduct hearings in July 1863, thus removing him from command at Gettysburg.

In 1863, M. Fay wrote "Irish Volunteers—Penn'a's Gallant 69th" "dedicated to the Sixty-ninth Regiment Pennsylvania Volunteers." As with comparable Irish Brigade and 69th New York wartime ballads, much of the song gave a traditional broadside account of the unit's enlistment, service record, campaigns, and involvement on Virginian battlefields throughout the two previous years. The 69th Pennsylvania's Irish-born and descended soldiers— described as "Philadelphia's adopted sons"—drove fear into Confederate hearts by making "the rebels run" away at their mere presence in the front line. Much of the song sang of the regiment's war history up to that time. It is worth quoting this particular broadside battle narrative at length to demonstrate how similar in style and content it was to more numerous contemporary Irish Brigade songs, especially by comparison to McDermott's "Irish Brigade" Fredericksburg verses. Starting with the Seven Days Battles, "Irish Volunteers" sang of how the 69th Pennsylvania:

> On bloody fields we left our track,
> When other Regiments falling back . . .
> Right manfully we fought our way in one unbroken line,
> And when our bullets were all spent, three cheers we for the Union sent,
> And charging at the grey coasts went, the Irish sixty-ninth.
> And on Antietam field again we boldly faced the Iron rain,
> Some of our boys upon the plain, they found a bloody grave . . .
> At Fredericksburg our old brigade, with Owens, who never was afraid,
> As soon as the Pontoon was laid, we crossed in the first line,
> And though the bullets flew around, we drove the grey coats from the town,
> Such work is always done up brown [done properly], by the Irish sixty-
>   ninth . . .
> The cannons blazing shot and shell, 'twas like the gaping jaws of hell,
> Where many a brave man round us fell, we boldly done our share . . .
> The grass was turning red with blood,
> And growing to a crimson flood, we still kept in our line,
> Though many got a bloody shroud, as Philadelphia's sons we are proud,
> And sing the deeds in praises loud of the gallant sixty-ninth.[85]

For all the 69th Pennsylvanians' heroism Fay portrayed, there was another motive beyond pure regimental eulogy behind the song. The lyric about Owen, "who was never afraid," was at odds with rumors of his cowardly command. The cultural image of Owen was one of acclaim, and the lyric "[he] never was afraid" was applicable to his entire 69th Pennsylvania war conduct. Reading the song in this light reveals how Fay was making a political military point: Owen was a brave commander who fought to the last like his men. Similar to examples about Meagher, the fact songs did not make direct reference to Owen's alleged cowardly behavior demonstrates how Civil War ballads presented different sentiments and depictions of wartime history when compared to more traditional accounts, particularly in relation to military figures.

Furthermore, if Owen and Pennsylvanian references are removed from these two 69th Pennsylvania Regiment song examples, both ballads could be altered to fit stories of the Irish Brigade and the 69th New York. Indeed, the 69th Pennsylvania were even named in honor of their more famous Northern diaspora military counterparts. That all these regiments fought alongside each other at major Civil War engagements provided a wider shared narrative that encompassed many of the diaspora's serving regiments. Stories about Antietam, Fredericksburg, Chancellorsville, and Gettysburg were not exclusive to just the Irish Brigade. This only enhances the impression of inescapable Irish Brigade narrative dominance.

That was the point of songs dedicated to regiments that sang of Irish American Civil War units' service and wartime history. Those on the home front, and soldiers throughout the Union Army, could *all* be part of the Irish Brigade. They could all follow the 69th New York's lead by extolling their example through ballad articulation and dissemination. Irish-born and descended soldiers actually created a homogenized narrative because they wrote it into wartime cultural accounts, especially through the use of songs. "Pat Murphy of Meagher's Brigade" (1863) was one of the best demonstrations of this mentality. Also published under the title "Pat Murphy of the Irish Brigade" (and sometimes under the more traditional-sounding folk air title "Land of Shillaly"), "Pat Murphy" was *any* Irish-born or descended soldier.

When the songs sang about *one* nameless battlefield encounter and its aftermath, its lyrics were applicable to *all* engagements and soldiers. Even the Irish fighting in the Confederate states could share the same sentiments. Although "Pat Murphy of Meagher's Brigade" mentioned the Union Army's Irish Brigade, two of its verses presented a generic battlefield scene familiar to all involved in the conflict regardless of ethnicity and nationality:

Then, the Irish Brigade in the battle were seen,
Their blood, in our cause, shedding freely,
With their bayonet charges they rushed on the foe.[86]

One of the many "Irish Volunteer" ballads echoed these same sentiments, signifying that the Irish in America shared in the same war experiences as the whole country. Describing another nameless engagement, and applicable to all regiments, companies, and brigades, Arthur McCann's "Irish Volunteer" (ca. 1862) painted a recognizable image of war service that was not necessarily pertinent to the Irish experience:

In the fearful hour of battle,
When the cannons loud do roar,
We'll think upon our loves,
That we left to see no more;
And if grim death appears to us,
Its terrors and its fears
Can never scare in freedom's war,
Our Irish Volunteers.[87]

Of course, when it came to finding Irish volunteering soldier examples to emulate, one figure was elevated above all others in American Civil War songs. There was an officer who appealed to both Irish and wider American sections of society and whose place as the ultimate "Irish Volunteer" was cemented in 1862. "Written and sung" by Tony Pastor, "The Irish Volunteer, No. 3" was an adapted version of many traditional and contemporary "Irish Volunteer" ballads. It sang:

Of a soldier, both gallant and brave,
Who fought like a hero the Union to save;
If you list to my ditty, you'll know who I mean.

Seven lines later, Pastor revealed this gallant Irish Volunteer was none other than Michael Corcoran. Written in response to Corcoran's return after his prisoner-of-war captivity, on the surface, this song was comparable to others about Northern joy that the Irish-born promoted general was back in the Union fray. Pastor drew on established First Battle of Bull Run history to remind audiences about Corcoran's early war service:

> You know how he fought on that terrible day,
> When the rebel masked batteries opened the fray—
> In the midst of the battle was Corcoran seen . . .
> Nobly he stood by his banner of green.

Then Pastor switched lyrical focus to detail Corcoran's captivity, drawing on information that had filtered back to the home front about his prison experiences. This particular song story would share similarities to the tale Corcoran himself later told in his wartime memoir, reinforcing narrative dissemination between song and personal account sources. Pastor stressed to the country that Corcoran was utterly selfless serving in the Union cause, and that he "showed . . . his heart was sound."

After returning to the Northern states in late summer 1862, Corcoran toured the main Eastern seaboard diasporic centers, telling his own tale and galvanizing Irish war support. His words and actions, and the many lyrical references to him in Irish American Civil War songs, hammered home that his was the example to follow. Corcoran was the literal personification of what Irish service in the Union Army was to be. Devoted to the United States, eager to fight, a proud representative of Irish heritage and American identity, it is little wonder he appeared in so many ballads. As the cultural embodiment of Irish wartime service, he stood for all. Corcoran was *the* Irish Volunteer, and Irish-born and descended soldiers were Corcoran-esque.

Tony Pastor's Corcoran "Irish Volunteer" song ended in grand lyrical terms with the sentiment of renewed optimism that the general's return would benefit the country:

> A bright sunshine has followed the rain,
> And back in New York we have got him again—
> At the head of his Brigade he now will be seen.
> And as such a valor and worth he displayed,
> A Brigadier-general he now has been made—

And the insults he met from the vile rebel crew—
He'll pay them all back; aye, and interest too—
Or he'll die for the Stars and the banner of green.[88]

In short, Michael Corcoran returned ready to face Confederates on the battlefield, with Irish-born and descended soldiers prepared to follow his example. "His Brigade" was both the Irish Brigade and his new Irish Legion. By extension, in song at least, he was leader of every Irish man and woman as the diaspora turned to this most preeminent Irish American chieftain. Culturally, it was an apt honor. Corcoran had familial connections to far older Irish foreign military legacies and fighting for causes greater than his own life. All the songs about Corcoran, his 69th New York, the Irish Brigade, and broader Irish military war service in the United States continued a longer fighting history. That tradition, combined with retaining a sense of cultural heritage, reinforced the way Irish memory of the past was sung alongside the American Civil War present.

Officers of the 69th New York State Militia pose at Fort Corcoran, Arlington, Virginia, in July 1861. The photograph was taken before the First Battle of Bull Run. Colonel Michael Corcoran is on the far left. Captain Thomas Francis Meagher is in the background, leaning his arms on the cannon. *Library of Congress, Civil War Photograph Collection.*

Scorebook cover commemorating the "100th Edition" of J. L. Geddes's "The Bonnie Flag with the Stripes and Stars" (St. Louis: Balmer & Weber, 1863). This was one of many Union adaptations of Harry Macarthy's 1861 Confederate anthem "The Bonnie Blue Flag." *Library of Congress, Civil War Sheet Music Collection.*

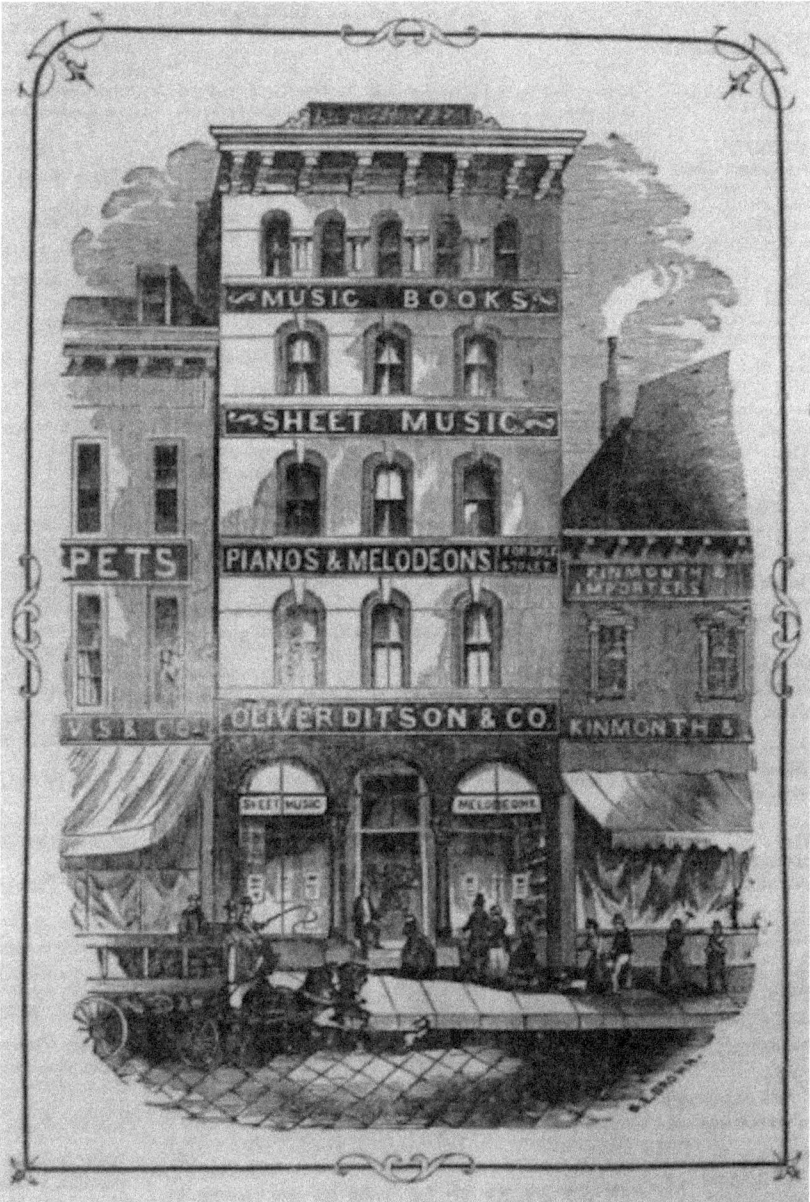

A sketch of one of Oliver Ditson's publishing houses in central Boston, Massachusetts. From here, Ditson sold instruments, songsheets, and periodicals such as *Dwight's Journal of Music*. *Author's collection.*

Carte de visite of General Michael Corcoran (ca. 1862–63), produced by E. & H. T. Anthony of New York, "manufacturers of the best photographic albums." *Author's collection.*

Irish harp and "Erin Go Bragh" banner illustration above the Confederate "Song for the Irish Brigade" (New Orleans: *Hopkins' New Orleans 5 Cent Song Book,* 1861). *Author's collection.*

Front cover of *The Camp Fire Songster* (New York: Dick & Fitzgerald, 1862). Described as "a collection of popular, patriotic, national, pathetic and jolly songs," the songster included several productions relating to Irish American Civil War service and Irish foreign military history. *Author's collection.*

A sketch of the fictional Private Miles O'Reilly in Charles Graham Halpine's *The Life and Adventures, Songs, Services and Speeches of Private Miles O'Reilly* (New York: Carleton, 1864). *Author's collection.*

Detail from one songsheet publication of the "Irish Volunteer, No. 3" (New York: H. De Marsan, 1862). A border of the Stars and Stripes and other American symbols framed the top of the ballad's lyrics. *Library of Congress, American Singing: Nineteenth-Century Song Sheets Collection.*

Detail of a postcard sent to Miss Hanna Coyle in Ireland from her friend on holiday in Detroit, Michigan, dated 10 October 1908, showing the continued emphasis of united dual American and Irish banner symbology. *Author's collection.*

4

———— ✠ ————

Lyrical Cultural Identity

A ccording to one "No Irish Need Apply" ballad, "sure the world knows Paddy's brave, for he's helped to fight their battles, both on the land and wave."[1] Emphasizing heroic Irish martial history, these lyrics related past service to the present Union and Confederate engagement. By singing about Irish involvement across the Crimea, India, and Europe, such "No Irish Need Apply" response rhetoric ensured Irish military legacies were shared with the wider American public. The two strands of remembering and reinforcing Irish foreign service and heritage combined to cement "the fighting Irish" concept in the Civil War. As Thomas Francis Meagher expressed at a New York recruiting rally on 25 July 1862: "Irishmen . . . long ago established for themselves a reputation for fighting with a consummate address and a superlative ability."[2] The Confederate "Erin's Dixie" was more blunt: "the Irishman is a fighting man, when fight he must."[3]

The expression of Irish pride in foreign military service, and the influence it played in volunteerism and fighting on the battlefield, were often extolled in Civil War songs. Moreover, ballads produced within Union and Confederate military and domestic settings sang about broader Irish cultural heritage identity. References to Ireland, symbols of Irishness, and American influence on Irish language articulation, all featured in wartime lyrics. In particular, the Irish Brigade used the example of their forefathers fighting in eighteenth-century Europe to generate numerous recollections in the mid-1800s United States. Tales were spread of the Wild Geese, the original Irish Brigade in the French Army, and past heroes that Generals Michael Corcoran and Thomas Francis Meagher emulated. The Civil War experience of Irish-born and descended soldiers added another page to the story of this foreign fighting legacy, as the warring United States became a fundamental part of Irish American cultural and martial heritage.

IRISH FOREIGN MILITARY SERVICE

Unsurprisingly, given that they were named in honor of their Irish European counterparts, the Union Army's Irish Brigade made particular reference to their martial past in the numerous wartime songs. Irish Brigade ballads often included explicit lyrical connections between the Civil War and the War of the Austrian Succession (1740–48). Irish Jacobite exiles, dubbed the "Wild Geese" to symbolize their flight from Ireland, could be found in Spanish, French, and other continental armies throughout the sixteenth to eighteenth centuries.[4] This included the French Army's original Irish Brigade who fought against British forces at the Battle of Fontenoy in 1745. The engagement became the foundation for Irish Brigade foreign army service history and was sung about in subsequent nineteenth-century ballads, including those produced in the United States. One of the earliest examples of Fontenoy fighting evocation appeared in Thomas J. MacEvily's "War Song of the Irish Brigade," submitted to the *Irish-American* newspaper in November 1861. It included reference to the Wild Geese's flight and how the Union Army's Irish Brigade would "ring out with great joy" the name and memory of "Fontenoy! Fontenoy!"[5]

Following praiseworthy service at the battles of Fair Oaks, Antietam, Fredericksburg, Chancellorsville, and Gettysburg, the Irish Brigade became the main focus of three ballads, all of which drew on Fontenoy imagery. Kate C. M.'s "The Irish Brigade" (1862) placed present actions in the context of the past, with Irish soldiers in America adding to former glory by showing: "You'll prove that no time can that name destroy / That you won by your valor on the plains of Fontenoy."[6] "The Irish Brigade in America" (1863) likewise reflected how the present version of the American Union Army's Irish Brigade was "like their noble ancestors, as in ancient days gone by." The song remembered how the original Irish Brigade in France was "led on by General Sarsfield at the siege of Fontenoy," creating a confused ballad history that linked the 1st Earl of Lucan Patrick Sarsfield, the 1690 siege of Limerick, and the 1745 Battle of Fontenoy together. Sarsfield, the Jacobite commander, had died over fifty years before. To be exact, the lyrics should have stated "the siege of Limerick" not "the siege of Fontenoy."[7] Written almost 120 years after that engagement, "The Irish Brigade in America" lyrics created a semifictional military past the diaspora could still draw inspiration from, even if it was not historically accurate.

By comparison, Hugh F. McDermott's "The Irish Brigade" (1863) included the motivating words Meagher had given his men before they marched on Marye's Heights, Fredericksburg, in December 1862. Adopting Meagher's commanding voice, McDermott's ballad sang of how the Brigade's regiments were rallied by the recall of past generations:

Again to the charge, old Erin's sons!
Again to the charge, and mount their guns!
Behold the Green! Think of its fame!
Think how your sires baptized its name!

In poetic terms, the song described how the Irish Brigade's five regiments were infused with the spirit of their fighting ancestors. Awaiting the charge against the Confederate line, McDermott's lyrics sang about how the Irish "soldier's soul is a harp of joy," which was "tuned to the glory of Fontenoy."

The image of these soldiers brimming with pride for their Irish Brigade heritage was furthered by McDermott's description of how they wore "green plums." Prior to marching out of the center of Fredericksburg to meet the Confederates' "bristling guns," Meagher ordered sprigs of boxwood to be given to each of his men.[8] Father Corby recounted the moments when "General Meagher advised every soldier to put a sprig of box-wood in his cap, so that he could be identified as a member of the brigade should he fall."[9] The floral arrangements were more than just identification though. As they placed it in their caps, soldiers called on cultural imagery "to symbolize the Irish heritage of the unit," with the green plant acting as a substitute for unavailable shamrocks, the well-known symbol of Ireland. "The boxwood would serve to remind friend and foe alike that these were Irishmen fighting for American union," and provided an "image of Ireland" on an American battlefield.[10]

Songs about the 69th New York Regiment echoed their Irish Brigade counterparts by drawing on Irish cultural martial heritage to reinforce their ethnic identity. "War Song of the New York 69th Regiment" (1861) made Irish-born and descended soldiers "swear [to] protect the Stars and Stripes" and—in a repeated refrain at the end of each verse—promised that the 69th

New York would "remember Fontenoy."[11] This story was recounted in the lyrics of "Return of Gen. Corcoran, of the Glorious 69th" (1862), which sang about how Meagher drew on the spirit of the original Irish Brigade at the Battle of Fontenoy to spur on the 69th New York from the start of the conflict at the First Battle of Bull Run and later at the Battle of Fair Oaks:

> As at the charge of "Fontenoy," our brave men of to-day,
> With gallant Meagher, drove the foe, in terror and dismay—
> For at the battle of "Fair Oaks, as at the "Seven Pines,"
> The Irish charge, with one wild yell, broke through the rebel lines.[12]

In addition to Fontenoy, 69th New York songs made lyrical reference to another famous battle that included Irish participation, though this time one that saw Irish soldiers fighting *for* the British Army *against* the French. The Battle of Waterloo (1815) had double resonance in Irish foreign military service history as it involved Irish regiments and was won by an Irishman Arthur Wellesley, Duke of Wellington.[13] "Glorious 69th" (1861) compared the 69th New York State Militia's journey from New York to Washington, DC, to the bivouac experience in Belgium as Wellington's forces gathered to meet Napoleon. When they "pitched our camp" at the side of the road, soldiers did not complain about their surroundings because they followed in the footsteps of their fighting ancestors:

> Without feather-bed or bedstead . . .
> We laid down in the damp, my Boys, as Soldiers ought to do,
> As did our famed Fathers on the plains of Waterloo.[14]

These famed Irish fathers were revered in transnational Irish military history and balladry. Kathleen O'Neil's 1863 "No Irish Need Apply" provided a satirical commentary about how the French would have appreciated the Irish being barred from army service because their contribution led to British victory at Waterloo:

> Och! The French must loudly crow to find we're slighted thus,
> For they can ne'er forget the blow that was dealt by one of us,

If the Iron Duke of Wellington had never drawn his sword,
Faith they might have "Napoleon Sauce" with their beef, upon my word.[15]

Waterloo and Wellington further made a lyrical appearance in "What Irish Boys Can Do" (1863). Referring to fighting spirit, one verse asked society to think of how Irish martial heritage might benefit the nation:

Did you ever know an Irishman from any danger flinch?
In fighting, too, he'd rather die than give his foe an inch;
Among the bravest in the world are the sons of Erin's green isle
Sure, the Iron Duke of Wellington was a native of the soil;
And didn't he badly whip the French on the plains of Waterloo?
Which plainly showed to the whole world what Irishmen can do.[16]

The implication here was that if Irish soldiers and an Irish-born general were instrumental in instigating one of the most successful military victories in history, then Irish-born and descended fighters in the United States could perform the same actions for the Union Army's benefit. Similarly, the Fenian "What Irishmen Have Done" (ca. 1870) commented on Wellington's Anglo-Irish identity by describing him as "England's honor . . . who fought at Waterloo."[17]

This postbellum ballad also raised a contradiction in relation to recounting foreign military history. During the Civil War, "What Irish Boys Can Do" had conflated Sarsfield's Wild Geese leadership and role during the Siege of Limerick with the Battle of Fontenoy. By comparison, "What Irishmen Have Done" combined Wild Geese service *against* the British in the sixteenth and seventeenth centuries with Irish service *for* the British during the Napoleonic Wars. "Wild Geese" as a term and diasporic identity do not appear explicitly in Irish American Civil War lyrics, yet they were alluded to as Fontenoy examples show. American wartime songs, and the general expansion of encompassing all Irish soldiers into one history, presented a ballad version of Wild Geese sentiment that was less about recalling specific conflict moments.

In ballads, Wild Geese history became applicable to *all* fighting Irish forefathers. This provides an interesting impression about how the diaspora learned Irish military history from oral and written broadside balladry. Accuracy was muffled for the sake of singing an inspiring story. Even when "The Irish Brigade in America" was published in Scotland under the title "The Soldier's Letter From America" in 1863, conflation of Wild Geese and Irish foreign military service was transmitted back across the Atlantic. As long as soldiers and the wider home-front community could be inspired by this military cultural heritage, *who* they were fighting for and/or against was not important. The lyrical point was that fighting—and the honor that came with it—mattered most.

Additionally, Wild Geese allusions appeared in the numerous "Irish Volunteer" ballads, which had circulated in traditional Irish song culture from the eighteenth century. "The use of the term [Irish Volunteers] . . . had deep meaning for Irish soldiers," it recalled the heritage of "various Irish Volunteers" in continental Europe who "had achieved glory on the battlefield." Irish units in the Union and Confederate armies sang of their own role as Irish Volunteers as a way to embrace "their ethnic heritage." Several Confederate militias and companies named themselves in honor of past Wild Geese heroes like Patrick Sarsfield and Irish nationalist figures like Robert Emmet.[18] Reverend Paul E. Gillen, a chaplain to both the Irish Bridge and Corcoran's Legion, even named his horse Sarsfield in a spur of equine emulation.[19]

The heroes drawn upon in Irish American Civil War songs were mostly battlefield figures, not Irish nationalist ones. One exception appeared in "The Irish Volunteer," "as sung by Joe English" in Union musical halls. Its lyrics presented the perspective of a former "native of the Isle" named Tim McDonald. He described how his father "fought in 'Ninety-eight, for liberty so dear," referring to the 1798 Rebellion against British rule. The senior McDonald "fell upon old Vinegar Hill, like an Irish volunteer," commenting that he had taken part at the Battle of Vinegar Hill, County Wexford (June 1798) against several thousand British soldiers who ended the uprising decisively. By fighting for liberty from secessionist treason (as the song described it), McDonald called on more Irish history to galvanize American Union loyalty among Irish-born and descended men and women: "Now if the traitors in the South should ever cross our roads, / We'll drive them to the devil, as Saint Patrick did the toads."[20]

American-produced song references to St. Patrick and 1798 reinforce that wider society would have been familiar with Irish nationalist and military histories, as well as with Ireland's patron saint.[21] Nonetheless, lyrics about past heroes' service were directed solely at the Irish American community. When

"Corcoran to His Regiment" (1861) sang of following in Irish military fore-fathers' footsteps, it asked possible Irish volunteers and recruited soldiers to:

Think how your brave fathers for your freedom fought;
Think of those bright deeds which Irishmen have wrought;
Meet advancing hosts, boys let them feel your steel,
And prove you're worthy of the land of Sarsfield and O'Neill.[22]

The emphasis on "your" was aimed at the Irish in America first and fore-most. Wider Union and Confederate society could draw inspiration from Irish military stories, but only the Irish could culturally and historically claim ownership and inheritance of that history. Only they could prove themselves worthy as the lyrics emphasized. This verse also referred to other past Irish heroes—the O'Neills, Ireland's famed chieftains who led resistance to English rule in the late sixteenth and seventeenth centuries. Unlike Sarsfield, the O'Neills made infrequent appearances in wartime songs.[23] They were, however, mentioned in the Confederate "Song for the Irish Brigade" (1861), which drew on O'Neill clan Red Hand of Ulster heraldry to describe how Union soldiers would be cleared from the battlefield by Irish-born and descended soldiers fighting in the Confederate states:

The Irish green shall again be seen
As our Irish fathers bore it . . .
O'Neil's red hand shall purge the land—
Rain fire on men and cattle.[24]

Writing this history into 1860s ballads helped continue an ethnic military identity that connected to immigrant home-front communities. It referred to traditional Irish tales disseminated generation to generation, reinforcing transnational cultural heritage transmission to immigrant populations. Such sentiment mattered to the Irish American Civil War generation, whose service was additionally put into the context of more recent nineteenth-century fighting examples—including reference to enlistment in the British Army across the British Empire, the Mexican-American War, and the Crimean War. Kathleen O'Neil's "No Irish Need Apply" ballad made reference to the former and latter, describing how "at the storming of Sebastopol, and beneath an Indian sky, Pat raised his head" as a British Army soldier because "their General said, 'All Irish might apply.'"[25] Another "No Irish Need Apply" version, published in 1864, drew on Irish Crimean War service to stress how their victorious battle actions would be reenacted on American battlefields:

> At Balaklava, Inkerman, and through the Russian War,
> Didn't Irishmen fight bravely as they've often done before?
> As in this War their loyal arms have made the rebels fly,
> So pray blot out forever, *that* "no Irish need apply."[26]

Song references to Irish involvement in conflicts prior to the Civil War contained vocabulary which later appeared in Irish American soldiers' postbellum memoirs. Major General St. Clair Augustine Mulholland, originally from Lisburn in Northern Ireland, wrote his recollections of serving with the 116th Pennsylvania Regiment in the Irish Brigade. Like ballads about their war experience, Mulholland saw Irish Brigade service as part of a longer history: "in every age, in every clime . . . in India, in Africa, in China, and on all the fields of Europe, they have left their footprints and the records of their valor."[27] This was comparable to Captain David Power Conyngham's Irish Brigade account written in 1867. He argued "there [were] few battle-fields in Europe in which the Irish soldier has not left his footprints."[28]

The Irish-born chaplain Father James M. Dillon used the same lyrical rhetoric in his sermon to the Irish Brigade's 63rd New York Regiment during their flag presentation ceremony when they joined the unit in 1861. He placed their service in the context of an established history: "The fathers of most of you have fought in every battlefield, from Fontenoy to Chapultepec, and their bayonets were ever in the van. Let it be said of you, ere this causeless rebellion is suppressed, that the soldiers of the Irish Brigade have emulated the heroism of their forefathers."[29] Father Dillon likely repeated this sermon's themes when he joined General Michael Corcoran's Legion two years later in February 1863. The Irish commander himself rarely drew overt attention to his Irish roots—which included descent from none other than Patrick Sarsfield—but during the establishment of his group of Irish New York regiments in 1863, Corcoran celebrated with pride that his men were marching on an esteemed Irish foreign service path. He was "fully confident that when the great hour of trial arrives," his soldiers would "do honor to their name and race!"[30]

LYRICAL IRISH LANGUAGE PHRASES

When news of Irish-born and descended volunteers' actions at the First Battle of Bull Run traveled across the Atlantic to Ireland in July 1861, one voice expressed sorrow at Irish battlefield involvement: "Poor Granu grieves unto herself, for those who lie far away, / And numbered with the dead, alas! All in America."[31] Granu—one of the many variations of Granuaile or Gráinne—was a figure of Irish folklore. During the eighteenth and nineteenth centuries, her presence could be found in Irish ballad tales that spread beyond the island through printed broadsides and the diaspora's maintenance of her mythical persona. Granuaile's name "became symbolic for Ireland and appears . . . in many songs" under several anglicized and Irish-language spellings, all of which ensured legends about her "were still very much alive," even in the United States of America. Granuaile tales and images appeared in Civil War songs as the metaphorical embodiment of the old Irish nation, another female figure who stood alongside personifications of Erin.[32] Both Granuaile and Erin were employed by songwriters to present motherly images of the shared grief and pride that Ireland, and the Irish in America, felt toward their soldier sons.

These allegorical images were just two of the main figurative ways lyrics expressed a sense of identity through cultural symbology use. While a pervading sense of American association could be heard in wartime ballads, songs about the Irish did not abandon their old homeland country entirely either. A diasporic sense of Irishness was reinforced, drawing on traditional images and symbols of Ireland—the harp, shamrocks, Erin and Granualie to name a few—alongside references to foreign military history. Considering the pride Irish soldiers took in their martial pasts, it is unsurprising that expressions of their Irish identity found their way into the Civil War songs. This went beyond simply reinforcing Irish ethnicity by setting songs to traditional Irish tunes such as "The Irish Jaunting Car." Lyrics sang explicitly of Irish symbols and phrases familiar to those from the old homeland and within diasporic settings. The proliferation of songsheets and songsters that included these references kept such allusions of Irish ethnic cultural heritage alive as they were disseminated beyond migrant communities.

By extension, Civil War songs indicate a broad familiarity with the Irish language, particularly through the not-infrequent lyrical use of three core phrases: "Cead Mile Failte," "Faugh a Ballagh," and "Erin go Bragh." These references could even form the titles of wartime songs; Thomas M. Brown's ballad for the 9th Massachusetts regiment, "Cead Mille Fealthe," used the expression to welcome back the unit to its home state in 1864. A description on the cover of the song's music scorebook explained that the common Irish saying translated to "A Hundred Thousand Welcomes"—an appropriate expression to sing to the returning Irish-born and descended 9th Massachusetts soldiers. Brown also used the phrase in the body of song, with one lyric expressing how the welcoming Boston crowds would sing "a Cead Mille Fealthe, our heroes, we give ye with heart, and with hand."[33] "Return of Gen. Corcoran, of the Glorious 69th" employed the phrase as the song cheered for Michael Corcoran's arrival from prisoner-of-war captivity with multiple Irish and American greetings:

A CEAD MAILLE FAILTHE we give to thee brave man,
Thou hero of the Sixty Ninth who nobly led the van,
With a hundred thousand welcomes we grasp thee by the hand,
And proudly claim thee, Corcoran, brave son of Erin's Land.[34]

While a hundred thousand "Cead Mile Failthe" references were not present in all Irish American Civil War songs, variations of the expression "Faugh a Ballagh" appear throughout lyrical sources. Translated as "Clear the Way," the Irish-language phrase had become a common military iteration, originating with Irish soldiers in the British Army in the previous century. Use of the phrase added another factor to the remembrance of Irish military service. When the "Glorious 69th" was sung about the 69th New York State Militia's journey to defend Washington, DC, in April 1861, its lyrics drew on this old Irish military phrase:

It was our whole intention to go through Baltimore,
And if attacked there by a mob, we'd show them what we could do;
We'd shout them out: FAUGH-A-BALLA! As we did at Waterloo.

The song returned to the expression in a subsequent verse, referring to the original Irish phrase and its English translation as it sang about the moment the 69th New York were reviewed by Union General Winfield Scott after reaching the capital. One stanza presented the lyrical story of how the senior military officer informed President Lincoln that the new arrivals came from a rich tradition of Irish martial service, and that this heritage would benefit the Union Army:

> They marched us by the White-House, reviewed by Gen. Scott;
> He said unto our President; Now, everything looks gay;
> Here comes the FAUGH-A-BALLAS that always clears the way![35]

As the war progressed, Irish American Civil War songs about the 69th New York continued to draw on "Faugh a Ballagh" for lyrical inspiration. "Corcoran to His Regiment" urged the men to join the war effort. Alongside recruitment propaganda, lyrics sang about using the war cry as rallying weapon against Confederate forces: "FAUGH-A-BALLAGH shout from the centre to your flanks, / And carry death and terror wild, into the foeman's ranks."[36] "The Irish Brigade in America," printed in early 1863, included a passing anglicized reference to the phrase that extended the notion of "clearing the way" as a form of battlefield tactic. In the song's Battle of Fredericksburg lyrical report, the Irish Brigade, "in six decisive charges . . . nobly cleared the way" as they participated in the Union attack along the base of Marye's Heights.[37]

A similar sentiment could be heard in "War Song of the New-York 69th Regiment," which contained a repeating chorus image about clearing Confederates from their lines. These lyrics used the phrase as both a military cry and an inspirational mantra to galvanize Irish support for the war effort in the Union states: "Then forward! From our homes and alters, all we hold most dear, / Our war-cry: Faugh-a-ballagh! Erin's sons will know no fear."[38] "The Irish-American Army" (ca. 1866) furthered this lyrical image by again adopting the refrain throughout, using the English translation: "Then hip, hurra! Come clear the way."[39] Soldiers took the expression and practice of "clearing the way" to heart, as revealed by the young Irish-born 28th Massachusetts soldier Patrick Kelly in early 1862. He informed his parents that it was "a fine thing to be a Faugh for [we] are bound to clear the way" when his regiment faced the opposition.[40] The rallying war cry became part of Civil War Union Irish identity and fighting service and was extolled through wartime songs. These were subsequently shared with wider Union communities.

In the Confederate states, Irish-born and descended soldiers sang "Faugh a Ballagh" in the "Song for the Irish Brigade." In this example, the image of "clearing the way" was reversed from Union examples. Instead, lyrics sang of Irish Louisianan soldiers clearing Union troops from battlefields:

> With pale affright and panic flight
> Shall dastard Yankees, base and hollow,
> Hear a Celtic race, from their battle-place;
> Charge to the shout of "Faugh a ballagh!"[41]

This sentiment was echoed in a general Confederate ballad about how the Irish "Celtic race" inspired the seceded states' fighting. "A Ballad for the Young South," written by Joseph Brenan in 1861, sang of Southern heritage. It praised "the clansmen of the Gael," and mentioned how Irish, Scottish, and Scots-Irish influence aided Confederate nationhood and fighting identity: "The fiery Celt's impassioned thought inspire the Southern heart."[42] "Faugh a Ballagh" thus enthused Irish American soldiers fighting for the Confederate cause just as it did in Union lyrical examples. It could also apply to more general secessionist mentality about clearing "dastard Yankees" from the battlefront and political fields of the conflict. The concept of "clearing the way" was not solely an Irish military and diasporic one.

Moreover, when publisher John Hopkins printed "Song for the Irish Brigade" in one of his Confederate-supporting five-cent songsters, he included a pictorial depiction of Irish cultural symbolism that complemented the song's lyrics. It referred to the third, and most common, Irish-language phrase heard in Irish American Civil War songs. Above the ballad's title was an engraving of an Irish harp decorated with shamrocks, the two dominant symbols of Irish national identity. Underneath was a banner with "ERIN GO BRAGH" emblazoned in bold, copying images seen on Irish regimental flags.[43] Translated commonly as "Ireland Forever," the expression "Erin go Bragh" appeared in several Union and Confederate ballads. The phrase roused support for the diaspora's wartime service and loyalty to their respective causes.

This national war cry would have been familiar to American audiences by the 1860s. For instance, it had appeared in the antebellum ballad "The Escape of Meagher," written in 1852 and disseminated as a broadside in both Ireland and the United States. It sang of Thomas Francis Meagher's escape from exile on Van Diemen's Land (present-day Tasmania, Australia). When he arrived in New York City, Meagher was greeted by diasporic enthusiasm: "it's plain to see, for Erin go Bragh, the sons they still have a grah." These lyrics used "Erin go Bragh" rhetoric and furthered Irish-language recall with the application of "grah." This latter word was an adaption of "gra," meaning "love." Therefore, the song was singing about the diaspora's affectionate love for the future Irish Brigade commander.

"The Escape of Meagher" included Irish lyrical references that explained how Meagher was "torn" from Ireland and taken "away from poor Granua in chains." Now in the United States, he was "an exile for life no more to return" to his native land.[44] Here again was the allegorical image of Granuaile, standing for the country of Ireland that Meagher had left following his imprisonment and exile after the failed 1848 Young Ireland revolt. These lyrics indicate a sense that such terms and Irish cultural knowledge were known beyond immigrant communities. Indeed, one traditional folk song that included reference to Granualie—"Granny Wales and the Mulberry Tree"—was written during the American Revolution. It was set to the tune "Old Gran Weal," whose music was "clearly . . . circulating in oral tradition" of 1770s America. The song certainly had Irish roots as it sang of an Irish story and historical figures and used "the spirit of Ireland . . . as a symbol for the struggle for independence in which the American colonies were engaged."[45] "Gran Weal" in the ballad's title was another corruption of Granuaile (like Granu), again revealing how she had existed as a figure in American musical culture long before Meagher's arrival inspired song lyrics that made reference to her.

"Erin go Bragh" was sustained as a war cry within pre–Civil War Irish American military culture as well. Its origins lay with the independence organization, the Society of United Irishmen in Ireland, and in manifestations of modern Irish nationalism in 1798. In the 1840s during the Mexican-American War, Irish Catholic San Patricios deserters who fought against the United States carried a "green silk" flag with "a crudely drawn figure of St. Patrick, a shamrock and a harp." The phrase "Erin go Bragh" was embroidered underneath.[46] This was much like subsequent Union and Confederate Irish regiment and army unit banners. Consequently, American audiences would have understood the inclusion of "Erin go Bragh" phrasing, such as in songs about the Union Army's Irish Brigade that often integrated the Irish-language expression into lyrics as well as symbols. As it sang of pride in Irish fighting heritage, one 1863 "Irish Brigade" ballad contained the exclamation: "O lone harp of Erin! O Erin go bragh!"[47] Hugh F. McDermott's "Irish Brigade" tied the saying to articulations of American loyalty: in the Union states, "the air is rent with a wild huzzah for the Stars and the Stripes and Erin-go-Bragh!"[48] "Erin's Dixie" conveyed Irish and Confederate loyalty with bold pride, through the use and exaltation of the war cry:

> For Dixie's land our wild "go bragh"
> Shall ring again—hurrah! hurrah!
> For Erin dear and gallant Dixie.[49]

Lyrical employment of "Cead Mile Failte," "Faugh a Ballagh," and "Erin go Bragh" reveal an attempted dual maintenance of Irish cultural linguistic heritage in the United States. However, their appearance was in the minority. The traditional Irish language itself, at least amongst the majority of surviving songs about the Irish American Civil War experience, was mostly limited to these phrases. Even in instances where songwriters would write in a mock-Irish dialect brogue to stress and parody the ethnic context of their productions, lyrics, and verses were first and foremost written in English. Publications like the *Fenian Songster,* where the songs were printed with bilingual English and Irish translated lyrics side-by-side, were uncommon in this era.[50]

In many of the examples quoted in this chapter, there are variations of Irish-language spelling. These three terms were also all presented in anglicized form.[51] This would have enabled performers to recognize and sing them phonetically. It indicates familiarity with a common Americanized Irish-language pronunciation. While it is beyond the scope of this book to assess the state of the Irish-language in 1860s America, certain expressions—both before and during the Civil War—found an established place within a transnational Irish American lexicon.[52] As songs spread throughout the Union and Confederacy, phonetic versions of Irish-language war cries and sayings were absorbed into the wider culture in a similar manner to traditional Irish music tunes. Their anglicized Americanization phrasing presents another example of Irish wartime lyrics being sung with an American voice.

* * *

GREEN FLAGS OF ERIN AND
THE STARS AND STRIPES

Alongside recollections of foreign military service, references to sprigs of shamrocks and boxwood, and smatterings of Irish-language phrases, the most visible manifestation of Irish cultural nationalism in Civil War songs were the green banners carried by several of the Irish-dominant Union and Confederate units, companies, regiments, and brigades. Song lyrics referring to banners provided stories about "the green" flying over the country's battlefields. As the lyrics of "The Irish-American Army" note, when Irish American soldiers "down Broadway . . . march'd," having "the Green Flag flying o'er us" generated "spirits quite uproarious."[53] This sentiment was one repeated throughout the conflict as the diaspora mobilized. When "Lamentation on the American War" reported the news about the Battle of Vicksburg, the song expressed praise that "Old Erin's flag on both sides hosied [hoisted]."[54]

Flags and regimental banners, especially if they recalled a sense of Irish identity, mattered a great deal. Marching under banner representations of Irish heritage strengthened their fighting spirit. Thomas Francis Meagher's account of the 69th New York State Militia before the First Bull Run described in highly lyrical language how Irish-born and descended soldiers would lift their eyes "in rapture to the Green Flag as it danced above the rushing column."[55] Meagher draw on similar language during an Irish Brigade recruiting rally at the 7th New York Regiment Armory in July 1862, where he tied regimental green banners to the beginnings of Irish proindependence history. In heightened rhetoric, he suggested enlistees would see the Irish nationalist republican Robert Emmet's legacy fulfilled as they took to the transnational stage in the Civil War's fight for democratic library. They would march under "the flag which flew in defiance from the walls of Limerick . . . The flag which Robert Emmet—the last of the consecrated martyrs of our race, lavished his wealth, his genius, his life . . . so that he might plant it high above the world, through the flashings of its emerald folds."[56]

The importance of the regimental flag as a symbol of national and military identity was a repeated sentiment throughout the history of conflict, and the Civil War did nothing to diminish this. Peter Welsh provided his wife with a vivid explanation of the pride he felt when he was made a color bearer for the 28th Massachusetts on St. Patrick's Day 1863: "I must tell you that I have the honor of carrying the green flag . . . I shall feel proud to bear up the flag of green the emblem of Ireland and Irish men and especially having received it on that day dear to every Irish heart the festival of St. Patrick."[57] Later that month, in response to his wife's less than enthusiastic reaction to the news of her husband's promotion, Welsh repeated his delight in "the green flag of Old Ireland . . . I will carry it as long as God gives me strength."[58]

What is intriguing about this particular relationship to the 28th Massachusetts's green banner is that Welsh was not Irish-born, nor originally from the diaspora in the United States. He was second-generation Irish, born in the Canadian province of Prince Edward Island. Being part of the Irish-dominated 28th Massachusetts had strengthened Welsh's sense of his own Irish roots and adoption of an Irish American identity. He was acting out the words of one Irish Brigade song, which explained that regardless of association and identity affiliation with other countries, there was:

Still one [flag] you love more, of an emerald hue;
'Tis the banner of Erin, 'tis the banner of green,
The emblem of true hearts where'er it is seen.[59]

Meagher and Welsh's reference to the green flags of the 69th New York State Militia and 28th Massachusetts are in keeping with arguments that "symbols and ceremonies," especially regimental flag presentations, assisted "the formation of nationalist ideas by transmitting certain messages to an intended audience and bringing together expressions of public unity." The green flags of Irish-dominated regiments, militias, and companies reinforced a simultaneous expression of Irish cultural and national symbolic identity while being raised in the service of the American Union and Confederacy; "flags and flag presentations," therefore, "joined in a visible public way Irish American service, identity and wartime claims to inclusion."[60] By extension, singing about these banners generated the same aural sentiment.

One example of this was the lyrical reference in "Cead Mille Fealthe" to the green banners of the 9th Massachusetts. Its Irish-born and descended soldiers had "fought for the Union, the Ninth, and its Banner of green." The songs also informed listeners that now that the unit had returned home, its regimental emblems were to be placed in the Massachusetts State House on proud display, in memory of the soldiers' service and sacrifice:

Go yonder where cover'd with glory,
Our State's war-torn banners are seen,
None tells a more eloquent story,
Than the Ninth's sacred Banner of green.

A footnote on the musical score of "Cead Mille Fealthe" emphasized these lyrics even more, stating: "the Flags are in the State House." This again urged those who heard and performed the piece, and who studied the scorebook, to go visit the emblems being sung about. These Irish banners were placed at the heart of American national civic patriotic display alongside other Massachusetts regiments' returned flags.

On the other hand, the lyrics of "Cead Mille Fealthe" betrayed a deeper national identity connection heard in Irish wartime songs that sang about devotion to symbolic banners. When the 9th Massachusetts Regiment returned their war-torn flags to the State House in Boston, they did so along with their other regimental standards that mirrored the design of the Star Spangled Banner. Their Irish flag was put on show:

The Sunburst beside the Star banner,
They bore them through war's iron rain!
Unstain'd by the touch of dishonor,
Massachusetts receives them again.[61]

Although the emblem of the sunburst was part of Irish nationalist symbology during the Civil War era, it was a relatively recent development for contemporary Irish identity in the mid-nineteenth century. Additionally, the mention of the sunburst in wartime songs was rare. As in the case of "Cead Mille Fealthe," it often appeared next to the image of American spangled stars. "Corcoran's Irish Legion" (1863) sang of a banner that bore similarity to the image of the 9th Massachusetts ethnic emblem, with the American eagle taking precedence over that Irish sunburst:

A song for our Flag proudly waving on high,
The Emblem of the old Irish Nation;
Its Glorious Sunburst ever shall fly
With the pennant of the Eagle in station![62]

The sunburst also appeared in the 1864 Confederate ballad "The Hero Without a Name," where lyricist Colonel W. S. Hawkins drew on an older Irish independence tradition in the hope it would generate more Southern support. In a parallel sentimental vein as Meagher's speech about Robert Emmet, the song recalled the spirit of 1798 Irish nationalists. Soldiers marched "[be]neath Erin's flag with its glad 'Sunburst,'" alongside the apparition of "Emmet, who stands in that martyr-van."[63] By comparison, the Union song "Corcoran to his Regiment" was bookended by beginning and concluding verses that recalled cultural symbols of Irish nationalism. Lyrics stated Irish-born and descended soldiers should:

> Bear aloft that Flag, boys, Erin's glorious green,
> Foremost in the fight, boys, be our "Sun-burst," seen,
> Onward with that uncrown'd harp to "victory or death" . . .
> Raise that glorious Sun-burst, raise it once again,
> Let me see it shining o'er the battle plain;
> With its bright rays beaming, Oh, my gallant band,
> For God and for the Union of our dear adopted land.[64]

Considering how this ballad was first performed at the Jones's Wood gathering in August 1861, where early support was galvanized for the Irish Brigade's founding, the final line of "Corcoran to His Regiment" is critical. Despite the grand Irish rhetoric, it was "for the Union" of America that green banners would be waved.

Other Irish American Union Civil War songs portrayed the green flag of Erin flying alongside the American national standard. "War Song of the Irish Brigade," set to the tune of "The Star Spangled Banner," sang from the point of view of the diaspora's fighting sons. They cheered when they hoisted the two banners of the Stars and Stripes and the flag of Erin: "And we'll up with our colors, the proudest e'er seen— / The red, white and blue, and the Emerald Green."[65] Equally, "The Irish Volunteer" expected dual banner symbology to last forever, singing: "may Erin's Harp and the Starry Flag united ever be."[66] Another volunteer ballad from 1862 called on society's aid to unite soldiers. Whatever their primary ethnic nationality, they were all "valiant sons of Mars," and the country should "let Erin's Harp united be, with your good Stripes and Stars."[67] "The Gallant 69th Regiment" was even stronger in its vocal articulation of banner unity, calling for American Union devotion to the tune of "Red, White and Blue." Its lyrics wished that "Columbia and Hibernia ne'er sever," and that "both to their colors prove true."[68] Finally, "War Song of the New-York 69th Regiment" (1862) expressed the same emotion that the two nations' flags would be carried in union together on the battlefields, in naval encounters, and in future fights to come:

> Unfurl, then, to the breeze,
> The OCEAN HARP, the STARS AND STRIPES,
> On land or on the seas.[69]

This lyrical articulation of Irish and American flag unity was repeated in Corcoran's and Meagher's wartime accounts. Both provided pictorial illustrations of their two nations' banners flying together during the conflict. In Meagher's description of the 69th New York State Militia's journey from Arlington Heights to Manassas in 1861, he recalled how "the Green Flag was planted on the deserted ramparts of the Confederates at Germantown [and] the Stars and Stripes were lifted opposite." The image of the two flags waving together generated an enthusiastic reaction, as Meagher detailed in highly poetical vocabulary: "The two beautiful and inspiring symbols—the one of their old home and the other of their new country—the 69th passed in triumph, hats and caps waiving on the bayonet points, and an Irish cheer, such as never before shook the woods of old Virginia, swelling and rolling far and wide into the gleaming air."[70]

While Meagher was relating what he actually witnessed, Corcoran went a stage further in his prisoner-of-war memoir when he described seeing the Irish and American flags united in his imagination. He conjured up this image while reading letters and snatched newspaper reports about the exploits of his previously commanded 69th New York, who were busy leading the way on battlefields in 1862 within the Irish Brigade. They were ready "to strike for the Star Spangled emblem of their adopted nationality," according to Corcoran. "In fancy," he dreamt of his soldiers marching under two banners, united in common cause and dual national identity. In his visions, "I saw them drawn up in line of battle behind the 'Banner of the Stars' and the 'Green Flag of Erin.'"[71] Corcoran and Meagher's portrayals of the green and the red, white and blue banners waving together mirror the lyrics of "Pat Murphy of Meagher's

Brigade" (1863), where "the Stars and the Stripes shall be seen along-side of the Flag of the Land of Shillaly!"[72] Another Irish Brigade ballad—"The Irish Brigade" (1862)—sang of how "Erin's Green flag" had become "blended along with the Red, White and Blue." To stress this coming together its lyrics, like many Irish wartime songs, were set to an American tune. Appropriately, in this example, the song employed the air of the "Red, White and Blue."

"The Irish Brigade" used more than just American music to stress the transnational unity between the two countries. It sang of a complication banner ballad lyrics sometimes presented when they established the image of dual flag symbology. The chorus of "The Irish Brigade" sang of a "long" desire to see:

> These flags be united,
> And on every hill-top displayed,
> Until Erin's wrongs shall be righted
> By many an Irish Brigade.[73]

These lyrical phrases repeated that of an earlier wartime song, the aptly titled "The Harp of Old Erin and Banner of Stars" (1861). Although most of the ballad was about Irish devotion to the American Union above all other affiliations, there was another sentiment being uttered quietly in its lyrics about continual Irish and American military banner association:

> Oh! Long may our flag wave in Union together,
> And the harp of green Erin still kiss the same breeze
> And brave ev'ry storm, that beclouds the fair weather,
> Till our harp, like the Stars, floats o'er river and seas.[74]

While less explicit than other examples, "The Harp of Old Erin and Banner of Stars" longed to see Erin's green banner wave over an independent Ireland.

This was an extension of the mutual transnational hope for republican democracy fought for on both sides of the Atlantic in the 1860s. Yet, lyrics articulated the confused relationship between Irish and American identity affiliation in the Civil War years. Such contradictory sentiment could be heard in passages of ballads that sung of Irish and Americans leading the fight *together* in Ireland under their united banners. While Kate C. M.'s "The Irish Brigade" sang about loving the banner of Erin's emerald hue over all others, it also sang about the defense of another banner: "Yes, that flag you'll defend, if you're Irish at all, / Into the hands of the enemy it never must fall." At first, in the more Irish elements of the song's context, it is unclear if this flag defense would be for the United States or Ireland. However, when considering the ballad's contemporary wartime authorship and performance, this defense was actually focused on America first and foremost. "The enemy" here was the Confederacy, not Britain. The final verses focused on collective Irish protection of the Star Spangled Banner, ensuring that it would not fall into Confederate hands. "For the Union forever, with your last dying breath," it expressed, cementing Irish support sentiment for the American Union at the song's conclusion.[75]

Confused national affiliation language spoke of simultaneous Irish independence desires and pride in the American Union cause. It contradicted *who* would be conducting such a fight by implying that several different groups would be involved in leading this future conflict. Lyrical rhetoric suggested first generation Irish-born settlers would return to Ireland, joined by those of second and subsequent generations who felt affiliated identity and association to both Ireland and the United States. By a wider extension, collective rhetoric about "our" and "we" in songs suggested that Americans themselves—both native born and the Irish in the country who had come to see themselves as Americans—would participate in future battles in Ireland. In songs at least, the latter identity appears to have come to the fore. This challenged a notion that the Irish were concerned *only* about, and wanted to bring forth, Ireland's independence from Great Britain in the mid-nineteenth century.

Irish American Civil War lyrical expressions reflected this sentiment of collective dual identity association, whereby the Irish in America sang and saw themselves as Americans by the time of the Civil War. As a result, the fight for Irish independence was described in United States-produced ballads as an *American* concern and an *American* engagement. With this lyrical identity association framework in mind, there would be repercussions for how members of the Irish diaspora—particularly those belonging to groups and networks that held strong Irish independence views—articulated their sense of Irish nationalism in ballads produced by and about them during the conflict. Singing Irish nationalist sympathies and sentiments with an American voice raises questions about the state and potency of such views in the middle of the conflict.

5

⁂

Fenian Sentiments and
Irish Nationalism Sympathies

W hen the fictional Irish soldier Tim McDonald sang about entering
Union Army service in "The Irish Volunteer," he explained he had
been "driven from my home by an oppressor's hand."[1] This was a
reference to recent troubles across the Atlantic in Ireland, where the Great
Famine's impact, anti-Irish sentiment toward British landlord tyranny, and
a belief that relief for the country's starving poor was negligible, were all
still being felt. The majority of Irish immigrants to the United States in the
fifteen years prior to the Civil War's outbreak had fled Ireland in the wake
of the Great Famine, particularly between 1845 and 1852, and after the failed
nationalist insurrection in 1848. For those first-generation Irish immigrants
who could remember Ireland in its darkest period, resentment toward Britain
still lingered and stoked some nationalist sympathizes in the 1860s, even as
they participated in their new country's civil conflict.[2]

The United States provided a welcoming home with its ideals of liberty,
democracy, and republican nationhood appealing to those holding Irish nationalist independence desires and anti-British views. Such sentiments were
not heard frequently in Irish American Civil War songs. The passage of over
a decade since the main Famine migration period meant specific recollections
of this past were muted in war ballads. Nonetheless, ardent anti-British sentiment did occasionally find its way into widely published songs, a reminder
that migration did not necessarily dampen this feeling, especially when tied
to expressions about a future fight for Irish self-rule. In particular, lyrics expressed specific Fenian Irish independence support. References focused on
this specific nationalist group, which had been founded in the United States in
1858 by John O'Mahony and Michael Dohney. Songs also referenced broader
and more general sympathies concerning Irish nationalism and future hopes

for independence from Britain. Ballads did not shy away from singing about nationalist expressions, although these were secondary to division between the American states. Lyrics about such aspirations were tied closely to other wartime concerns and were not sung separately, which raises questions about the very nature of Irish nationalism sympathy, support, and Fenian attitudes toward independence in the context of American civil conflict.

IRISH INDEPENDENCE SYMPATHIES
IN THE UNITED STATES

When "The Irish Brigade in America" was published on both sides of the Atlantic in 1863, it repeated the view presented previously by Tim McDonald in "The Irish Volunteer." Sung from an Irish point of view on the American home front, it explained how recent migrants had come to their new nation:

> It was the cursed landlords' tyranny that forced them from their home,
> To cross the fierce Atlantic, in foreign lands to roam.
> John Bull's deception is found out, but he yet may see the day,
> That Paddy's sons, with sword and gun, will show him Irish play.[3]

Occasionally, these sentiments materialized within the context of songs that appeared initially to be about Irish war service. The best example of this was by lyricist F. Collins, who produced "The 69th Brigade" in 1862. Unlike any other examples in this study, the verses in the second half of this ballad turned into protracted vitriol about the past twenty years of Irish history and Ireland's relationship to Britain during the Famine.

Whereas "The Irish Jaunting Car" discussed in chapter 1 had sung about Queen Victoria's visit to Ireland in 1849 in jovial terms, Collins was far more critical of the monarch's response to the potato blight crisis and ended with a threat that Irish American Civil War soldiers would soon be paying her a visit of their own. Directed at Ireland itself, one verse sang:

> Were [Victoria] to come among you, on a visit every day,
> Do not pay attention nor give heed to what she'll say;
> She's trembling in her skin, she's so very much afraid,
> She'll shortly get a visit from the Sixty-Ninth Brigade.

The song went on to criticize Victoria's lack of immediate response to the Famine. Here the monarch was put to use as both a lyrical representation of herself and, by proxy, Westminster and the British state. All were culpable in abandoning Ireland according to the ballad:

> When hunger death and famine, sent one million to their grave,
> She did not come among you then, their precious lives to save,
> She made up a subscription and sent you fifty pounds,
> Wasn't that a blessed offering from the British royal crown.[4]

Relief to Ireland continued to be a pressing concern in the 1860s, and the diaspora in both the Union and Confederacy routinely gathered money to send to those in need. One of the largest fundraising drives was instigated by prominent members of the Irish American community at New York City's Delmonico's Hotel "for the purpose of inaugurating a relief fund for the suffering Poor of Ireland."[5] Irish Brigade regiments themselves collected as much as they could among the ranks through the spring of 1863. Their chaplain Father William Corby wrote to New York's Catholic Archbishop John Hughes with an enclosed contribution of over one thousand dollars given by "a portion of the offices and men of two regiments of this brigade . . . to the fund now being raised for the relief of the suffering poor of Ireland." Even though the Irish Brigade was much diminished by this point in the conflict, Corby was proud that "the remaining few of the Irish Brigade have spontaneously, and without any concert of action, come forward to contribute their mite to the general subscription."[6] At the same time, General Michael Corcoran raised money within his Legion regiments as "part of the contribution for the relief of Ireland." He entrusted John O'Mahony, leader of the Fenian Brotherhood, with "several packages of money to be deposited" with the relief fund organizers.[7]

Monetary aid for those impacted by the Famine was one notable contribution, but another was referred to regularly in wartime ballads: the fighting contribution made by the soldiers themselves. The final verse of "The 69th Brigade" repeated its threat that Britain would receive a visit from Civil War soldiers once the conflict between the states was concluded. Servicemen would return to Ireland in a triumphant Irish Brigade led by Generals Corcoran and Thomas Francis Meagher. After they achieved Union victory, they would bring forth Ireland's independence:

The day is fast approaching, that all the world can see,
That there must be a total end to British tyranny;
Corcoran and brave Meagher, whose deeds shall never fade
Will free Erin's sons and daughters with the Sixty-Ninth Brigade.

Among those who would serve with this unit was the soldier whose "voice" was singing the song's lyrics. The ballad begins by focusing on the perspective of a Union home-front woman, who details what her "true love William" is experiencing in the war. As the ballad's second half turns toward Ireland, William takes up the tale himself:

If this war was over, I'd leave you but once more,
That would be to cross the sea, to Erin's lovely shore;
To put an end for ever to the landlord's crow-bar brigade
Under the gallant leaders, of the Sixty-Ninth Brigade.[8]

"The 69th Brigade" was reflective of nationalist sympathetic sentiments that appeared in some, though by no means not all, Irish American Civil War songs. One 1865 American version of the traditional ballad "St. Patrick's Day" contained concluding verses that turned attention back to Ireland. Like "The 69th Brigade," it hoped the famed 69th New York Irish would return to their old homeland. The diaspora was to "wish for the time, when with the Sixty-Ninth to land in old Ireland, on St. Patrick's Day."[9] The notion of Union Army Irish regiments and soldiers returning to fight for independence under the command of their leaders was also expressed in one 1862 ballad. Despite continued battlefield heroics, "The Irish Volunteers" was already looking forward to war's end, when Irish veterans would carry the bright prospects of Irish independence across the ocean. This would be achieved under Meagher's leadership:

Long life to Colonel Meagher, he is a man of birth and fame
And while our Union does exists applauded be his name.
Our land once more to peace restored, and brighter prospects near
We will not lack to welcome back, the Irish Volunteers.[10]

The verse's rhetoric can be understood in two ways—"our land" meant America and Irish volunteer soldiers aiding the restoration of the united

Union. The "we" in the final line had a dual association. To those in the Union home front it meant the collective "we" of the American nation, welcoming back all soldiers after victory. They were alongside the "we" of the diaspora, who could take pride in the loyal fighting service performed by Irish-born and descended soldiers fighting under Meagher (which at this early stage of the Civil War meant the 69th New York State Militia and, even more specifically, Meagher's company of Zouaves raised before the First Battle of Bull Run). The "we" could also mean Ireland, as the country herself would "welcome back" her fighting sons when the Civil War was over. Here, lyrical messages adopted parallel meanings depending on who was performing and who was listening to the song. It sang to both the Irish in America and to wider American society.

Most references about returning to fight for independence were far more explicit in their language about this hopeful postbellum plan. "Pat Murphy of Meagher's Brigade" was particularly unequivocal, with the eponymous Pat singing that he would rather be facing the British in 1863 than the Confederacy, armed with his "shillaly" (an Irish wooden fighting stick). Though the song did not diminish the fighting spirit of the Irish, Pat's view implied they would be even stronger in combat if they faced a different, non-Confederate, enemy:

> Now, if it was only John Bull to the fore,
> I'd rush into battle quite gaily;
> For the spalpeen [rascal] I'd rap with a heart an' a half,
> With my elegant Sprig of Shillaly.[11]

This sentiment was one shared by the young 28th Massachusetts soldier Daniel Crowley as he and his fellow Irish soldiers laid siege to Petersburg, Virginia. One night in September 1864, he "had a little chat" with a Confederate soldier across the entrenchment who "said he was an Irishman." After engaging in a mutual enquiry about when they "left the old land," if they heard news "from there and how things were looking at present" in Ireland, the Confederate Irish soldier began to discuss the forthcoming 1864 presidential election. "He expects when McClellan is elected President there will be peace," Crowley reported. This peace would bring with it a new fight, this time in Ireland. According to the Confederate Irishman, "we will all have a chance of trying our mettle for the old sod." Crowley stated how he likewise hoped that "day is not far distant." In the same manner as the fictional Pat Murphy, Crowley commented, "I would rather spill my blood in that cause than in the present one."[12]

Correspondingly, Timothy O'Regan's "Save the Constitution" (1862), while about the Irish 9th Connecticut Volunteers, discusses Ireland's future independence in its final verse. The song expresses desires for peace and Union restoration. Calling again on the symbology of the Irish green flag, it holds the expectation that Irish American Civil War soldiers would aid in the battle, and subsequent victory, against British rule in Ireland:

When peace once more will bless this shore for what it was intended,
When trade and commerce will revive and civil war is ended;
Oh steer your barks to Erin's Isle, whose proud soul is kept under,
To rise her Green flag to the breeze and burst her claims asunder.[13]

Regardless of longing for Irish independence after the Civil War's conclusion, most lyrics sympathetic to such a contest believed it would occur in the *future*. Returning to Ireland to fight, and actually achieving freedom from British authority, was not necessarily envisioned as a course that would occur more immediately. Crowley's aspiration for a "not far distant" fight for independence was not supported in the lyrical examples quoted. These conflict ballads were produced at times when fighting and secession looked far from finished. Instead, ballads thought Irish independence would come *after* Union restoration. As "Save the Constitution" had indicated, Ireland's liberation would be obtained once peace was returned to the states as the United States. In addition, concord with the Confederacy did not solely imply an end to fighting. It meant reconciliation and reconstruction, with the Irish in America being involved in both processes.

Placing Irish independence in a lyrical future like this was also a suggestion made by Peter Welsh when he wrote to his father-in-law in Ireland in mid-1863: "if the day should arrive within ten years after this war is ended an army can be raised in this country that will strike terror to the Saxon's heart."[14] While the 28th Massachusetts soldier thought a possible invasion would happen one day, it would be a future, not immediate, possibility. This suggests a doubt over the level of nationalist belief, support, and sympathy to this Irish cause. A misgiving air around this issue could be heard, particularly in Fenian wartime ballads.

THE FENIAN BROTHERHOOD

Five years after the group's founding, the Illinois' *Ottawa Free Trader* described the Fenian Brotherhood in November 1863 as "an organization of Irishmen of a secret and military character, whose members are pledged to strike for the independence of Ireland whenever an opportunity arises . . . In the United States they are numbered by hundreds of thousands . . . [with] representatives from all parts of the United States, Canada and Ireland."[15] Given their presence in the United States over the course of the Civil War era, Fenians are impossible to ignore in relation to Irish conflict experiences and sentiments. It is certainly important not to overemphasize "to the point where readers see every Irish American soldier as a Fenian" because that was certainly not the case.[16] Yet, Fenians utilized print culture and propaganda in the mid-nineteenth century, and their views appeared alongside other non-Fenian/Irish nationalist sympathetic voices. They also drew a usable shared knowledge of Irish wartime service as part of their own arguments for independence and celebrations of Irish heritage within an American setting.

This practice started in the initial years of the Fenian movement. First written in the early 1840s by Young Irelander lyricist Thomas Davis, "The Green Above the Red" was one of the more popular nationalist ballads that remained in transnational print circulation almost twenty years after its first publication. In original versions, the lyrical image of the green flag of Erin was placed above red British emblem colors. By 1860, several ballad outputs were in existence that had reappropriated Davis's song by using the same style and traditional Irish air ("There's Whiskey in the Jar") but gave the original more American-focused words. One example, "composed and sung by William H. Lindsay," was a Fenian edition "dedicated to the St. Lawrence Order of the F.B." This was a Fenian Brotherhood chapter in St. Lawrence, New York, on the Canadian border. Lindsay's "The Green Above the Red" celebrated members joining "the Fenian cause." Those who pledged their support to the organization "have nought to fear, with Bold O'Mahony to lead us."[17] The postbellum "What Irishmen Have Done" (ca. 1870) returned to Davis-inspired rhetoric about the triumphant green flag of Erin when it prayed:

"God grant the day may soon draw near, when the Fenian band, / Will raise the green above the red, in their own native land."[18]

The same hope was echoed in "Our Own Flag of Green," which was printed as a broadside ballad first in Dublin and subsequently in America in 1860. It told the people of Ireland that the diaspora would return:

Soon shall our Green Flag wave o'er us,
Soon, soon shall we march to meet the foe . . .
The standard of England shall be torn,
And no more in our Island shall be seen.

Despite this rhetoric, such Irish independence jubilation contained a problem. Halfway through the ballad, lyrics stopped focusing on just the Irish returning to fight in Ireland. Instead, they concentrated on the familiar idea of dual banner symbolism as the United States and Ireland joined together in the fight: "when the Eagle and our Shamrock are united . . . Then the wrongs of our lands shall be righted."[19] The united appearance of the eagle—America's metaphysical embodiment—alongside Irish symbolism casts doubt on the nature of the pro-Irish language in the rest of the song. Additionally, these sentiments were set to a tune that recalled banner duality, as "Our Own Flag of Green" used the American air of "Red, White, and Blue" to support its nationalist expressions. Other ballads were even more direct in this conflation of dual nations fighting for Irish independence. "The Fenian's Welcome to Ireland," also written around early 1860, sang of how both Fenians and the American Navy would be sailing across the Atlantic, ready to be welcomed in Ireland:

The Fenians are coming without more delay,
The brave ships are ready to cross o'er the sea.
The American fleet now will shortly appear,
The Fenians will bid a happy new year.[20]

The American Civil War had lasting implications for the Fenian Brotherhood. While "tentative plans for insurrection in Ireland were concocted," the conflict's outbreak had "thwarted plans for any immediate action" to bring about successful independence.[21] With the nation's primary concern focused on Confederate secession and the fight to keep the American Union together, active support and aid for Fenian Irish independence was a secondary concern. That did not stop the number of Fenian members from rising during the conflict, with membership totals peaking between 1865 and 1866.[22] Nor was the organization present on just the home front. Scholars of the Irish in America have noted how "Fenian recruiters were busy in both camps enlisting talent for the republican cause."[23] Indeed, Fenians "freely recruited their own military organization from within" both armies.[24] The Brotherhood was most active in the Northern states, with its organizational stronghold in New York City during the conflict. The Union Army's Irish Brigade regiments, Corcoran's Legion, and the 9th Massachusetts Regiment all had notable internal Fenian branches. This regional dominance is reflected by Fenian American Civil War songs originating predominately in Union publishing houses rather than Confederate ones.

Initially, the war provided an opportunity for the Fenians, but this had a detrimental impact on the level of active support for the movement after 1865. In its report of the 1863 Fenian Convention, the *Ottawa Free Trader* explained how the group's leaders urged "younger members of the Brotherhood to study military tactics."[25] As numerous Fenian studies have argued, the conflict "served as a training ground to prepare for war" when the diaspora would lead the fight for independence against Britain.[26] Enlistment in the "Union and Confederate armies [was] a means of acquiring military expertise"—a golden opportunity on a larger scale than previous Irish nationalist uprisings had presented.[27] Yet, with enlistment and war service came great sacrifice.

Meagher alluded to the problem Fenians—and wider Irish nationalism—faced in one Irish Brigade recruiting rally speech: "It is a moral certainty that many of our countrymen who enlist in this struggle for the maintenance of the Union will fall in the contest. But, even so, I hold that one in ten of us come back when this war is over, the military experience gained by that *one* will be of more service in the fight for Ireland's freedom than . . . the entire ten."[28] The general was being overly optimistic in the face of a stark reality. Fighting in wars runs a considerable risk of injury and death, and Irish-born and descended soldiers on both sides fell, thinning the ranks "of potential freedom fighters" for Ireland to call upon.[29] O'Mahony went so far as to declare this problem as "an impediment to Fenianism" at the group's first convention in Chicago. By the time the meeting was held, the Irish Brigade was reduced considerably in its fighting strength, and Irish-dominant units were suffering severe casualties.[30]

The wartime reality of losing the possible foot soldiers of the Fenian movement was a concern expressed in Irish American Civil War songs. The depiction of the Vicksburg dead in "Lamentation on the American War," including fallen Union and Confederate Irish soldiers, highlighted the cost this had to the Irish American diaspora and to families back in Ireland. The ballad's lyricist P. J. Fitzpatrick articulated this sentiment with great lyrical emotion. Describing how news of the 1863 battle spread across the Atlantic, the broadside reported:

Many a mother anxiously to the Post Office ran,
In hopes a welcome letter should return from her son,
Alas but little do they know they fell in crimson gore,
Their bones lie moldering with the dust all on Columbia's shore.[31]

"Lamentation on the American War" was certainly one of the most vivid ballads in its blunt retelling of the loss of lives in the conflict and the implied impact this experience would have on galvanizing an experienced force for Irish liberty. It also sang of another problematic reality with which the Fenians had to contend.[32] At Vicksburg, as at almost every Civil War encounter, the diaspora's sons faced each other on the battlefield. From the First Battle of Bull Run—where the 69th New York State Militia fought Louisianan regiments also comprised of Irishmen—to Antietam, Fredericksburg, Gettysburg, and all other battles and skirmishes, soldiers from and connected to Ireland were fighting each other as members of Union and Confederate forces. While some may have "entered the ranks with the same hopes of . . . gaining military experience that could be used to free Ireland from British rule," the conflict's reality soon revealed a truth that hampered Irish nationalist and Fenian hopes.[33] By fighting, killing, and wounding each other, they were reducing those who could serve the cause of Irish independence.

This reality was reflected in a lyrical poem submitted by "Bessie" to the *Irish-American* newspaper in July 1864. It lamented the diminished nature of the Union Army's Irish Brigade, commenting how "Our Brigade exists no longer." This referred to its reduction to a brigade in-name-only for a brief time over the summer of 1864 after its regimental numbers fell in the after-

math of two and one-half years of costly service in Virginia. "Bessie" portrayed the impact this had on those who could one day muster and fight for
Ireland against British rule. The poem's final stanza claimed how the Brigade's
soldiers:

> Had hoped to free from the tyrant's chain the dear old "sainted Isle."
> And again behold its emerald sod, unprofaned by Saxon guile . . .
> Their hopes, bright dreams, alas!
> Themselves, with the mournful past, have fled.

The loss of Irish-born and descended soldiers was presented as a transnational
tragedy for the diaspora and for Ireland. Those harboring independence plans
on both sides of the Atlantic would shed "many a tear," and give "tender
thought" to "the lonely graves" of the dead who would not return.[34] The only
way to counter the loss was to emphasize notions of an Irish and American
unified alliance.

As previous examples have shown, uniting the banners of Erin and America was a common trope in Civil War ballads. This lyrical rhetoric of dual-
emblem imagery influenced how those sympathetic to Irish nationalist independence desires, including Fenians, articulated their plans about battling
Britain. Frequently those retuning to Ireland were not alone. Songs implied
that Americans would be involved in this future conflict. Nationalists in the
diaspora realized that due to a lack of substantial funds and a lack of available men, help was needed from elsewhere; they "saw allying their cause with
American power as necessary if they were to achieve their ends."[35] This was
apparent to Meagher when he observed how the Irish "could not hope to suc-
ceed in our effort to make Ireland a Republic without the moral and material
aid of the liberty-loving citizens of these United States."[36]

Wartime ballads expressed the fighting benefits of united Irish and American soldiers. Directed initially at the Confederates, "The Irish Volunteer"
painted a battlefield image of how the two nations would be a formidable
foe. These lyrics, by extension, were comparably applicable to the nationalists'
desires to fight the British: "May traitors quake, and rebels shake, and tremble
in their fears, / When next they meet the Yankee boys and Irish volunteers!"[37]
The same sentiment could be heard in the postbellum Fenian ballad "Fenians
Ever More" (1866), which noted how "Poor Johnny Bull [Britain] will quickly

find what united hearts can do." This attitude incorporated Americans into the "what Irish boys can do" ethos.[38] In 1863, "Paddy the Loyal" went even further to taunt the British with the thought of Irish and American soldiers combining to fight against them. Recalling anti-British sentiment, the ballad sang of a sense that the Irish were owed justice and autonomy from tyrannical rule. Its lyrics mocked the British by recalling the American War of Independence and revolutionary successes—an example of a colonial dominion gaining triumphant self-rule:

> Well Erin's sons know old John Bull,
> And long to pay him off in full;
> Faith Uncle Sam's his match you know!
> Bull found that out some time ago.[39]

On the other hand, while singing about this dual Irish and American fighting force crossing the Atlantic to Ireland emphasized a spirit of transnational unity in the name of democratic republicanism, it betrayed an underlying issue in the "distinctive diaspora nationalism" forged by Fenians.[40] The fact that the Fenians needed United States support challenges precisely *who* would be leading the forces to Ireland, if such plans came to fruition. Singing about Irish and American soldiers carrying out this task together pointed out a damaging truth for any near-future independence bids. Despite diaspora sympathy and active support, the loss of skilled veteran soldiers in the Civil War was an unavoidable blow. Those who survived the conflict were simply not enough in number to carry out the ambitious task alone. The Fenians themselves recognized this, as one letter from the Fenian Society in Chicago to Secretary of State William Seward revealed in September 1865. They appealed to Seward and the restored United States "for your aid, we want money . . . we have the men, we want the means." Elsewhere in the letter, they acknowledged the "need [for] the sympathy and material aid of the American men." While promising "this is the last time that Ireland as a mendicant shall pass the beggars box," such an appeal, even when the organization was at its peak size, lays bare the realistic level of strength it could muster for an immediate "day of Ireland's trial."[41]

Around the time of Chicago's Fenians post–Civil War appeal to Seward, one ballad revealed the same desires for money and men to support the Irish cause. The "Irish-American Army," printed in the Fenian-specific songbook *Stephens' Fenian Songster* in 1866, suggested:

> When comes the hour to fight the Power
> That tramples Irish freedom,
> Columbia, then, will give us men,
> A Grant, too, if we need him?[42]

The final line was a pun—newly reunited America would provide a monetary grant to the Fenian cause and, more specifically, an American general to gather soldiers together to fight against the British. "A Grant" was the Union's General Ulysses S. Grant. The commander would be enlisted to help the Irish, and the United States would "give" men to fill nationalist ranks. Such suggestions present an overt sense of surety in the Fenian cause not only to obtain but to also receive help. Again, it stresses the Irish could not battle alone. The 1866 "Fenians Ever More" shared the same lyrical impression of the United States coming to Ireland's aid: "with Yankee ships and Irish hearts," the two countries' soldiers would "cross the mighty Main." The "starry flag" of America "shall then protect the Fenians ever more."[43]

In ballad rhetoric views, the United States would support Fenian and Irish nationalist causes because it owed a debt of service to Ireland for the military support Irish-born and descended soldiers had given to the war effort. Kate C. M.'s "The Irish Brigade" told Irish soldiers:

> Hope on, then, soldiers, the day yet you'll see,
> When true love of freedom shall set Ireland free;
> And believe that the country for which Haggerty died,
> In peace or in war, will stand by your side.[44]

This was another reference to the County Donegal-born Captain James Haggerty of the 69th New York State Militia, the first Union Army Irish officer to die in the Civil War at the First Battle of Bull Run in 1861 (mentioned in chapter 3). Even in 1863 when "The Irish Brigade" was published, Haggerty's spirit was being recalled to stress that if he had given his life for the Union, then the Union should return the same fighting favor to help Ireland's independence. The Fenian Society expressed this sentiment to Seward in 1865, reminding him of Irish soldiers' sacrifice. They argued that the "hundreds of brave men whose lives went out side-by-side with your countrymen" all fought believing "America would not forget the many brave Irish hearts who marched to death beneath the starry banner."[45]

No Irish American Civil War verse articulated this view better than the final stanza of "Pat Murphy of Meagher's Brigade":

> Then, surely Columbia can never forget,
> While valor and fame hold communion,
> How nobly the brave Irish Volunteers fought,
> In defense of the Flag of our Union—
> And, if ever Old Ireland for Freedom should strike,
> We'll a helping hand offer quite freely.
> And the Stars and the Stripes shall be seen alongside,
> Of the flag of the Land of Shillaly.[46]

As with the title of the Fenian ballad "The Irish-American Army" and the lyrical examples of the United States of America answering Ireland's call in "Pat Murphy of Meagher's Brigade," there was, again, the confused the issue of *who* would offer "a helping hand" to Ireland. The first part of the verse was directed initially to America itself, asking the country not to forget the diaspora's Civil War contribution. The second half, however, returned to the collective pronoun fusion of "our" and "we" that revealed the combination of Irish and American identity together. The song sang of the Irish experience of the war, of service in the Irish Brigade, and the sacrifice of the eponymous Pat Murphy—he stood for all Irish-born and descended soldiers. Yet, here was an Irish voice singing about "our Union," meaning the American Union, and the collective "we" of the Irish *as Americans*.[47]

What "Pat Murphy of Meagher's Brigade" exposed was how general Irish nationalist sentiment, and specific Fenian sentiment, was instilled with the same sense of American association and identity seen elsewhere in Civil War ballads. Both Irish American Civil War songs and Fenian American Civil War songs contain sentiments that support suggestions of how "Irish nationalism in America evolved during the Civil War into a context of loyalty to the United States" and that "the Fenian movement [revealed] a surprising level of Americanization within Irish America."[48] Diasporic home-front and front-line senses of their own relationships to American identity were strongly supportive of Union and Confederate causes in ballad expressions. While nationalist sentiments and retention of Irish cultural heritage remained for first- and second-generation migrants, years of living in the antebellum United States—along with the enhanced patriotism of conflict—infused a sense of Americanness. Americanization of Irish nationalism did not start in the 1860s; this process began far earlier. The Civil War added a new dimension to this development, and wartime songs gave it voice.

Fenian articulations of this American construction of Irish nationalism reveal the conflict loyalty and association to dual identities ultimately had for the Fenian cause for independence. Alongside seeking American manpower, materials, and money, Fenians turned to American music to bolster their nationalist articulations. Like other more general examples, the air of "Red, White and Blue" was adapted specifically by the Fenians to create contrafacta using 1840s American-produced music with new lyrics. One such example was "Camp Song of the Irish Brigade," which called on the traditional figure of Granuaile to it describe Irish devotion to the Union cause in 1861:

Old "Grann" now looks over the ocean,
And hears the fierce bugle of Mars,
And the strength of her hearts high devotion,
Is rou'd for the Stripes and the Stars.[49]

The following year in 1862, James Wrigley published "The Fenian Brigade." This was effectively an altered Fenian version of "Camp Song of the Irish Brigade," sung to the same "Red, White, and Blue" American tune. For the most part, the ballad was unchanged, except that instead of singing about Irish Brigade fighting spirit, this new version added a chorus refrain about how "the English will fly in terror before you, when charged by the Fenian Brigade." The most obvious alteration came in the verse relating to Granuaile's own view of the American Civil War:

Old Granna has looked o'er the ocean,
And heard the fierce bugle of Mars;
And the strength of her heart's high devotion
Was roused for the stripes and the stars;

Now she raises her voice loud as thunder . . .
Saying: "Boys, cut the English, asunder,
With the swords of your Fenian Brigade!"[50]

Here Granuaile was used to represent American and Irish identity duality that Fenians had to resolve and accommodate simultaneously. Given the more overt American rhetoric of the original version, however, alongside its American tune, devotion to the Union dominated over Fenian expressions.

Another song "sung around the Camp Fir[es] of the Irish Brigade" was included at the end of the Chicago Fenian Society's letter to Seward. To underline their argument that the United States should help them, the correspondents included quotes from the 1863 universal wartime ballad "Comrades of the Cannon." It sang about "comrades around our Camp Fire bright" who represented the transnational composition of the Union forces. "Freedom's Fight is all the same," lyrics explained, whether soldiers were bivouacking "by Hudson, Rhine or Shannon"—referring to New York, German, and Irish American soldiers, respectively. The song also included a rallying American cry: "Here's to our Starry Banner."[51] The Fenians were making their nationalist point by using a song that still articulated American sentiments first and foremost.

Furthermore, the most important Irish song written immediately after the Civil War—"God Save Ireland"—was itself set to an American tune. T. D. Sullivan's 1867 proto-Irish nationalist anthem spread throughout Ireland and the Irish diaspora. One of the fundamental reasons for its quick adoption in the United States was because Sullivan used the music of the Civil War song "Tramp! Tramp! Tramp! The Prisoner's Hope" for his composition.[52] The influential songwriter and music publisher George F. Root had written the original lyrics and music in 1863. "Tramp! Tramp! Tramp!" was fundamentally an American cultural output with no specific Irish connections as it sung generally about Union prisoners of war and their uplifting hope of release. Root's composition inspired numerous sequel versions across the Union and Confederacy, such as "On! On! On! The Boys Came Marching" (1865), which again sang about prison release and victorious Union fighting.[53] Other parody ballad contrafactum appeared in the final two years of the war using Root's original version for inspiration. It quickly became a tune used for different songs in its own right, including "Grant to Washington Shall Go," produced after Ulysses S. Grant's successful presidential election campaign in 1869.[54]

Sullivan's use of Root's ballad tune for "God Save Ireland" is not surprising given the practice of setting words to familiar tunes to aid their success. In many ways, Root's "Tramp! Tramp! Tramp!" followed the reverse dissemination journey of "The Irish Jaunting Car" and Harry Macarthy's "The Bonnie Blue Flag." Instead, this was an American-produced song and tune that traveled across the Atlantic to Ireland and essentially became Irish. It also, ironically for the Fenian Irish nationalists, became a Canadian tune in the second half of the nineteenth century. It was used for ballads written in response to the first of several failed attempts by a group of veteran Fenians, starting in 1866, to invade Canada and seize British forts along the Niagara Frontier. "Canadian volunteers . . . celebrated their victory over the Fenians by singing," which included one song that explained:

> When the news spread through the land that the Fenians were at hand,
> At our country's call we'll cheerfully obey . . .
> For beneath the Union Jack we will drive the Fenians back,
> And we'll fight for our beloved Canadian home.[55]

Here was an example of an anti-Fenian Canadian song, set to an American tune, directed at the Irish diaspora in the United States in 1866, who, in turn, would take up the same American tune the following year while singing a song that extolled Irish nationalism. The myriad of identities Sullivan's "God Save Ireland" carried with it in the nineteenth century exemplifies the fluid nature of transnational musical culture.

WHO WOULD FIGHT FOR IRELAND?
LYRICAL INDEPENDENCE AND FENIAN DOUBTS

The need for supportive aid for any credible attempt at a fight for Irish independence in the direct aftermath of the Civil War raises questions of how solid a construct and practice Fenian nationalism, specifically, and Irish nationalism, more broadly, was in the 1860s. Divisions within the organization and factional arguments generated by "botched . . . incursions" and "misadventures" into Canada fragmented the Fenian Brotherhood.[56] Additionally, "transnational factionalism" between the Fenians and the Irish Republican Brotherhood and postbellum Anglo-American diplomatic relationships added to tensions that were already appearing during the Civil War. Another failed invasion attempt, this time in Britain, led by Confederate Colonel Thomas Kelly in 1867 "triggered a major political split within the ranks" of American Fenians, resulting in the effective end of the organization by the 1870s.[57] The "singular harmony of feeling and unanimity of purpose" found at the 1863 Chicago convention, and the hope of rising membership numbers and two further 1865 conventions in Cincinnati and Philadelphia, diminished fairly quickly for this particular branch of Irish nationalist activity.[58]

The American Fenians' fracture certainly relates to understandings of the Irish during the Civil War and their respective relationship to "being Irish" and "being American." As Irish American nationalist scholarship has observed, the undeveloped "inchoate nature" of nationalist organizations was impacted by events beyond Ireland and its diasporas across the globe, especially in the United States of America. By the time of the Fenian Brotherhood's decline, the group "had only been active for ten years, four of which were spent fighting . . . in the American Civil War."[59] Wartime era ballads that articulated Fenian and Irish nationalist ideas and desires alongside dual loyalty, identity, and dependency on the United States exposed cultural expressions and doubts about tensions, support levels, and articulation of strength in the Irish American nationalist diaspora. Undoubtedly, specific Fenian, Irish nationalist, and Irish cultural heritage lyrics were in the minority of outputs during the Civil War years. Few songs were dedicated to specific chapters, and Fenian activities were mentioned infrequently.

One reason for this was that these songs were being disseminated to the larger American public. While they sang with sympathetic tones that showed a level of nationalist hope for independence one day, the United States was emphasized over Ireland as the foremost nation to turn attention toward. Ballads did not report actual Fenian activity unless it was tied to aspirations about American support for Irish independence. The same relative silence appears in the letters and memoirs of those most frequently sung about in Irish American Civil War songs. Although Michael Corcoran referred to Ireland as "still beneath the iron heel of a despotic [British] power," his wartime records do not focus on independence visions. That being said, John O'Mahony visited Corcoran's camp in 1863, and known Fenians served under the Irish-born general in his Legion and in the 69th New York State Militia.[60]

By comparison, Thomas Francis Meagher used the Fenian movement when it served his military and political purposes, but his overall level of public support is similarly questionable. Ever since the Young Irelander arrived in the United States in 1852, his relationship to Irish nationalism in the diaspora vacillated. In March 1861, the *Irish-American* reported the "unusual absence of . . . T. F. Meagher, and others of the Irish nationalist party" at the Friendly Sons of St. Patrick's dinner in honor of Ireland's patron saint.[61] This may well be because "in the mid-nineteenth century, the Society of Friendly Sons was not particularly nationalist" enough for the former rebel.[62] Meagher did have connections to the Fenian Brotherhood, but so did many prominent Irish Americans in New York City. On 22 January 1864, the group organized a second "performance" of Meagher's funeral elegy for Corcoran at the Cooper Institute, and Meagher likewise met with O'Mahony in Irish Brigade military encampments.[63] After the war, Meagher appears to have shunned the Fenians altogether in the open. Not long after he became the Territory of Montana's Acting Governor in fall 1865, "industrious and enterprising Irishmen— members of the Fenian Brotherhood" paid him a visit. Meagher wrote to William Seward to inform him about this meeting because "as an officer of the United States, I felt bound in honor, as well as by a conscientious regard to my official obligations, not to say or do anything which might be at variance with the policy and duty of the Government." Irrespective of personal "feeling and convictions" that "made it impossible for me not sympathize with an organization which has the liberation of Ireland at heart," publicly Meagher refused to interact with local Fenian chapters.

These Fenian members had gone to meet Meagher to inform him of their intention in "this city, and the neighboring mining districts, to give . . . a serenade in honor" of his arrival in the region. This was a reference to a common American nineteenth-century political culture practice whereby groups would sing songs and lyrical ballad compositions to political figures, serenading them with praise and support in front of crowds. Meagher told Seward the "serenade took place" and that "several hundreds of citizens in no way connected with the Fenian Brotherhood attended," although members of the organization were present.[64] He was alluding to the fact that the United States government would have to deal with possible Anglo-Canadian-American diplomacy issues concerning the Fenians' interests in British military sites across the border.

Montana's close northern boundary with its Canadian neighbor meant that peace might not always be possible in the region, something borne out the following year when tensions erupted over the Fenians' attempted invasion raids.[65] In an act of Republican government loyalty, Meagher was making sure Seward knew he would not "speak in relation to the Brotherhood," or deal with them in secret. He sent his account in case he was ever "officially called in [to] question" about his postbellum Irish nationalist stance. Amid the currying favor with Seward, Meagher gave a good impression here that his personal Irish nationalism was no longer publicly active.[66]

Despite what some ballads wished for in their lyrics concerning Meagher and Corcoran leading their Irish soldiers back to Ireland to fight for independence, such a reality was impossible. Corcoran died in December 1863 and Meagher, prior to his death in 1867, showed no sign of active support for the Fenian cause after the war. Had the circumstances differed and both lived longer, it is doubtful the two most prominent Irish American Civil War generals would have returned to Ireland. Neither appeared to show enormous open enthusiasm for Fenian activities. Evidence suggests their level of support was not much more than sympathetic and passive. Like the ballads about them, Meagher and Corcoran put their loyalty to the United States above that to their old home nation.

The dawn of a new era for the diaspora after the Civil War brought with it a cemented sense of American nationality. When a "Mr. Mullaly" wrote "Long Live the Sixty-Ninth," he returned to a familiar Irish American lyrical trope. Notwithstanding calling upon Irish cultural heritage, symbols, and language, the song demonstrated how these too had become American. In a similar way to "Cead Mille Fealthe" welcoming home the 9th Massachusetts, "Long Live the Sixty-Ninth" sang in celebration of the returning Irish-born and descended soldiers of the 69th New York in 1861, with their home city singing in dual Irish and American jubilation:

Hail to the men now in triumph returning . . .
Ireland is proud, and America is grateful,
The heart of each Irish girl bounds at their names.
"Caed millea failtha, men!"
Out on the air again—
Rings the clear sound of the Irish hurrah . . .
Long live the Sixty-ninth! Erin go Bragh! . . .

The honor of Ireland was safe in their keeping,
The "Sunburst" and "Stars and Stripes" safe in their hands
No marvel they fought with a strength superhuman,
For each man in the Sixty-ninth struck for TWO lands.[67]

The "two lands" had two meanings—America and Ireland, as well as America and the Irish American nation the diaspora had constructed and brought to the fore. Irish America was its own entity, a mixture of American patriotism with an Irish cultural heritage, where vestiges of the language and emblems were placed alongside those belonging to the United States.

Not even the most prolific Irish songwriter could fully escape the pull of the American nation when writing about Irish nationalism after the Civil War. In 1866, Charles Graham Halpine published *Baked Meats of the Funeral,* "a collection of essays, poems, speeches, histories and banquets" that continued the adventures of his fictional Irish soldier Private Miles O'Reilly.[68] As with his earlier works, *Baked Meats* was disseminated widely throughout the country and furthered Halpine's message of Irish loyalty to Union society. It also contained commentary on the state of Irish nationalism at the end of the conflict. Just after the outbreak of hostilities in spring 1861, Halpine had produced "Old Ireland," a poem which promised how Ireland's "sons now abroad, arming themselves, would soon come to her rescue."[69] This suggested that the Irish in America would return to liberate the island nation once the fight between the Union and Confederacy was over. He repeated this notion after the war in "The Fenian Rallying Song," printed within an essay on the Fenian Brotherhood in *Baked Meats.* Most of the song sang of a hope that the day would soon be granted when "we may press our native sod" to bring an end "Ireland's long eclipse."

Again, however, Fenian independence soldiers were not returning alone. One line stated: "let them give us arms and ships"—a hope for American military aid. The penultimate verse likewise included lyrics about how American forces would be involved "when the Stars and Stripes may burn . . . against our foes," and "when Yankee guns shall thunder on Britain's coast."[70] Halpine, like Corcoran and Meagher, indicated signs of a less-than-committed overall level of Fenian support. He was undoubtedly connected to the organization: he addressed them at one meeting in Jersey City in May 1865 and wrote editorials in the *New York Herald* about Irish nationalism and the Fenians specifically.[71] Nonetheless, in his extensive biography on the Irish songwriter, William Hanchett has highlighted that Halpine "never states publicly that he himself was a member of the Fenian Brotherhood." He thought the Canadian raids were "criminal and irresponsible" and "denounced [them] as folly and a crime."[72] While sympathetic to independence, Halpine described Fenianism as a "curious and erratic movement."[73] It was a fitting depiction for the entire state of Irish nationalism in the diaspora.

It is also one that suits the nature of song lyrics that discussed Irish nationalism, cultural nationalism, Irish heritage, and Fenianism. As the public singing voice of Irish America Civil War sentiment on the home front, Halpine articulated sympathetic cultural nationalism over active supportive Fenian nationalism and American loyalty over Irish identity. In turn, this signifies much about the retention of Irishness across the whole of the country during the conflict. The Irish sang of Ireland in symbolic form; hopeful wartime lyrics about Ireland's independence would be carried to fruition by another generation some sixty years later. Irish American lyrical politics in the 1860s was itself more urgent. It focused on present American concerns caused by the conflict between the Union and Confederacy rather than on Ireland's nationalist republican dreams.

6

---·❧·---

Lyrical Expressions
of Wartime Politics

ithin its commentary on the state of local New York politics and
Democrat Party machinations, Charles Graham Halpine's "Song of
the National Democracy" contained two lines that encapsulated attitudes expressed in Irish American Civil War songs. Combining articulations of
Irish loyalty to the Stars and Stripes with criticism of Confederate secessionists
and racist reference to slave emancipation, Halpine's 1864 lyrics saw continued
fighting for a Union victory as fundamental: "To the flag we are pledged—
all its foes we abhor; / And we ain't for the nigger, but are for the war!"[1]

Expressions of pledging support to the Star Spangled Banner and the
Union cause echoed those heard in ballads about the Irish experience in the
1860s. In contrast, sentiments relating to nativist responses, racial views about
Blacks and emancipation, and overarching political arguments—especially
in relation to secession, the Democratic Party, and the 1864 presidential
election—were heard less frequently. The actions of Irish-born and descended
soldiers impacted home-front opinions voiced in wartime songs, and their
service was used to shape specific attitudes about these matters. Halpine's
pointed lyrical arguments, in particular, did much to influence attitudes about
these subjects.

The County Meath-born songwriter's lyrical commentary played to both
perceived and real Irish racism toward freedmen and the enslaved, hostility to the Emancipation Proclamation, and years of bitter resentment about
anti-Catholic nativist attacks originating in the antebellum decades. Military
enlistment and bounty policies culminated with these resentments over four
of the darkest days of Irish American history: the New York City Draft Riots.
Taking place from 13 July to 16 July 1863, the riots created further dissonance
and tensions between Irish views on the war's policies. Many (though by no

means all) of New York City's disparate diaspora members attacked institutions associated with Union conscription policies and emancipation, including targeting abolitionist presses and the Colored Orphan Asylum on Fifth Avenue. By the end of the rioting, over one hundred people had died, and more than two thousand were injured, with many victims being from the city's Black population. The Irish community was blamed heavily for events.

The experience of New York in 1863, where these tensions were put into starkest relief and came to the most violent boiling point, was not the norm. What is undeniable is that the Civil War provided a platform for such tensions to fester and form in public discourse as the Irish, themselves recent subjects of racist nativist attacks, turned into the persecutors of the people they were also fighting (in the Union) to set free. Each suburb, city, state, and region, and each Irish military unit and home-front community during the war, had their own varying degrees of racial hostility toward the free and enslaved Blacks in the country. Part of their racism was a sign of Irish assimilation and adoption of American attitudes, alongside the fact that recent poor, working-class, urban Irish migrants were concerned emancipated slaves would journey northward and cause economic and employment strain as both groups competed for work. In many ways, the Irish migrants' relationship to Blacks in urban enclaves—especially in Eastern seaboard cities such as New York where the large population and constant influxes of workers created the most employment and economic pressures—played to notions of racial hierarchies among migrant groups. As nativist anti-immigrant attacks abated during the war years, and the diaspora's Catholic Irish members were accepted into American working-class society, attention turned to attacking those beneath them on the social ladder of acceptance—namely, free Blacks and slaves along with those aligned with bringing about emancipation.[2]

The homogenized New York Irish diaspora's example, and impact, on Irish American Civil War studies has led to an unbalanced assessment of this particular period of their history. The participation of some of the city's Irish population in the Draft Riot's worst acts, especially in actions against Blacks and supportive abolition institutions, has created a persistent narrative that stresses a lack of Irish support for the Civil War. Its events were unquestionably "harmful for the Irish," as Susannah Ural has argued: "the riots . . . renewed or reinforced nearly every negative stereotype about the Irish in America."[3] Regardless of extensive conflicting contemporary evidence that indicate internal divisions and contrary opinions about the actions of Irish rioters from fellow members of the diaspora, pervading scholarship has suggested home-front views and actions applied to the entire Irish community in the United States.

This narrative runs counter to Irish American Civil War song sentiments. The culminating issues of the Draft Riots—nativism, racism, enlistment, political sympathies, and views about the war's aims, policies, generals, and government leaders—are relatively mute in Irish American wartime ballads. The events in New York City in July 1863 themselves appear in a handful of veiled references. Riots and religion, two of the most common topics of Irish American nineteenth-century studies, are removed from the contemporary lyrical lexicon. Their omission says as much, perhaps even more, than their inclusion. One reason is basic commercial interest related to widespread dissemination of songs into society and a consequent desire to leave out more unpalatable topics. That explains the lack of religious references in songs, so as not to draw attention to soldiers' Catholicism in a climate of nativist suspicion. While targeted anti-Irish nativist ballad responses attacked hostile attitudes about the place of the Irish in American society, such as "No Irish Need Apply" song examples, they did not draw on the diaspora's religious affairs or identities.

On the other hand, the lack of reference to the other contributing Draft Riot factors of Irish attitudes toward slavery, emancipation, and the Black population cannot be explained by simple omission of controversial issues. The continual popularity of music hall blackface minstrel show tunes and songs, which Irish urban communities enjoyed watching, alongside the frequent use of racist rhetoric in general Union and Confederate ballads and even the depiction of caricatured slaves on songsheet border illustrations all point toward the everyday reality of immovable and inherent American racism. That is not to say the Irish in America were not racist because they did not sing frequently about their racial prejudices.[4] Instead, their singing focus was more frequently centered on other topics, with sentiments about loyalty to the Union and Confederacy, American identity articulation, Irish cultural nationalism, and the fighting experiences of soldiers coming to the fore. When a handful of lyrics on the subject *did* appear, they were placed in broader commentary related to wider American political issues.

The Irish rarely responded to community fears about immediate emancipation and racialized economic competition by singing about them, at odds with the fact that virtually every other topic central to 1860s society appears in Civil War ballads. When sentiments about nativism, the enslaved, and wartime politics were printed, they were connected to interlocking issues that paint an often-contradictory picture. They highlight how an homogenized opinion of Irish Americans in the mid-nineteenth century, centered mostly on the home-front view of the New York diaspora, presents too narrow and simple a view of complicated, ever-evolving attitudes. Contrary to arguments that "countless . . . Irish American poems and songs complained of nativist prejudice and the injustice of the war," Irish American Civil War songs in fact provided numerous examples that the diaspora's home-front mentality toward the major issues of the conflict was *overwhelmingly* proactive, positive, and articulated a strong voice of Irish inclusion in the pressing issues of the day.[5] If anything, the Irish made use of song culture to present a counternarrative of wartime sentiments and attitudes, thus illuminating a constant shaping and reshaping of soldier and home-front views. They challenge a more linear approach to assessing the Civil War's influence on Irish Americans' relationship to their new position in society and their adoption of contemporary concerns.

IRISH VIEWS OF CONFEDERATE SECESSION

Considering the Civil War centered on the cornerstone issue of slavery, Irish ballads produced early in the conflict barely mentioned the institution. There was a subtle slavery hint in "The Gallant 69th Regiment" (1862) when it made a passing comment that the United States was "the home of the brave, though not the free."[6] After the Emancipation Proclamation was issued in 1 January 1863, songs altered the way they sang about slavery on the rare occasion the subject appeared. Hugh F. McDermott's "The Irish Brigade," written in the same month the policy came into effect, described the coming day "when Slavery's power hath passed away and nature's laws"—meaning the natural rights of men, freedom and liberty—"shall rule again" in the country.[7] "The Irish Brigade in America" (1863) commented how Irish-born and descended soldiers were now fighting not just for reunification but overall abolition as well. The song began with a description of the: "Gallant sons of Erin's isle, of high and low degree, / Who are fighting in the American states to put down slavery."[8]

Another 1863 ballad production revealed that there could be critical vocalizations of abolitionist rhetoric alongside more supportive expressions. The eponymous Pat of "Pat Murphy of Meagher's Brigade" chastised those whom he saw as responsible for pushing the Confederate states into secession and hostility. He reflected one particularly vehement view heard in some communities about emancipation and attacked the abolitionists directly for pushing the policy onto the Union administration's political agenda. Sung from the soldier's own voice, thick with a mock-Irish brogue, lyrics commented:

> There's a crowd in the North, too, an' they're just as bad;
> Abolitionist spouters so scaly—
> For throubling the naigers I think they deserve
> A Whack from a Sprig of Shillaly!

Pat Murphy's violent note about attacking abolitionists foreshadowed the New York Draft Riots, but it must be stressed that such an extreme opinion was not reflected in counterpart ballads. Attacks against abolitionist views were, on the whole, kept off Irish wartime songsheets.

It is also important to contextualize these particular lyrics in relation to the main subject of Pat Murphy's ire. The description of the abolitionists being "just as bad" was a comparison to the Confederates themselves and one secessionist in particular. Four lines prior to those quotes, the start of the verse focused on Jefferson Davis. Pat Murphy's main desire was to see the Confederate leader punished for disrupting American unity:

> Jeff. Davis, you thief! If I had you but here,
> Your beautiful plans I'd be ruinin'—
> Faix! I'd give ye a taste of my bayonet, bedad!
> For trying to burst up the Union.[9]

This Irish lyrical threat to attack Davis with a bayonet echoed violent expressions in "Corcoran's Ball!" (1863). In the final verse, it explained that if "old Jeff Davis raise but his finger now," Irish soldiers would "soon . . . be smashing his ugly old sconce."[10]

Pat Murphy reiterated a common Irish wartime sentiment. Ballads may have been relatively muted in reference to slavery but anti-secession and anti-Confederate attacks were more frequent. This presents a subtle distinction: while the Irish in America may not have been singing about the institution at the heart of the Confederacy, they *were* singing about slavery's impact and reason for why the conflict was happening. They were also deeply critical about Confederate states' secession in general. Lyrics adopted Union rhetoric, depicting Southern separatists as traitorous rebels who would be beaten by Irish soldiers. This helped further lyrical sentiments about fighting spirits and military service pride. Additionally, it was not only those on the front line who could sing these broader views. Everyone (in lyrical terms) shared in Columbia's "mandates made by thy heroes assemble" as "The Gallant 69th Regiment" explained, avenging the Union "when secession's cursed form stood in view."[11]

Numerous songs justified soldiers' war service and the diaspora's support for the Union in relation to their condemnation of Confederate secession. "Corcoran's Irish Legion" (1863) explained that when the Irish general "again" took command of Irish regiments after his prisoner captivity, he would fight until "the bonds of Rebellion" were reconnected "and peace restored to our dear adopted land." The song also reminded listeners how the Irish had been involved in this war aim from the start, as they "rushed hand in hand . . . to crush out the traitors forever and ever" following Lincoln's call for troops in April 1861. The phrase "traitors are crushed forever"—yet more violent sentiment waged against the Confederacy—was a repeated refrain throughout the ballad.[12] "Glorious 69th" further described Irish service as being a response to Lincoln's orders as it detailed the moment in May 1861 when:

Our President commanded us, and we must hasten o'er,
For to put down Secession, on the Old Virginny shore . . .
For we must go to Washington, to put down the Rebel band.[13]

"The New York Volunteer" (1861) also recalled the 69th New York's reason for going southward to the seat of war. "Dedicated to the brave Sixty-Ninth," it was another song performed by Thomas L. Donnelly, where the self-described "Comedian and Vocalist" adopted the singing persona of an Irish soldier. With a mock-Irish accent, the fictional soldier explained his enlistment before presenting his view of the battlefield enemy:

I wint down to Virginny, with Corcoran's bould Haroes,
To have a hand at skivering [skewer] the Southern would-be Neros . . .
The rebels soon must yield; they cannot stand our banging.[14]

Three months after they left their New York homes, the "gallant soldiers" of the 69th New York, who had "gone to face the enemy and put rebellion down," met on fields around Manassas, Virginia. The broadside account of the fighting in "Battle of Bull Run" (1861) described how the militia had "put to flight with shame, each proud secession leader with bayonet sword and gun." Future Union service would "make them pay severely for the battle at Bull Run," a lyrical thereat again aimed at the Confederate "them" who won that particular engagement.[15] The underlying tone was clear: the Irish were prepared to seek fighting justice for their honor, both for the soldiers they sacrificed and for the American nation.

Lyrics articulated challenges and doubts about secessionist aspirations to break the United States apart. As part of that questioning, Irish ballads vocalized ardent belief in the ideals of truly unified states. John F. Poole's self-explanatory ballad entitled "Pat's Opinion of the Stars and Stripes" (1862) labeled secessionists as "blackguards" who were "ruining" not just *the* country, but also "*our* country." By "trying to bust up the Union and pull *down* the Stars and the Stripes," this particular "Pat" informed listeners that "we'll"—referring to the Irish in the Union's Army and Navy—would "soon bate the blackguards afloat and ashore." They would ensure "our flag o'er Fort Sumter be waving once more," referring to the location of the war's outbreak on 12 April 1861.

The final verse of "Pat's Opinion of the Stars and Stripes" even suggested Confederate forces "better give in" as there was no point prolonging the conflict. The Union, together with its Irish military and civilian support, would "soon gain the day."[16] "New War Song of the 69th Regiment" (1862) even questioned why the Southern states had seceded and engaged in a battle for their independence in the first place. It gave a "curse on those bloody traitors and seceeders of the South" for their attempt to go "out of this happy Union." The 69th New York "Erin's sons with swords and guns" would soon "let them know" they would be beaten on the battlefield. Another aspect would further "prove their overthrow," with one line questioning the very nature of Confederate mentality in taking the ambitious action to sever the bonds of unity: "If they knew what they were doing, they never would go out."[17]

Songs about the famed 69th New York and the Irish Brigade were not the only ones to stress anti-Confederate and anti-secession rhetoric. The 69th Pennsylvania ballad "Col. Owens' Gallant Irish Volunteers" (1861) described how the unit would likewise join in the fight:

When we march away down south
The Rebels will get their fill.
Davis, Lee and General Bragg,
We'll make them all stand clear.[18]

Their Irish compatriots in the 9th Connecticut Volunteers sang of anti-Confederate retribution in one verse of "Save the Constitution" (1862) about the group's mobilization:

When foul rebellious fictions laws this great republic branded,
As loyal subjects to the cause, the gallant Ninth responded;
And drew the sword to share her woes and keep down vile disunion
Until they see this country once more a perfect Union.[19]

Other nationalities voiced comparable views about fighting secession and restoring the Union. The 69th New York's Scottish diaspora cousins in the 79th New York Highlanders sang of the same anti-Confederate rhetoric in their "War Song of the 79th Regiment." Written at the start of the war in 1861, its lyrics described the seceded states as abhorrent "knaves." It warned the "rebels who our flag have spurned" that they would not win, as "our Union shall not be o'erturned."[20]

Irish-born and descended Confederate counterpart ballads were coy about the true reasons behind their nationalist independence defense but were also equally vocal in their anti-Union rhetoric. "Song for the Irish Brigade" (1861) contained comments about the Union's Irish Brigade, describing those who fought in the Army of the Potomac as "Lincoln snakes." The Irish in the Confederacy would eliminate Republican, abolitionist, and Union policies from the land in the same manner as St. Patrick removing serpents from Ireland. Using identical language as the Scottish New York community, this particular Confederate Irish song described Republicans at the start of the war as "knaves that rest on Columbia's breast, and the voice of true men stifle."[21] This alluded to sectional political concerns that the rights of the Southern states, including the right to own slaves, would be curtailed. "Erin's Dixie" reiterated Irish support for the Confederate cause two years later in 1863 by championing "Old Virginia's rights and Dixie." It described in proud voice that "the Irishman is a fighting man" who would continue to "make a stand for Dixie."[22]

In a similar vein, "Kelly's Irish Brigade" (1862) sang of Confederate criticism of Lincoln and Irish support for secession. Directed at "all ye that hold communion with Southern Confederates so bold," the ballad discussed regional diaspora support for Missouri's right to leave the Union: "'Tis but State's Rights and Liberty we ask . . . Let the voice of Missouri be obeyed." The Missouri Irish were thus singing that if the erring state wished to leave the Union, then she had the right to do so. Pro-Union supporters "called us Rebels and Traitors" for taking such a stance, but that did not concern them. When they met "Kelly's Irish Brigade" on the field as they fought in defense of Missouri's right to join the Confederacy, the "cowardly Lincolnites [would] tremble . . . The Northern fanatics will tremble."[23] This was a reference to Captain Joseph Kelly's regiment in the Missouri State Guards, a unit comprised of predominantly Irish-born and descended men.[24] While the ballad revealed pro-Confederate sentiments among some of the Irish community, as well as local civil strife tensions, they also applied to wider Irish support for Confederate aims.

By extension, some general Confederate songs were not just critical of the Union and those fighting to end secession. "Yankee Doodle's Ride to Richmond" (1862) contained many anti-Union phrases that were disparaging about the very ethnic composition of federal military forces. It described the Union Army as "a crew of dirty vagabonds," and hurled derogatory criticism at "thieving Yankees, filthy Dutch [German], and Irish from the Bogs."[25] One Irish soldier who would likely take offence at that was General Michael Corcoran, who also engaged in his own fair share of anti-Confederate attack in his prisoner-of-war memoir. Just as Irish wartime songs were critical of the Confederacy's perceived treachery against the nation and the Constitution, so too did Corcoran note how it was his "firm belief that" the United States government and the country had "been subjected to the insidious power of treachery" by the Southern states' secession. He adopted a vitriolic tone to argue how the Confederate states should be returned to the Union in "the shortest way to crush out the horrid civil war that is wasting our land."[26]

"Return of Gen. Corcoran, of the Glorious 69th" (1862) reflected Corcoran's attitude in its presentation of the diaspora's shared defense of American national ideals in reaction to secession. As with previous examples, it sang about how a united Irish American force would stop "Southern traitors." "In one loud, united voice that rent the very sky," they would swear to "put base traitors down, and conquer them or die." More than that, through their overall Union support the Irish would beat "the Rebel foe, who would destroy the land that gave them birth and nurtured them, the dastard rebel band." These lyrics had dual meaning: the nurturing land "that gave them birth" encompassed not only the seceded Southerners but also second and subsequent generation Irish men and women in America. Such lyrics reiterated the sentiment that the United States was a true Irish homeland by the 1860s. "The land" was *their* land.

However, "Return of Gen. Corcoran" contained a verse that raised the complicated issue of war support, its causes, and why the Irish were participating in its unifying cause. Written in the aftermath of Lincoln issuing the Preliminary Emancipation Proclamation in September 1862, these lyrics offered the first Irish wartime song reference to the specific issue of slave emancipation. It was not one that sang of the action with overwhelming positivity. The Irish had provided their military service because:

'Twas not to subjugate the South, those Irish braves went forth,
Nor emancipated their negroes to satisfy the North—
But bring them back unto the laws, their noble sires had made,
And place again, beneath our Flag, each Southern renegade.[27]

Although the emphasis was still on ending secession, slavery was the quiet voice in the background. This particular song reference made the issue louder. The notion of emancipating the slaves "to satisfy the North" was another thinly veiled attack at abolitionists and Republicans. It was also, as the date of the Emancipation Proclamation's enactment came closer, the first musical rumblings that the diaspora was not fully supportive of this particular Union war aim.

IRISH VIEWS OF EMANCIPATION

The Irish American relationship to the issue of slavery and African Americans during the nineteenth century was complicated to say the least. The Civil War brought to the fore significant racial tensions and attacks against enslaved and free Blacks in the divided nation. The multifaceted reasons behind the perceived broader Irish stance require qualification. There was a difference between views on abolition and emancipation, for instance. On the rare occasion the topic came up, Irish wartime songs would sing about *abolitionists*—in other words, those pushing for the ending of slavery—and not the actual practice of *abolition* itself. It was the instigators of civil divisions around slavery who were blamed for exacerbating sectional tensions, not the object of their antislavery campaign. Abolition was tolerable when it did not form a perceived threat to the Irish community. Emancipation during the war did, however, because its potential consequences—namely the freeing of former slaves into the labor market—raised concerns centered on the issue of employability competition in the Northern states and a sense that emancipation altered the Union's agenda.

Focus on New York City's reaction to the Emancipation Proclamation in 1863 creates the impression that the views from its Irish community applied to the whole of Irish America. This muddies the combining streams of discontent explaining Irish home-front disquiet. While they may have been infrequent with lyrical expressions about it, the Irish were not necessarily quiet about expressing that they were not fighting for abolitionist aims. Emancipation was simply not a topic in any American-produced song about the Irish American Civil War experience that appears in this study. The only notable mention came in a ballad written and published on the other side of the Atlantic in Ireland in summer 1863. One passage of "Lamentation on the American War" described the Emancipation Proclamation as altering Irish understanding about what the conflict was ultimately about and the perceived detrimental impact this would have on the immigrant community. This issue was expressed in inflated lyrical language:

> America once happy land, but now a scene of woe,
> President Lincoln and his slave bill has proved an overthrow,
> For the thousands of our Irish boys without employment strong,
> The widows and their orphans dear, all in America.[28]

In keeping with a sentiment hinted at in these lyrics—but not necessarily the only interpretation of them—some scholars have argued that racial tensions between Irish Americans and Blacks were exacerbated by "learning of the horrifying losses" Irish-born and descended soldiers were suffering on the battlefield, especially in the wake of the Battle of Antietam and Lincoln's Preliminary Emancipation in September 1862. The combination of the diaspora's sons dying and Union policy meant "the Irish community in America learned that the war was moving in a direction they could not support," which led to anti-emancipation stances, continued racial hostility toward Blacks, despondency, and a decline in willingness to engage in the conflict.[29]

This impression of the Irish response to events in the middle of the Civil War is too constricted when considering the complex reaction that took place throughout Union society to battlefield losses, the Proclamation, the draft, and debates about the conflict's meaning and ultimate goals. Both the broader Irish community in the Northern states more generally, and the New York Irish particularly, expressed a myriad of positions across differing sections of the diaspora concerning all of these issues. Beyond doubt, "resentment was intensified by the Emancipation Proclamation, which, in Irish eyes, changed the character of the war for the worse." The policies of freeing slaves and drafting civilians certainly stirred deeper tensions. In relation to the diaspora in New York City, "much of the accumulated anger was vented against Blacks" in the area. However, the Draft Riots did not spring solely from the war itself. Violence "was an eruption of the frustrations that had accumulated" by the middle of 1863. They also revealed dissatisfaction spawned from disquiet about residual antebellum anti-Irish policies. The riot served "both as a catharsis for past feelings" first and then "more tangibly as a modifier of draft policy."[30]

Even so, when considering these combined tensions and amalgamated influences during the New York City Draft Riots, what is often overlooked is the fact that during this same period a significant ideological split started to develop between the Irish soldiers on the front line and the rest of the diaspora on the home front. It is a divide that Michael Corcoran himself articulated in one letter to Irish American Judge Charles P. Daly ten days after the Emancipation Proclamation came into effect. "I must acknowledge that I am not as full of hope and confidence as to the probable ultimate results of this most unhappy contest as when I last saw you," the Irish-born general told his friend. He indicated a sign of war-weariness that reflected more general sentiments across the country by the middle point of the conflict. Corcoran admitted to his friend that his mood was likely exacerbated by recent events, commenting: "I may be unnecessarily disappointed on account of the results of late battles." This was a passing reference not just to the encounters of his own Corcoran's Legion but also to the events of the Battle of Fredericksburg in December 1862, which had occurred one month prior to the penning of his correspondence. He would have known about the detrimental fighting losses encountered by the Irish Brigade on Marye's Heights, which included the remnants of his own former 69th New York.

Additionally, Corcoran attributed his apparent malaise to the "anticipated result of the Proclamation etc.," the only time in his letter conversations with Daly where he mentioned wider Union government administration policies. As with contemporary Irish wartime songs, he made no other reference to the Emancipation Proclamation or to what his own views were on the matter. It is possible to read his comment from a military point of view—such a policy might cause further low spirits in a bruised Union Army, which would, in turn, impact home-front war spirit and morale. It is also possible (and likely, given the nature of nineteenth-century society) Corcoran shared the racial prejudices of his Irish and American countrymen, even though there is little indication of this in his surviving writings. He ended this commentary to Daly by stating how "I almost earnestly hope that matters may soon assume a much more favorable aspect," both in terms of the Union Army achieving victories and a hope any disquiet about emancipation would soon diminish.[31] Such a view highlights discord in the diaspora that emerged over the course of 1863 and 1864 as wartime policies seeped into soldier and civilian discussions and Irish wartime balladry.

THE NEW YORK CITY DRAFT RIOTS

"I am very sorry that the Irish men of New York took so large a part in them disgraceful riots" Peter Welsh wrote in 1863. This was the third letter he sent to his wife Margaret between 17 July and 2 August that year on the subject of the New York Draft Riots and Irish involvement in their violent nature. His prolonged commentary reveals how news was disseminated between the front line and home front and also how deeply the actions of his fellow diaspora countrymen bothered him. "God help the Irish," Welsh stated, "they are to easily led into such snares which give their enemys an opportunity to malign and abuse them."[32] The enemies were both Confederate supporters and Union nativist sympathizers. It was a view directed at the discord of opinions about the draft, enlistment, and the place of the diaspora in American society over the summer of 1863.

The Enrollment Act of March 1863, coming after the Emancipation Proclamation's introduction that New Year's, furthered social tensions. A culmination of varying strains came together; "for the Irish, conscription was particularly objectionable since it came almost simultaneously with emancipation." It raised disquiet because the act "required the Irishman to fight for" former slaves who would become their "competitor in the labor market" at the end of the war, at least from the point of view of some in the diaspora.[33] It also raised the pressure over the Irish American Union home front's level of involvement and willingness to volunteer support for the war effort. A clear divide appeared to have been drawn between the service in the first two years of the conflict and the peak of tensions in summer 1863.

The impact of heavy Irish Brigade losses and Thomas Francis Meagher's fair (but relatively small) recruitment drive successes by the middle of 1863 gives the impression that Irish soldiers' eagerness to fight had diminished. Sections of the diaspora perceived the draft as punishment on the community and that the previous battlefield service of fathers, husbands, brothers, and sons was not recognized by American society. This led to suggestions that "increasing numbers of Irishmen saw their sacrifices as unappreciated," a fact exacerbated by "news reports questioning the quality of Irish military service" and negative commentary accusing "the Irish of serving in numbers far below their representation in the populace." By 1863, such criticisms, and a seemingly unfair draft policy, led the diaspora to argue that conscripting their men was "a means for allowing native-born Americans to avoid the hardships of war."[34]

This approach discounts conflicting voices within the diaspora about the draft and what its implementation meant to the place of the Irish in American Union society. Irish American Civil War songs provided readers, listeners, and performers of balladry with more positive commentary regarding the service of Irishmen. They acted as encouragement for the home front to join the war effort voluntarily, which, it must be stressed, they continued to do for the rest of the conflict. Irish-born and descended soldiers still enlisted—and sung about enlisting—even after the events in New York City in July 1863. There was not one pervasive negative view of the draft to which the whole diaspora ascribed. The homogenizing of Irish American Civil War experience falls short of focusing on competing and complex views on the front line and home front.[35] Indeed, in his work on non-New York Irish regiments, Ryan Keating has criticized the way in which the Draft Riots have come seemingly to represent the whole Irish American Civil War experience "despite the fact that this event was hardly emblematic of the sentiments of Irish Americans." The Draft Riots should not be "symbolic of lingering questions surrounding loyalty to the United States."[36]

Before the introduction of the draft, songs directed to the home front sang of Irish enlistment. The comic music-hall style ballad "O'Toole & McFinnigan On the War" depicted a lyrical conversation between "two Irishmen out of employ," Paddy O'Toole and "Misther McFinnigan." The two men "were smoking about taking it lazily" as they talked about enlisting in the Union Army. O'Toole stated:

> I think of enlistin'. . .
> Because, do you see what o'clock it is?
> There's nothin' adoin' at all.'

This presents a view that enlistment was a way of removing boredom but with an economic benefit as the army would provide Irishmen with jobs. O'Toole continued this vein by singing about how there would be no jobs "until after the war," so there was some immediate value in donning a uniform. Both O'Toole and McFinnigan eventually enlist, inspired "to think of bould Corcoran leading us right into the camps" of the Confederacy, reiterating the influence Michael Corcoran had on views of Irish fighting service. They also echoed ongoing anti-Confederate views, arguing: "Secession's . . . so black the divil himself ought to father it!" This song was written when Corcoran was recruiting for his Legion of New York regiments in fall 1863. These fictional Irish enlistees were telling the home front in both New York and in Boston, where the ballad was also published, to join with the famed commander: "'Tis Corcoran will lead 'em, d'ye mind, / And I will go with them," said McFinnigan.[37]

Irish songs were equally uncritical of the Union draft's conscripted service after the policy commenced. In Eugene T. Johnston's 1863 "Who Will Care for Micky Now?"—"a parody on 'Who Will Care for Mother Now?'"—there was brief allusion to the act, but it did not bemoan the Irish soldier's lot or intone criticism of its perceived diaspora discriminatory nature. A note on James Wrigley's songsheet publication of Johnson's ballad described how the fictional Limerick-born "Micky," whose "voice" was singing the song, was one "amongst the many heroic fellows who drew a prize in the U.S. lottery" when the draft came to his state. The lyrics detailed Micky's conversation with "his sweetheart" in which he informed her bluntly: "I am drafted." Micky acknowledged he must become a soldier "to fight the rebel foe," and "soon 'gainst ribels I'll be marching."[38]

Apart from this reasoning, the rest of the song is about how this fictional Irishman would cope with being a soldier. The refrain "who will care for Micky now?" referred to the fact that he had never survived by himself. It was not about being drafted. Johnston's music hall parody on the popular wartime sentimental ballad "Who Will Care for Mother Now?" removed all of the lamenting tone and expressions of the original version. Instead, it created a satire of masculine soldiery with the image of a terrified Micky learning to cope with a soldier's life. This was in contrast to other depictions of valor and brave self-sacrifice presented in songs about Irish soldiers. "Who Will Care for Micky Now?" was a comment to the home front that now that the draft had been enforced, Irishmen were ready to take up the heroic mantle of dutiful American Union defenders but were understandably anxious about what awaited them on the front line.

A further contemporaneous song that sang of the Irish in relation to the consequences of drafted service was "When This Cruel War is Over—No. 2." Another parody song, this was a specific Irish version of Charles Carroll Sawyer's 1863 Union and Confederate ballad "When This Cruel War Is Over." It was sung from the perspective of an already-enlisted Irish soldier who had bravely "shoulder'd my ould musket" and, "With spirits light and airy, Marched off to the wars." War weariness had begun to creep in, though, as the soldier sang, "I am homesick I fear." He would "give this world for a substitute" to swap with him and "take my place here" in the ranks.[39] This was a reference to the fact that the draft opened up the possibility of substitutes to stand in for draftees if they were able. Yet, instead of becoming a commentary on how draft and substitution policies would impact recruits from the diaspora, the song overall adopted a more traditional folk song theme about an Irishman and his sweetheart. There was even a verse on the quality of soldiers' food but nothing about the war itself. This again made it apparent that Irish wartime balladry did not dwell on draft vagaries to any great extent.

Members of the diaspora did not have a uniform view of events concerning the draft and recruitment. Judge Charles P. Daly's wife, Maria Lydig Daly, witnessed many of the New York Draft Riots' initial developments while her husband helped to restore order in the city. She was extremely critical of the implementation of the draft in New York. In her well-maintained wartime diary, on the second day of the riots (14 July 1863), she stated that the measure was "very foolishly ordered by the government, who supposed these Union victories would make the people willing to submit." This was a reference to recent successes at Gettysburg and Vicksburg ten days before rioting broke out. In her mind, "the principal cause of discontent was the provision that by paying three hundred dollars any man could avoid serving if drafted, thus obliging all who could not beg, borrow, or steal this sum to go to the war. This is exceedingly unjust. The laboring classes say that they are sold for three hundred dollars."[40]

In her next entry, Maria Daly reflected on the "four days of great anxiety" and the "fighting [which] went on constantly in the streets between the military and police and the mob." She reported, "the greatest atrocities have been perpetuated . . . the mob [had] such a brutal manner that nothing in the French Revolution exceeded it." She claimed to now "feel quite differently" about events after the passage of a few days and "very sorry and much outraged at the cruelties inflicted." Yet, this wife a of prominent member of New York's Irish American elite could not hide her racial prejudice, negative views about emancipation, or her ethnic and racial blindness about who she thought was responsible for what had happened: "I hope it will give the Negroes a lesson, for since the war commenced, they have been so insolent as to be unbearable. I cannot endure free Blacks. They are immoral, with all their piety. The principal actors in this mob were boys, and I think they were American."[41] While mentioning the fact that rioters had Blacks "hung in the streets!" Maria Daly never condemned the Irish instigators of such actions.[42] She refused to acknowledge her husband's own parental countrymen had carried out much of the worst violence; her diary entries justified the brutal actions in the riots by members of New York's Irish diaspora.

The reaction of the rioters was based on politics, namely, anti-draft and anti-emancipation attitudes. Maria Daly explained that the reason for their targeted violence was because "this mob seems to have a curious sense of justice. They attacked and destroyed many disreputable houses and did not always spare secessionists,'" thus bringing together objects of wartime discontent in New York City.[43] Although she did not mention him, one leading member of the Irish American military community also received his own share of hostility during this destructive attack. Former 69th New York officer and Irish Brigade Colonel Robert Nugent served as a provost marshal in July 1863 while recovering from wounds sustained at the Battle of Fredericksburg the previous December. His position as "director of the draft in the city" made him a target for the Irish rioters, regardless of his status as a member of the famed Irish Brigade or his status as a County Down immigrant. During the riot, "the Irish mob . . . broke into his home, raced through his rooms, destroying the furniture and slashing photographs," both of Nugent himself and (allegedly) of Thomas Francis Meagher. This selected vandalism indicated that "Irishmen blamed Nugent for the draft and Meagher for the high casualties" sustained by Irish soldiers by that point in the conflict.[44] Nugent's house was certainly attacked, but his role as one of New York's draft instigators was never referred to in the three occasions he appears in Irish American wartime ballads.

Like Meagher and Corcoran, Robert Nugent was only sung about with praise. Another epitome of a successful Irish American Union Army officer, he appeared in songs about both the 69th New York and the Irish Brigade. When "The Irish Brigade in America" depicted the unit's memorable encounter with Confederate forces at Fredericksburg, lyrics boasted how "the 69th and 88th [New York] were first upon the field." They were "led on by Col. Nugent, determined not to yield."[45] He also appeared alongside Meagher as an example of a typical Irish soldier. One "Irish Volunteer" song from the time of the Irish Brigade's formation wished "success to Meagher and Nugent, and their Irish volunteers."[46] Furthermore, the Irish-born commander appeared in "Our Brave Irish Champions" to commemorate the Irish contribution to the First Battle of Bull Run in July 1861. Here Nugent's lyrical appearance did not end well, as the song sang erroneously of how "Nugent fell dead of his horse, all bleeding in his gore."[47] His subsequent Civil War service, eventual command of the Irish Brigade as its last leading general, and later American Indian Wars service made Nugent the longest surviving Irish-born American Union officer sung about in ballads. Even though these song examples were written prior to the Draft Riots, no evidence of Irish rioters' hostility toward Nugent appears in contemporary 1863 popular balladry (or in subsequent years).

Nugent's example served as reminder that there were Irish-born and descended men and women who were not against the policy of conscripted service and did not see it as being unduly unfair on the Irish home-front community in the Union. As Susannah Ural has argued, "it is significant that not all Irish Catholic volunteers and civilians opposed the draft."[48] In addition, "almost all of the policemen and a large number of the soldiers on riot duty were as Irish as their opponents," including some of the returning Irish soldiers from Gettysburg who helped subdue the unrest.[49] Given that the wider Irish community was not united on the issues of the draft and emancipation and did not universally sympathize with the rioters, the lack of anti-draft and riot rhetoric in wartime songs is understandable.

Peter Welsh's continued correspondence and criticism of home-front actions is perhaps the most-quoted example in Irish American Civil War era studies, but it is also the best articulation of an anti-Draft Riot perspective from an Irish American soldier. Welsh told his wife how he was "sorry to hear there is such disgraceful riots in New York," caused by "bloody cutthroats" who "should be hung like dogs."[50] He believed ardently that "every leader and instigator of those riots should be made an example of," including Irish men and women. Welsh was a strong supporter of the Enrollment Act. In his mind, "no conscription could be fairer than the one" being imposed. Acknowledging that "it would be impossible to frame it to satisfy every one," Welsh saw the draft as important to the wider Union cause: "[It] will show the south that we have the determination and the power to prosecute the war and they have no possible means of raising an adequate force to oppose the army we can raise by this conscription."[51] Both Welsh and Maria Daly hinted at a sentiment in their writings that New York's reaction to the draft was damaging to the war effort and would provide substantiation to Confederate comments on internal Union divisions. It also revealed concerns that if some in the Union civilian community were not in support of the war, it weakened the acknowledgement of battlefield service and sacrifice.

Welsh's strong anti-Draft Riot views were heard in one Irish American Civil War song that made clear reference to the policy and to the riots themselves. Printed in *The Continental Songster* in 1863 after the events in New York City, "Paddy the Loyal" emphasized the need for the Irish home-front diaspora to show strong American Union support. Although disagreeing with them herself, Maria Daly had raised concern that violent displays of seeming disloyalty to Union war policies "will give the rebels encouragement."[52] "Paddy the Loyal" took this a step further by stating that those not supportive of the

Union were effectively pro-secession and Confederate sympathizers. The final verse sang directly to rioters and anti-draft members of the diaspora:

Oh! Ye secesh sympathizers,
Hould your hush, that my advice is;
If ye's won't fight, don't talk disloyal,
Nor aid the scamps who would destroy all.[53]

These lyrics reveal the overwhelming sentiment in song articulations by and about the Irish in relation to issues of emancipation and the draft. The message was one of fervent Union support and pointed commentary at the Irish home-front diaspora. Lyrics urged them to show loyalty and assist the war's policies, at least publicly. Not doing so would raise questions over how genuinely committed they were to the American nation.

NO IRISH NEED APPLY AND LYRICAL LOYALTY TO THE AMERICAN UNION

There was one crucial reason behind the emphasis Irish American Civil War songs placed on articulating this loyalty and why lyrics sought to remind the diaspora that it needed to show American Union allegiance to the fullest extent through continued volunteer enlistment and Lincoln administration support. Although muted by comparison to its peak in the 1850s, anti-Irish nativist views were still directed at pockets of the diaspora, especially in Eastern urban centers. The notion the Irish had not contributed a fair share to war service touched on latent concerns about the diaspora's devotion. The draft riots did nothing to "strengthen the position of those who hoped to display Irish American military service as proof" of reliability and patriotism. Instead the action helped "nativists' portrayal of them as violent, selfish, and untrustworthy" across Irish America.[54] The sentiments in "Paddy the Loyal" correspond to this opinion.

Conversely, there are questions over how widespread nativist views still were during the Civil War. Some Irish transnationalist studies have argued that "anti-Catholicism had receded as a public passion" by 1856, as the stance took "a subordinate position to the sectional tensions between North and

South."[55] It is critical to see the nativist American Party's "Know Nothing" political views in regional context. Their anti-immigrant approach "fared less well away from the eastern seaboard"; the differing "political climate and economic prospects between the most densely populated East Coast cities and inland regions" impacted how much of the diaspora were subjected to attack from those sympathetic to this political view.[56] This speaks to debate over the relative national strength of the American Party's local political influence. Their anti-immigrant arguments, aimed mostly at German and Irish Catholics in the country, took hold in the broader political system evolution of the early 1850s antebellum United States.

Arguments about regional nativist political strengths and weakness also tie to how long such opinions were maintained by society across the country, particularly as anti-immigration became supplanted in the immediate political climate of the secession crisis and eventual war.[57] Such sentiments were supported by bold claims heard in the penultimate verse of "The Irish Brigade," written in January 1862:

> The Know-Nothing warfare is ended—
> No longer they say we're untrue;
> And now Erin's Green flag is blended
> Among with the Red, White and Blue.[58]

In the song's view, the main body of anti-Irish and anti-Catholic attack in the form of Know Nothing supporters had collapsed by the time of the Civil War, a reference to the American Party's decline after the 1856 presidential election. Their ideas may have dissipated into the political climate of the late 1850s and 1860s war period, but in this Irish American ballad's view, it was an anti-Irish stance that the diaspora need not worry about. The first six months of the war had helped expel latent nativist attacks as Irish-born and descended soldiers established they were not "untrue" to the nation. The reference to the two dual flags of Ireland and America united on the battlefields reinforced the sense of loyalty to the Union cause. This "Irish Brigade" ballad had been written in Woburn, Massachusetts, but it sang of a wider view about the central part the Irish played in defense of the country. Its lyrics could be interpreted by the Irish on the home front as saying they needed to adopt the same steadfast mentality and support as the soldiers on the front line. Former nativist social and political "warfare [was] ended"; the only concern for the Irish in America was now the conflict between the Union and Confederate states.

The most important Irish cultural responses to mid-nineteenth-century American nativism were lyrical replies to the rhetoric of "No Irish Need Apply" (NINA) in employment stances. At least three "No Irish Need Apply" ballads were written during the Civil War, making these social commentaries wartime songs in their own right. They mostly sang to wider home-front society, but they also served to remind the Irish to maintain their American national association. This sentiment was used to make a pointed and satirical attack at those stoking nativist sentiment. Exalting the military service of the Irish in the Civil War demonstrated that the group had the right to apply to any position in the country. In Richard Jensen's analysis of NINA cases, he argues these songs were "sung only by the Irish."[59] That cannot be corroborated, and there is no evidence to support this conclusion. These songs were published by printers unconnected to the diaspora, they were disseminated and performed across society that spread the familiar phrase, and they could be sung with an American voice just as much as an Irish one to emphasize the point that NINA rhetoric needed to end. Jensen does not provide wartime contextualization for the production of these songs, nor does his brief analysis of these cultural outputs mention that their lyrics were overwhelmingly positive about the conflict and Irish service in it.

For example, in music hall performer and "Irish Vocalist" Kathleen O'Neil's 1862 version, lyrics began with a description about a "simple Irish girl . . . looking for a place" of work. The ballad then sang of anti-Irish nativist attacks and defended the Irish as being hardworking and making valuable contributions to the country. It stressed former Irish foreign military service as one of the most important contributions. Lyrics reminded American society of the service of Irish-born and descended soldiers on the battlefields and how this was evidence of loyalty that would make nativist attacks stop. Its final verse also made a comment that feelings toward the Irish in America were changing in this period: "I can see by your kind faces, that you will not deny / A place in your hearts for Kathleen, and All Irish may apply." These lyrics were not only a reference to Irish home-front employability but also to men serving in Army and Navy ranks. Multiple copies of this NINA ballad were circulated after its first performance in spring 1862, and publishers in New York, Boston, and Philadelphia kept the song in production throughout the conflict.[60]

In John F. Poole's lyric version of "No Irish Need Apply," also first written in 1862 and performed on the home front by the non-Irish "great Comic Vocalist of the age, Tony Pastor," the same sentiments were expressed, but this time from a more recent male immigrant perspective. Lyrics described, "in America . . . an Irishman is just as good as any other man." Any nativist and NINA attitudes were a minority-held view. As American conflict broke out in the final verse of Poole's ballad narrative, the "lasting fame" of Irish foreign military endeavors suddenly made them attractive fellow fighting citizens: "yet when they want good fighting-men, the Irish may apply." Nativist "fools may flout and bigots rave" at the thought of this Irish contribution to the Union war effort, but the song returned to the sentiment that the group were willing to participate: "for freedom and the right they raise the battle-cry." This action would dampen anti-Irish commentary. The song ended on a satirical comment that the only people who should protest Irish fighting service were Confederates because the Irish were such good fighters that their soldiering contributions would only serve to strengthen the Union cause. Lyrics joked that when seen on the battlefields, "then the Rebel ranks begin to think: No Irish need apply."[61]

The link between combating any anti-Irish sentiment with lyrical expressions of Irish fighting praise was heard in "What Irish Boys Can Do," the subtitle of which was "Answer to "No Irish Need Apply."" The song was both an "answer" to NINA songs such as Poole and O'Neil's and an "answer" to wider NINA viewpoints in society. Written in 1863, the song was a product of the atmosphere of societal suspicion about Irish loyalty to the war. "What Irish Boys Can Do" was directed toward American and Irish critics of the draft policy who questioned military enrollment and those who "insult an Irishman . . . [and] call him green." Battlefield examples would be the "answer to those dirty words: No Irish need apply!" Like O'Neil and Poole's songs, the final verses focused specifically on the conflict. Its lyrics recalled Corcoran, Meagher, James Shields, and the Irish Brigade's fighting examples and how the sacrifice and displays of Union devotion by Irish-born and descended soldiers should not be ignored by the home front:

And then, too, in the present war between the North and South
Let no dirty slur on Irish ever escape your mouth;
Sure, did you ne'er hear tell of the 69th who bravely fought at Bull-Run?

. . . Then, why slur upon the Irish? Why are they treated so?
What is it you've against them? Is what I want to know;
Sure, they work for all they get, and that you can't deny!
Then, why insult them with the words: No Irish need apply?

The song ended with a reminder that society would "find all things that's noble the Irish folks can do," a strident sentiment about how the Irish in America were committed citizens of the nation's prosperity.[62] It was also singing suggestion to the diaspora and the New York City Irish rioters. Continued public disagreement with war policies would undo the work of Irish military service and reignite nativist slurs against much of the Irish Catholic community.

NINA-related wartime song lyrics all emphasized the need for collective Union civilian unity. The Irish in the United States were, and should remain, committed to their new homeland. This sentiment could be heard in another wartime "No Irish Need Apply" ballad production written in 1864. It reinforced the need to emphasize support through military service and overall loyalty in the aftermath of draft conscription and African American emancipation. The reason for this was a universal sense of common brotherhood as united Americans:

Let us all united be, and true men all around,
And let no petty feelings yet in any heart be found . . .
Let us join both heart and hand, and this the reason why,
We all should meet in Heaven, where all nations *may* apply.[63]

NINA song responses, and the examples of "Paddy the Loyal" and "O'Toole & McFinnigan On the War," were singing to both American society and the home-front diaspora that the Irish were committed to the Union cause and nation. They also served to stress, through broad popular culture, a message of unity and loyalty that runs counter to many of the more biased, negative commentary in nativist and diaspora presses that questioned Irish war involvement and government administration actions, respectively. Ballads served to influence the diaspora's attitudes across the country while singing simultaneously of American association to the whole of society. Consequently, songs were used to emphasize particular messages to communities. In the aftermath of the New York Draft Riots, one Irish-born songwriter would demonstrate this practice better than any of his wartime lyricist contemporaries.

CHARLES GRAHAM HALPINE

Having been a resident in the United States for over a decade by the outbreak of the Civil War, Charles Graham Halpine was already a familiar in New York's Irish American community as a writer, poet-lyricist, and journalist. His poetry collection *Lyrics by the Letter H,* published in 1854, and his subsequent story serializations, newspaper writings, and books—many of which were produced during the conflict—made him one of the most prolific Irish writers in the Civil War era. Halpine's early military career was also tied to the beginnings of the Irish wartime service. He acted as an aide to then-Colonel Michael Corcoran when the 69th New York State Militia mobilized in immediate response to Lincoln's call for troops. He traveled to Washington, DC, with the unit before transferring to serve under General David Hunter as his adjutant. In addition, Halpine was well-connected to New York Democratic circles, including those dominated by the Irish American political elite in the city, and for a time he served as a "Democratic party propagandist." As the war continued, and particularly in the wake of the Emancipation Proclamation and draft reactions, he shifted his political leanings and "aggressively backed the efforts of Lincoln's administration to build popular support for the war." He did this "especially among the New York Irish after the July 1863 riots."[64]

Halpine "publicized the communal meanings of Irish American service" by employing the services of a fictional Irish soldier he created in 1863.[65] The character of Private Miles O'Reilly, of the 47th Regiment New York Volunteers, was self-described by Halpine as "one very humble soldier."[66] Halpine's initial stories, printed in the *New York Herald,* began on 8 September 1863. He depicted O'Reilly as a seasoned soldier who had: "Become quite famous in a small way . . . for [his] comic songs and impromptu verses about the incidents of the day . . . An odd character named Miles O'Reilly, who has frequently relieved the monotony of camp life by scribbling songs on all sorts of subjects, and writing librettos for the various 'minstrel companies' . . . Printed in regular street ballad form."[67] Through his fictional depiction of O'Reilly as a songwriting soldier, Halpine described the dissemination process of lyrics from the front line to the home front, as well as the practice of passing on the Irish tunes many of his songs were set to, in the same way as traditional folk tunes had passed into American musical culture: "He got them printed, and they soon were in the hands of nearly every soldier—the men singing them with intense and uproarious relish to an old Irish air, slightly altered . . . which Private O'Reilly taught them."[68]

So convincing were Miles O'Reilly's initial stories that on the home front "many viewed Halpine's writings as genuine expressions of soldier opinion." That made Halpine's creation the perfect lyrical voice to sing pro-Union and pro-Lincoln administration sentiments from 1863 onward. After laying the fictional foundation of a soldier-songwriter career, Halpine employed Miles to spread messages about war policies and politics, which began with commentary directed at the diaspora itself. In the aftermath of the New York Draft Riots, General John A. Dix "was charged with pacifying the city" and restoring order, especially among aggrieved Irish communities. Aware that "the majority of the rioters were Irish," and likely familiar with Halpine's lyrical verse talents, "Dix appointed Halpine as his assistant general and asked him to bolster Irish support for the war." Halpine responded by penning songs and stories that were "intended to shape both the public image of the Irish and Northern political views."[69] He began with a song that attempted to sing to the whole of society about an issue that was mute in every other Irish wartime ballad: the service of African American soldiers.

Halpine's and O'Reilly's "Sambo's Right to be Kilt" reflected "the occasionally intense debate among Union white soldiers" and civilians of all backgrounds about the issue of African American Union Army enlistment.[70] Lyrics claimed:

> Some tell us 'tis a burnin' shame
> To make the naygers fight;
> And that the thrade [trade] of bein' kilt
> Belongs but to the white.

Yet, the song went on to explain that "the right to be kilt"—or "killed" in a non-mock Irish accent—should be divided equally between white and Black men in uniform. The singing voice of Miles himself argued:

I shouldn't at all object
If Sambo's body should stop a ball
That was comin' for me direct.[71]

In essence, the song presented a view that if African Americans wanted to fight, serve, and die instead of white soldiers, then that should be supported. Breaking from O'Reilly's direct voice, Halpine commented under the song that its sentiment was full of racist impressions and language; despite its apparent liberal approach, it was still heavy with prejudice: "Whatever may be thought of the spirit animating this ditty—which certainly is extremely devoid of any philanthropic or humanitarian cant . . . its popular diffusion resounded undoubtedly to the best interest of the service."[72] Halpine was making a satirical point about racial views toward the military service of free Blacks and former slaves while still exhibiting the same deeply offensive sentiments for public resonance. In his mind, the song served to highlight to white society that more men serving was good, and if Black soldiers wanted to be placed in the front line before white soldiers then that could well reduce casualty lists. All this was done in the spirit of honoring the right to fight and die for the country's unity, albeit in a way that was not based on any sense of equality.[73]

The issue of Black military service was a familiar one to the Irish officer. When Halpine served with Hunter in the early years of the conflict, he had seen the general's abolitionist stance in support of former slaves fighting firsthand.[74] His experience of the debate around this issue was reflected in *Life and Adventures of Private Miles O'Reilly,* published in 1864 when Halpine's initial O'Reilly songs and stories were collected together. After reprinting "Sambo's Right to be Kilt," Halpine discussed Hunter's own position in great detail: "General Hunter . . . urged the matter forward purely as a military measure, and without one syllable or thought of any 'humanitarian proletarianism.' Every Black regiment in garrison would relieve a white regiment for service in the field. Every ball stopped by a Black man would save the life of a white soldier."[75] Halpine both recirculated this argument in the middle of the conflict to justify the Union's need for African American service, and, through his song, Halpine gave a subtle reminder to the diaspora, and to wider society, that any racial prejudice they held was misdirected. Not only would free Blacks and former slaves provide more soldiers to bolster Union forces, but they would also serve in the fight for democratic republican freedom. This wider aim was something the Irish, especially those holding nationalist sympathies, supported.

Halpine's clever establishment of O'Reilly's songs and stories aided the dissemination from a fictional cultural output to a real one. Using "several techniques," the Irish soldier-songwriter "accomplished several goals. By claiming the song was popular and authentic, it became both."[76] Circulated first in the *New York Herald*, and later in Halpine's Miles O'Reilly books, "Sambo's Right to be Kilt" spread throughout the Irish communities and wider Union society. It was also reprinted in 1864, along with the sheet music for five other ballad pieces, in *Songs of the War by Private Miles O'Reilly*. By publishing his works in non-diaspora specific settings—in other words not printing his songs in the diaspora's dominant *Irish-American* or Boston *Pilot* newspapers—Halpine reinforced Irish concerns within larger societal contexts.

That is not to say he abandoned his Irish roots entirely. One fundamental reason why "Sambo's Right to be Kilt" was "immediately popular . . . extensively reprinted" and successful was because it had been "written to a familiar melody . . . which nearly everybody could sing."[77] This recognizable air was "The Low-backed Car," another variant title of "The Irish Jaunting Car" air. "Sambo's Right to be Kilt" was thus another contrafactum connected back to the initial "The Irish Jaunting Car" pieces discussed in chapter 1. It is telling that Halpine, like Harry Macarthy when he penned the Confederate "Bonnie Blue Flag" to the same tune in 1861, used this established Irish and American musical melody for this particular song and subject matter. His choice was deliberate, knowing how common the musical tune was across the country. He was following a practice of setting lyrics to popular melody airs to aid their dissemination, particularly when the song's important subject matter needed to be picked up with speed to spread its message throughout communities.

After "Sambo's Right to be Kilt," Halpine's O'Reilly songs "focused on the Americanizing, communal experience of military service" and electoral issues in the second half of the conflict.[78] His songs centered on unity, including commentary about local politics involving members of the Irish American community. In particular, Halpine drew attention to internal divisions within New York City's Democratic and political organizations. He described the situation in the 1863 production "The Bust Up of the Machines":

Things looks mighty quarely
In the dimmycratic party of this daycint [decent] town;
The maines is busted.[79]

Halpine was most critical of Democrat divisions over how the war should be conducted and concluded, hinting at divisions emerging in 1863 and 1864 between soldiers' views and home-front political opinions. "Song of the National Democracy" was especially aimed at splits among Democrats: "in November we'll have an almighty big row" as the war, peace, and Copperhead elements of the party would debate at local and national level about what political stance to take in relation to Lincoln, Republicans, and the Union war effort. The song described "November's slate smashing grand row"—initially a reference to the 1863 New York state elections when it was first circulated and later applied to the 1864 presidential election when reprinted in *Life and Adventures*.[80] Halpine himself was connected to many of the New York political actors who appeared in his satirical songs, including those in the Irish-dominated Tammany Hall sections. His words were directed deliberately at those who had diasporic political influence. Above all, he argued that the whole of the Democrat Party's machinations needed to unite for the sake of the war. This was mostly because Halpine, by this point in the conflict, exhibited strong Lincoln and Republican leanings.[81]

The Irish-born Union Army officer wordsmith had strong ties to Lincoln and his closest advisors and secretaries, which influenced his favorable view of the administration. Halpine moved in the highest political and military circles throughout the Civil War, serving as a close confidante and aide to Generals Corcoran, Dix, Halleck, and Hunter. He often visited the White House with many of them and had "frequent contacts with Lincoln." He even visited the president at his summer cottage on the outskirts of Washington, DC, and Lincoln himself made several written and pictorial appearances in Miles O'Reilly stories as the fictional soldier met and sang to him. Halpine, in reality, was a pro-Lincoln War Democrat who "supported the administration's war at the same time as he opposed the administration."[82] If anything, his personal experience indicated the complicated nature of Union politics, especially near the war's end. While a homogenized view of the Irish in the mid-nineteenth century has suggested they were all ardent Democrat Party supporters, the Civil War raised complications to this depiction.

Although direct Democrat and Republican Party rhetoric is absent in Irish balladry, the diaspora would have been familiar with how the community's leaders altered their stances in relation to wartime politics. Corcoran and Meagher, like Halpine, supported Lincoln's administration. Meagher especially "embraced the Republican Party and its broader view of rights."[83] By the end of the war, he was "willing to abandon his former soldiers for the lure of political office with the Republicans," leading to his appointment first as secretary to Montana, and then as Acting Governor of the territory in September 1865.[84] Toward the conflict's end, "prominent Fenians" and leading diaspora figures seemed to embrace more radical Republican elements as the atmosphere of American politics changed as a result of four years of fighting, secession, emancipation, and realignment. Echoing Halpine's O'Reilly song messages, in 1865 some Fenians "offered Black regiments" support, which Christian Samito has seen as "a surprising moment of radicalism linking some Irish Americans with African Americans during the Civil War."[85] Halpine, therefore, expressed the core themes underlying Irish American Civil War songs: the diaspora could well be Democrat-leaning, but their Union support came before all other concerns.

Nevertheless, one particular political issue in 1864 did find its way into the balladry produced by soldiers and civilians: the presidential election and George B. McClellan's candidacy. McClellan was no stranger to wartime songs. The general appeared in compositions from the start of the conflict and was the prime subject of the popular and controversial "Give Us Back Our Old Commander"—which circulated Union society despite attempts to ban it on account of its critical administration rhetoric. He also made appearances in early Irish wartime ballads. "The Irish Volunteer" by Joe English gave a lyrical cheer to the general: "Here's to brave McClellan, whom the army now reveres—/ He'll lead us on to victory, the Irish volunteers."[86] The Irish even penned their own call for McClellan's continued Army of Potomac command after his removal in November 1862. "We'll Fight for Uncle Sam" (1863) explained how Irish-born and descended soldiers would fight better when led by the general:

We soon will use the Rebels up, and make them all surrender,
And, once again, the Stars and Stripes will to the breeze be swellin,'
If Uncle Abe will give us back our darling boys McClellan
Oh! We'll follow Little Mac.[87]

McClellan earned the reverence of Irish soldiers during the war mostly because of the mutual respect he had shown them after the Battle of Antietam in 1862. His report of the engagement praised the contributions of "the brave Irish Brigade" who "sustained its well-earned reputation" during the fighting.[88] When McClellan left his command, the tribute was returned when he "passed the Irish Brigade during his final farewell." As McClellan reached them, "Meagher ordered the Irish men to throw down their green battle flags in an act of devotion."[89] By the 1864 election, the Irish continued displays of "Little Mac" devotion by writing ballads in support of his presidential campaign. Several of these came direct from the home front, continuing a practice started in 1862, when verses from "War Democratic View of McClellan's Nomination" were printed in the *New York World* and republished in the *Irish-American* before local November elections.[90] Two years later, "The Cry Is Mac, My Darling" followed the same dissemination route after being "written by an Irish soldier in the 1st Division, 2nd Army Corps" (in which the Irish Brigade served). Set to the traditional Irish air of "Oh, My Nora Creina Dear," the song expressed Irish delight "to hear that you've been nominated," referring to McClellan's presidential candidacy. He would be proclaimed as "our chosen chief" come the election.[91]

Similar sentiment was heard in October 1864 when the *Irish-American* printed "The Irish for McClellan," penned by a "T. F. L." This ballad-verse described McClellan as "a soldier right sterling and true . . . a statesman and patriot too." Recalling Irish cultural heritage, it stated: "McClellan will, therefore, receive, without fail, / The votes of the sons of Old Graineumhail." The final lyrics hoped that when McClellan became president, he would help the Irish win their own independence fight and achieve "the great stroke of Freedom for Graineumhail."[92] Some soldiers on the front line also shared the wish to have both a reinstated commanding General and eventual President McClellan. The 28th Massachusetts Irish Brigade enlistee Daniel Crowley wrote about how McClellan needed to return to army command in August 1864. Until he did so, "no good [would] be done here," commenting specifically about how he was entrenched in the siege around Petersburg, Virginia.[93] Referring to the wait for election ballot news and outcome, Crowley reported: "We have received no authentic information so far as to who will be President of the United States for the next four years. Some say Lincoln and . . . [others] little Mack. I hope it's the latter for the country's sake." Ultimately,

McClellan lost the election and Irish songs ceased to sing about him. In many ways, Crowley articulated a pervading war-weary emotion about the situation in the aftermath of the 1864 election: "not that I care a great deal for my part as I am rather indifferent."[94]

Halpine was not indifferent to the politics of 1864; neither did he follow an expected Irish pro-Democrat and pro-McClellan party line. Instead, through his Miles O'Reilly singing voice, he urged the Irish diaspora and wider Union society to keep faith in Lincoln's presidency. Halpine's "Song of the Soldiers"—printed in the *New York Herald,* recirculated in *Life and Adventures,* and published in song collections of O'Reilly ballads—explained that political divisions did not matter. Soldiers were soldiers; they acted as one body and thought with one mind. Soldiers believed Lincoln was where "the future government of the United States is centered," telling the home front of front-line voting intentions. While never saying "vote for Lincoln" directly, Halpine made a preelection heartfelt plea to put the United States of America first in the final verse:

> By communion of the banner—
> Battle-scarred but victor banner,
> By the baptism of the banner,
> Brothers of one church are we!
> Creed nor faction can divide us,
> Race nor language can divide us,
> Still, whatever fate betide us,
> Children of the flag are we![95]

Likewise, Halpine's "The Blue Cap and Button" emphasized how Lincoln had the majority of support. Voting for him was the only option despite other possible military and political opinions. While undoubtedly "there are some, you know, for McClellan will go"—solider voters that Halpine called "the 'old braves' who still admired" the former general-in-chief—this particular O'Reilly song was used to stress that many more men remained loyal to the president. Irish-born and descended soldiers were "the boys of the host that has suffered the most," part of "the Army of Potomac who have dyed with their blood Virginia's fields." Regardless of their wartime suffering, Halpine stressed the praise this Irish soldiery felt toward Lincoln:

In West and in East there's one . . .
Around whom the army might gather—
"Uncle Abe," it is you, honest, kindly and true—
To us boys you have been a father.[96]

The lyrical point was clear: return Abraham Lincoln to the White House and all would be well across the nation in the eventual outcome of the war.

It is questionable how "Irish" Halpine's later war lyrical outputs really were. Halpine articulated a strong sense of Americanness and American national identity, something also apparent in the O'Reilly's voice of his fictional story song creations. O'Reilly's mock Irish brogue was dropped, as can be heard and observed in ballads about the 1864 election. Nonetheless, Halpine's works were still singing *to* the diaspora and were singing *about* the diaspora to wider Union home-front society. He created clever song and satire arguments that showed how the war was, in his view, doing away with anti-Irish nativist prejudice. Secession had brought the ideal of a united Union together. Through publication and circulation in the *New York Herald*, reprinting in *Life and Adventures* in 1864, production of *Baked Meats of the Funeral* in 1866, dissemination of song music scorebooks, and in his postwar writings, Halpine's expressions of an Irish Americanness—and Irish conceptualization of American commitment to the war and political administration policies—were all reinforced, recirculated, and reached further across society than any of his lyricist contemporaries. *Life and Adventures of Miles O'Reilly* was "an immediate success, selling three thousand copies on the first day, exhausting the first printing." They were met with widespread praise and "enthusiastic reviews . . . all over the country."[97]

Halpine's message of unity spread extensively. As the sheer relentlessness of warfare took its toll on soldier and home-front mentality from 1863 onward, it was also met with growing support from all sections of society. One of the final O'Reilly wartime songs was "The Blue-Bellies to the Grey-Backs: A Dream of Universal Dominion." An "entirely pathetic, and yet entirely manly" ballad, it called for the Union and Confederacy to reunite for the future prosperity of the nation. Arguing that the conflict had become "a fight ye cannot win" and telling the Confederacy to surrender, Halpine's lyrics were aimed toward the entire country:

Brethren, thus we stand confronted . . .
Tired and bloody but undaunted—
Shall the work again begin?
Shall the cry again be slaughter,
Your blood, our blood shed like water . . .
Brethren, join us—stand beside us—
Both have wrongs to wipe away . . .
Let our flag, with forces blended,
O'er the world, serene and splendid,
Henceforth bear imperial sway![98]

Halpine urged every state to think of reconciliation and the nearing time when the Union North and Confederate South would come together as a powerful, united, global nation that all citizens would help bring forth. This echoed the dedication Halpine "respectfully inscribed" for *Life and Adventures*: "to our Navy and our Army; to all good citizens . . . and to patriots of every class and nationality throughout the United States."[99]

Those "patriots of every class and nationality" included his fellow Irish countrymen and women. Halpine's words were similar to a sentiment heard in "Pat Murphy of Meagher's Brigade," which expressed the diaspora's sadness at the fraternal damage civil conflict was doing to the country. "It's a shame for to see Brothers fighting in such a quare [queer] manner" it sang, mirroring Halpine's continual call for reunion.[100] His belief in unity permeated every aspect of his wartime writings: he wished for rioters and the home front to share the same war position as their fighting family members in 1863, he wished for local and national party unity to strengthen Union administration war policies, and he wished for eventual unity between the warring states in 1865. Charles Graham Halpine was a consummate believer in the union of the United States, an Irishman born across the Atlantic who had come to value the ideals of his second homeland nation as paramount. That was the message he spread to his Irish and American brethren. It was in keeping with cultural articulations by Irish soldiers and civilians who likewise expressed their devotion to the United States and their sense of Americanness through song.

7

---·⊰✦⊱·---

Irish American Loyalty and Identity
in Civil War Songs

No individual Irish American Civil War song ever centered on a single issue—lyrics about volunteering, fighting, home-front matters, and occasional nationalist sentiments combined to form verses covering multiple themes. Through their words and lyrical emphasis, however, one attitude kept coming to the fore and underlined every opinion and articulation discussed in this book. Above all other sentiments in Irish American Civil War song lyrics, wartime ballads were infused with messages of inherent loyalty and entrenched nascent patriotism to the United States, to ideals of freedom and liberty, to the Star Spangled Banner, and to the American home nation where the diaspora resided. Songs often concluded with strong statements that reinforced Irish support for the United States as citizens that shared in the nation's beliefs and reconciled future, encapsulated by fixing on the Stars and Stripes as the emblem of their American identity association. This was demonstrated in "Battle of Bull Run" (1861), which explained that in the aftermath of the conflict's first engagements, Irish regiments and "gallant soldiers" had "gone to fight a glorious cause" and to "defend the glorious Stars and Stripes." Soldiers and the home front upheld the right "to defend the Flag and Union, the Government and its laws."[1]

In other words, the Irish in America served to defend the very structure of the nation they now inhabited. Irish American Civil War songs articulated patriotic allegiance to the nation through singing about how the diaspora shared in the ideals of liberty, democratic republicanism and freedom, and how these were bound up in American national symbols and anthems associated with devotion to the Star Spangled Banner. Instead of continuous laments about Ireland and anti-British feeling from this past, the sentiments of the diaspora's songs focused first and foremost on defending the United States of America and adopting the Stars and Stripes as their own flag. The Irish who fought and sung in the Civil War thus cemented their commitment to the American Union and articulated their allegiance to the nation as Americans.

Even in fewer existing Confederate songs about the Irish fighting for the seceded Southern states, a pervading sense of loyalty to the American side of dual Irish American identity comes to the fore. The fact that these songs circulated in home-front society through publications and performances in music halls ensured Irish lyrics about American sentiments permeated wartime culture. They stressed to the diaspora and wider society that the United States was central to the Irish experience of living, working, and fighting in the country to which many had emigrated, resided in, and were raising their families in. What such lyrics demonstrate is the manner in which the diaspora expressed its sense of participatory American citizenship as naturalized citizens in the 1860s.

The concept of "national citizenship" was "vague . . . prior the Civil War" and, for the most part, "largely functioned to determine whether one owed allegiance and certain obligations to the United States." Additionally, "even the meaning of naturalization remained unsettled" at this time. Irish American Army and Navy volunteers framed their allegiance and obligations within the mentality of doing one's duty by serving the country in which they settled. Through singing about home front and battlefield contributions, the Irish in the Civil War era reflected what Christian Samito has described as the "interrelated sides of citizenship." Aside from being "a political creation and a legal concept," citizenship also existed on a more encompassing "social and cultural level."[2] Wartime songs certainly reflect this notion. When Irish American Civil War ballads sang about America, they also sang about the concept and association of the United States as "home." This reflected the final aspect of how the diaspora perceived the nation in which they lived and fought to defend.

IRISH ADOPTION OF PATRIOTIC AMERICAN IDEALS

Immigrant communities' contribution to, and understanding of, "a distinctively American citizenship crystallized" and enhanced in the 1860s by involvement in the conflict. This became a concept "that eventually integrated national rights and duties along with notions of loyalty and the embrace of

American ideals."[3] With regards to the latter point, songs expressed how the Irish embraced the ideals of freedom, liberty, democracy, and republicanism that the United States had expounded since its founding.

In early 1862, one Irish Brigade song stressed how Irish-born and descended soldiers "rushed to Columbia's aid" when Confederate "traitors, unholy, conspired to pull down the flag of the free." These fighting "brave sons of Erin desired" to become "the vanguard of freedom" in the Union Army, serving at the forefront to calm the erring Southern states and restore the nation once again.[4] By singing about how the Irish Brigade was critical to the Union's military might, the song emphasized the impression that war service was tied to a ready desire to see the United States reunited as a bastion of liberty and freedom in the world. This sentiment was shared in ballads produced on the other side of the Atlantic, such as "The Soldier's Letter from America" (1863), which likewise sang about Irish Brigade exploits. The Irish unit fought "in the loyal cause of freedom on the American shore."[5] Even when Hugh F. McDermott's epic ballad verse about the Irish Brigade's experience at the 1862 Battle of Fredericksburg sang of the death and loss of so many sons of Erin, lyrics still stressed the sacrifice was worth it for the cause of freedom embodied by the American Union. In the ballad's final fours lines, it explained how soldiers had "died for glory more sublime" fighting for the future of democratic freedom over secessionist slave tyranny:

> Fame blushed for Fame, as heroes fell . . .
> While Freedom struck their funeral knell,
> Which rings for aye on the ear of Time.[6]

The same sentiment could be heard in "The Sons of Erin's Isle," published in London in 1864. The ballad sang about how the Irish "sons of Erin's isle" who had "left their native soil" of Ireland were greeted with warmth in the American land to which they had emigrated. Omitting any mention of anti-Irish nativist feeling, they "will be welcome to that noble land of freedom." The Irish fighting in the Union Army would be serving because the United States had become "their country for to save," and "their lives they freely gave in the right of their countrymen."[7] This notion was reinforced in "Freedom's Guide" (ca. 1862), a song about the Irish 69th New York. Its final line stressed how they would "show them how the Sixty-Ninth can fight." The "them" meant both the Confederacy and wider American nation, highlighting continual Irish fighting commitment. The rest of the song sang about "countless [Irish] throngs shall fill the land" to ensure "our country's rights maintain." Once more, the collective rhetoric of "our country" was America, not Ireland. "Our guide is Freedom's banner," one lyric stated, singing how the Stars and Stripes would guide soldiers on the battlefield. They would serve not just because they were Irish-born and descended citizens living in the country. "Freedom's Guide" explained the Irish in the Union Army were fighting "as Yankee boys."[8] They fought as Americans.

Irish wartime songs that communicated commitment to ideals of freedom echoed sentiments Peter Welsh articulated to his father-in-law when he explained why he had joined the war effort. Couching his justification in a global framework, he argued American values were the same as Irish values: "we have the same national, political, and social interests" to ensure democratic republicanism survived. This was important not just "for ourselves but for coming generations and the oppressed of every nation" because American freedom, and the country, "was a common asylum for all." For the Irish, "America is Ireland's refuge, Ireland's last hope. Destroy this republic and her hopes are blasted," the 28th Massachusetts sergeant believed.[9] This presented a view of the United States as the last best hope on earth for a nation conceived in liberty: sentiments Abraham Lincoln discussed in his address at Gettysburg five months after Welsh was writing. At the end of the war, one Fenian song presented a similar opinion as it sung about the possible return to Ireland by the diaspora's soldiers in a future fight for independence against Britain. Reiterating the Fenian lyrical articulation about the need for American aid to ensure Irish independence success, "The Gleam of Hope!" (1865) described the moment when returning nationalists would "plant the Flag of Liberty" on Ireland's shores.[10]

Michael Corcoran also conveyed the rhetoric of liberty when he made an appearance in the verses of "Corcoran to His Regiment" (1861). According to the ballad, he told his "gallant band . . . 'Liberty and Union' [was to] be your battle-cry" as they volunteered and marched to war.[11] Such grand concepts of "Liberty and Union" harkened back to older American history. Adopting the language of the Revolution reinforced the sense of Americanness behind Irish service. In Thomas J. MacEvily's "War Song of the Irish Brigade" (1861), Revolutionary rhetoric was evoked as citizens "once more . . . awaken to liberty's call" and "rise up in might in defense of the nation." To enforce the American sentiments of this particular Irish Brigade-dedicated ballad, MacEvily set his lyrics to the anthemic tune of "The Star Spangled Banner."[12] Furthermore, "William," the fictional lyrical focus of "The 69th Brigade," was described as "a Patriot, and a soldier, in the Sixty-Ninth Brigade."[13] Here "Patriot" did not mean the Irish Patriots of the 1700s. This particular Irish soldier followed in the spirit of the Revolution's Patriots fighters.

The same universal notions of American liberty could be heard in Irish wartime ballads written about the diaspora's contributions to the Confederate Amy. By comparison to songs about American Union loyalty, "Erin's Dixie" (1863) emphasized how the Irish in the seceded Southern states would "make a stand for Dixie," and "swear to stand or fall with Dixie" during the course of the war. This sentiment was reiterated throughout the song, enhanced by the repetitive final chorus refrain:

> We'll stand or fall with Dixie, hurrah! hurrah!
> Dixie's land we'll take our stand,
> And strike a blow for Dixie.

The song stated the reason for this ardent Confederate support was because the Irish were fighting for freedom. Using the same justifications for secession as heard throughout the Confederacy, "Erin's Dixie" explained how the Irish would shed their blood against the Union: "For Faith and Freedom freely flows it, / Each battlefield in Dixie shows it."[14]

"Kelly's Irish Brigade" conveyed the same outlook. Within its focus on Missouri's right to secede, it stressed that the state's Irish population would support the Confederate cause because secession represented liberty and freedom. It called on those who served in this particular Irish Confederate Army unit to fight for "State's Rights and Liberty, and Missouri." These were the three united bodies that Irish Missourians would "ever defend . . . no matter how hard may be the task."[15] The ballad stressed to wider Confederate society that the Irish in the seceded Southern states would be dedicated to their separatist cause, and these ballads did so using the same lyrical language as their Union counterparts.

One of Missouri's residents who penned "additional words to 'Bonnie Blue Flag' as sung by the Missourians during the war" in 1861 echoed the sentiments of "Kelly's Irish Brigade." Sung to the old traditional Irish tune of "The Irish Jaunting Car," these supplementary lyrics to Harry Macarthy's pro-Confederate secession anthem called for Missouri to join her Southern state sisters in secession. In the middle of its two verses, this personal "Bonnie Blue Flag" version used rhetorical concepts of freedom and liberty to validate Missouri's right to become part of the Confederate States of America:

Now ye southern patriots
A nation you have made
We'll fight for life and liberty
Until oppressions stayed.[16]

Both Missouri songs—one connected directly to Irish residents in the border state and the other with set lyrics to an Irish musical tune—reflect the way the Irish experience in the South contained both American and Confederate national identities while also retaining a sense of ethnic cultural heritage from Ireland. They were part of a broader and evolving Irish Confederate American nationalism, a sentiment that has received attention from David Gleeson. He argues, "the Irish . . . had to negotiate their identity with a developing American one" in the middle of the nineteenth century. As "Confederate nationalism was basically negative, confused and contradictory" itself, the diaspora had find a way to articulate their Confederate loyalty in opposition to Union support while still using rhetoric about fighting for American concepts of freedom and liberty.[17] These two Irish-related Missouri examples are in many ways microcosms of broader Confederate identity development tensions during the Civil War.

"Song for the Irish Brigade" (1861) furthered this rhetoric across the Confederacy by singing about how the Irish would fight for their Southern state homes and uphold secession. This again created opposite comparative arguments to songs about the official Union Army Irish Brigade ballads that used the same lyrical stances in defense of the American nation. The Irish Confederate ballad aimed its anti-Union opinion at the federal government, with its words presenting the impression that the Irish in the Southern states would head to Washington, DC, to "free" the capital. By extension, they would "free" the country itself from anti-states' rights politicians and perceived Republican tyranny. The men of the Confederate "Irish Brigade" would "exorcise from the rescued prize" all those who opposed secession in Congress and in the Lincoln administration.[18] The song's lyrics created a mentality that the Irish were part of the "true" American identity represented. They, in turn, were inheritors of the nation's ideals.

Unsurprisingly, the opposing view of *who* constituted an American Union national could be heard in Irish wartime ballads produced in the Northern states. When "The New York Volunteer" (1862) praised the service of "our City Regiments" in the Union Army, lyrics described how soldiers from the region were quick to answer Lincoln's call for troops at the start of the conflict. Among the city regiments were, of course, the Irish 69th New York:

> Now, there's our City Regiments
> Just see what they have done:
> The first to offer to the State
> To go to Washington
> To protect the Federal Capital.
> And the Flag they love so dear!
> And they've done their duty nobly,
> Like New York Volunteers.[19]

The noble duty of defending freedom and liberty as New Yorkers and as Americans also extended to lyrical articulations that reinforced the strength of "the Union." This was not just a side to fight for in the war. "The Union" was the very embodiment of the entire United States. Consequently, the vast majority of songs made it clear that the American Union was the country uppermost in the minds of the singing diaspora.

Even lingering anti-Irish views during the war years could not diminish Union praise, at least according to Kathleen O'Neil's "No Irish Need Apply" 1862 version. The final verse described an Irish immigrant girl's delight at being "in the land of the 'Glorious and Free,'" again drawing on the United States of America as a symbolic country of freedom by comparison to an Ireland then under British rule. The song's singer—in this NINA version Kathleen O'Neil herself—was "proud . . . to own it, this country dear to me." This expressed how the United States had become the immigrant's own country of associated identity, with shared values and principles. As a result of contributing to society and displaying loyalty, America in turn was shedding anti-Irish prejudices. It welcomed the Irish as citizens. In return for this mutual affection between Irish immigrants and the American nation, O'Neil ended her song with a toast, hoping the country and its ideals would last forever: "Then long may the Union flourish, and ever may it be, / A pattern to the world, and the "Home of Liberty!"[20]

Similar sentiments could be heard in ballads that used fictional Irish soldiers' voices as their lyrical focus, with the added emphasis that those fighting would do everything in their military power to preserve the Union. When O'Toole and McFinnigan decide to join the war effort in "O'Toole & McFinnigan On the War" (1863), they exclaimed "Hurroo! For the Union, me boys." They also criticized the Confederacy and secession supporters for trying to disrupt states' unity, singing how they wished the "devil take all who bother it."[21] The same attitude was presented in Thomas Donnelly's "New York Volunteer" (ca. 1862). This music hall ballad gave an Irish soldier's explanation as to why he volunteered in the Union Army's New York regiments to defend the country and stop secessionist disturbers of the peace. So great was the Union association felt by this fictional Irish soldier that his ardent fervor would sustain him on the battlefield. It even provided him the confidence to challenge Jefferson Davis:

> A gallant hero the Southerners ne'er could frighten,
> And all I want's a belly-full of drinking or of fightin';
> I'd die to guard the Union, as that alone can save us,
> And I'd rather be a blind jackass than that damn fool, Jeff Davis.[22]

Tony Pastor penned the account of another fictional lyrical Irish soldier singing about Union loyalty in "Young America and Ould Ireland" in 1862. Although part of the song included references to soldiers returning to Ireland to fight for independence, the ballad's ultimate message was that fighting for the American Union was the present and chief concern. "Sure, it's the Union I fight for, till Ireland is free," the song's singing soldier expressed. Yet, "with my knapsack and gun, wheresoever I be," the soldier stressed throughout the song that the Union came first above other national allegiance. At the end of each verse, Pastor repeated the phrase "America's Irish Brigade." This made it clear to listeners that the Union Army's Irish Brigade was an American military entity.[23]

General Union wartime ballads would likewise articulate the views of Irish soldiers being American soldiers who fought for their shared stake in the country's future. "Free and Easy of Our Union!" (1861) explained how "those sons of Erin . . . they were for the Union still." The whole nation should "raise your voices all united" in praise of the diaspora's commitment and willingness to send its sons to the battlefront alongside their American compatriots. "Let us give three hearty cheers . . . for our Volunteers" the song concluded.[24] Here, the "our" encompassed Irish-born and American-born soldiers in one collective national volunteering soldiering body.

All these songs reiterated the sentiment that the Union, and by extension the entire nation, was fundamental to the diaspora's American experience. They also reveal how the Irish in the country adopted the ideals of the Union and the American concepts of nationhood. The 9th Connecticut's regimental ballad "Save the Constitution" (1862) exhibited this better than comparative Irish Brigade regiment song dedications, as the title drew directly on allegorical images of the United States as tangible entities to defend. "The Constitution" was both the actual document and the idea that it was the united American nation itself. The song called to "all you gallant volunteers" to come and listen to a song about how the Irish 9th Connecticut volunteers "so manfully are fighting" to uphold "the laws and freedom's cause" of the American Union.

Where the song differed, however, was its focus on describing the nation as a ship, extending a metaphor that the United States was encapsulated in the body of the famous USS *Constitution*—one of the American Navy's leading flagships during the War of 1812 and still in active service during the Civil War. The 9th Connecticut, the song explained, were serving the Union "to navigate the ship of State, and keep her in full motion, / That she may brave the stormy wave and sail on freedom's ocean." The song's chorus reiterated the idea of secession being akin to a storm threatening to drown the nation and all it stood for. By singing about how the 9th Connecticut pinned their colors to the country's ship mast "with bould courage," these particular Irish soldiers would "uphold each noble institution and navigate the ship of state to save the Constitution," bringing about ultimate Union victory and Confederate defeat.[25]

While these expressions were centered on a regional and local show of Union support from one Irish Connecticut regiment, they echoed the lyrics of another passionate pro-Union ballad, "Hurrah for the Union" (1861). The two examples bear striking similarity in how they articulated a metaphorical concept of the nation bound to the Constitution (both the document and the ship), with "Hurrah for the Union" singing about how the country was like "our ship's the Constitution" with "good patriots at the helm." This lyrical comparison was more a reflection of how widespread such views were around society rather than a conscious link between the Irish-focused version and a more general ballad. However, their similarity reinforced that the diaspora shared, adopted, and developed the same sentiments about pro-American Union loyalty, ideals, and shared nationhood. Indeed, "Hurrah for the Union" contained sentiments that would not be out of place in Irish ballads sung by all members of Union society:

> We fight to save the Union, and God is on our side,
> We fight to put down traitors who the Union would divide,
> And millions rally round the flag, which no power can subdue
> We can die—but we cannot pull down the Red, White and Blue.[26]

Furthermore, that members of the diaspora were part of a mutual American Union identity was repeated to the wider public in another general wartime ballad. "We Will Have the Union Still" (1861) included lyrics about the 69th New York's fighting service at the First Battle of Bull Run. The song was set to the tune of "Free and Easy Still," and had been written in response to "Free and Easy of Our Union!" Continuing the latter ballad's theme about Union loyalty and defending the country from further secession, "We Will Have the Union Still" included the Irish directly as part of a national body of soldiers fighting "for Uncle Sam" who were adamant they would "have the Union still." The Union was forever and could not be defeated. Its lyrics told the public that soldiers would be revered because of the sacrifice and service they gave to the national cause. The Confederacy "shall find we'll die for freedom," and witness that they would never yield "to traitors" in the seceded states. This united body of Union Army soldiery were committed to giving their last full measure of devotion to the country. This was what the home front would praise as they went to battle:

> Then hurrah for those brave fellows,
> Who have gone forth to the wars,

They'll return soon full of glory
Waving high our Flag of stars.[27]

Those returning from the war as part of this American army included Irish-born and descended soldiers marching under a starry flag that also belonged to them. This was a reference to the Star Spangled Banner, the emblem of the Union Army and the United States. It was a symbol the Irish fighting in the war especially attached themselves to alongside and above green banners that recalled their ethnic heritage (as discussed in chapter 4). The Stars and Stripes were waved metaphorically throughout wartime ballads, acting as the most visible lyrical symbol of the Irish expressing their American identity.

IRISH DEVOTION TO THE STAR SPANGLED BANNER

Printed in *The Continental Songster* in 1863, Kate C. M.'s "The Irish Brigade" bound together all the themes of fighting for freedom, liberty, and Union heard in earlier war song examples. Although this particular version of an Irish Brigade-dedicated ballad sang of Irish cultural heritage and nationalist wishes, the majority of lyrics stressed to wider American society that the Irish in the Union Army would put American allegiance first. To demonstrate this, Irish-born and descended soldiers, and the broader home front, pledged their allegiance to the Stars and Stripes banner because "our American flag you love, it is true." Here, "our" was simultaneously the country and the diaspora combined. It again stressed the American focus of the Irish wartime experience. The song began with the pledge:

To the Banner of Freedom, to the red, white and blue,
The brave Irish soldier must ever prove;
The Stars and the Stripes no stain can defile,
While defended by sons of the Emerald Isle.

After singing about Ireland and the green flag of Erin, the conclusion of Kate C. M.'s Irish Brigade song returned to the Star Spangled Banner in the final verses, leaving an impression of an American image in the minds of those reading, performing, and listening to *The Continental Songster*'s ballads. Lyrics reinforced how "our flag you'll protect, for Liberty's dear" and that the

American Union banner was of paramount importance to the diaspora. They would guard it if "you're Irish in heart, and a true volunteer."

That ultimate line about being a true Irish-hearted volunteer fighting for liberty evoked Irish Volunteer and Irish Patriot heritage of the late 1700s alongside American Patriot rhetoric from the Revolution. It also provided one of the best summations of what Union Army service meant to the Irish. Their "true" volunteerism was an expression of how willing the diaspora was to support the war cause on the battlefield and home front. Once more, the focus was on the Union and how the American flag embodied the united nation concept. The final few lines of "The Irish Brigade" rallied the diaspora:

> Onward to victory—yes, victory or death!
> And the Union forever, with your last dying breath;
> Let the Stars and the Stripes be henceforth your boast,
> "And the Union forever," the Irishman's toast.[28]

"Camp Song of the (Chicago) Irish Brigade" (1861) galvanized Irish to the fight in a similar manner by singing about the flag as the emblem of Union victory that their war service would bring about:

> Bearthe [bear] stars and the stripes o'er you proudly,
> And ne'er let your march be delay'd,
> Till the foe flies in terror before you,
> When charg'd by the Irish Brigade.[29]

By singing constantly about it, the American flag acted as a reminder of what the soldiers were fighting for. Each star on the banner, including those representing the seceded states that remained on the standard, was representative of the whole country. "Battle of Bull's Run" painted a lyrical image of:

> The Sons of Old Ireland, led forth in their glory . . .
> Their name will shine brighter in the fame written story,
> With that grand constellation—THE AMERICAN STAR.
> They raised that banner aloft, with its heaven born splendor,
> It was true patriot's hearts could true glory behold.[30]

To emphasize Irish service as something spurred on by a sense of true American patriotism, Arthur McCann, lyricist for "Battle of Bull's Run," set these words to the tune "American Star" in 1861, creating both a lyrical and musical dual connection to the Star Spangled Banner being upheld by the Irish in the country. Singing about national devotion to American musical tunes strengthened the sense of American identity that the conflict brought to the cultural fore—though it must be noted that "American Star" itself was an 1850 contrafactum of an older traditional Irish air, "The Humours of the Glen."[31]

On occasion, this sentiment of a heightened display of American identity was reflected on songsheet publications themselves, such as one copy of Tony Pastor's "Irish Volunteer, No. 3" about Michael Corcoran's American Union loyalty. When H. De Marsan printed the song, the lyrics were illustrated by a design that contained the Stars and Stripes draped around the border. This made the contrast between a ballad about an Irish soldier enfolded in emblematic American illustrations all the greater. While songsheet borders were often printed in stockpiles with ballad lyrics added to the middle of the page at a later point, this particular example provided visual emphasis about Irish connections to the United States. It complemented the aural message of Pastor's song. Marsan printed other copies of this ballad, as did fellow New York printer James Wrigley, but of the multiple reproductions produced and circulated in 1862, this particular edition intensified Irish cultural adoption of American symbols and identity.

The sense of the Irish adopting an American identity association was similarly heard in Civil War songs that were not solely related to the dominant Irish Brigade narrative. Other examples reiterated the lyrical narrative about how the Stars and Stripes were carried by Irish regiments, with the flag serving as the embodiment of the nation. The 9th Connecticut's "Save the Constitution" sang proudly about how the regiment carried "the Stars and Stripes before them."[32] The 69th Pennsylvania went to great lengths to extol the American flag as their unit's standard in one of their regimental ballads. If anything, "Col. Owens' Gallant Irish Volunteers" (1861) was more a song about Star Spangled Banner attachment than praising the unit's service. Its lyrics described how the regiment fought for the Union and how the country and flag belonged to them as Americans. These devotional lyrics and constant banner references dominate throughout and are bound up in the rhetorical concepts of true fighting patriotism. These Pennsylvania Irish embodied the Union cause as American citizens:

> Our country we are bound to save,
> And keep for ever more
> And soon the stars and stripes shall wave
> On all our glorious shore:—
> The stars and stripes—our own true flag—
> That we do prize so dear . . .
> Now we'll give three cheers for the 69th,
> And for our country too;
> Likewise unto our Volunteers,
> For they are all true blue;
> We are all of a noble band,
> And are prepared to fight.
> We'll all stand by the stars and stripes,
> The flag we know is right. . . .
> We'll all stand by our glorious flag,
> And for our country fight . . .
> Like true Irish Volunteers.[33]

The 69th New York's soldiers donned "true blue" Union Army uniforms and sang about their own connections to the Star Spangled Banner in several of their wartime ballads. "The New York Volunteer" discussed the way in which the city's regiments offered cheers "for the Stars and Stripes hurrah!" as "the flag to float o'er us . . . and to guide us through the fray." This sentiment was repeated throughout the song. Lyrics continued to describe how New York's Union regiments, with Irish-born and descended soldiers serving in them, would ensure the Confederacy's defeat, punish secessionist leaders, and ensure the American flag was returned to prominence across the country:

> The rebels soon must yield; they cannot stand our banging,
> And Davis, Wise, and Beauregard will in the air be hanging;
> The Stars and Stripes will wave aloft, from Oregon to Maine,
> And while the sun shines o'er us, they'll ne'er come down again.[34]

"The Gallant 69th Regiment" (1862) reiterated the image of "the Stars and Stripes, so gloriously, floating o'er them" as they marched "in defense of the Red, White and Blue." Soldiers pledged themselves to the country and sang of the nation as being "the Shrine of each Irishman's devotion." This recalled the opinion that United States was welcoming to the diaspora.[35]

One earlier wartime ballad about the 69th New York State Militia depicted this Irish American Union Army association with the flag as a symbol with which to beat the Confederacy. A verse in the "Glorious 69th" (1861) portrayed an account of how the unit's Chaplain Father Mooney—a man "of honor and renown"—went with the soldiers to Washington, DC, at the start of the conflict. While he "did escort our Heroes unto the battle-ground," Mooney allegedly "said unto our colonel" Corcoran: "Now, we must fight hand to hand, / Until we plant the Stars and Stripes way down in Dixie's Land." Here the flag acted as a physical symbol of reunion. The song stressed how Irish soldiers' actions, such as planting flags in Southern soil, would help bring an end to secession. Lyrics concluded with yet another cheer of "here's to the Stars and Stripes," affirming Irish connections to the American banner they marched under.[36]

This portrayal was enhanced in "Pat's Opinion of the Stars and Stripes" (1862). The soldier Pat, whose voice was singing the ballad in the lyrical first-person, described how Irish American Union Army soldiers "fought like the divil, upholding the Stars and Stripes."[37] So committed were the diaspora's soldiers to keeping the Star Spangled Banner streaming gallantly over the entire United States that when O'Toole and McFinnigan sang about the flag in 1863, they commented, "the Stars and the Stripes here, at home" in the United States soon "to Canada walls we would pin."[38] This was not a reference to Fenian and Irish nationalist desires to trouble the Canadian border after the Civil War but an expression of desire to see Canada as part of an even greater United States of North America.

Expressions praising the Star Spangled Banner generated a sense of shared ownership of the flag by soldiers and the home front. These were comparable to language used by senior members of the diaspora in their wartime memoirs, which likewise spread the sense of Irish flag association to the nation. General Thomas Francis Meagher suggested that when the 69th New York State Militia's three-month initial war service ended in July 1861, its soldiers would remain with Union forces instead of returning to New York before the battle at Bull Run commenced. In Meagher's mind, "the 69th would not abandon the Stars and Stripes."[39] Michael Corcoran went even further with his repeated calling upon the image of the banner in his prisoner-of-war account. During his Confederate captivity in 1861, he stated in his usual lyrical writing fashion: "Night after night have I lain absorbed in thought upon my miserable cot, and gazed listlessly up into the far-away sky, spangled with its thousands of beaming stars . . . I have often prayed that, like that distance dome above, the azure field of our own Starry Standard would in the future be studded as thickly with stars, each representing some nation or people of the earth."[40]

Corcoran, as with Irish wartime song expressions, saw the American flag as an emblem of the country, liberty, and democracy. In his dreamy state, he evoked future expansion of statehood making up the United States. He even suggested he would aid this national expansion if he survived the conflict, and he would give his life to ensure Union prosperity. This personal devotion appeared in Tony Pastor's "Irish Volunteer" 1862 song about the Irish-born commander, in which the musical hall impresario declared, "Corcoran would die for the Stars and the banner of green."[41]

As has been observed, Corcoran often turned to song and music to stress his American identity association, especially in connection to the Star Spangled Banner and Francis Scott Key's 1814 anthemic ballad of the same name. Throughout his prisoner-of-war account, several descriptions of concerts and Union song performances appear, including one passage in which he recounted the times he and his fellow prisoners would sing at length: "How gloriously did we then used to ring out the soul-stirring national anthem, 'The Star Spangled Banner'! The air would first be exquisitely rendered by some one of our best vocalists . . . when the chorus 'Oh, long may it wave!' came in, every man of us joined in it with our whole souls." During these performances, Corcoran would think of his Irish 69th New York State Militia command: "at these times . . . I wished to be once more at the head of the gallant old Sixty Ninth, with that dear old standard floating over me." He then told his memoir's American readers that singing about the flag, and singing "The Star Spangled Banner" in particular, made him feel fervently American and yet more devoted to the Union cause. His words mirror contemporary Irish ballad sentiments: "Oh America! Could you . . . have looked within my breast, you would have seen my heart beating, with all its Irish fervor, for your welfare and success."[42]

None of these articulations in wartime memoirs or songs are unique to the Irish experience of the Civil War. Star Spangled Banner devotion was comparable, to some extent, to Bonnie Blue Flag lyrical focus and repetition in the Confederacy. In the additional "Bonnie Blue Flag" lyrics penned in Missouri, the same image of praising a flag standard appeared. It adopted the idea of each star representing a state, commenting on the hope that the border state would join the Confederacy:

> So cheer for our emblem
> Our battle flag I mean
> For the single star of the Bonnie blue flag
> Has grown to be thirteen.[43]

Harry Macarthy actually attempted to reconcile the two Union and Confederate flags at the end of the war in an effort to bring about lyrical banner reunion. His collective "patriotic song" "Our Country's Flag" (1867) was aimed at the former seceded states but presented a national message of unity under the Stars and Stripes. The song hoped, "the Patriot's love of Country" would "ever join them heart and hand" as the nation moved forward from the war. Yet, the Scots-Irish songwriter could not miss one final opportunity to use his popular "Bonnie Blue Flag" refrain. Several of the lines in "Our Country's Flag" came from his early war anthem. Focusing on the Stars and Stripes, Macarthy told Confederate supporters:

> We're still the "Band of Brothers" that proudly once unful'd
> The Bonnie Blue Flag whose
> "Single Star" was sung throughout the world
> But now that war no longer reigns,
> Let the cry be heard afar,
> Hurrah, Hurrah for
> Our Country's Flag,
> Yes, each and ev'ry Star![44]

The Star Spangled Banner itself made regular appearances in Union balladry, with flag songs forming their own genre. In 1862 the famous refrain of

"The Battle Cry of Freedom" called the country to "rally round the flag"—a phrase that became embedded throughout Union culture.[45] Moreover, German Americans combined flag symbology and rhetoric about American ideals in their wartime ballads, comparable to what is found in Irish examples. One German language song chorus, "sung by the Blenker Division of the Army of the Potomac" to the tune of "John Brown's Body," expressed how Union Army German Americans in the Eleventh Army Corps under their commander Louis Blenker would, "Rally for Lincoln and for Liberty . . . For the Banner of the Union." One verse even included an American ballad reference to enhance German American identity association:

We are Germans and we're fighting
For the Freedom of the Union . . .
[With] Yankee-Doodle on our lips . . .
For the banner of the Union![46]

In addition to penning Irish wartime songs, F. Collins wrote the national Union flag ballad "The Glorious Stripes & Stars" in 1861. It stressed the practice of pledging allegiance to the banner and created a message of national unity. This was in keeping with the way Irish American Civil War song lyrics presented the impression of an American identity:

To the Union Stripes and stars which unite us all in one,
A more glorious Flag the sun never shone upon;
Then with our blood and money we'll defend it that we can,
And drive every rebel traitor out of this once happy land . . .
When unity and peace and good order we obtain . . .
Then no more we will hear of such fighting and such wars,
For all the nations round us must respect the Stripes and Stars.[47]

As with references to Irish regiments carrying green banners and depictions of Ireland's cultural symbols, wartime ballads placed great emphasis on the image of flags as visual and lyrical entities that held great meaning to the diaspora and wider society. Of course in the case of the Star Spangled Banner, it was the national American banner, and the majority of Union Army regiments marched under its broad stripes and bright stars. Dual flag rhetoric could certainly be heard in Irish songs, as already discussed. However, Stars and Stripes references dominate the songs in this study. They are mentioned to a far greater extent than any green regimental banners, which were only carried by some units. The focus on America's flag in song reinforced that the diaspora, in the Union at least, used the symbolic image of the United States to stress national identity and allegiance to the country.

The Stars and Stripes, like green Irish flags, were part of a "symbols and ceremonies" culture. This culture, enhanced by the war, assisted "the formation of nationalist ideas by transmitting certain messages to an intended audience" and brought those who shared these ideas "together in expressions of public unity." The nationalist ideas here were fundamentally American in nature. "Flags and flag presentations"—and by extension singing about the Star Spangled Banner—were part of the way in which the Irish in America molded their "service, identity and wartime claims to inclusion" in a "visible public way."[48] This inclusion, as shown by wartime lyric examples, was bound to a sense of Irish ownership of the Stars and Stripes.

The reason why Irish American Civil War songs stressed the national flag belonged to the diaspora and its soldiers was also provided in lyrics that expressed the blood sacrifice Irish-born and descended men gave, particularly to the Union cause. Captain W. F. Lyons created a strong lyrical image of the Irish Brigade and Union Army banners passing through war together in one passage of his biography about Thomas Francis Meagher. Describing the image of "the Stars and Stripes and the green flag . . . borne in every fight," these banners "came out riddled with shot; torn with shells; ripped often times into shreds; but they came out unsullied."[49] Several wartime song lyrics, especially about those relating to the Irish Brigade's war service, challenged this unblemished impression. "The Irish Brigade" ballad written in January 1862 painted a different scene of battle where the Stars and the Stripes were stained proudly with Irish blood. Irish-born and descended soldiers had literally "Poured out their life-blood like water, / Upholding the Red, White and Blue."[50] Kate C. M.'s ballad drew on the lyrical image of the unit's soldiers bleeding over the national banner, with one verse portraying the moment when its constituent regimental banners were returned to their respective states. Irish blood was seen in a positive light as a sign of how far the diaspora's soldiering sons were prepared to go to uphold the Union:

If covered with blood, they are covered with glory;
For the bright stars of Liberty never can fade,
While shielded they are by our Irish Brigade.[51]

The notion of pouring out a Christ-like blood sacrifice was expressed on more than one occasion during the war. Charles Graham Halpine drew on this perception in one of his Miles O'Reilly stories in which the soldier visited the White House along with Meagher. Halpine penned a fictional speech by the Irish-born general that brought together themes of military battlefield service, the American banner, and blood sacrifice for the country: "By adoption of the banner, and by the communion of bloody grave-trenches on every field, from Bull Run to where the Chickamauga rolls down its waters of death, the race that were heretofore only exiles, receiving generous hospitality in the land, are now proud peers of the proudest and brave brothers of the best."[52] After the war, Halpine returned to the image of Irish blood sacrifice for the American nation in one of his final cultural productions before his death. Printed in the *New York Herald* in November 1867, he penned a song that described how all soldiers, including his fellow Irishmen, fought and bled for the Star Spangled Banner:

Oh, as citizens—Americans—
We gloried in the name,
And on many a field our blood we shed
To guard your flag of fame.[53]

Halpine, and other wartime lyricists, drew on inspirational battlefield stories of injured and dying soldiers. Irish American Civil War accounts all contain stories of heroic sacrifice and bleeding wounds in the midst of fighting, but one tale in particular gained widespread attention in 1862. At the Battle of Fredericksburg, Irish-born Thomas Plunkett, serving in the 21st Massachusetts, picked up the regimental banner, which to all intents and purposes looked like the Stars and Stripes. During the Union Army's ill-fated charge upon Marye's Heights—the same engagement that caused such heavy Irish Brigade losses and generated lyrical outpourings—Plunkett received multiple injuries. Carrying the color made him a Confederate target. When the banner underwent twentieth-century restoration, in the "center, large irregular brown stains . . . from a liquid" were still present.[54] This was Plunkett's Irish blood, still discoloring the flag. The evidence corresponds to reports that when he was carried from the field at Fredericksburg, the standard he held onto was "soaked . . . [in] the Irishman's 'life blood.'" Clara Barton, the famed nurse who founded the American Red Cross and who treated the soldier briefly, later "observed that his blood 'literally obliterated the stripes.'"[55] Thomas Plunkett lost both arms at Fredericksburg in his efforts to keep the standard flying and was awarded the Medal of Honor for his actions.[56]

Plunkett's story added poignancy to Irish American Civil War lyrics depicting soldiers' sacrifices staining the Stars and Stripes as Irish blood mingled with American symbolic imagery. "To the Glorious 69th!" (1861) sang about why this Irish blood in particular mattered to the American nation:

> Those noble sons of Erin, who to this country came,
> The people call them Irish, which sure is no mean name;
> For, patriotic blood does run, quite richly, through their veins,
> Unwilling that this Country's Flag should suffer rebel stains.[57]

As these lyrics made clear, Irish soldiers were showing true patriotic loyalty to the American nation by honoring its flag with their blood. Confederate "rebel stains," by comparison, were not pure. They could not taint the Stars and Stripes because their secession had removed any sense of patriotism. Another 69th New York song repeated this message of Irish service, sacrifice, and defense of the Stars and Stripes as being more worthy—and more American—than Confederate actions. One verse explained the moment when the diaspora answered the Union's call to arms in the wake of secession:

> When traitors rise in might and power
> To humble its proud name,
> Rise, one and all, as Erin's sons,
> Protect its noble fame;
> Proclaim abroad to all the world
> THAT FLAG THEY'LL NE'ER DESTROY
> Swear to defend the Stars and Stripes.[58]

All Irish-born and descended soldiers fighting in the Union Army defended the Stars and Stripes. They upheld the banner and all the ideals of the American nation encapsulated by the flag. Irish wartime song references to the national banner reveal that these soldiers bled Irish green, Confederate grey, and Union American red, white, and blue in equal measure. The latter ran through lyrical articulations of Irish love and devotion to the starry standard of the United States of America stronger than the rest. Irish American Civil War ballads provide an explanation for why the United States and American identity came to the fore frequently in cultural articulations. The nation had become more than just a symbolic entity of grand inspirational ideals to the diaspora. By the Civil War era, it had also become *home*. The home nation to defend was America, not Ireland.

THE IRISH AMERICAN HOME

By the outbreak of the Civil War, the Irish diaspora was well established in the United States. Many immigrants had been in the country for several years, decades, or generations. Even the Famine migrants of the 1840s and 1850s had been resident for at least ten years before Fort Sumter was fired upon. They, along with several prominent diaspora leaders, established families and livelihoods for years before 1861. Michael Corcoran had been in the United States for over twelve years before the conflict began, while Thomas Francis Meagher had likewise been in the country for almost a decade before. Then there were the younger, first-generation soldiers who had been born in Ireland but raised across the Atlantic in America, like Daniel Crowley and Patrick Kelly mentioned in previous chapters. Serving alongside them were those like Peter Welsh of second- and subsequent generation extraction born in North America. While they all retained a sense of Irish cultural heritage, they also expressed their American identities because they had come to share an inherent association with the nation by the 1860s. In addition, notable diaspora figures such as James A. Mulligan, leader of his own band of Irish regiments, and army chaplains like William Corby, were second-generation Irish Americans. Mulligan was born in New York State before residing in Chicago in the 1850s, while Corby, who had been born in Detroit, Michigan, stated very clearly in his postwar memoir that he was not Irish: "I write not as a foreigner but as a native-born American citizen" as he discussed the Irish experience in his country.[59]

While national identity is personal and fluid, especially among immigrants, scholarship of the Irish in the Civil War era often indicates that the conflict was used to express various aspects of "dual" Irish identity and a developing American identity. This has led to an impression of the diaspora being Irish and being American, finding simultaneous ways to articulate their Irishness and their Americanness alongside their United States patriotism. The war "gave Irish Americans an opportunity to prove their patriotism" by supporting Union (and Confederate) causes.[60] By extension, the conflict gave an opportunity to expresses patriotism through cultural outputs, like ballads. However, some have suggested that even before the war, "American patriotism was firmly established among Irish Americans."[61] These differing opinions create too much of a binary position along a spectrum of "when did the Irish become American?"

Complex challenges to this sense of national identity articulation have been raised in arguments that "some Irish Americans gained a greater appreciation for their American identity." Thus, the Irish in the United States "increasingly felt they could be considered Americans even when they did not completely abandon their ethnicity." This was a long process of identity evolution in a "climate" where the diaspora "increasingly recognized the American component of their identity and allegiance."[62] Conversely, the opposite has also been suggested, with the diaspora viewing "the war through Irish lenses," not American ones.[63] In terms of the contemporary cultural articulation of Irish identity transition in America and this historiographical debate, wartime ballads support statements about American identity appreciation more so, with the added caveat that the Irish had *already* become American in their identity focus and national sympathies. Using lyrics as evidence highlights that the Irish both in the Union and in the Confederacy viewed the war through American lenses.

Songs provide the clearest popular articulations of the United States being an Irish home nation. The reason they fought for the country, adopted its ideals, upheld and bled for the flag was because they were the manifestations of home. It was home that was ultimately being fought for and sung about during the conflict. Home defense was paramount. As Peter Welsh told his brother-in-law in 1864: "It is the right and duty of citizens and those who have lived in this country long enough to become citizens to fight for the maintenance of law and order and nationality."[64] What Welsh meant was that because the United States had become an established home for the diaspora, it was thus only right that its members took up arms as American citizens to defend its unity. Although Welsh discussed Union war service, the same argument can be applied to those upholding Confederate secession.

Irish American Civil War songs articulated the expression of American home identity as part of their overall message of Irish loyalty to the nation on the battlefield and in the home front. One lyric in "War Song of the New-York 69th Regiment," sung from the perspective of the 69th New York's soldiers marching off to war, gave the cry: "Then forward! For our homes and altars, all we hold most dear" to rally those to enlist.[65] Although singing specifically about one regiment, this sentiment could be expressed by any soldier or sailor on either side, Union, Confederate, Irish or otherwise. They were marching forward to fight for and defend what they all held closest to them. Their homes and families mattered above all else.

In wartime ballads, these families resided in fundamentally American home residences. This sentiment could be heard in "Off for a Soldier" (ca. 1863), a Union song about a fictional soldier Micky O'Flaherty going to "march with the boys 'till rebellion is done." In a mock-Irish brogue, Micky described to his wife Peggy what his reason was for heading to war. Using familiar concepts of American national rhetoric, he explained his actions:

> The stars and the stripes shall float over my head,
> And Peggy, you know I must help save the counthry
> That affords me protection and gives me my bread.

By going to war and safeguarding the United States as an all-protecting nation of liberty welcoming migrant populations, Micky would "return a hero to be pointed at as America's pride." Lyrics described how his defense of his family on the battlefield was more important than defending them in the home front simply because of the severity of American unity being at stake. The song stressed Micky would not return with his family until the war was over:

> Niver 'till traitors
> Have fired their last gun at the flag of the free . . .

The drums then came beating, the colors were flying,
A kiss for his wife and his children three
And Mickey O'Flaherty marched with the soldiers
To fight for the flag of the faithful and free.[66]

"Off for a Soldier" sang of an Irish soldier (albeit a fictional one) who conflated the image of home in America with the symbol of the Star Spangled Banner. One real Irish-born soldier likewise expressed these sentiments in extremely passionate language in both the ballads written about him and his own wartime writings. Once again, Michael Corcoran used the rhetoric of the United States as being his home nation at length throughout his prisoner-of-war memoir, comparable to the extent he mentioned the Star Spangled Banner. Corcoran described how "my heart constantly yearned for home" while he was imprisoned. When he was moved to various prison holdings in the Southern states, "the greater the distance from the latter [that is, his home state] became, the stronger grew the tie that still held me to it."[67] Home was foremost in Corcoran's mind. Crucially, he meant home as in New York City, not Ireland.

Occasionally, Corcoran combined the home and the flag together, equating their association. He did this most markedly in the memoir's final passages when he wrote about returning to New York City after being released from Confederate captivity. Describing the boat journey reaching its destination, he saw "Home, with its loved ones and friends" spring up before his "eyes like an enchanting vision." As he reached closer, Corcoran continued in the same vein: "Eagerly, very eagerly, did I strain my eyes down the river to catch the first glimpse of the Starry Flag . . . In due time I saw it, and, as my eyes fell upon its bright stars and stripes, my soul thrilled to its center, and my Irish heart welled up with emotion." His thirteen-months of incarceration notwithstanding, at the conclusion of his account, Corcoran informed his American public readership that he had once "again taken up the sword," now serving at the head of his own Legion named after him. Like Micky O'Flaherty, Corcoran stressed he would continue to fight for his home country until secession ended. He would "Never sheathe [his sword] until victory perches upon the national banner of America, or Michael Corcoran is numbered among those who did not return home from the battle-field."[68] This was in keeping with his Corcoran's erstwhile belief that soldiers fighting for the Union should defend the country to the very end. For Corcoran, giving his life for his American home was a sentiment he expressed wholeheartedly and without question.

This expression of home devotion ties into Corcoran's overall image as a truly gallant Irish-born American patriot serving the Union Army, an impression which wartime songs emphasized all the more. Certainly, his prisoner-of-war account was written with a wider readership in mind, showing his allegiance to the American public beyond the diaspora. Nevertheless, Corcoran's devotion to the nation and commitment to the military fight against the Confederacy were recurring sentiments in Irish American Civil War ballads. His views were also more than just expressions for show. His own private letters, and the intimate way song lyrics portrayed his character, demonstrated his inherent sense of Americanness. This had been developed over a decade of living in New York City before the start of the conflict. "Corcoran's Ball!" depicted Corcoran as the ultimate loyal American officer. Aimed at the whole country, one verse of the song exclaimed:

> You've all heard of the Great Michael Corcoran,
> That true Son of Erin, so brave in the strife;
> The National cause he was ever a worker in,
> And the Union to him was more precious than life.
> When dastard Secession raised its dark crest upon
> This Glorious Country, he answered her call;
> And though, at the moment, he sorely was press'd upon
> He went off, right gladly, to open the ball.[69]

"Corcoran's Irish Legion" expressed the same sense that the general was defending "the National cause," and would aid the peaceful reconciliation of the reunited country. "Corcoran's Irish Legion" and "Corcoran's Ball!" were written in 1863, around the time Corcoran penned his memoir, and both celebrated his renewed army service after his imprisonment. The former, "Corcoran's Irish Legion," returned to the broader context of the conflict to explain why the one-time commander of the 69th New York led his soldiers to the war effort in 1861. Drawing on American ideals and the Star Spangled Banner, lyrics expressed the dominant message that Corcoran did this because secession was a treacherous act. The whole of the United States had to be defended, with a swift response from the diaspora's soldiers:

When Treason's black Flag was raised in the land
By a ruthless foe that did hate it,
And the Capitol threatened by a dastardly band,
Who would have Washington's tomb desecrated . . .
We rushed hand in hand. . . .
To fight for our home our dear adopted land,
And to crush out the traitors forever and ever.[70]

The continual return to Corcoran's example raises the question of whether the County Sligo native turned ardent American citizen was atypical of wider Irish fighting service and wartime experiences. Certainly, Corcoran himself was more vocal in his expressions of what the American Union meant to him than most others, but his sentiments could be heard in the accounts of other Irish-born and descended serving soldiers and in other outputs from the home front. In addition, the description of Corcoran going to fight in "Corcoran's Irish Legion" applied not just to those who went with him but to all of those of Irish descent who fought across the Union. If the sentiments were reversed to one that extolled Confederate defense, then these lyrical views could extend to all on both sides of the divided nation. Love of country and nationality is a malleable construct. Corcoran provided the diaspora with a solid example that could be used to inspire everyone. He may have been one man, but his wartime experience and sentiments, especially in his expressions of devotion to the United States, could apply to anyone. Ballads helped stress this universal association. Corcoran had assimilated into American identity, society, and alliance by the Civil War. This was only enhanced by his service in the conflict. Lyrics reinforced and disseminated his transnational transition.

In addition, "Glorious 69th," written over two years before Corcoran's memoir appeared, uttered the same feeling of an Irish-born American citizen inspired by the perception of home. Singing directly about the 69th New York State Militia marching to war, and indirectly about *any* New York volunteer and Union military enlistee, lyrics sang from a generic enlistee's perspective about their parting journey to war: "Farewell unto New York, shall I never see it more? / It fills my heart withy pity, to leave its sylvan shore."[71] The sylvan home-front shore was fought for, defended, and protected on the Civil War's battlefields by Ireland's sons, who served to ensure its future could be maintained and that the home would remain central to their community's experience of American life.

This view of the United States as a home, a sentiment only enhanced by the conflict, was central to Irish American cultural productions. It could be heard, for instance, in the folk ballad "The Return of Pat Malloy" (ca. 1865). Written around the Civil War's end, it was a sequel response to the prewar song "Pat Malloy" (ca. 1860). The latter original example sang of an Irish-born immigrant "Pat" who left Ireland for England before traveling to the United States. Verses expressed how his mother missed Pat terribly.[72] In "The Return of Pat Malloy," the eponymous Irish migrant is settled with his family in the United States, including his mother who had now also migrated. The final verse paints an idyllic home scene as this family is settled in postbellum society. Lyrics described Pat's "mother's in her rocking-chair, her children pay the rent." She was living "in New York, relieved from work, each happy hour spent . . . free from every toil her care her heart is light and free." This was the peaceful home life hundreds of thousands of Erin's sons and daughters, like Pat Malloy, had fought for and upheld during the Civil War. Here, an American-produced Irish traditional ballad was "composed for, and sung with unbounded applause by William H. Lindsay" on the musical hall stages of the 1860s, disseminating the message that the Irish were effectively living undisturbed lives in the country they had fought to defend and reunite.

Placed in a residential home setting, "The Return of Pat Malloy" reinforced the transmission of Irish cultural heritage within American constructs. Its last lyrics painted the picture of Pat Malloy's Irish-born mother settled across the Atlantic with her American-born grandchildren in a new family abode. Here she told tales of Irish traditions and sang songs to new generations of the diaspora who were Americans by birth and association: "She sings a good old Irish song, with 'young Pat' on her knee . . . She sings, and talks, and plays with him, both morning, noon and night."[73] Yet, for all of Pat Malloy's mother's singing Irish songs to her grandson, by the end of the Civil War most of the Irish ballads written in the United States were about Irish service in the conflict and were extremely American in their focus. Songs by and about the Irish who fought pulled together all the strands of American loyalty, identity, and home nation association. While still including references that sang of traditional Irish heritage, new outputs returned continually to the rhetoric of innate kinship with the United States via expressions of sharing American ideals and adopting national symbols.

The constant collective terminology heard in writings and lyrics—when "our" meant the Irish in America expressing themselves as Americans—shows how by the 1860s, an inherent sense of Americanness pervaded the diaspora's understanding of their place in the United States. They were Americans. The Civil War gave them cause and opportunities to demonstrate this through song, fighting service, and support for the united home nation's future. Singing about the country's ideals, claiming emblems like the Star Spangled Banner for their own, and sharing in collective war effort contributions reveal how Irish identity had become American very quickly in the mid-nineteenth century. The Civil War provided the platform on which this transnational identity transition could be observed, and exalted, across society.

Conclusion

The amalgamation of national loyalty, symbolic adoption, home country association, and identity articulation by the Irish in the Civil War era was brought together right at the start of the conflict in Thomas Kean's 1861 "The Harp of Old Erin and Banner of Stars." It bound all the themes about how the Irish and Americans were one entity who shared and ultimately emphasized America above all else. In the rhetorical construct of Irish America, this song sang of how the Irish in the United States stressed the importance of the American side of their dual identity. The overall strength of their American association was reinforced by the fact that the country represented home. Lyrics explained the reason why the diaspora's Irish-born and descended sons had joined the war effort and answered the call to defend the unity of the United States. It was their land, as embodied by their adoption and ownership of the American flag. Their service would generate home-front support that put loyalty to the American Union first. Kean's song summarized every sentiment heard throughout subsequent Irish American Civil War balladry. It sang of lyrical thoughts embedded with American expressions and demonstrated a paramount sense of Americanness coming to the fore as the Irish put their Civil War experiences into song:

> I swear . . . [by] the vows we have pledged to this home of the free,
> As we'd sheathe our swords in the foes of dear Ireland,
> We will use them as freely 'gainst traitors to thee . . .
> Strike in their might for the Banner of Stars.
> No, no, with their life blood they'll guard the rich treasure;
> See how they respond to the call, "shoulder arms" . . .

They'll conquer though traitors their cannon may rattle,
And bring back triumphant the Banner of Stars.[1]

These same beliefs would appear again in the early twentieth century. As the United States mobilized its countrymen in 1917, lyricist Edward Harry Kelly penned a song that informed the nation how its population of Irish descent would once again don American military uniform and join the war effort on the fields of Flanders and France. "America, Ireland Loves You" stressed Irish commitment to this new military cause, reiterating ballad sentiments written during the Civil War. Soldiers would again march under the Stars and Stripes:

America, Ireland loves you,
She's with you in this hour of trial . . .
Ev'ry son of Old Erin in allegiance is swearin'
They're rarin' to fight for the Red, White and Blue.[2]

This example was one of several ballads written from the perspective of Irish communities in the United States during World War I. They reinforced that the Irish, as Americans, were just as ready to fight for liberty and democracy at the turn of the twentieth century as they had been over fifty years before at Bull Run, Fredericksburg, Gettysburg, Chancellorsville, and every other engagement. Irish American World War I songs expressed similar sentiments heard throughout the rest of this study. They also demonstrated the predominant place Irish war service ballads still had in American musical culture into the 1900s.

Even before the outbreak of conflict in Europe, lyricists continued to stress the diaspora's eagerness to defend their United States home nation. In 1913, yet another Irish Volunteer rhetoric ballad appeared, entitled "Marching Song of the Irish Volunteers." It discussed Irish foreign military service in the Spanish-American War (1898) and the American Indian Wars during the second half of the nineteenth century. Lyrics described how "the Irish race, united, new, the youngest nation of the earth" by bringing it back together following Confederate secession.[3] After the United States joined the world war effort four years later, songwriter and publisher Michael J. Fitzpatrick wrote a new "Irish Volunteer"-entitled song. In addition to continuing the popular Irish volunteer ballad theme, it articulated long-standing devotion to the Star Spangled Banner as the embodiment of the United States, expressing a similar sentiment to that heard in "America, Ireland Loves You" and throughout the Civil War.[4]

Although there remained a sense of Irish cultural heritage, these early 1900s songs continued to express how American identity was engrained in the diaspora's mindset. This attitude had been cemented in Irish American Civil War ballads. At the end of the conflict in 1865, Charles Graham Halpine dedicated "The Review: A Picture of Our Veterans" to all those who fought. Halpine depicted soldiers disbanding, mourning the loss of the nation's sons on both Union and Confederate sides, and waving battle emblems in the direction of the country's reconciled future. Commenting how the ballad was "already . . . on the lips and in the hearts of many of our veterans," Halpine exclaimed:

> Oh, our comrades! Gone before us
> In the last review to pass,
> Never more to earthly chieftain
> Dipping colors as you pass . . .
> To the souls of all our perished
> We, who still saluting, pass,
> Dip the flag and trail the sabre
> As with wasted ranks we pass.[5]

Just as his Miles O'Reilly songs and fictional stories spread messages of Irish loyalty to the American Union cause, Halpine used his lyrical pen to create ballads such as "The Review" that established the idea of one united martial experience. Sectional divisions were forgotten; sentiments about soldiers, grief, and thanks for battlefield sacrifice became central. The final verse of Halpine's "Song of the Soldiers" was "frequently recited at Grand Army of the Republic gatherings into the late 1880s," repeating the message that veterans on both sides were "brothers of one church."[6]

This American unity had nothing to do with transnational associations. It was about a fundamental sense of Americanness. Halpine even used Miles O'Reilly to emphasize this feeling in one of his fictional character's final appearances. In November 1867, the *New York Herald* published a poem that described O'Reilly as a "gallant soldier, genuine Irishman, and true American." Halpine's phrase summarized more than O'Reilly's identity. Effectively, he described Irish-born and descended residents in the United States:

> We are citizens twice over,
> By the law and by the sword,
> By adoption and by service.[7]

Although these lyrics can be read as articulating a sense of the Irish "becoming" American through their war experience, they were actually more reflective of examples that stressed how the Irish had *become* American by the time the war started. It was an expression heard in songs from the Civil War's earliest days. In 1861, the last verse of "To The Glorious 69th!" combined sentiments about fighting and dying for the home nation with a spiritual idea that dead soldiers would reunite in the choir invisible to sing about American ideals:

> I think those noble soldiers deserve a heavenly sphere . . .
> And when the Angel Army shall gather in one throng,
> The . . . boys will sing the freedom song.[8]

Another New York 69th ballad sang of the same emotion in the succinct phrase, "Ireland is proud, and America is grateful."[9] Earning a place in American wartime cultural memory was just reward for military and home-front commitment to reuniting the nation once again.

Had Halpine lived longer, he would likely have become one of the leading voices of postbellum Irish America, articulating the diaspora's identity as Americans through more writings, poems, and songs and using the memory of Civil War service to stress how devoted the Irish were to the country they called home. Halpine, however, died in August 1868 from an accidental opiate overdose to aid his insomnia before he could fulfill more of his lyrical and literary promise. Indeed, his death was the culmination of several significant voices disappearing from the diaspora. The collective demise of prominent members of the Irish American community during the war and within a decade of the conflict's end—including Halpine, Michael Corcoran, Thomas Francis Meagher, James A. Mulligan, and several Irish Brigade commanders—silenced this strain of American Irish articulation. Certainly, something of their overall American identity ethos lived on in later nineteenth-century ballad lyrics about upholding the country's values. In 1868, the song "America to Ireland" suggested the Irish fighting in the United States Army and living in the reconstructed nation were carrying on the legacy of past Irish American Civil War heroes:

> The leaves of the Shamrock are spreading a-far,
> And we honor the heroes who bare them,
> Where Sheridan, Corcoran, Mulligan, Meagher,
> Like pillars of fire went before them.[10]

Corcoran, Meagher, and Mulligan slowly passed out of American cultural memory. Corcoran, the man with "the soul of a hero . . . easily seen" throughout wartime balladry, all but vanished from broader Irish American commentaries.[11] This is despite the fact that for three years of the conflict, his contribution to the war effort, his example, and his articulations of American loyalty had an enormous impact on Irish lyrical expressions about their experiences in the divided nation. The last notable lament to this exemplar Irish American Union Army general appeared not long after his funeral and eulogy performances in January 1864. A ballad verse published in the *Irish-American* newspaper mourned his death and exalted his gallant character:

> With sorrowing hearts we'll plant it
> Above our hero's tomb;
> And where fond, bright hopes lie,
> With manhood's early bloom;
> While Erin with her tear and smile,
> Unrolls her scroll of fame,
> And writes, in sunlight pencilling,
> Beloved Corcoran's name.[12]

The omission of Corcoran in most subsequent histories of Irish American Civil War experience is surprising given his predominance among wartime society. His cultural influence alone is significant. The way he absorbed the United States of America and all it stood for as part of his own identity, that he was sung about the most, and the manner in which he was employed by songwriters as *the* symbolic figure for the diaspora to aspire to, raises comparisons to—and questions about—the contrasting prevailing attention on Thomas Francis Meagher's own standing in Irish American studies. Corcoran was just as, if not more, important. In one postbellum fictional wartime story, Corcoran's presence in Union Army ranks was described as having "an almost magical effect on" the soldiers serving under him.[13] It was a fitting description for the lyrical hagiography that surrounded the general in the 1860s. Nonetheless, the magic of Corcoran's cultural appeal faded with time.

Thomas Francis Meagher continues to emerge in historical biographies, though his presence in wartime singing culture and ballads has been largely ignored. The focus has been on his public speeches and journalism in the United States, not in how society wrote and sung about him.[14] The former Young Ireland nationalist returned to some level of prominence across the Atlantic in Ireland among twentieth-century republican circles during the era of revolution, independence, and civil war, although his American past was rarely alluded to. In 1916, Sinn Féin founder Arthur Griffith compiled *Meagher of the Sword* but the book focused on Meagher's Young Ireland political speeches up to the time of his sentencing to Van Diemen's Land in 1848. His life and fighting service across the Atlantic did not fit the Irish Rising's rhetorical and historical messages of nationalism that Griffith created.[15]

In the United States, memory of Meagher remained fairly muted and local. His short-lived acting governorship role is remembered with a large statue in Helena, Montana, erected in the early 1900s—which inspired a similar monument placed in his Irish hometown of Waterford one hundred years later; a frieze depicts him saluting General Fitz John Porter at the Battle of Malvern Hill on a monument in New Hampshire, where he appears to be more visible to the viewer than the rest of the monument relief; a memorial on the banks of the Missouri River near Fort Benton marks his final days; and a bust of his head was placed next to his wife Elizabeth's grave in Brooklyn's Green-Wood Cemetery in July 2017 to mark the 150th anniversary of his death.[16] In addition, Meagher is prominent on the Irish Brigade monument at Antietam positioned at the end of the Sunken Road (later known as Bloody Lane after the battle) where many Irish-born and descended soldiers fell in September 1862. This commemorative structure continues the conflation heard in wartime song lyrics about Corcoran's 69th New York and Meagher's Irish Brigade. The soldiers on the front of the stone are 69th New Yorkers, whereas

Meagher's face graces the reverse side, confusing the two entities while concurrently reinforcing the 69th New York's predominance within the brigade's history.

These Irish American Civil War monuments are modern constructs, but on 2 July 1888 one of the first memorials to Irish-born and descended soldiers appeared on "the field that drank in the blood of so many of our dead companions."[17] At the Battle of Gettysburg's twenty-fifth anniversary, the Irish Brigade was remembered at a service presided over by their last commander, General Robert Nugent. It was attended by surviving members of the unit, including chaplain William Corby, who later reported details of the event in his memoir. Attendees gathered for "the dedication of the monument erected to the memory of the Irish Brigade, a beautiful structure." Its unveiling ceremony focused on the same themes heard in songs a quarter-century earlier about how the Irish Brigade "fought on many well-stricken fields for the preservation of the Union and in the Cause of Universal Liberty."[18]

Corby's account highlighted how songs were still being sung in the Irish Brigade's honor after the war at commemorative events. During the Gettysburg 1888 anniversary, several ballad and poetry performances repeated past sentiments heard in wartime iterations. One example was William Geoghegan's "The Irish Brigade at Gettysburg," which recalled Irish and American flags waving over soldiers at the 1863 battle:

Two banners o'er them flew—
The emblem of the land they left
And the land they came unto.[19]

"In Memory of the Fallen Dead of the Irish Brigade" by William Collins was also recited, which again emphasized allegiance to the Star Spangled Banner. Like countless Civil War song examples, it stressed the view that the Irish Brigade and its soldiers were a crucial part of the fighting American spirit. They upheld the Union's ideals, gained overall victory, and reunited the United States:

Where'er that blue, by valor nerved, in serried ranks was seen
There flashed between it and the foe the daring Irish Green!
And never yet, on any land, rushed forth to Freedom's aid
A braver or more dauntless band than Ireland's brave Brigade . . .

[They] Fought in the strife for Liberty
And sealed their faith in blood;
But never yet beat hearts as proud
As those which Ireland gave.[20]

* * *

The sentiments heard within American Civil War songs written by and about the Irish experience of the conflict reveal accounts of the military service of Irish-born and descended soldiers in the Union and Confederate armies. They extolled their actions in engagements and the reasons they served, proclaimed what they fought for, provided home-front support and opinions, sang messages of ultimate faithfulness to the United States of America, and furthered commitment to the nation's ideals. They highlight an additional way the diaspora articulated their war views. These ballad sources should be placed alongside public speeches, wartime writings, and memoirs. They are important because they detail another understanding of how the diaspora reacted to the Civil War and how some of its members used song and music culture to spread communications about their battlefield engagements alongside their attitudes about contemporary political issues. They gave voice to the unsung influence of Irish culture and devotion to the Union and Confederate causes, and later to reconciliation and propagation of the United States' future. Their sentiments and expressions of American identity; commitment to the causes, of liberty, democracy, and republicanism; and the continued articulation of American identity provides an expressive narrative of an established sense of Americanness.

On the surface, the vast majority of the approximately 150 songs and lyrical pieces analyzed for this book centered on the military side of the Irish American Civil War experience. Verses penned in honor of the Union Army's Irish Brigade and its composite regiments, especially its founding 69th New York Regiment and its previous state militia incarnation, dominated the singing culture of Irish soldiers and their families. Despite examples relating to comparable Irish Pennsylvania, Massachusetts, Connecticut, and Illinois Union Army regiments, and equivalent Irish Louisiana and other Confederate units, the 69th New York and Irish Brigade received the strongest lyrical emphasis. While further Irish American Civil War studies will likely continue a developing trend away from Irish Brigade and Irish New York prominence, culturally there remains an argument that the reason these two main subjects have received so much attention is because they were the most predominant across society and wartime recollections.

All of the examples quoted within these chapters sang to the experience of all Irish-born and descended soldiers and, by extension, their home-front families. A song about a 69th New York soldier could apply to a 9th Massachusetts soldier. If passing references to a fictional lyrical soldier's ethnicity are removed, lyrics could further apply to anyone fighting. As seen specifically with the conflation of "Camp Song of the Irish Brigade"—which began as a ballad about Illinois regiments and became one about those from the Eastern states—in most lyrical cases it did not matter which particular unit was the central focus. The common sentiments of fighting bravely on the battlefield, of defending the Union (or in some cases Confederate) cause, upholding the flag, and defending the ideals of the home nation were universal themes. This lyrical and thematic malleability was crucial to songwriters' intent: it added to the message that the Irish fought in the Civil War for the same reasons and in the same manner as their American compatriots. Hence, much of the lyrical Irish Brigade focus and experience could apply beyond the diaspora.

To be sure, some song lyrics were more specific to detailed events in Irish American Civil War history. The military focus included references to battles that were, for example, just about the engagement of the 69th New York State Militia at the First Battle of Bull Run in 1861 or the Irish Brigade at the Battle of Fredericksburg in 1862. These lyrical reports and song stories followed traditional balladry news reporting styles, providing accounts that could be disseminated throughout society alongside official war and newspaper reports. Just this aspect of song lyrics alone, including the many hundreds that were not solely focused on Irish Union and Confederate military examples, is an area of further exploration. Songs provide distinct interpretations of battles, skirmishes, and overall war service. They present a differing source of military culture and examples that compare, and run counter to, more traditional conflict writings.

By extension, songs about the Irish American Civil War experience expose how important the *military* aspect was to the diaspora. That so many songs were about key figures for society to emulate, like Generals Michael

Corcoran and Thomas Francis Meagher, and used military service to reinforce diaspora loyalty to the nation indicates that these were part of a continued response to latent anti-Irish nativism. Mostly, they served as a way to repeat sentiments that Erin's sons had become Columbia's sons as well. There was, additionally, a link between cultural articulations generated in response to political developments during the war, again reflecting the sense of American interest being expressed. Either songs did not bother to mention conscription and draft policy protests, or—as the sentiments heard in "Paddy the Loyal" expressed—they sought to criticize the diaspora itself for any seeming sign of Union disloyalty. Serving the country, sacrificing for the country, showing commitment to the country: these were all fundamental lyrical messages heard within Irish wartime ballads.

At the core of Irish American Civil War songs was the recurring refrain about how *American* the Irish service and singing culture was in the 1860s. The sentiments expressed were essentially American and reflected Union or Confederate national identity. Lyrics suggest those impacted by the war were not *becoming* American. Nor, to an extent, had they *become* American. They *were* Americans. Fighting service reinforced this. It is noticeable how often lyrics sung about American solidarity first and foremost. Michael Corcoran's case in particular highlights this fundamental aspect to the greatest extent. Yet, arguably, what Irish American Civil War ballads sung about in relation to this identity expression was the essential feeling that the United States had become the Irish diaspora's home. The American identity portrayed in ballad verses was also one of home identity and association. This had implications for the way a sense of Irish identity was still present in the form of references to Irish symbology, anglicized Irish-language phrases, and references to past foreign military history. These Irish cultural tropes were circulating throughout society, stressing a broader familiarity and dilution of this heritage within Union and Confederate states.

This had broader implications in relation to Irish nationalist views and the Fenians' fight for a future independent Ireland brought about with American soldiering aid. As shown, if lyrics are taken literally then the collective pronoun use of "our"—as heard at the end of "Pat Murphy of Meagher's Brigade" (1863)—confuses *who* would fight on the island of Ireland. The "helping hand" offered freely in the ballad was an American one.[21] If Irish-born and descended soldiers returned to Ireland, lyrical rhetoric presented the argument that American soldiers would be fighting too. Fenian cultural arguments and articulations uncover how the Civil War impacted and hampered Irish independence goals in the 1860s. They articulated doubts and conflicts within Irish transnational nationalist stances.

In addition, traditional Irish music and song influence and contribution to the formation of American musical culture—especially through the repeated and adapted use of old eighteenth-century tunes to form the foundation for Civil War songs—was extensive. Ballads written in the wartime period entered a preexisting American musical culture shaped by, and including, many popular strands of Irish, Scottish, and Celtic ballad traditions. The pervasive use of Thomas Moore's *Irish Melodies* song tunes, American cultural adoption of Irish language phrases and ethnic symbology, and the presence of numerous Irish related ballads within wider wartime lyrical productions reflected the inherent Irishness of American music by the mid-nineteenth century. While songs may have been sung with an Irish accent, they were also sung with an American voice. Undeniably, Irish American Civil War ballads exhibit how American the diaspora's music had become. The use of American tunes such as "Hail, Columbia," and the ever-evolving Irish, Union, and Confederate use of "The Irish Jaunting Car" and Harry Macarthy's "Bonnie Blue Flag" air, underscore how music and song origins were not limited to the communities that created them. Traditional Irish songs and musical tunes were, therefore, American. They were not exclusive to the diaspora by the Civil War era.

While this book has focused on the sentiments and culture of Irish American Civil War songs, predominately from the four years of the conflict itself, the broader culture of Irish song and music within the United States contributed to an extensive interconnected network of Irish and American lyrical and ballad melody publications. Publishers and musical hall patrons circulated Irish wartime songs, which, in turn, projected the overall message of the diaspora's willingness to see the war effort through and the nation reconciled. The symbiotic relationship between song printing production and their performance—particularly (though not exclusively) relating to Irish examples in the Civil War era—played a crucial role in disseminating these ballads' cultural expressions. The role that music hall theaters and patrons like Tony Pastor had in constructing and shaping the mainstream culture of the war through the use of contemporary Irish songs and traditional ballad tunes is a deeply significant and influential aspect of nineteenth-century American music culture, theater history, and Irish American transnational cultural history.

Continued production of Irish American Civil War songs also reflected the fundamental fact that Irish-born and descended soldiers enlisted and served throughout the conflict, even as war-weariness pervaded Union and Confederate societies. Later enlistees had their own experiences that needed to be written into song in 1864 and 1865. Sentiments, and the memory of their fighting legacy, were still expressed in American balladry up through and including World War I. This cultural continuation challenges the impression of an Irish abandonment of the war effort. Irish American Civil War songs produced and disseminated during the conflict, postbellum recollections and writings that included reference to them, and echoes of their sentiments and themes in American songs at the turn of the twentieth century all expose the expansive nature of Irish musical and lyrical influence.

This cultural transnationalism was similar to a sentiment expressed by Peter Welsh in June 1863. Although discussing the diaspora's impact across the United States, the same description can be applied to the level of importance Irish cultural productions, including songs and music, had throughout the nation: "[Ireland's] sons . . . are interwoven like a network over the whole face of the country. Their influence is felt in every section and it is increasing . . . The Irish element will be the most powerful and influential in the land."[22] Welsh's words about the establishment of Irish America would be echoed over 150 years later at the White House. In his 2017 St. Patrick's Day speech, former Irish Taoiseach Enda Kenny commented on the significant contribution Irish and Scots-Irish migrants had made in United States history. He included reference to the countless Irish soldiers whose names were scattered in the wind, who fought and died in the fields of Civil War battles for the Union and Confederacy, and in subsequent American conflicts. He observed how Irish soldiers "beat the daylights out of each other in Fredericksburg and Gettysburg . . . They fought in every war for America and died for America."[23]

Kenny tied this service to a suggestion—the same suggestion heard in Civil War ballads—that the Irish fought for the United States because of their commitment to the ideals of the nation that became their home. This was in keeping with what is now a very well-established tradition of celebrating and championing Irish American heritage in the United States, something first done with gusto by President John F. Kennedy during his visit to Ireland in

June 1963, where famously he addressed the Irish Parliament in front of a returned Irish Brigade Civil War banner.[24] This remembrance of Irish American martial service has echoed through numerous events and St. Patrick's Day celebrations to this day and will no doubt continue with President Joe Biden, who (even more so than Kennedy) draws on his own direct generational Irish roots.

Enda Kenny went further, however, than just discussing loyalty and past fighting service in 2017. When talking about the Irish American home nation, he stressed that this was a home infused with Irish song. He referred to the enormous social impact Erin's sons and daughters had "through music and culture, and so many other areas."[25] As Bill Clinton exalted over twenty years before on a visit to Dublin: "I believe that if you want to grasp the global culture, you need to come to Ireland."[26] Irish American Civil War ballads were part of this transnational legacy. Certainly within the context of the war specifically and within mid-nineteenth century Irish American migration history more broadly, the approximately 200,000-born—and greater numbers of subsequent descended soldiers and their families—are a minority. That does not take away from their significance to the history of the conflict and the diaspora's experience in the 1860s.

When describing the devastation caused to Irish Brigade numbers after the Battle of Chancellorsville in May 1863, W. F. Lyons stated how the Irish contribution to the war effort was "few, and faint, but fearless still!"[27] It was an apt portrayal and, by extension, applied to the whole Irish experience of the conflict. Irish-born and descended American citizens' martial and cultural contribution was the embodiment of true American patriotism: "The Soldier, bard and Patriot, were mingled in the man!" as Michael O'Riely's "Irish Volunteers" song extolled.[28] Another contemporaneous ballad reiterated this same point. "Music, mirth and song, through our land, predominate," its lyrics sang.[29] Much of that music, mirth, and song during the war was sung with an Irish spirit enthused with an inherent sense of American identity and association.

When Pat Murphy sang around the campfire with his lilting voice, Irish traditional tunes and expressions could be heard, but they were couched with red, white, and blue feeling. These sentiments, strewn through the pages of surviving songsheets, songsters, and in memoirs and accounts, gave voice to the Irish American Civil War contribution. The spirit they sung about was one of an Irish Americanness, where American identity came to the fore, was enhanced by the conflict, and spread throughout wartime musical culture and song expressions. They should neither be forgotten or remain unsung in transnational studies that seek to understand the sentiments and culture of the Irish American Civil War experience.

NOTES

✦·✦·✦·✦·✦

ABBREVIATIONS

BA   Boston Athenaeum
CPDPL   Charles P. Daly Papers and Letters, New York Public Library
CWWP   Civil War Widows Pensions, US National Archives

INTRODUCTION

1. Unknown Lyricist, "Pat Murphy of Meagher's Brigade" (Boston: Horace Partridge, 1863).

2. Traditional figures held that some 140,000–150,000 Irish-born fought in the Civil War, but recent work by Damian Shiels has uncovered greater dominance of Irish soldiers and sailors on both Union and Confederate sides than previously believed. This study uses the larger figure of 200,000 total Irish-born—approximately 180,000 for the Union (which is still an underexaggeration) and 20,000 for the Confederacy. See http://irishamericancivilwar.com for the most up-to-date analysis on these statistics.

3. See *Statistics of the United States in 1860* for "Irish-born Populations in Major U.S. Cities, 1860" census records (Washington, DC, 1866). By 1861, the Irish-born population in the United States was approximately 1.6 million. Alan O'Day, "Imagined Irish Communities: Networks of Social Communication of the Irish Diaspora in the United States and Britain in the Late Nineteenth and Early Twentieth Centuries," *Immigrants & Minorities: Historical Studies in Ethnicity, Migration and Diaspora* 23, nos. 2–3 (2005): 403.

4. The complexity of a lack of lyricist biographical information relates particularly to women writers, as male songwriters adopted female personas in order for songs to gain wider receivership. In addition, some songwriters wrote under pseudonyms, making it more difficult to track an author. Billy Coleman has observed that political campaign songs in the early 1800s had a "tendency to lack authorial attribution." This was true not only for ballad lyricists but also with "newspaper columns, poems, and pamphlets . . . often [appearing] in print anonymously or under pseudonyms"—a practice that continued into and beyond the Civil War era. Billy Coleman, *Harnessing Harmony: Music, Power, and Politics in the United States, 1788–1865* (Chapel Hill: University of North Carolina Press,

2020), 99. As this book focuses on Irish American Civil War song and music sentiments and culture, that ballads were written, published, and spread articulations about the Irish wartime experience is a primary and greater investigative concern than unclear ballad authorship.

5. Alfred M. Williams, "Folk-Songs of the Civil War," *Journal of American Folklore* 5, no. 19 (1892): 267.

6. Steven H. Cornelius, *Music of the Civil War Era* (Westport, CT: Greenwood Press, 2004); Christian McWhirter, *Battle Hymns: The Power and Popularity of Music in the Civil War* (Chapel Hill: University of North Carolina Press, 2012); Christian McWhirter, "Music," in *A Companion to the U.S. Civil War*, ed. Aaron Sheehan-Dean (Hoboken, NJ: Wiley-Blackwell, 2014), 1003–20. New studies on the wider context of American music and song culture and history have expanded interdisciplinary approaches to American musicological history and demonstrate the importance of songs in shaping national culture. See Coleman, *Harnessing Harmony*; Laura Lohman, *Hail Columbia! American Music and Politics in the Early Nation* (New York: Oxford University Press, 2020).

7. Willard A. Heaps and Porter W. Heaps, *The Singing Sixties: The Spirit of Civil War Days Drawn from the Music of the Times* (Norman: University of Oklahoma Press, 1960).

8. E. Lawrence Abel, *Singing the New Nation: How Music Shaped the Confederacy, 1861–1865* (Mechanicsburg, PA: Stackpole Books, 2000).

9. The last decade has witnessed the growth of studies about specific American ballads, including John Stauffer and Benjamin Soskis's *The Battle Hymn of the Republic: A Biography of the Song That Marches On* (New York: Oxford University Press, 2013) about both "John Brown's Body" and "Battle Hymn of the Republic" before, during, and after the Civil War. James A. Davis recently produced *Maryland, My Maryland: Music and Patriotism During the American Civil War* (Lincoln: University of Nebraska Press, 2019) about the Confederate anthem "Maryland, My Maryland," its wartime creation, and ongoing musical legacy. For non–Civil War examples of works about specific American songs, see Sheryl Kaskowitz, *God Bless America: The Surprising History of an Iconic Song* (New York: Oxford University Press, 2013), and Scott Reynolds Nelson, *Steel Drivin' Man: John Henry, The Untold Story of an American Legend* (New York: Oxford University Press, 2008).

10. James H. Stone, "War Music and War Psychology in the Civil War, *Journal of Abnormal and Social Psychology* 36, no. 4 (1941): 556.

11. McWhirter, *Battle Hymns*, 112.

12. James A. Davis, *Music Along the Rapidan: Civil War Soldiers, Music and Community During Winter Quarters, Virginia* (Lincoln: University of Nebraska Press, 2014), 14, 73, and 42.

13. Ibid., 42.

14. "Preface," *War Songs of the South* (Richmond, VA: J. W. Randolph, 1862), 4.

15. Davis, *Music Along the Rapidan*, 58.

16. Dale Cockrell, "Nineteenth Century Popular Music," in *The Cambridge History of American Music*, ed. David Nicholls (Cambridge: Cambridge University Press, 1998), 181–82.

17. McWhirter, *Battle Hymns*, 125–26.

18. Davis, *Music Along the Rapidan*, 52.

19. Robert L. Wright, *Irish Emigrant Ballads and Songs* (Bowling Green, OH: Bowling Green Popular Press, 1975). Some ballads quoted in this study use Wright's source evidence.

20. Mick Moloney, "Irish-American Popular Music," in *Making the Irish American: History and Heritage of the Irish in the United States*, ed. J. J. Lee and Marion R. Casey (New York: New

York University Press), 381–405; Rebecca S. Miller, "Irish Traditional Music in the United States," in Lee and Casey, *Making the Irish American,* 411–16. This is in keeping with Mick Moloney's own New York University archive holding, where many Irish American ballad records date from the postbellum period and twentieth century (The Mick Moloney Irish-American Music and Popular Culture Irish Americana Collection, The Tamimnet Library and Robert F. Wagner Labor Archives, New York University).

21. William H. A. Williams, *'Twas Only an Irishman's Dream: The Image of Ireland and the Irish in American Popular Song Lyrics, 1800–1920* (Champaign: University of Illinois Press, 1996).

22. Dan Milner, *The Unstoppable Irish: Songs and Integration of the New York Irish, 1783–1883* (Notre Dame, IN: University of Notre Dame Press, 2019).

23. Michael Saffle, "Across a Great Divide: Irish American Music and Musicians of the Civil War Era," in *Bugle Resounding: Musicians and Music of the Civil War Era,* ed. Bruce C. Kelley and Mark A. Snell (Columbia: University of Missouri Press, 2004), 186.

24. Saffle's definition of the Irishness of American songs and music also relies heavily on analysis from William L. Burton's *Melting Pot Soldiers,* which centers on the experience of the Union Army's ethnic regiments. William L. Burton, *Melting Pot Soldiers: The Union Ethnic Regiments* (New York: Fordham University Press, 1998).

25. Williams, *'Twas Only An Irishman's Dream,* 9.

26. Georges-Denis Zimmerman, *Songs of Irish Rebellion: Political Street Ballads and Rebel Songs, 1780–1900* (Hatboro: Folklore Associates, 1967), 12.

27. Susannah J. Ural, "'Ye Sons of Green Erin Assemble': Northern Irish American Catholics and the Union War Effort, 1861–1865," in *Civil War Citizens: Race, Ethnicity, and Identity in America's Bloodiest Conflict,* ed. S. J. Ural (New York: New York University Press), 125 and 127.

28. James McPherson, *For Cause and Comrades: Why Men Fought in the Civil War* (New York: Oxford University Press, 1997), 9.

29. Robert R. Grimes, *How Shall We Sing in a Foreign Land? Music of Irish Catholic Immigrants in the Antebellum United States* (Notre Dame, IN: University of Notre Dame Press, 1996), 176.

30. Davis, *Music Along the Rapidan,* 239 and 250.

31. Leonie Hannan and Sarah Longair, *History through Material Culture* (Manchester: Manchester University Press, 2017), 2.

32. Ibid., 6; 1.

33. Benedict Anderson, *Imagined Communities: Reflections on the Origin and Spread of Nationalism* (London: Verso, 2006), 18, 24, 34, 36. For exploration of print culture capitalism, song publishing and production intertextuality before the American Civil War, see Meredith L. McGill, *American Literature and the Culture of Reprinting, 1834–1853* (Philadelphia: University of Pennsylvania Press, 2003).

34. Hannan and Longair, *History through Material Culture,* xiii.

35. For studies on the nineteenth-century practice of collecting songsheets, scrapbooking, and personal/private collation of musical scorebooks and works in the United States of America (both classical and traditional folk examples), see Candace Bailey, *Charleston Belles Abroad: The Music of Harriet Lowndes, Henrietta Aiken, and Louisa Rebecca McCord* (Columbia: University of South Carolina Press, 2019); Ellen Gruber Garvey, *Writing With Scissors: American Scrapbooks from the Civil War to the Harlem Renaissance* (New York: Oxford University Press, 2013).

36. Hannan and Longair, *History through Material Culture,* 4.

37. Thomas N. Brown, *Irish-American Nationalism, 1870–1890* (Philadelphia: Lippincott, 1966). Modern scholarship on the Irish migrant diaspora in the United States of America has its foundations in Carl Wittke, *The Irish in America* (Baton Rouge: Louisiana State University Press, 1956). However, "Brown's influence . . . permeate[d] the thinking of an entire generation" more with regard to the whole discourse of Irish American history and studies, J. J. Lee, "Introduction: Interpreting Irish America," in Lee and Casey, *Making the Irish American,* 10.

38. See Kerby Miller, *Emigrants and Exiles: Ireland and the Irish Exodus to North America* (New York: Oxford University Press, 1985).

39. The Great Famine, or An Gorta Mór in the Irish language, lasted between 1845 and 1849, with its effects reaching into the early 1850s. The period saw mass disease and starvation spread across the island of Ireland and led to a significant decline of the population through death (approximately one million) and emigration to Britain, North and South America, Europe, and Australasia (approximately over another one million people).

40. Kevin Kenny, *The American Irish: A History* (Harlow: Longman, 2000); Kevin Kenny, "Diaspora and Comparison: The Global Irish as a Case Study," *Journal of American History* 90, no. 1 (2003): 134–62; Kevin Kenny, "Twenty Years of Irish American Historiography," *Journal of American Ethnic History* 28, no. 4 (2009): 67–75.

41. This is why the number of 200,000 Irish who fought in the Civil War centers on those born in Ireland (that is, the first generation). The overall figure of those claiming Irish ethnicity through subsequent descended generations—including the children, grandchildren, and great-grandchildren of pre-Famine migrants—makes the total ethnic-Irish soldiers and sailors participation count higher. Irish-born soldiers were found throughout non-Irish dominant Union and Confederate army and naval units, revealing how widespread second and subsequent generation enlistment was during the conflict. Surname evidence in particular can be used to trace these generations and obtain a more accurate number of total ethnic-Irish serving in the wartime military.

42. Kenny, *American Irish,* 138.

43. David Fitzpatrick, "Irish Emigration in the Later Nineteenth Century," *Irish Historical Studies* 22, no. 86 (1980): 137. In a similar line of argument, Marjorie Fallows observed how Irish American historiography has repeatedly ignored that "not all Irishmen [and women] had the same experience" of the United States. Marjorie R. Fallows, *Irish Americans: Identity and Assimilation* (Hoboken, NJ: Prentice Hall, 1979), 42.

44. Christian G. Samito, *Becoming American Under Fire: Irish Americans, African Americans, and the Politics of Citizenship During the Civil War Era* (Ithaca, NY: Cornell University Press, 2009), 103–4. Samito focuses on the 1860s, but the Irish served in previous military engagements in the United States from the War of Independence onward. Civil War songs barely discussed this part of Irish foreign military history (see chap. 4).

45. Linda Dowling Almeida, *Irish Immigrants in New York City, 1945–1995* (Bloomington: Indiana University Press, 2001), 5. For further studies on the New York Irish experience in the Civil War era, see Tyler Anbinder, *Five Points: The 19th Century New York City Neighborhood That Invented Tap Dance, Stole Elections, and Became the World's Most Notorious Slum* (New York: The Free Press, 2001); Ronald H. Bayor and Timothy J. Meagher, eds., *The New York Irish* (Baltimore: Johns Hopkins University Press, 1996); Mary C. Kelly, *The Shamrock and the Lily: The New York Irish and the Creation of a Transatlantic Identity, 1845–1921* (New York: Peter Lang, 2007).

46. Susannah J. Ural, *The Harp and the Eagle: Irish-American Volunteers and the Union Army, 1861–1865* (New York: New York University Press, 2006); Susannah J. Ural, "'Remember Your Country and Keep Up Its Credit': Irish Volunteers and the Union Army, 1861–1865," *Journal of Military History* 69, no. 2 (2005): 331–59; Ural, "'Ye Sons of Green Erin Assemble.'"

47. Ural, "'Ye Sons of Green Erin Assemble,'" 115.

48. David T. Gleeson, *The Green and the Gray: The Irish in the Confederate States of America* (Chapel Hill: University of North Carolina Press, 2013); David T. Gleeson, "'To Live and Die [for] Dixie': Irish Civilians and the Confederate States of America," *Irish Studies Review* 18, no. 2 (2010): 139–53; David T. Gleeson and Brendan J. Buttimer, "'We Are Irish Everywhere': Irish Immigrant Networks in Charleston, South Carolina, and Savannah, Georgia," *Immigrants & Minorities: Historical Studies in Ethnicity, Migration and Diaspora* 23, nos. 2–3 (2005): 183–205.

49. Ryan Keating, *Shades of Green: Irish Regiments, American Soldiers and Local Communities in the Civil War Era* (New York: Fordham University Press, 2017), 2, 12, 14.

50. Damian Shiels, *The Irish in the American Civil War* (Dublin: The History Press, 2013); Damian Shiels, *The Forgotten Irish: Irish Experiences in America* (Dublin: The History Press, 2016); Damian Shiels website, "Irish in the American Civil War," *http://irishamericancivilwar.com*.

51. Don H. Doyle, *The Cause of All Nations: An International History of the American Civil War* (New York: Basic Books, 2015); Amanda Foreman, *A World on Fire: An Epic History of Two Nations Divided* (London: Penguin, 2011); Ann L. Tucker, *Newest Born of Nations: European Nationalist Movements and the Making of the Confederacy* (Charlottesville: University of Virginia Press, 2020).

52. Unknown Lyricist, "War Song for the 79th Regiment" (New York: James Wrigley, 1861).

53. "Our German Volunteers," in *The Camp-Fire Songster: A Collection of Popular, Patriotic, National, Pathetic, and Jolly Songs, Suited for the Camp or March, Containing a Number of Songs Never Before Printed* (New York: Dick & Fitzgerald, 1862), 31–32.

54. Thomas Kean, "The Harp of Old Erin and Banner of Stars" (New York: H. De Marsan, 1861).

1. IRISH MUSIC AND SONGS IN MID-NINETEENTH-CENTURY AMERICA

1. E. P. Thompson, *Customs in Common: Studies in Traditional Popular Culture* (New York: The New Press, 1993), 8.

2. Hugh Shields, *Narrative Singing in Ireland: Lays, Ballads, Come-All-Yes and Other Songs* (Blackrock: Irish Academic Press, 1993), 52.

3. James Quinn, *Young Ireland and the Writing of Irish History* (Dublin: University College Dublin Press, 2015), 190.

4. Michael Broyles, "Immigrant, Folk, and Regional Musics in the Nineteenth Century," in *The Cambridge History of American Music,* ed. David Nicholls (Cambridge: Cambridge University Press, 1988), 138.

5. Cockrell, "Nineteenth Century Popular Music," 180.

6. Michael Broyles, "Art Music from 1860 to 1920," in *The Cambridge History of American Music,* ed. David Nicholls (Cambridge: Cambridge University Press, 1988), 240.

7. Quinn, *Young Ireland* , 45; Williams, *'Twas Only an Irishman's Dream,* 19.

8. Williams, *'Twas Only an Irishman's Dream*, 29.

9. Ibid., 31.

10. Grimes, *How Shall We Sing in a Foreign Land?*, 171.

11. The Bostonian classical music scholar John Sullivan Dwight established *Dwight's Journal of Music, A Paper of Art and Literature* in 1852. Despite holding "lofty views of music," Dwight "considered the role of music in a globalised space." He used his eponymous *Journal*, and other writings, to promote and report European music and Celtic folk outputs. Catherine Jones, *Literature and Music in the Atlantic World, 1767–1867* (Edinburgh: Edinburgh University Press, 2014), 117, 194. For discussion of Dwight's influence in relation to American musical interest as a form of high culture that was integral to social convictions and politics, see Coleman, *Harnessing Harmony*, chap. 4.

12. *Irish Melodies* advertisement, *Dwight's Journal of Music*, 9 March 1861.

13. *Irish-American*, 18 March 1861.

14. *Irish-American*, 18 March 1862.

15. *One Hundred Songs of Ireland* advertisement, *Dwight's Journal of Music*, 26 January 1861.

16. For more on the Young Ireland movement and the work of the *Nation* in the 1840s, see Quinn, *Young Ireland*. Following the split with Daniel O'Connell's Repeal Association, which called for reform of Ireland's relationship and position under British rule in 1847, and their revolutionary actions in the 1848 Young Irelander Rebellion, many of the group's followers dispersed. Its leaders were imprisoned and later transported to outposts of the British Empire. John Mitchel was sent to Bermuda and then Van Dieman's Land (present-day Tasmania), where he was reunited with Thomas Francis Meagher. From their exiled positions, Young Irelanders managed to integrate themselves into Australian, Canadian, and American political and military circles in the 1850s and 1860s.

17. Quinn, *Young Ireland*, 50.

18. Thomas Francis Meagher, *The Last Days of the 69th in Virginia, A Narrative in Three Parts* (New York: Lynch & Cole, 1861), 3–4.

19. Julia Crawford, "Kathleen Mavourneen" (ca. 1838). Musicological debate surrounds when Crouch published the song: 1838 is the likely date, although a version possibly appeared in 1835. Doubt also exists about Crawford's identity and whether she was Crouch's wife. See Williams, *'Twas Only an Irishman's Dream*, 41; Cornelius, *Music of the Civil War Era*, 84.

20. Seán O'Boyle, *The Irish Song Tradition* (Dublin: Gilbert Dalton, 1976), 16.

21. Williams, *'Twas Only an Irishman's Dream*, 41.

22. McWhirter, *Battle Hymns*, 24.

23. Cornelius, *Music of the Civil War Era*, 86.

24. John Poole, "I Goes To Fight Mit Sigel," New York: H. De Marsan, 1861. "Mit," meaning "with" in English, reflects the ballad's use of anglicized German words and German phrasing (the song's title translates as "I Go To Fight With Sigel").

25. Bayard Taylor, "Songs of the Camp," in *The Camp-Fire Songster: A Collection of Popular, Patriotic, National, Pathetic, and Jolly Songs, Suited for the Camp or March, Containing a Number of Songs Never Before Printed* (New York: Dick & Fitzgerald, 1862), 65–66. Four-nations transnational approaches focus on the comparative histories of all nations of the British Isles—England, Scotland, and Wales—and the island of Ireland (also encompassing Northern Ireland).

26. Bayard Taylor, "A Crimean Episode," *Dwight's Journal of Music*, 28 September 1861. For musicological and aural studies of the Crimean War, see Gavin Williams, ed., *Hearing the Crimean War: Wartime Sound and the Unmaking of Sense* (New York: Oxford University Press, 2019).

27. "The Irishman's Shanty" (ca. 1859), in *Hopkins' New-Orleans 5 Cent Song-Book* (New Orleans: John Hopkins, 1861), 10–11.

28. "Limerick Races," in *Hopkins' New-Orleans 5 Cent Song-Book* (New Orleans: John Hopkins, ca. 1861), 17–18.

29. By 1860, Louisiana's Irish population was over 28,000: "in South Carolina and Louisiana over 70 percent of the Irish lived in the largest cities, Charleston and New Orleans." See Gleeson, *The Green and the Gray*, 7.

30. A detailed genre of study has developed the specific history of minstrelsy, blackface theater, vaudeville, and musical hall culture in the United States over the 1800s and early 1900s. For a small relevant example of this scholarship, see Annemarie Bean, James V. Hatch, and Brooks McNamara, eds., *Inside the Minstrel Mask: Readings in Nineteenth-Century Blackface Minstrelsy* (Middletown: Wesleyan University Press, 1996); Nicholas Gebhardt, *Vaudeville Melodies: Popular Musicians and Mass Entertainment in American Culture, 1870–1929* (Chicago: University of Chicago Press, 2017); Eric Lott, *Love & Theft: Blackface Minstrelsy and the American Working Class* (New York: Oxford University Press, 2013); William J. Mahar, *Behind the Burnt Cork Mask: Early Blackface Minstrelsy and Antebellum American Popular Culture* (Champaign: University of Illinois Press, 1999); David Monod, *Vaudeville and the Making of Modern Entertainment, 1890–1925* (Chapel Hill: University of North Carolina Press, 2020).

31. For more on the practice of exoticism as a form of cultural adoption, see Georgina Born and David Hesmondhalgh, eds., *Western Music and Its Others: Difference, Representation, and Appropriation in Music* (Berkeley: University of California Press, 2000); W. Anthony Sheppard, "Exoticism," in *Oxford Bibliography in Music*, ed. Kate van Orden (New York: Oxford University Press, 2016): https://www.oxfordbibliographies.com/view/document/obo-9780199757824/obo-9780199757824-0123.xml?rskey=mCBY94&result=1&q=Exoticism#firstMatch.

32. Michael T. Bernath, *Confederate Minds: The Struggle For Intellectual Independence in the Civil War South* (Chapel Hill: University of North Carolina Press, 2010), 231–32.

33. *The Southern Soldier's Prize Songster: Containing Material and Patriotic Pieces (Chiefly Original) Applicable to the Present War* (Mobile: W. F. Wisley, 1864), 3–4.

34. The complex origin of "Yankee Doodle" has long generated musicological debate and was even the subject of an American article published at the start of the Civil War. According to that piece, the tune for "Yankee Doodle" tune could be traced to a mid-1600s English nursery rhyme. There was a suggestion that it evolved from contemporary German music. The tune's American identity was formed "it was supposed, in the spring of 1775, after the skirmishes at Lexington and Concord." See "The Origin of Yankee Doodle," *Dwight's Journal of Music*, 6 July 1861.

35. "Clocknaben," in *Southern Soldier's Prize Songster*, 96.

36. O'Boyle, *Irish Song Tradition*, 16.

37. Welsh song and music traditions remained predominantly within Welsh American diasporic settings: smaller community numbers and language difference limited dissemination. However, *Dwight's* printed an advertisement for "The Harp of Wales," "a fine parlour song" by Welsh composer Brinley Richards, suggesting some more widespread song sharing into American society. *Dwight's Journal of Music*, 28 September 1861.

38. Williams, *'Twas Only An Irishman's Dream*, 78.

39. *One Hundred Songs of Scotland*, advertisement, *Dwight's Journal of Music*, 28 February 1861.

40. For more on Scottish song and music influence in the United States and its relationship to

Irish examples, see Broyles, "Immigrant, Folk, and Regional Musics," 139–41; Williams, *'Twas Only and Irishman's Dream,* 78–81; Michael C. Scroggins, *The Scotch-Irish Influence on Country Music in the Carolinas: Border Ballads, Fiddle Tunes and Sacred Songs* (Charleston: The History Press, 2013); David Atkinson and Steve Roud, eds., *Street Ballads in the Nineteenth-Century Britain, Ireland, and North America: The Interface Between Print and Oral Traditions* (London: Routledge, 2014). For work on the influence of Robert Burns on American culture, see Arun Sood, *Robert Burns and the United States of America: Poetry, Print, and Memory, 1786–1866* (London: Palgrave Macmillan, 2018).

41. "Texan General's Address to His Army" in *The Rebel Songster: Containing a Choice Collection of Sentimental, Patriotic and Comic Songs, Compiled by a Musical Gentleman of this City* (Richmond, VA: Ayres & Wade, 1864), 25–26.

42. "War Song for the 79th Regiment" (New York: J. Wrigley, 1861).

43. Rowland Berthoff, "Celtic Mist Over the South," *Journal of Southern History* 52, no. 4 (1986): 535.

44. For analysis of perceived Southern Celtic cultural heritage and Civil War military traditions, see Grady McWhiney and Perry D. Jamison, *Attack and Die: Civil War Military Tactics and the Southern Heritage* (Tuscaloosa: University of Alabama Press, 1982), 172–91; W. J. Cash, *The Mind of the South* (New York: Vintage Books, 1991).

45. Caroline Moseley, "Irrepressible Conflict: Differences Between Northern and Southern Songs of the Civil War," *Journal of Popular Culture* 25, no. 2 (1991): 49–50.

46. Williams, *'Twas Only An Irishman's Dream,* 80.

47. Advertisement, *New Orleans Daily Crescent* (New Orleans), 12 August 1861.

48. Valentine Vousden, "The Irish Jaunting Car" (Dublin, 1854).

49. "The Irish Jaunting Car" (London: H. Such, 1854). Other versions focused directly on the driver-narrator, named as Larry Doolan, Larry Doolain, or Mickey Doolin in different examples.

50. "The Irish Jaunting Car" (New York: Andrews, ca. 1854–55). Aside from the popular tune and divergent antebellum song versions, Americans were also aware of what Irish jaunting cars actually were. References to the transportation mode appeared in travel accounts written in mid-1800s American newspapers. One report described the carriage as a "peculiar and distinctive Irish vehicle, an outside jaunting-car, which has the merit of giving you a variety in the way of exercise—joltings, backwards, forwards, and sideways—a vigilant and vigorous endeavor to keep yourself and your luggage on," "Greenwood Leaves from Over the Sea" in the *National Era* (Washington, DC), 23 September 1852.

51. "New Songs at Richardson's," *Daily Dispatch* (Richmond), 8 August 1857.

52. Cornelius, *Music of the Civil War Era,* 42. For exploration of "Maryland, My Maryland," see James A. Davis, *Maryland, My Maryland: Music and Patriotism During the American Civil War* (Lincoln: University of Nebraska Press, 2019). "Lauriger Horatius" is not only the tune for "Maryland, My Maryland"—it provides the melody for the German song "O Tannenbaum," known in English as the carol "O Christmas Tree." It is also the air for the international socialist and labor anthem "The Red Flag" (1889).

53. *Winchester Daily Bulletin* (Tennessee), 13 March 1863.

54. "An Addition to the Bonnie Blue Flag" in *War Lyrics and Songs of the South* (London: Spottiswoode & Co., 1866), 129.

55. "Additional words to 'Bonnie Blue Flag' as sung by the Missourians during the war" (ca.

1861), handwritten page of verses placed inside a copy of *Virginia Songster* (Richmond, VA: J. W. Randolph, 1863), Boston Athenaeum Confederate Collection [cited hereafter as BA].

56. Armand and his brother Henry Clay Blackmar produced over 230 wartime compositions, "more than any other firm" in the Confederacy (Cornelius, *Music of the Civil War Era*, 17).

57. Harry Macarthy, "The Bonnie Blue Flag" (New Orleans: A. E. Blackmar & Bro., 1861–62). Blackmar produced numerous editions of the song in New Orleans. When the Union occupied the city, General Benjamin F. Butler banned "The Bonnie Blue Flag," and Blackmar and Macarthy fled the region. The former reopened his business in Augusta, Georgia, where he continued to print Macarthy's Confederate songs. See Billy Coleman, "Confederate Music and the Politics of Treason and Disloyalty in the American Civil War," *Journal of Southern History* 86, no. 1 (2020): 75–116.

58. Harry Macarthy, "The Bonnie Blue Flag" (New York: H. De Marsan, ca. 1861); Boston's Horace Partridge printed other songsheet copies between 1861 and 1862.

59. Harry Macarthy, "The Bonnie Blue Flag" (Liverpool: Hime & Son, ca. 1862). Sister publishing houses in London and Manchester also produced copies.

60. Harry Macarthy, "The Bonnie Blue Flag" (Cheltenham: Edward Hale & Co., 1864).

61. "Bonnie Blue Flag" pianoforte variations were published by several printing houses, including Baltimore's Miller & Beacham, Philadelphia's Lee & Walker (1862), and Blackmar & Bro. (1862–64).

62. *The Bonnie Blue Flag Song Book*, 3rd ed. (Augusta, GA: A. E. Blackmar & Bro., 1863).

63. Carrie Bell Sinclair, "The Homespun Dress" (New Orleans: A. E. Blackmar, 1864).

64. John C. Cross, "Mother on the Brain" (New York: H. De Marsan, 1864).

65. Davis, *Music Along the Rapidan*, 147.

66. In ten specific Confederate songster publications analyzed in detail for this study, "The Homespun Dress" appears only once. It is possible the tone of women's home-front sacrifice was too melancholy, although many sentimental, lamenting, and mournful Confederate and Union songs about the conflict's impact on society appeared regularly in publications. If anything, "The Homespun Dress" has become more popular retrospectively in American Civil War music memory.

67. Harry Macarthy, "Our Country's Flag" (1865). Macarthy's end-of-war song failed to gain widespread Union and Confederate success precisely because of its unifying attempt. The original "Bonnie Blue Flag" and subsequent adaptations were centered on sectional divides and galvanized fighting and secessionist spirit throughout the war. "The Bonnie Blue Flag" remained a Confederate anthem in American music culture memory after 1865, but Union versions fell out of postbellum circulation (as did "Our Country's Flag"—see chap. 7 for further discussion of this ballad).

68. C. Sterett, "A Reply to the Bonnie Blue Flag" (New York: S. T. Gordon, 1862). The song was also published under the title "The Bonnie Blue Flag."

69. "The Bonnie Blue Flag, Or Our Beautiful Flag," advertisement, *Dwight's Journal of Music*, 6 February 1862.

70. "Glorious Old Flag, A Reply to the Bonnie Blue Flag" (Philadelphia: Marsh, 1862); "The Flag with the Thirty Four Stars" (Cincinnati: A. C. Peters & Bro., 1862).

71. J. L. Geddes, "The Bonnie Flag with the Stars and Stripes" (St. Louis: Balmer and Weber, 1862). Geddes wrote his version while imprisoned in Cahaba/Castle Morgan Prison near Selma, Alabama, where his regiment enjoyed singing his composition to answer Macarthy's "Bonnie Blue Flag" Confederate anthem. In one account of life at the prison, the 8th Iowa Infantry band—who

"sang patriotic and sentimental songs nearly every night"—were described as bringing "halcyon days" to the incarcerated. Jesse Hawes, *Cahaba: A Story of Captive Boys in Blue* (New York: Burr Printing House, 1888), 238–39.

72. "Hurrah for the Banner of Red, White and Blue" advertisement in *Dwight's Journal of Music*, 22 June 1861.

73. Throughout the eighteenth century, a number of political groups claimed the Irish Patriot Party name to campaign for stronger Irish self-government independent from British and Westminster oversight. Their efforts brought about the Constitution of 1782, which gave the island of Ireland legal and legislative independence from Britain for six years before nationalist campaigns by the United Irishman failed to achieve republican independence. Ireland became part of the United Kingdom of Great Britain and Ireland in 1801.

74. "The Irish Volunteers of 1860" (Ireland, ca. 1860).

75. A different group of American Civil War "Irish Volunteer" songs were also set to another air, "The Yankee Man of War" (such as "Irish Volunteer," printed by A. W. Auner in Philadelphia around 1862). The lyrical and musical pattern of these songs do not match the melody of "The Irish Jaunting Car." The tune for "The Yankee Man of War" was possibly of English origin.

76. Michael O'Riely, "The Irish Volunteers" (New York: H De Marsan and J. Wrigley, 1862). It is unclear if an Irish soldier or a music hall performer under a pseudonym wrote this version. The name is similar to Charles Graham Halpine's fictional Irish wartime character Miles O'Reilly, but he appeared later in the conflict. Moreover, the lyrical style of O'Riely's "The Irish Volunteer" ballad does not fit Halpine's usual writing form.

77. Tony Pastor, "The Irish Volunteer No. 3" (New York: H De Marsan and James Wrigley, 1862).

78. Arthur McFadden, "Col. Owens' Gallant Irish Volunteers" (Philadelphia: A. W. Auner, 1861).

79. Frank Spear, "The New York Volunteer" (New York: Dick and Fitzgerald, 1862).

80. "The New York Volunteer," in *Camp-Fire Songster*, 23–24.

81. By the Civil War, most anti-immigrant nativist sentiment diminished while secession and abolition politics dominated concerns, but rhetorical anti-Irish articulations could still be heard. This is evidenced by the various 1860s "No Irish Need Apply" songs that presented a pro-Irish lyrical voice to combat hostility toward some sections of the Irish Catholic diaspora. Specific anti-Irish lyrical responses are discussed in chap. 6.

82. William Sutherland, "What Irish Boys Can Do—Answer to 'No Irish Need Apply'" (New York: H. De Marsan, 1863).

83. Eugene T. Johnston, "What Irish Boys Have Done" (New York: Charles Magnus, ca. 1870).

84. "Dublin Jaunting Car," advertisement, *Dwight's Journal of Music*, 18 April 1863. In addition, songsheet publications of "Larry Maher's Big Five Gallon Jar" listed its air as "The Irish Jaunting Car." This example was contemporaneous with Irish American drinking songs (New York: H. De Marsan, ca. 1860s).

85. Jonathan Lighter, *The Best Antiwar Song Ever Written* (Windsor: Loomis House Press, 2012).

86. Patrick Gilmore, "When Johnny Comes Marching Home" (Boston: Henry Tolman & Co., 1863). Gilmore wrote songs under the pseudonym Louis Lambert.

87. Eugene T. Johnston, *Corcoran's Irish Legion* (Boston: Horace Partridge, 1863).

88. "The Irish Brigade" (Boston: Horace Partridge, January 1862). Not all Irish Brigade songs

were set to American musical tunes. For example, Kate C. M.'s "The Irish Brigade" was set to an Irish air, "My Heart's in Old Ireland," in *The Continental Songster: A Collection of New, Spirited Patriotic Songs for the Times* (Philadelphia: A. Winch, 1863), 58–59.

89. Unknown Lyricist, "The Gallant 69th Regiment" (New York: H. De Marsan, 1862).

90. "Our Own Flag of Green" (New York: J. Wrigley, ca. 1865).

2. THE PRODUCTION OF IRISH AMERICAN CIVIL WAR SONGS

1. "Cead Mille Fealthe" advertisement, *Dwight's Journal of Music, A Paper of Art and Literature* (Boston: Oliver Ditson), 25 June 1864.

2. Thomas M. Brown, "Cead Mille Fealthe—A Hundred Thousand Welcomes" (Boston: Oliver Ditson, 1864). In some instances, Brown's name was printed in error as "Browne." "Cead Mille Fealthe" followed Brown's other Massachusetts regiment composition "Hurrah for the Banner of Red, White and Blue," dedicated to the 13th Massachusetts Infantry in the summer of 1861 (mentioned in chap. 1).

3. McWhirter, *Battle Hymns*, 3.

4. Cornelius, *Music of the Civil War Era*, 16.

5. Moseley, "Irrepressible Conflict," 46.

6. Grimes, *How Shall We Sing in a Foreign Land?*, x.

7. Davis, *Music Along the Rapidan*, 42.

8. Cornelius, *Music of the Civil War Era*, 82.

9. Ural, *Harp and the Eagle*, 60. Both Ural and David Gleeson—in *The Green and the Gray*—discuss the myriad reasons for Irish enlistment in the Union and Confederate Armies, how they were recruited, and how Irish-dominant militia units became part of regular military service during the Civil War.

10. John Dougherty to Ann Dougherty, 4 September 1862, Application WC93207, *Approved Pension Applications of Widows and Other Dependents of Civil War Veterans*, Civil War Widows Pensions, US National Archives (cited hereafter as CWWP).

11. William McCarter, *My Life in the Irish Brigade: The Civil War Memoirs of Private William McCarter, 116th Pennsylvania Infantry*, ed. Kevin O'Brien (De Capo Press, 2003), 2.

12. Davis, *Music Along the Rapidan*, 53.

13. Michael Corcoran, *The Captivity of General Corcoran: The Only Authentic and Reliable Narrative of the Trials and Sufferings Endured, During his Twelve Months' Imprisonment in Richmond and Other Southern Cities, by Brigadier-General Michael Corcoran, the Hero of Bull Run* (Philadelphia: Barclay & Co, 1864), 65. This passage was in a section of Corcoran's account that detailed his short-lived prison diary, 16 October 1861.

14. McWhirter, *Battle Hymns*, 34.

15. Corcoran, *Captivity of General Corcoran*, 93. Corcoran's role in Irish wartime balladry will be discussed further in chap. 4.

16. William H. Rogers, *The Great Civil War—William H. Rogers's Personal Experiences* (Boston: Bivouac, 1888), 9.

17. Ibid., 6.

18. Zenas T. Haines, 21 March 1863, in *Letters from the Forty-Fourth Regiment M. V. M.: A Record of the Experience of a Nine Months' Regiment in the Department of North Carolina in 1862–1863* (Boston: The Herald Job Office, 1863). Haines also noted: "the musical world will be glad to know that the organs of our principal singers are as yet unaffected by the severe trials of picket duty: a fact the more noticeable, perhaps, considering that those organs have not been lubricated with whiskey rations from first to last of our severe trials as soldiers," 87–88.

19. John G. Jones to his parents, 24 October 1862, in Clare Taylor, ed., *Wales and the American Civil War* (Aberystwyth: William Reese Co., 1972), 8. Between his enlistment in Company G of the 23rd Wisconsin Infantry Regiment in 1862 until his death in 1864, Jones maintained regular correspondence with his Welsh family residing in Wisconsin. As well as writing frequently about singing culture and maintenance of the Welsh language among the diaspora's Wisconsin soldiery, Jones's letters detail his experiences at the Battle of Vicksburg in July 1863. Taylor's volume provides a good source of Jones's correspondence, along with Jerry Hunter's analysis in *Sons of Arthur, Children of Lincoln: Welsh Writing from the American Civil War* (Cardiff: University of Wales Press, 2007).

20. Jones to his parents, 12 October 1862, in Taylor, *Wales and the American Civil War*, 8.

21. Corcoran, *Captivity of General Corcoran*, 30.

22. David Power Conyngham, *The Irish Brigade and Its Campaigns* (Glasgow: Cameron & Ferguson, 1868), 39.

23. Davis, *Music Along the Rapidan*, 54–56.

24. Patrick Kinnane to Elizabeth Kinnane, 10 April 1863. The purchase is understandable considering Patrick and Elizabeth Kinnane's antebellum music careers—the siblings were fiddlers who played accompanying violin music at dances and gatherings. Patrick very likely performed fiddle music for his fellow soldiers in camp with his new purchase. Application WC75830, *Approved Pension Applications of Widows and Other Dependents of Civil War Veterans*, CWWP.

25. Patrick Kelly to his parents, 19 January 1862, quoted by Damian Shiels, *Forgotten Irish*, 119.

26. William Corby, *Memoirs of Chaplain Life: Three Years in the Famous Irish Brigade* (Chicago: La Monte, 1893), 116–17.

27. McCarter, *Life in the Irish Brigade*, 50.

28. Jones to his parents, 24 October 1861, in Taylor, *Wales and the American Civil War*, 8–9.

29. Corcoran, *Captivity of General Corcoran*, 30. Sadly, Corcoran did not write any of Hart's lyrical constructions in his memoir.

30. Michael Corcoran to Charles P. Daly, 13 May 1863, Charles P. Daly Papers and Letters, New York Public Library (cited hereafter as CPDPL). "All Quiet Along the Potomac Tonight" was a poem written by Ethel Lynn Beers and published in *Harper's Weekly* in November 1861. Popularity of the piece led to J. H. Hewitt setting the words to music, and it was published as a song in 1863. By comparison, Michael Corcoran's counterpart Thomas Francis Meagher's letters and writings did not show the same lyrical style as his fellow Irish-born commander. That is not to say he was not musical: Meagher was known to play the clarinet in his youth. While studying in England at Stonyhurst College, he was a member of the school orchestra. One account details Meagher's early anti-British sentiment after refusing to "sound a note of praise for England's victory" at Stonyhurt's annual Battle of Waterloo commemoration. David Knight, "Thomas Francis Meagher: His Stonyhurst Years," *Decis: Journal of the Waterford Archaeological and Historical Society* 59 (2003): 41–52. As a Young Irelander, Meagher also wrote poetry compositions—such as "Prison

Thoughts"—though did not set these to music. Arthur Griffith, ed., *Meagher of the Sword: Speeches of Thomas Francis Meagher in Ireland, 1846–1848* (Dublin: M. H. Gill & Son, 1916), 330–33. When compared to Corcoran, however, there is no indication Meagher engaged with Civil War song and music culture to any significant extent.

31. McCarter, *Life in the Irish Brigade*, 2.

32. Kelly to his parents, 15 January 1862, quoted by Shiels, *Forgotten Irish*, 118. William McCarter also referred to marching Irish soldiers singing "John Brown's Body," McCarter, *Life in the Irish Brigade*, 57–58. For more on this ballad's influence, see Stauffer and Soskis, *Battle Hymn of the Republic*.

33. Kelly to his parents, 27 November 1862, quoted by Shiels, *Forgotten Irish*, 122. Given the letter's date, Kelly likely heard the song during 28th Massachusetts Thanksgiving commemorations.

34. "Mary Le More" (Glasgow: Robert McIntosh, ca. 1849). "Mary Le More" has been described as an Irish land laborer/tenant farmer clearance and eviction song in Shiels, *Forgotten Irish*, 124. Scottish broadside copies reveal its lyrical origins across the Irish Sea in Liverpool, home to sizable Irish and Scots-Irish communities in the mid-nineteenth century. See "'Mary Le More' Commentary," National Library of Scotland, http://digital.nls.uk/broadsides/broadside.cfm/id/16531.

35. Davis, *Music Along the Rapidan*, 45; 61–62.

36. Shields, *Narrative Singing in Ireland*, 52.

37. Shiels, *Forgotten Irish*, 117.

38. Davis, *Music Along the Rapidan*, 61–62.

39. Daniel Crowley to Cornelius Flynn, 6 December 1864, Daniel Crowley Letters to Cornelius Flynn, BA. Given the correspondence's date, Crowley possibly gifted the war ballad to his friend around the Thanksgiving or Christmas period, and the reference to "A. and W." were likely friends or family relations familiar to both Crowley and Flynn.

40. Jones to his parents, 27 August 1863, in Taylor, *Wales and the American Civil War*, 44.

41. Charles Graham Halpine, *The Life and Adventures, Songs, Services and Speeches of Private Miles O'Reilly [Pseud.], 47th Regiment, New York Volunteers, with Comic Illustrations by Mullen, from the Authentic Records of the 'New York Herald'* (New York: Carleton, 1864). Halpine also asked his wife Margaret "to send him volumes of Irish poems and ballads" for performances in camp and to aid his own lyrical productions. William Hanchett, *Irish: Charles Graham Halpine in Civil War America* (Syracuse: Syracuse University Press, 1970), 46. For further analysis of Halpine's wartime lyrical productions and O'Reilly's songs, see chaps. 6 and 7.

42. Richard Oulahan, "Camp Song of the Sixty-Ninth," *Irish-American*, 15 June 1861.

43. Thomas J. MacEvily, "War Song of the Irish Brigade," *Irish-American*, 30 November 1861.

44. "Editor's Drawer," *Harper's New Monthly Magazine*, April 1864 (New York). Given the date that this Canadian Corcoran composition was sent to the periodical, it was likely written as a eulogy after Corcoran's death in December 1863. Its full title was: "A Copy of Four Verses of Poetry Being Verses . . . Composed On The Pedigree—Emigration and Military-Career Of, Brigadier General Corcoran, Up to the Time That He Left New York the Second Time for the Battlefield." That one stanza printed by the periodical was from the sixteenth verse provides a reason why it was turned down for full publication—wartime lyrical productions were rarely overly long (eight to ten stanzas, with an average of six).

45. Charles Bryne, "Campaign Song of the Democracy!" (1858).

46. John Savage to Charles P. Daly, 10 September 1861, CPDPL.

47. Maria Lydig Daly, 28 July 1861, *Diary of a Union Lady, 1861–1865,* ed. Harold Earl Hammond (Lincoln: University of Nebraska Press, 2000), 43. Savage produced Irish nationalist poems prior to emigrating in 1848 and continued to do so after arriving in the United States of America.

48. 17 October 1861, ibid., 64.

49. 2 January 1864, ibid., 273.

50. 7 November 1861, ibid., 73.

51. 13 October 1862, ibid., 186–87.

52. "Words and Music by an Irishman," "Corcoran to His Regiment—Or 'I Would Not Take Parole'" (Boston: Horace Partridge, 1861).

53. "The Monster Festival: Aid for the Widows and Orphans of the Sixty-ninth Regiment,' *New York Times* (New York), 30 August 1861.

54. "Pat Murphy of Meagher's Brigade" (New York: H. De Marsan, 1863).

55. See Anbinder, *Five Points.*

56. Williams, *'Twas Only an Irishman's Dream,* 118–19. Pastor also produced a number of his own songster collections, including *Tony Pastor's Irish Comic Songster* (New York: Dick & Fitzgerald, ca. 1860s).

57. McWhirter, *Battle Hymns,* 16 and 2.

58. Alfred M. Williams, "Folk-Songs of the Civil War," 268.

59. Steven R. Boyd, *Patriotic Envelopes of the Civil War: The Iconography of Union and Confederate Covers* (Baton Rouge: Louisiana State University Press, 2010), 14, 60.

60. F. Collins, "Battle of Bull Run" (New York: J. Wrigley, 1861).

61. Unknown Lyricist, "Free and Easy of Our Union!" (Boston: Horace Partridge. 1861).

62. Magnus migrated from Germany in the 1840s, Ditson's family had Scottish roots but the printer was born in Boston, and Partridge came from Massachusetts. Marsan's naturalization documentation from 24 October 1860 notes he had French familial connections, but the record gives no reference to his place of birth. It also fails to include his occupation but lists his address as "38 Chatham Street," one of the locations—along with number 60 Chatham Street—where Marsan produced and sold his songsheets and other singing, musical, and printed ephemera. Common Pleas Court, Petitions for Naturalization Index—New York City/New York County Courts (1860), National Archives.

63. The centrality of Boston's publishing world demonstrates how close companies were in the nineteenth century, and their connections can still be seen on ghost signs and remaining buildings to this day. Ditson began his print culture career with a counter at the Old Corner Book Store at 277 Washington Street, close to the Old State House, Faneuil Hall Marketplace, and beside the modern-day Boston Irish Famine memorial. Until 1865, Ticknor and Fields, who also published the *Atlantic Monthly* nearby in their Tremont Street building, owned the store. Ditson himself had more property interests along Washington Street. Within five minutes walk from these locations, Horace Partridge's wartime emporium was based at 27 Hanover Street (now the site of the New England Holocaust Memorial, across from the Yankee Publishing House building).

64. For examples of this collection practice and how young women particularly created their own musical scorebooks comprised of European classical and operatic pieces alongside traditional Irish and Scottish folk items, see Bailey, *Charleston Belles Abroad.*

65. McWhirter, *Battle Hymns,* 121.

66. *Virginia Songster* (Richmond, VA: J. W. Randolph, 1863).

67. *Camp Songs* advertisement, *Dwight's Journal of Music*, 8 June 1861.

68. *War Songs for Freemen* advertisement, *Dwight's Journal of Music*, 5 March 1864.

69. "Song for the Irish Brigade," in *Hopkins's New-Orleans 5 Cent Song-Book* (New Orleans: Hopkins, ca. 1861), 14–15.

70. "New Orleans Song of the Times" (15–16) and "Song of the Times" (4–5), both in *Hopkins's New-Orleans 5 Cent Song-Book*.

71. "Erin's Dixie," in *The Southern Flag Song Book* (Vicksburg & Augusta: H. C. Clarke, 1863), 20–21.

72. Gleeson, *Green and the Gray*, 47, 52.

73. Kate C. M., "The Irish Brigade," 58–59; "By Himself," "Paddy the Loyal," 36–37; H. Angelo, "How Are You Jeffy Davis," 9–11; H. Angelo, "A National Melody," 34–36, in *The Continental Songster: A Collection of New, Spirited, Patriotic Songs, for the Times* (Philadelphia: A. Winch, 1863).

74. John F. Poole, "Pat's Opinion of the Stars and Stripes," in *The Camp-Fire Songster*, 67–68.

75. Davis, *Music Along the Rapidan*, 52.

76. *Combination Song* Advertisement, *Dwight's Journal of Music*, 1 May 1864.

77. William Dunn, "The Father of All Songs" (New York: H. De Marsan, 1864).

3. BATTLEFIELD BALLADRY

1. Meagher, *Last Days of the 69th in Virginia*, 12–13.

2. Ibid., 12–13.

3. Unknown Lyricist, "To the Glorious 69th!" (New York: H. De Marsan, 1861).

4. "The Gallant Sons of Erin" (New York: H. De Marsan, 1861).

5. F. Collins, "Battle of Bull Run" (New York: James Wrigley, 1861). The reference to Johnson's forces appears to be a conflation of Confederate Generals Jackson and Johnston who the Irish faced at the First Bull Run.

6. Arthur McCann, "Battle of Bull's Run," in Wright, *Irish Emigrant Ballads and Songs*, 457–58.

7. For exploration of cultural expressions about martial identity in Irish history, see Daithi O'Hogain, *The Hero in Irish Folklore* (Dublin: Gill and Macmillan, 1985).

8. Thomas Walsh, "Our Brave Irish Champions—A New Song on the GREAT BATTLE FOUGHT IN AMERICA! On Sunday, 21st of July, 1861" (Cork: Haly, 1861).

9. "New Song on the Dreadful Engagement, and Tremendous Loss of the Irish in America" (1862), in Wright, *Irish Emigrant Ballads and Songs*, 461.

10. "A New Song on the Last Battle Fought in America" (Ireland, 1862), in Wright, *Irish Emigrant Ballads and Songs*, 463.

11. P. J. Fitzpatrick, "A Lamentation on the American War—Awful Battle at Vicksburg" (Ireland, 1863), in Wright, *Irish Emigrant Ballads and Songs*, 459–60.

12. Corcoran, *Captivity of General Corcoran*, 23–24.

13. Meagher, *Last Days of the 69th in Virginia*, 11.

14. Mr. Mullaly, "Long Live the Sixty-Ninth" (New York: James Wrigley, 1861); Robert Smith, "We Will Have the Union Still" (New York: James Wrigley, 1861).

15. Unknown Lyricist, "The Gallant 69th Regiment" (New York: H. De Marsan, 1862).

16. "The Irish Brigade" (Boston: Horace Partridge, January 1862).

17. Daniel Crowley to Cornelius Flynn, 2 April 1864, Daniel Crowley Letters to Cornelius Flynn, BA.

18. P. T. Hade, "Camp Song of the Chicago Irish Brigade" (Chicago: Root & Cady, 1861). Archive catalogues confuse and acknowledge the local, regional, and national fluidity of Hade's song title. Root & Cady's music scorebook often appears simultaneously as both "Camp Song of the Chicago Irish Brigade" and as "Camp Song of the Irish Brigade" in library records. The ballad is, at times, referred to as "Camp Song of the (Chicago) Irish Brigade" in this book to reflect this song's subject conflation.

19. P. T. Hade, "Camp Song of the Irish Brigade" (Philadelphia: A. W. Auner, ca. 1862).

20. "Song for the Irish Brigade," in *Hopkins' New-Orleans 5 Cent Song-Book* (New Orleans: John Hopkins, 1861), 14–15.

21. Unknown Lyricist, "Young Ireland and Ould America" (New York: H. De Marsan, 1862).

22. Corby, *Memoirs of Chaplain Life*, 63.

23. "Young Ireland and Ould America."

24. Ural, *The Harp and the Eagle*, 101, 120.

25. Patrick Collins to his sister, 24 January 1864, Application WC94716, *Approved Pension Applications of Widows and Other Dependents of Civil War Veterans*, CWWP.

26. Unknown Lyricist, "The Irish Brigade in America," also known as "The Soldier's Letter from America" (Glasgow: James Lindsay, 1863).

27. The estimated 45 percent Irish Brigade loss at Fredericksburg through death, injury, and missing soldiers was spread across its five regiments. See Ural, *Harp and the Eagle*, 132–33.

28. Corby described the battle slaughter and Irish Brigade's post-Fredericksburg mood as "sad, very sad," Corby, *Memoirs of a Chaplain Life*, 133–34.

29. "Irish Brigade in America."

30. Ural, *Harp and Eagle*, 134.

31. "Alexis," "The Irish Brigade at Fredericksburg," *Irish-American* (New York: Lynch & Cole), 31 January 1863.

32. Kate M. Boylan, "The Irish Dead on Fredericksburg Heights," *Irish-American,* 2 May 1863.

33. Ural, "'Ye Sons of Green Erin Assemble,'" 113.

34. For example, few general song lyrics exist about the Battle of Gettysburg's three days of fighting, a marked contrast to how the engagement has dominated postwar memory and Civil War studies.

35. P. J. Fitzpatrick, "A Lamentation of the American War—Awful Battle at Vicksburg" (Ireland: Unknown Publisher, 1863).

36. Hugh F. McDermott, "The Irish Brigade" (New York: Frank McElroy, 1863).

37. Crowley to Flynn, 17 May 1865. Daniel Crowley Letters to Cornelius Flynn, BA.

38. Corcoran, *Captivity of General Corcoran,* 94–95.

39. M. B. Fields to Charles P. Daly, Invitation to "The Ball in Honor of the Prince of Wales," 3 October 1860, CPDPL. Queen Victoria's heir, Prince Edward of Wales (later Britain's King Edward VII), toured North America for five months from 10 July–15 November 1860, visiting Canada and the United States.

40. Charles Graham Halpine, one of Corcoran's acquaintances, later wrote that the refusal to march in the parade "was an Irish demonstration for an Irish object to illustrate an Irish sentiment."

Corcoran was not punished because there was "a token of sympathy that exists between the American and Irish people" in relation to Irish nationalism. See Halpine, *The Life and Adventures,* 86.

41. "Col. Corcoran and the Prince of Wales" (New York: James Wrigley, 1861).

42. Although Irish American Civil War songs stopped referring to the story after 1861, Corcoran's Prince of Wales incident remained well-known after the war. In 1868, when Prince Edward visited Ireland, one American newspaper commented that New York's Knights of St. Patrick should give Edward the same Order of St. Patrick he would receive across the Atlantic. This would "make reparation to their royal brother for the plebeian patriotism of the 69th, who refused the Prince" in 1861, "Attention Sir Knights," *Irish Republican* (Chicago), 28 March 1868.

43. Robert Smith, "We Will Have the Union Still" (New York: James Wrigley, 1861).

44. Unknown Lyricist, "Free and Easy of Our Union!" (Boston: Horace Partridge, 1861). Elsewhere in this general Union song, lyrics sang about the 69th New York's Bull Run actions:

Glory to those sons of Erin,
Who fought with an Iron will;
Told the Southrons what may happen,
They were for the Union still.

45. Richard Oulahan, "Corcoran! The Prisoner of War," *Irish-American,* 6 September 1862.

46. John F. Poole, "Pat's Opinion of the Stars and Stripes," in *The Camp-Fire Songster,* 67–68.

47. William P. Ferris, "Return of Gen. Corcoran, of the Glorious 69th" (Boston: Horace Partridge, 1862).

48. "Monthly Record of Current Events," in *Harper's New Monthly Magazine* (New York), October 1862.

49. "Editor's Easy Chair," in *Harper's New Monthly Magazine,* October 1862. Castle Green was the former name of Castle Clinton in the Battery Park area on the tip of Manhattan Island where immigrant arrivals first docked prior to the opening of Ellis Island across the water in 1892. During the Civil War, troops (including many Union Army Irish soldiers) embarked and disembarked from the fort as they headed to the Southern states and returned from theaters of the conflict. An image of what Corcoran's return would have looked like can be gleaned from Louis Lang's 1862 painting, *Return of the 69th (Irish) Regiment, N.Y.S.M. from the Seat of War* (now held by the New York Historical Society Museum and Library). The German-born artist captured Thomas Francis Meagher leading the 69th New York back to the city after the First Bull Run, although the painting also depicts enthusiastic enlistment spirits. Corcoran himself appears on a newspaper cover in the bottom right of the painting, which references his prisoner captivity at the time Lang's work was produced.

50. Crowley to Flynn, 12 November 1864. Daniel Crowley Letters to Cornelius Flynn, BA.

51. F. Collins, "The 69th Brigade" (New York: James Wrigley, 1862).

52. Frank Spear, "The New York Volunteer," in *Camp-Fire Songster,* 23–24. Also published by James Wrigley in New York (1862).

53. Thomas Francis Meagher to Charles P. Daly, 23 August 1861, CPDPL.

54. Charles Corkery to Charles P. Daly, 13 September 1861, CPDPL.

55. Ural, *Harp and Eagle,* 89.

56. Arthur McCann, "Battle of Bull's Run."

57. William Corby defended Meagher's memory, arguing his "character, is, I think, not well understood by many." He argued Meagher had "the bearing of a prince . . . was polite and gentlemanly, even when under the influence of liquor," Corby, *Memoirs of Chaplain Life,* 28–30. Meagher was a wartime alcoholic who, at times, struggled with command and the horrors of conflict. Circumstantial evidence and omissions from soldiers such as William McCarter (who served as his temporary secretary prior to Fredericksburg) add weight to home-front rumors about his character and conduct. In contrast to Corcoran, Meagher's wartime behavior was markedly different. The former was selfless, the latter more selfish. Yet, on the basis of contemporary song sentiments alone, another side of Meagher appears. Despite his character flaws, ballads portrayed him in an inspirational and uncritical light, akin to how many of his men described and remembered him.

58. McDermott, "Irish Brigade."

59. Thomas J. MacEvily, "War Song of the Irish Brigade," *Irish-American,* 30 November 1861.

60. Michael O'Riely, "The Irish Volunteers" (New York: James Wrigley, 1862).

61. Halpine, *Life and Adventures,* 187.

62. William Sutherland, "What Irish Boys Can Do—Answer to 'No Irish Need Apply'" (New York: H. De Marsan, 1863).

63. Unknown Lyricist, "O'Toole & McFinnigan on the War" (Boston: Horace Partridge, 1863).

64. Ural, *Harp and Eagle,* 110.

65. Richard Oulahan, "Corcoran's Zouaves," *Irish-American,* 21 November 1863.

66. Michael Corcoran to Charles P. Daly, 28 November 1862, CPDPL.

67. Richard Oulahan, "Corcoran's Irish Legion," *Irish-American,* 29 August 1863. Whatever Oulahan's views of his 1863 war service, his commander did not share this lyrical frustration. In the Legion's early days, Corcoran wrote: "the Irish Legion is now everything its most ardent friends could desire," Corcoran to Daly, 13 January 1863, CPDPL.

68. Eugene T. Johnston, "Corcoran's Irish Legion" (Boston: Horace Partridge, 1863). The lyrical depiction of giving "old Stone wall Irish thunder" is a reference to how Corcoran's 69th New York State Militia faced Confederate General Stonewall Jackson at the First Battle of Bull Run in July 1861 (another ballad reference to the memory of Irish service at that particular battle engagement).

69. John Mahon, "Corcoran's Ball!" (New York: H. De Marsan, 1863). The "New" Bowery Theater was at the cultural heart of New York's immigrant neighborhoods.

70. Corcoran to Daly, 13 January 1863, CPDPL.

71. Corcoran, *Captivity of General Corcoran,* 27.

72. "Mary of Montreal," "Written on Hearing the Death of General Corcoran," *Irish-American,* 30 January 1864. The Canadian location of the ballad poem's author is the same as "A Copy of Four Verses of Poetry Being Verses about Corcoran" sent to *Harper's New Monthly Magazine* in April 1864, as discussed in chap. 2.

73. Crowley to Flynn, 30 June 1864. Daniel Crowley Letters to Cornelius Flynn, BA.

74. "Bessie of Clifton, Long Island," "The Irish Brigade," *Irish-American,* 30 July 1864.

75. David Gleeson, "Irish Rebels, Southern Rebels: The Irish Confederates," in *Civil War Citizens,* ed. Susannah J. Ural (New York: New York University Press, 2010), 141–42.

76. "Erin's Dixie," in *The Southern Flag Song Book* (Vicksburg & Augusta: H. C. Clarke, 1863), 20–21.

77. Gleeson, "Irish Rebels, Southern Rebels," 139.

78. A. B. Meek, "Our Country's Heroes," in *The Southern Soldier's Prize Songster: Containing Material and Patriotic Pieces (Chiefly Original) Applicable to the Present War* (Mobile: W. F. Wisley, 1864), 9–12.

79. "The Late Captain E. K. Butler," *Irish-American,* 23 July 1864.

80. "Pat Rooney and His Little Ones," *Irish-American,* 24 May 1862.

81. Thomas Donnelly, "The New York Volunteer" (ca. 1862), in Wright, *Irish Emigrant Ballads and Songs,* 453.

82. Timothy B. O'Regan, "Save the Constitution" (New York: James Wrigley, 1862).

83. Thomas Francis Meagher, quoted by W. F. Lyons, *Brigadier General T. F. Meagher; His Political and Military Career, with Selections from His Speeches and Writings* (Glasgow: Cameron and Ferguson, 1871), 79.

84. Arthur McFadden, "Col. Owens' Gallant Irish Volunteers" (Philadelphia: A. W. Auner, 1861).

85. M. Fay, "Irish Volunteers—Penn'a's Gallant 69th" (Philadelphia: Johnson, 1863).

86. Unknown Lyricist, "Pat Murphy of Meagher's Brigade" (Boston: Horace Partridge, 1863).

87. Arthur McCann, "Irish Volunteer" (Philadelphia: A. W. Auner, ca. 1862).

88. Tony Pastor, "The Irish Volunteer, No. 3" (New York: James Wrigley 1862).

4. LYRICAL CULTURAL IDENTITY

1. Kathleen O'Neil, "No Irish Need Apply" (Philadelphia: J. H. Johnson, 1862).

2. "Cead Mille Failthe—General Meagher Recruiting the Irish Brigade—Enthusiastic Gathering at the Seventh New York Regiment Armory—Speech by General Meagher—A Rousing Meeting!" *New York Herald* (New York), 26 July 1862.

3. "Erin's Dixie," in *The Southern Flag Song Book* (Vicksburg & Augusta: H. C. Clarke, 1863), 20–21.

4. Stephen McGarry, *Irish Brigades Abroad: From the Wild Geese to the Napoleonic Wars* (Dublin: The History Press Ireland, 2013).

5. Thomas J. MacEvily, "War Song of the Irish Brigade," *Irish-American,* 30 November 1861.

6. Kate C. M., "The Irish Brigade," in *The Continental Songster,* 58–59.

7. Unknown Lyricist, "The Irish Brigade in America," also known as "The Soldier's Letter from America" (Glasgow: James Lindsay, 1863).

8. Hugh F. McDermott, "The Irish Brigade" (New York: Frank McElroy, 1863). Boxwood (buxus) have small green leaves similar to shamrock.

9. Corby, *Memoirs of Chaplain Life,* 132.

10. Ural, *Harp and the Eagle,* 125.

11. "War Song of the New-York 69th Regiment" (New York: H. De Marsan, 1861).

12. William P. Ferris, "Return of Gen. Corcoran, of the Glorious 69th" (Boston: Horace Partridge, 1862).

13. Wellington's Irish roots should not be confused for a sense of Irishness. His family had several estates in Ireland and were part of the upper-class Anglo-Irish Protestant social order. Wellington himself was seen as the epitome of eighteenth- and nineteenth-century British (Anglo) military identity.

14. Unknown Lyricist, "Glorious 69th" (New York: James Wrigley, 1861).

15. O'Neil, "No Irish Need Apply."

16. William Sutherland, "What Irish Boys Can Do—Answer to 'No Irish Need Apply'" (New York: H. De Marsan, 1863).

17. Eugene T. Johnston, "What Irishmen Have Done" (New York: Charles Magnus, ca. 1866–70).

18. Gleeson, "Irish Rebels, Southern Rebels," 135.

19. Corby, *Memoirs of Chaplain Life,* 307.

20. "The Irish Volunteer," quoted by Wright, *Irish Emigrant Ballads and Songs,* 472–73. The lyrics here allude to St. Patrick's famed removal of snakes from the island of Ireland in the fifth century. For a recent analysis of the Battle of Vinegar Hill, see Ronan O'Flaherty and Jacqui Hynes, eds., *Vinegar Hill: The Last Stand of the Wexford Rebels of 1798* (Dublin: Four Courts Press, 2021).

21. Alongside Fontenoy, Waterloo, and the Crimean War, the Confederate ballad "On to Richmond" described the Union's advance around the Confederate capital as "worse than Culloden," referring to the infamous Scottish 1745 battle that aided the destruction of the Jacobite rising against the British Crown. See "On to Richmond," in *Virginia Songster* (Richmond, VA: J. W. Randolph, 1863), 59–63.

22. "Words and Music by an Irishman," "Corcoran to his Regiment—Or, 'I Would Not Take Parole'" (Boston: Horace Partridge, 1861).

23. It is unclear *which* O'Neill was being referred to in these lyrics: Hugh O'Neill, Earl of Tyrone ("The O'Neill") who resisted Tudor rule and conquest of the island of Ireland in the late 1500s, or Owen Roe O'Neill, the Gaelic chieftain who fought in Spain in the 1600s with the Spanish Irish Brigade. The lyrical conflation of all again highlights the lack of historical accuracy in songwriting memory.

24. "Song for the Irish Brigade," in *Hopkins' New-Orleans 5 Cent Song-Book* (New Orleans: John Hopkins, 1861), 14–15.

25. O'Neil, "No Irish Need Apply."

26. "No Irish Need Apply" (Philadelphia: William. A. Stephens, 1864), quoted by Wright, *Irish Emigrant Ballads and Songs,* 526.

27. St. Clair Augustine Mulholland, quoted by Corby, *Memoirs of Chaplain Life,* 351.

28. Conyngham, *The Irish Brigade and Its Campaigns,* 6.

29. Father James M. Dillon, quoted by Corby, *Memoirs of Chaplain Life,* 296. The Battle of Chapultepec took place during the Mexican-American War in September 1847.

30. Michael Corcoran to Charles P. Daly, 13 January 1863, CPDPL.

31. Thomas Walsh, "Our Brave Irish Champions—A New Song on the GREAT BATTLE FOUGHT IN AMERICA! On Sunday 21st of July, 1861" (Cork: Haly, 1861).

32. Aloys Fleischmann, "Granny Wales, and the Mulberry Tree," *Isaiah Thomas Broadside Ballads Project,* http://www.americanantiquarian.org/thomasballads/items/show/120.

33. Thomas M. Brown, "Cead Mille Fealthe" (Boston: Oliver Ditson, 1864).

34. Ferris, "Return of Gen. Corcoran, of the Glorious 69th."

35. Unknown Lyricist, "Glorious 69th."

36. "Words and Music by an Irishman," "Corcoran to His Regiment, Or 'I Would Not Take Parole'" (Boston: Horace Partridge, 1861).

37. Unknown Lyricist, "The Irish Brigade in America."

38. Unknown Lyricist, "War Song of the New-York 69th Regiment."

39. "By Corporal Barney," "The Irish-American Army," in *Stephens' Fenian Songster* (ca. 1866), quoted by Wright, *Irish Emigrant Ballads and Songs*, 439–40.

40. Patrick Kelly to his parents, 19 January 1862, quoted by Shiels, *Forgotten Irish*, 119.

41. Unknown Lyricist, "Song for the Irish Brigade."

42. Joseph Brenan, "A Ballad for the Young South," in *War Songs of the South* (Richmond, VA: West & Johnson, 1862), 25–29.

43. Unknown Lyricist, "Song for the Irish Brigade."

44. "The Escape of Meagher" (1852), quoted by Zimmermann, *Songs of Irish Rebellion*, 242–43. In more anglicized (and less poetical) phrasing, the song's lyrics translate as: "It's plain to see, for Ireland Forever they still have a love."

45. Fleischmann, "Granny Wales."

46. Kenny, *The American Irish*, 121. The San Patricios's flag had the Mexican coat of arms on the other side, presenting a complex display of Irish and Mexican transnational identity affiliation. See Samito, *Becoming American Under Fire*, 23. The San Patricios were comprised of several hundred deserters from American service, including many Irish Catholic migrants and soldiers from other European nations. They were led by John Patrick Riley, an Irish-born former British Army and United States Army enlistee.

47. Kate C. M., "Irish Brigade."

48. McDermott, "Irish Brigade."

49. "Erin's Dixie," in *The Southern Flag Song Book* (Vicksburg & Augusta: H. C. Clarke, 1863), 20–21.

50. *Fenian Songster* (ca. 1867), The Mick Moloney Irish-American Music and Popular Culture Irish Americana Collection, The Tamimnet Library and Robert F. Wagner Labor Archives, New York University. Songsters solely in Irish were rarer still in mid-nineteenth-century American public print circulation.

51. "Cead Mile Fealthe" should be written in Irish as "Céad Míle Fáilte." "Erin go Bragh" was the common anglicized form of the original "Érinn go Brách," although there are other Irish spelling variations. Likewise, "Faugh a Ballagh" had several alternatives, including "Fág an Bealach." Multiple English and Irish spellings of Granuaile follow a similar practice. The lack of one standard Irish spelling (a common occurrence in Celtic languages) contributes to the myriad of anglicized translations. Various Civil War lyrical differences reflect this linguistic custom.

52. For current research on the use of Irish in the nineteenth century in the United States, see Bobbie Nolan, "Language and Identity among Irish migrants in London, Philadelphia and San Francisco, 1850–1920" (PhD diss., University of Edinburgh, 2020).

53. Corporal Barney, "Irish-American Army."

54. P. J. Fitzpatrick, "A Lamentation on the American War—Awful Battle at Vicksburg" (1863), quoted by Wright, *Irish Emigrant Ballads*, 459–60.

55. Meagher, *Last Days of the 69th in Virginia*, 9.

56. Thomas Francis Meagher, "Recruiting the Irish Brigade," quoted in the *New York Times*, 26 July 1862. Mention of Robert Emmet's name was met with "loud cheers" according to reports. In his famous 1803 "Speech from Dock," Emmet declared: "Let no man write my epitaph . . . When my country takes her place among the nations of the earth, then and not till then, let my epitaph be written." His words inspired Young Irelanders and Fenians involved in the American Civil War,

but he rarely appeared in contemporary American song lyrics and ballads about transnational support for Irish nationalism.

57. Peter Welsh to Margaret Welsh, 31 March 1863, in Peter Welsh, *Irish Green and Union Blue: The Civil War Letters of Peter Welsh, Color Sergeant 28th Regiment Massachusetts Volunteers,* ed. Lawrence Frederick Kohl and Margaret Cassé Richard (New York: Fordham University, 1986), 79–80.

58. Welsh to Margaret Welsh, 31 March 1863, ibid., 81–82. Margaret Welsh's hesitation was understandable: carrying the standard made her husband a target for Confederate sharpshooters. By the time Welsh was made color bearer, the story of Irish-born Thomas Plunkett's heroic efforts to keep the 21st Massachusetts regimental flag aloft at the Battle of Fredericksburg in December 1862 was known across the nation—while upholding the banner, Plunkett was shot several times, eventually losing both his arms through sustained injury (see chap. 7 for further discussion of this incident). Welsh attempted to pacify his wife's concerns, explaining how Irish-dominated 28th Massachusetts had "been in seven battles and had one color bearer killed . . . he carried the national flag. In all the seven battles there was but two men wounded carrying the green flag."

59. Kate C. M., "Irish Brigade."

60. Samito, *Becoming American Under Fire,* 104.

61. Brown, "Cead Mille Fealthe."

62. Eugene T. Johnston, "Corcoran's Irish Legion" (Boston: Horace Partridge, 1863).

63. Colonel W. S. Hawkins, "The Hero Without a Name" (October 1864), in *War Lyrics and Songs of the South* (London: Spottiswoode & Co., 1866), 69–73.

64. "Words and Music by an Irishman," "Corcoran to His Regiment."

65. Unknown Lyricist, "War Song of the Irish Brigade."

66. "Irish Volunteer," quoted by Wright, *Irish Emigrant Songs and Battles,* 472–73.

67. Michael O'Riely, "The Irish Volunteers" (New York: James Wrigley, 1862).

68. Unknown Lyricist, "The Gallant 69th Regiment" (New York: H. De Marsan, 1862).

69. Unknown Lyricist, "War Song of the New-York 69th Regiment."

70. Meagher, *Last Days of the 69th in Virginia,* 6.

71. Corcoran, *Captivity of General Corcoran,* 95.

72. Unknown Lyricist, "Pat Murphy of Meagher's Brigade" (Boston: Horace Partridge, 1863).

73. Unknown Lyricist, "The Irish Brigade" (Boston: Horace Partridge, January 1862).

74. Unknown Lyricist, "The Harp of Old Erin and Banner of Stars" (New York: H. De Marsan, 1861).

75. Kate C. M., "Irish Brigade."

5. FENIAN SENTIMENTS AND IRISH NATIONALISM SYMPATHIES

1. "The Irish Volunteer," quoted by Wright, *Irish Emigrant Ballads and Songs.* When the Southern states seceded, McDonald headed "to a recruiting-office . . . that happened to be near, and joined the good old 'Sixty-ninth,'" like an Irish volunteer"—a reference to 69th New York State Militia enlistment.

2. Sentiments about Famine suffering and anti-British hostility were expressed on a mostly

equal basis across immigrant generations. The influence of disseminated contemporary opinions by Young Ireland exiles, such as John Mitchel, kept the argument that the British were to blame in Irish transnational discourse. Studies on the diaspora's intergenerational memory transmission reveal how attitudes and trauma were passed along to children and grandchildren—even among those with no direct lived experience of events. See John Herson's work on the Irish in Britain and the central role family played in shaping generational lives, identity, memory-making, and community family history knowledge. John Herson, *Divergent Paths: Family Histories of Irish Emigrants in Britain, 1820–1920* (Manchester: Manchester University Press, 2015).

3. "The Irish Brigade in America," also known as "The Soldier's Letter from America" (Glasgow: James Lindsay, 1863).

4. F. Collins, "The 69th Brigade" (New York: James Wrigley, 1862). The reference to Queen Victoria's subscription fund was a lyrical comment about the monarch's personal Famine relief donation (around £2,000 pounds, not the £50 mentioned in the song). For more on immediate relief efforts sent from the United States in the 1840s, see Stephen Puleo, *Voyage of Mercy: The USS Jamestown, The Irish Famine, and the Remarkable Story of America's First Humanitarian Mission* (New York: St. Martin's Press, 2020).

5. New York Friendly Sons of St. Patrick Invitation, 24 March 1863, CPDPL.

6. Corby, *Memoirs of Chaplain Life,* 147.

7. Michael Corcoran to Charles P. Daly, 13 May 1863, CPDPL.

8. F. Collins, "The 69th Brigade."

9. "St. Patrick's Day" (New York: James Wrigley, ca. 1865).

10. Michael O'Riely, "The Irish Volunteers" (New York: James Wrigley, 1862).

11. Unknown Lyricist, "Pat Murphy of Meagher's Brigade" (Boston: Horace Partridge, 1863).

12. Daniel Crowley to Cornelius Flynn, 29 September 1864, Daniel Crowley Letters to Cornelius Flynn, BA.

13. O'Regan, "Save the Constitution" (New York: James Wrigley, 1862).

14. Peter Welsh to Patrick Prendergast, 1 June 1863, in Welsh, *Irish Green and Union Blue,* 103.

15. *The Ottawa Free Trader* (Illinois), 28 November 1863. The report detailed events at the Fenians' first national convention and described how attendees swore allegiance "to the Constitution and laws of the United States of America," alongside voicing Union support. Fenian Congress Resolution, Chicago, November 1863, quoted by William D. Griffin, ed., *The Irish in America, 550–1972: A Chronology and Fact Book* (New York: Oceana Publications, 1973), 86.

16. Ural, "'Ye Sons of Green Erin Assemble,'" 127.

17. William H. Lindsay, "The Green Above the Red" (New York: H. De Marsan, ca. 1860). In reference to the dual flag symbology seen in Fenian ballads discussed in this chapter, it is worth noting that one Marsan-printed copy of Lindsay's song included a decorative border with the image of a Union Army general rallying soldiers while waving the Stars and Stripes, cementing pictorially an American connection to the lyrics published beside it.

18. Eugene T. Johnston, "What Irishmen Have Done" (New York: Charles Magnus, ca. 1866–70).

19. Unknown Lyricist, "Our Own Flag of Green" (New York: James Wrigley, ca. 1860).

20. "The Fenian's Welcome to Ireland" (ca. 1860), quoted by Zimmermann, *Songs of Irish Rebellion,* 31.

21. Malcolm Campbell, *Ireland's New Worlds: Immigrants, Politics and Society in the United States and Australia, 1815–1922* (Madison: University of Wisconsin Press, 2008), 107.

22. Exact Fenian Brotherhood numbers vary. Snay estimates the figure as around 45,000. Mitchel Snay, *Fenians, Freedmen, and Southern Whites: Race and Nationality in the Era of Reconstruction* (Baton Rouge: Louisiana State University Press, 2007), 56. Brundage argues the organization claimed there were 50,000 members in 1865. David Brundage, *Irish Nationalist in America: The Politics of Exile, 1798–1998* (New York: Oxford University Press, 2016), 103. That represents around a quarter of Irish-born Union and Confederate soldiers. Kevin Kenny suggests the figure was as high as 250,000 members by 1865, "many of them Civil War veterans." See Kenny, *The American Irish,* 128. Active Fenians were a minority in the Irish American diaspora, but sympathies for Irish nationalism were more widespread.

23. Lawrence J. McCaffrey, *The Irish Diaspora in America* (Bloomington: Indiana University Press, 1976), 121.

24. Fallows, *Irish American: Identity and Assimilation,* 54. David Sim has also highlighted how the Irish Republican Brotherhood (the Fenian's sister organization in Ireland) paid close attention to Civil War recruitment. In spring 1864, their leader James Stephens traveled across the Atlantic to tour Union Army camps in an effort to raise money and build nationalist networks. David Sim, *A Union Forever: The Irish Question and U.S. Foreign Relations in the Victorian Age* (Ithaca, NY: Cornell University Press, 2013), 87–88.

25. *Ottawa Free Trader,* 28 November 1863.

26. Ural, *Harp and the Eagle,* 55.

27. McCaffrey, *Irish Diaspora in America,* 121.

28. Thomas Francis Meagher, quoted by Ural, *Harp and the Eagle,* 55.

29. Ural, *Harp and the Eagle,* 190.

30. Samito, *Becoming American Under Fire,* 121–22.

31. P. J. Fitzpatrick, "Lamentation on the American War—Awful Battle at Vicksburg," quoted by Wright, *Irish Emigrant Ballads and Songs,* 459–60.

32. Ural has called this issue "a larger tragedy for the Irish in America." Ural, *Harp and the Eagle,* 76.

33. Ibid.

34. "Bessie," "The Irish Brigade," *Irish-American,* 30 July 1864.

35. Sim, *Union Forever,* 7.

36. Thomas Francis Meagher, quoted by Ural, *Harp and the Eagle,* 52.

37. "The Irish Volunteer," quoted by Wright, *Irish Emigrant Ballads and Songs,* 472–73.

38. Unknown Lyricist, *Fenians Ever More* (Boston: George D. Russell & Company, 1866).

39. "By Himself," "Paddy the Loyal," in *The Continental Songster,* 36–38.

40. Snay, *Fenians, Freedmen, and Southern Whites,* 140.

41. The Fenian Society (Chicago) to William H. Seward, 21 September 1865, The Papers of William H. Seward, Vere Harmsworth Library.

42. "By Corporal Barney," "The Irish-American Army," in *Stephens' Fenian Songster* (ca. 1866), quoted by Wright, *Irish Emigrant Ballads and Songs,* 439–40.

43. Unknown Lyricist, "Fenians Ever More."

44. Kate C. M., "The Irish Brigade," in *Continental Songster,* 58–59.

45. Fenian Society to Seward, 21 September 1865, Papers of William H. Seward, Vere Harmsworth Library.

46. Unknown Lyricist, "Pat Murphy of Meagher's Brigade."

47. Pat Murphy returned from his lyrical death in the postbellum ballad "The Finnegins," an anti-British song supportive of the "Finnegins" cause (dialect for "Fenians"). It sang of how "Pat Murphy, he stood on the shore . . . waiting to hear the Lion" after he captured a British flag in Eastport, Maine. This was a fictional reference to the real Fenian Canada raids in 1866. Frank Wilder, "The Finnegins, Or Down to Eastport Town" (Boston: Oliver Ditson, 1866).

48. Samito, *Becoming American Under Fire,* 102.

49. P. T. Hade, "Camp Song of the (Chicago) Irish Brigade" (Chicago: Root & Cady, 1861).

50. Unknown Lyricist, "The Fenian Brigade" (New York: James Wrigley, 1862).

51. "Comrades of the Cannon" (ca. 1863), quoted by the Fenian Society to Seward, 21 September 1865, Papers of William H. Seward, Vere Harmsworth Library.

52. George F. Root, "Tramp! Tramp! Tramp! The Prisoner's Hope" (Chicago: Root & Cady, 1863).

53. George F. Root, "On! On! On! The Boys Came Marching, Or, The Prisoner Free—Sequel to Tramp! Tramp! Tramp!" (Boston: Horace Partridge, 1865).

54. Unknown lyricist, "Grant to Washington Shall Go" (Boston: Horace Partridge, 1869).

55. Edith Fowke, "Canadian Variations of a Civil War Song," *Midwest Folklore* 13, no. 2 (1963): 102. Fowke's study of the Canadian legacy of "Tramp! Tramp! Tramp!" reveals that Root's American tune achieved "continued popularity . . . in Canada." It was also used for subsequent Canadian ballads produced during the Boar War (1899–1902) and World War I (1914–18). For more on the Fenian Canadian attacks, see Lawrence E. Cline, *Rebels on the Niagara: The Fenian Invasion of Canada, 1866* (New York: State University of New York Press, 2018).

56. Campbell, *Ireland's New Worlds,* 109–10. Gillian O'Brien has gone further, arguing "the movement [was] never entirely united" even before its 1866–1867 split. Gillian O'Brien, *Blood Runs Green: The Murder That Transfixed Gilded Age Chicago* (Chicago: University of Chicago Press, 2015), 22.

57. Brundage, *Irish Nationalists in America,* 103–5.

58. *Ottawa Free Trader,* 28 November 1863.

59. James H. Adams, "The Negotiated Hibernian: Discourse on the Fenian in England and America," *American Nineteenth Century History* 11, no. 1 (2010): 47, 53.

60. Corcoran, *Captivity of General Corcoran,* 22. In one letter Corcoran reported he was "expecting a visit from [Meagher] and O'Mahony," Corcoran to Daly, 11 September 1863, CPDPL. The plaque outside the house in Fairfax, Virginia, where Corcoran died in December 1863 states: "he commanded the Fenian Brotherhood of N.Y.," though most histories of the Fenian movement do not mention him as a prominent leading figure (William P. Gunnell House, Fairfax, Virginia).

61. *Irish-American,* 18 March 1861.

62. Kenneth Moss, "St. Patrick's Day Celebrations and the Foundation of Irish-American Identity, 1845–1875," *Journal of Social History* 29, no. 1 (1995): 134.

63. "Funeral Oration of the late Brigadier General Corcoran, to be delivered by Brigadier General Meagher" Invitation from John O'Mahony to Charles P. Daly, 16 January 1864, CPDPL. As the Friendly Sons of St. Patrick's president and a member of the New York Irish American elite, Daly often received invitations to Fenian Brotherhood events. Maria Lydig Daly's diary also

attests her husband was an acquaintance of O'Mahony. The Fenian leader visited the couple on several occasions, but Maria Daly—despite commenting on Irish political views in her almost-daily record—never mentioned the Fenian organization by name.

64. Thomas Francis Meagher to William H. Seward, 10 October 1865, Papers of William H. Seward, Vere Harmsworth Library.

65. Meagher's display of American loyalty in relation to Fenian politics hinted at a sentiment heard after the 1866 Fenian Canada raids when the Republican administration began to question the place of Irish nationalism in wider society, which in turn showed the division and difference between the diaspora's Fenian support and sympathy. For example, Irish-born Colonel Patrick Guiney saw himself as an American citizen, an identity reinforced by the war. Like Meagher, however, he understood Irish nationalist sympathies, stating he was "no Fenian, properly so called; but I think well of those who are, and better of their cause." Patrick Guiney to Benjamin F. Butler, 25 November 1867, quoted by Samito, *Becoming American Under Fire,* 202.

66. Meagher to Seward, 10 October 1865. The Fenians who visited Meagher were likely from the John Mitchel Circle of Montana Territory, which had approximately 150 members. Snay, *Fenians, Freedmen, and Southern Whites,* 56.

67. "Words by Mr. Mullaly," "Long Live the Sixty-Ninth" (New York: James Wrigley, 1861).

68. Charles Graham Halpine, *Baked Meats of the Funeral: A Collection of Essays, Poems, Speeches, Histories and Banquets, by Private Miles O'Reilly, Late of the 47th Regiment New York Volunteer Infantry, 10th Army Corps* (New York: Carleton, 1866).

69. Charles Graham Halpine, "Old Ireland" (1861), quoted by William Hanchett, *Irish: Charles Graham Halpine in Civil War America* (Syracuse, NY: Syracuse University Press, 1970), 153.

70. Halpine, "The Fenian Rallying Song," in *Baked Meats of the Funeral,* 236–37.

71. "Miles and the Fenians—Private Miles O'Riley in Jersey City—Major Chas. G. Halpine ('Private Miles O'Riley') is announced to speak before the Fenians, at Washington Hall, Jersey City, on Sunday evening," *New York Times,* 28 May 1865.

72. Hanchett, *Irish,* 153–55.

73. Halpine, *Baked Meats of the Funeral,* ii.

6. LYRICAL EXPRESSIONS OF WARTIME POLITICS

1. Halpine, "Song of the National Democracy," in *Life and Adventures,* 69–71.

2. For greater assessment of the New York City's Draft Riots' broader social and political tensions in relation to Civil War era racial and migrant views, see Iver Bernstein, *The New York City Draft Riots: Their Significance for American Society and Politics in the Age of the Civil War* (New York: Oxford University Press, 1990).

3. Ural, *Harp and the Eagle,* 188, 182.

4. In his study of New York Irish political violence, Michael A. Gordon observes that the Irish in New York City (and in many other Northern cities and states) were "often racist and usually loyal Democrats." Regardless, "thousands eagerly joined" Union Army Irish regiments and supported the Union cause in the 1860s. Michael A. Gordon, *The Orange Riots: Irish Political Violence in New York City, 1870 and 1871* (Ithaca, NY: Cornell University Press, 2009), 15.

5. Ural, *Harp and the Eagle,* 212.

6. Unknown Lyricist, "The Gallant 69th Regiment" (New York: H. De Marsan, 1862).

7. Hugh F. McDermott, "The Irish Brigade" (New York: Frank McElroy, 1863).

8. Unknown Lyricist, "The Irish Brigade in America," also known as "The Soldier's Letter from America" (Glasgow: James Lindsay, 1863).

9. Unknown Lyricist, "Pat Murphy of Meagher's Brigade" (Boston: Horace Partridge, 1863).

10. "Corcoran's Ball!" (1863), quoted by Sara Breitenfeldt, *The Harp of Old Erin and Banner of Stars: Irish Music from the American Civil War* (Ward Irish Music Archive, Milwaukee, WI; Lulu Press, 2011), 46. "Sconce" is a colloquial expression for "head."

11. Unknown Lyricist, "The Gallant 69th Regiment."

12. Eugene T. Johnston, *Corcoran's Irish Legion* (Boston: Horace Partridge, 1863).

13. Unknown Lyricist, "Glorious 69th" (New York: James Wrigley, 1861).

14. "The New York Volunteer" (1861), quoted by Wright, *Irish Emigrant Ballads and Songs,* 452. Donnelly's stage-name was also printed on songsheets as "Thomas Donnelly, Esquire." The line about "Southern would-be Neros" was a reference to the Roman Emperor Nero, tying the Confederacy to an image of attempted tyrannical national rule.

15. F. Collins, "Battle of Bull Run" (New York: James Wrigley, 1861).

16. John F. Poole, "Pat's Opinion of the Stars and Stripes," in *The Camp-Fire Songster,* 67–68.

17. "By D. S. F. of East Brooklyn," "New War Song of the 69th Regiment" (Boston: Horace Partridge, 1862).

18. Arthur McFadden, "Col. Owens' Gallant Irish Volunteers" (Philadelphia: A. W. Auner, 1861). "All stand clear" is another corruption of "clear the way" rhetoric discussed in chap. 4.

19. Timothy B. O'Regan, "Save the Constitution" (New York: James Wrigley, 1862).

20. Unknown Lyricist, "War Song for the 79th Regiment" (New York: James Wrigley, 1861).

21. "Song for the Irish Brigade," in *Hopkins's New-Orleans 5 Cent Song-Book* (New Orleans: John Hopkins, ca. 1861), 14–15.

22. "Erin's Dixie," in *The Southern Flag Song Book* (Vicksburg & Augusta: H. C. Clarke, 1863), 20–21.

23. "Kelly's Irish Brigade," quoted by Wright, *Irish Emigrant Ballads and Songs,* 469.

24. Cornelius, *Music of the Civil War Era,* 99.

25. "Yankee Doodle's Ride to Richmond," in *War Songs of the South* (Richmond, VA: West & Johnson, 1862), 113–19. The song also criticized "vagrant Hoosiers from the West—a herd of drunken hogs," a reference to soldiers from Indiana.

26. Corcoran, *Captivity of General Corcoran,* 43–44.

27. William P. Ferris, "Return of Gen. Corcoran, of the Glorious 69th" (Boston: Horace Partridge, 1862).

28. P. J. Fitzpatrick, "Lamentation on the American War—Awful Battle at Vicksburg," quoted by Wright, *Irish Emigrant Ballads and Songs,* 459–60.

29. Ural, "'Ye Sons of Green Erin Assemble,'" 115.

30. Edward K. Spann, "Union Green: The Irish Community and the Civil War," in *The New York Irish,* 203–4.

31. Michael Corcoran to Charles P. Daly, 13 January 1863, CPDPL.

32. Peter Welsh to Margaret Welsh, 2 August 1863, in Welsh, *Irish Green and Union Blue,* 115.

33. Fallows, *Irish Americans: Identity and Assimilation,* 38.

34. Ural, *Harp and the Eagle,* 176.

35. Draft Riot studies are part of the wider issue of Irish American homogenization discussed in the Introduction. Again, the New York City experience is often applied to broader diaspora views, which is a problem for Draft Riot analysis as many Irish communities did not see the same violent riotous reaction and many decried the behavior of those in New York. See Bayor and Meagher, eds., *The New York Irish,* and Kelly, *The Shamrock and the Lily,* for examples and essays that demonstrate how this regional microlevel focus transposed onto broader macrolevel national Irish American history.

36. Keating, *Shades of Green,* 11.

37. Unknown Lyricist, "O'Toole & McFinnigan On the War" (Boston: Horace Partridge, 1863).

38. Eugene T. Johnston, *Who Will Care for Micky Now?* (New York: James Wrigley, 1863). Given the propensities of attitudes in Irish songs originating from New York City, it is likely Johnston's "Micky" was referring to the draft coming to the city in summer 1863 (thus was printed before the Draft Riots).

39. Unknown Lyricist, "When This Cruel War is Over—No. 2" (Boston: Horace Partridge, 1863).

40. Maria Lydig Daly, 14 July 1863, *Diary of a Union Lady, 1861–1865,* ed. Harold Earl Hammond (Lincoln: University of Nebraska Press, 2000), 246–48.

41. Daly, 23 July, 1863, ibid., 249–51.

42. Daly, 14 July 1863, ibid., 246–48.

43. Daly, 23 July 1863, ibid., 249–51.

44. Ural, *Harp and the Eagle,* 180.

45. Unknown Lyricist, "The Irish Brigade in America."

46. "The Irish Volunteer," quoted by Wright, *Irish Emigrant Ballads and Songs,* 472–73.

47. Thomas Walsh, "Our Brave Irish Champions: A New War Song on the GREAT BATTLE FOUGHT IN AMERICA! On Sunday, 21st of July, 1861" (Cork: Haly, 1861).

48. Ural, "'Ye Sons of Green Erin Assemble,'" 124.

49. McCaffrey, *Irish Diaspora in America,* 69.

50. Welsh to Margaret Welsh, 17 July 1863, in Welsh, *Irish Green and Union Blue,* 110.

51. Welsh to Margaret Welsh, 22 July 1863, ibid., 113–14.

52. Daly, 14 July 1863, *Diary of a Union Lady,* 248.

53. "By Himself," "Paddy the Loyal," in *The Continental Songster,* 36–37.

54. Ural, *Harp and the Eagle,* 180.

55. McCaffrey, *Irish Diaspora in America,* 95.

56. Campbell, *Ireland's New Worlds,* 51.

57. The political peaking of the Native American Party, later known simply as the American Party, can be observed in the 1854 elections: they declined as political attention turned toward debates over slavery's continuance and territorial expansion in the late 1850s. Those in the party opposed to slavery were subsumed into the rising Republican Party machine. The colloquial "Know Nothing" moniker originated in the group's early secret organization when members denied its existence. The term was common in contemporary discourse, as reflected in Irish wartime lyrics that recalled this nativist stance against their place in American society.

58. Unknown Lyricist, "The Irish Brigade" (Boston: Horace Partridge, January 1862).

59. Richard Jensen, "'No Irish Need Apply': A Myth of Victimization," *Journal of Social History* 36, no. 2 (2002): 140.

60. Kathleen O'Neil, "No Irish Need Apply" (Ohio: S. Brainard & Co., 1863). When Brainard's Ohio-based publishing house printed this musical scorebook in 1863, the O'Neil NINA song had already been produced and sold by Oliver Ditson in Boston and by the Philadelphia printing houses of J. H. Johnson and Lee & Walker, who published the song in 1862. O'Neil's version was also the only NINA ballad to provide context for why the song was written and the origin of the derogatory phrase. A note was added above songsheet and music scorebooks that reprinted the February 1862 *London Times Newspaper* notice: "WANTED—A smart active girl to do the general house work of a large family; one who can cook, clean plate, and get up fine linen preferred. N.B.—No Irish need apply."

61. John F. Poole, "No Irish Need Apply" (New York, H. De Marsan, 1862).

62. William Sutherland, "What Irish Boys Can Do—Answer to 'No Irish Need Apply'" (New York: H. De Marsan, 1863).

63. Unknown Lyricist, "No Irish Need Apply" (Philadelphia: William A. Stephens, 1864).

64. Hanchett, *Irish,* xiii.

65. Samito, *Becoming American Under Fire,* 112.

66. Halpine, *Life and Adventures,* x.

67. Ibid., 19, 26. Halpine described these fictional references to O'Reilly's earlier song productions as "containing little poetry [and] are as full of sense as an egg is full of meat."

68. Ibid., 26.

69. McWhirter, *Battle Hymns,* 92. Halpine only mentioned the Draft Riots in a brief comment when Miles O'Reilly visited New York City and passed "the black open space on Fifth avenue where the Colored Orphan Asylum lately stood. You see similar black spaces in Third avenue and elsewhere. These are the vestigia nigra of our late anti-draft, anti-negro riot" (Halpine, *Life and Adventures,* 121).

70. Cornelius, *Music of the Civil War Era,* 99–100.

71. Charles Graham Halpine, "Sambo's Right to be Kilt" (New York, 1863).

72. Halpine, *Life and Adventures,* 55–56.

73. Ibid., 57. Halpine's biographer William Hanchett further argued that the humor in "Sambo's Right to be Kilt" "was cruel and cold-blooded, but that was the secret of its success. Halpine's reasoning could persuade whites to accept blacks as soldiers without in the least disturbing their fundamental prejudices" (Hanchett, *Irish,* 70).

74. Major General David Hunter, described by Erin Foner as one of "the few abolitionists in the officer corps," was also one of the first Union commanders to free enslaved people in the Department of the South in May 1862. Hunter let male runaway slaves volunteer to serve, acting on his own military plan. This led to congressional concern that Hunter was going against Lincoln's pre-Emancipation military policies and forming Black regiments. See Eric Foner, *The Fiery Trial: Abraham Lincoln and American Slavery* (New York: W. W. Norton & Company, 2010), 206–8. That Halpine alluded to this story over a year after Hunter's actions indicates the impact it had on contemporary debates over emancipation and subsequent Black Union military service.

75. Halpine, *Life and Adventures,* 57.

76. McWhirter, *Battle Hymns,* 94. Halpine described that in fictional life, "white soldiers . . . began singing it around their camp-fires at night, and humming it to themselves on their sentry-beats." The story become true as "Sambo's Right to be Kilt" began circulating in reality throughout the Union (Halpine, *Life and Adventures,* 56).

77. Hanchett, *Irish,* 70.

78. Samito, *Becoming American Under Fire,* 112.

79. Halpine, "The Bust Up of the Machines," in *Life and Adventures,* 63–67.

80. "Song of the National Democracy"; Halpine set this song to the Scottish air "Bonnie Dundee."

81. Halpine was particularly scathing about the corrupt state of New York politics. In one satirical story, he described "the clock in the cupola of the City Hall . . . had a musical box attached to its machinery, which, as time slipped on, poured forth such popular airs as 'That's the Way the Money Goes' [aka 'Pop Goes the Weasel'], and 'Come, Brothers, Join the Mystic Ring,' in one continuous melody" (*Life and Adventures,* 123–24).

82. Hanchett, *Irish,* 55, 132.

83. Samito, *Becoming American Under Fire,* 186.

84. David T. Gleeson, "Ethnicity," in *A Companion to the U.S. Civil War,* ed. Aaron Sheehan-Dean (Hoboken, NJ: Wiley-Blackwell, 2014), 786.

85. Samito, *Becoming American Under Fire,* 186.

86. Joe English, "The Irish Volunteer." The Irish were not the only ethnic group to praise McClellan in song. One German American version of "New York Volunteers" included him in lyrics alongside veteran commander Union General Winfield Scott and German-born Major General Franz Sigel: "Raise your voices with one accord, and give them hearty cheers, for McClellan, Scott and Siegel, and their Union Volunteers!" See "Our German Volunteers," in *Camp-Fire Songster* (1862), 31–32.

87. "We'll Fight for Uncle Sam" (New York: H. De Marsan, 1863) in Wright, *Irish Emigrant Ballads and Songs,* 473.

88. George B. McClellan, quoted by Lyons, *Brigadier General T. F. Meagher,* 90.

89. Ural, "'Ye Sons of Green Erin Assemble,'" 115.

90. Corporal Casey Solus, "War Democratic View of McClellan's Nomination," *Irish-American,* 8 October 1864.

91. "The Cry is Mac, My Darling," *Irish-American,* 17 September 1864.

92. "T. F. L," "The Irish for McClellan," *Irish-American,* 22 October 1864. "Graineumhail" was another iteration of "Granuaile" (as discussed in chap. 4).

93. Daniel Crowley to Cornelius Flynn, 7 August 1864, Daniel Crowley Letters to Cornelius Flynn, BA.

94. Crowley to Flynn, 12 November 1864, ibid.

95. Halpine, "Song of the Soldiers," in *Life and Adventures,* 178–80.

96. Halpine, "The Blue Cap and Button," ibid., 187–88. The blood-soaked Virginian fields were described as turning "the color of the sumac," like the deep red color ground spice and dye.

97. Hanchett, *Irish,* 94.

98. Halpine, "The Blue-Bellies to the Grey-Backs: A Dream of Universal Dominion," in *Life and Adventures,* 214–15.

99. Halpine, *Life and Adventures,* iv.

100. Unknown Lyricist, "Pat Murphy of Meagher's Brigade."

7. IRISH AMERICAN LOYALTY AND IDENTITY IN CIVIL WAR SONGS

1. F. Collins, "Battle of Bull Run" (New York: James Wrigley, 1861).

2. Samito, *Becoming American Under Fire,* 1–2, 15. For further analysis of wider discussions about racial and ethnic citizenship definitions in the mid-nineteenth century, see Martha S. Jones, *Birthright Citizens: A History of Race and Rights in Antebellum America* (Cambridge: Cambridge University Press, 2018).

3. Samito, *Becoming American Under Fire,* 2.

4. Unknown Lyricist, "The Irish Brigade" (Boston: Horace Partridge, January 1862).

5. Unknown Lyricist, "The Irish Brigade in America," also known as "The Soldier's Letter from America" (Glasgow: James Lindsay, 1863).

6. McDermott, "The Irish Brigade" (New York: Frank McElroy, 1863).

7. *The Sons of Erin's Isle* (London: W. S. Fortey, ca. 1864).

8. "Freedom's Guide" (ca. 1862), quoted by Alfred M. Williams, "Folk-Songs of the Civil War," *Journal of American Folklore* 5, no. 19 (1892): 269.

9. Peter Welsh to Patrick Prendergast, 1 June 1863, in Welsh, *Irish Green and Union Blue,* 101–3.

10. Jason Tully, "The Gleam of Hope!" (New York: James Wrigley, 1865).

11. "Words and Music by an Irishman," "Corcoran to His Regiment, Or 'I Would Not Take Parole'" (Boston: Horace Partridge, 1861).

12. Thomas J. MacEvily, "War Song of the Irish Brigade," *Irish-American,* 30 November 1861.

13. F. Collins, "The 69th Brigade" (New York: James Wrigley, 1862).

14. "Erin's Dixie," in *The Southern Flag Song Book,* 20–21.

15. "Kelly's Irish Brigade," quoted by Wright, *Irish Emigrant Ballads and Songs,* 469.

16. "Additional words to 'Bonnie Blue Flag' as sung by the Missourians during the war" (ca. 1861), handwritten page of verses placed inside a copy of the *Virginia Songster* (Richmond, VA: J. W. Randolph, 1863), BA Confederate Collection.

17. Gleeson, "'To live and die [for] Dixie,'" 141, 147.

18. "Song for the Irish Brigade," in *Hopkins' New-Orleans 5 Cent Song-Book* (New Orleans: John Hopkins, 1861), 14–15.

19. "The New York Volunteer," in *The Camp-Fire Songster,* 23–24.

20. Kathleen O'Neil, "No Irish Need Apply" (Philadelphia: J. H. Johnson, 1862).

21. Unknown Lyricist, "O'Toole & McFinnigan On the War" (Boston: Horace Partridge, 1863).

22. Donnelly, "The New York Volunteer" (ca. 1862), quoted by Wright, *Irish Emigrant Ballads and Songs,* 453.

23. Tony Pastor, "Young America and Ould Ireland" (New York: H. De Marsan, 1862).

24. Unknown Lyricist, "Free and Easy of Our Union!" (Boston: Horace Partridge, 1861).

25. Timothy B. O'Regan, "Save the Constitution" (New York: James Wrigley, 1862). The lyrics about sailing on the USS *Constitution* had another resonance for the 9th Connecticut: the unit boarded the ship when they headed southward to the war after their mobilization.

26. "Hurrah for the Union" (New York: James Wrigley, 1861).

27. Robert Smith, "We Will Have the Union Still" (New York: James Wrigley, 1861).

28. Kate C. M., "The Irish Brigade," in *The Continental Songster,* 58–59.

29. P. T. Hade, "Camp Song of the (Chicago) Irish Brigade" (Chicago: Root & Cady, 1861).

30. Arthur McCann, "Battle of Bull's Run," (1861), quoted by Wright, *Irish Emigrant Ballads and Songs,* 457.

31. John McCreery, "The American Star, National Song" (Baltimore: F. D. Benteen, 1850). Several traditional Irish and Scottish folk ballads and airs originated in the late 1700s and early 1800s with the title "The Humours of the Glen." Music score copies of McCreery's 1850 composition do not mention the song's Irish musical roots, suggesting how the tune had become subsumed into American culture by the middle of the nineteenth century (similar to the transmission of musical tunes examples discussed in chap. 1).

32. O'Regan, "Save the Constitution" (New York: James Wrigley, 1862).

33. McFadden, "Col. Owens' Gallant Irish Volunteers" (Philadelphia: A. W. Auner, 1861).

34. Frank Spear, "The New York Volunteer" (New York: Dick and Fitzgerald, 1862).

35. Unknown Lyricist, "The Gallant 69th Regiment." (New York: H. De Marsan, 1862). The song was set to the air "Red, White, and Blue," reinforcing these American lyrical banner sentiments.

36. Unknown Lyricist, "Glorious 69th" (New York: James Wrigley, 1861).

37. John F. Poole, "Pat's Opinion of the Stars and Stripes," in *Camp-Fire Songster,* 67–68.

38. Unknown Lyricist, "O'Toole & McFinnigan On the War" (Boston: Horace Partridge, 1863).

39. Meagher, *Last Days of the 69th in Virginia,* 11.

40. Corcoran, *Captivity of General Corcoran,* 28.

41. Pastor, "The Irish Volunteer, No. 3" (New York: James Wrigley, 1862).

42. Corcoran, *Captivity of General Corcoran,* 30. Corcoran knew Francis Scott Key's "Star Spangled Banner" lyrics well: the quote he used appears in the song's second verse. What is intriguing about his adoption of the "Star Spangled Banner"—along with its appearance across other Irish and American Civil War music sources—is that the 1814 composition was not the official national anthem of the United States (it become so in 1931). The song was one of many unofficial nineteenth-century American national anthems that were used as popular tune foundations for songwriters to set their lyrical compositions to (alongside the likes of "Hail, Columbia" and "Red, White, and Blue"). For "Star Spangled Banner" studies, see McWhirter, *Battle Hymns,* 33–36; Billy Coleman, "'The Music of a Well Tun'd State': *The Star Spangled Banner* and the Development of a Federalist Music Tradition," *Journal of the Early Republic,* 35, no. 4 (2015), 599–629; Lohman, *Hail Columbia!*; Michael Corcoran, *For Which It Stands: An Anecdotal Biography of the American Flag* (New York: Simon & Schuster, 2002).

43. "Additional words to 'Bonnie Blue Flag' as sung by the Missourians during the war" (ca. 1861).

44. Harry Macarthy, "Our Country's Flag" (New Orleans: A. F. Blackmar, 1867).

45. George F. Root, "The Battle Cry of Freedom" (Chicago: Root & Cady, 1862).

46. German American version of "John Brown's Body" "sung by the Blenker Division of the Army of the Potomac," quoted by Cornelius, *Music of the Civil War Era,* 29.

47. F. Collins, "The Glorious Stripes & Stars" (New York: James Wrigley, 1861).

48. Samito, *Becoming American Under Fire,* 104.

49. W. F. Lyons, *Brigadier General T. F. Meagher,* 67.

50. Unknown Lyricist. "The Irish Brigade." Boston: Horace Partridge, January 1862.

51. Kate C. M., "The Irish Brigade."

52. Halpine, *The Life and Adventures*, , 159–60. Halpine's rhetoric about the banner echoes the language used in his "Song of the Soldiers" discussed in chap. 6.

53. Charles Graham Halpine, quoted by Samito, *Becoming American Under Fire*, 206.

54. Flag No. F100 Case D, Massachusetts Volunteer 21st Regiment Infantry banner in *Massachusetts State House Flag Project Examination Report* (Boston, 1984), Burrill File, State Library of Massachusetts Special Collections.

55. Shiels, *The Irish in the American Civil War*, 90.

56. Plunkett was also commemorated at the fortification on Georges Island in Boston Harbor that was used throughout the Civil War as a prison for Confederate soldiers and politicians (including, famously, Confederate Vice-President Alexander H. Stephens and the *Trent* Affair diplomats James M. Mason and John Slidell). In the late 1890s, a new gun emplacement at the fort was named Battery Plunkett in honor of Thomas Plunkett's memory. See Jay Schmidt, *Fort Warren: New England's Most Historic Civil War Site* (Amherst: UBT Press, 2003), 127. Fort Warren also has Civil War song history connections, as 12th Massachusetts Infantry soldiers wrote "John Brown's Body" in 1861 at the military encampment. See Stauffer and Soskis, *The Battle Hymn of the Republic*, chap. 2.

57. Unknown Lyricist, "To The Glorious 69th!" (New York: H. De Marsan, 1861).

58. Unknown Lyricist, "War Song of the New-York 69th Regiment" (New York: H. De Marsan, 1862).

59. Corby, *Memoirs of Chaplain Life*, 66.

60. McCaffrey, *Irish Diaspora in America*, 95.

61. Bernard Aspinwall, "Irish Americans and American Nationality, 1848–66," in *Contemporary Irish Studies*, ed. Tom Gallagher and James O'Connell (Manchester: Manchester University Press, 1983), 112.

62. Samito, *Becoming American Under Fire*, 112, 133.

63. Ural, *Harp and the Eagle*, 41.

64. Peter Welsh to Francis Prendergast, 25 April 1864, in Welsh, *Irish Green and Union Blue*, 155.

65. Unknown Lyricist, "War Song of the New-York 69th Regiment" (New York: H. De Marsan, 1861).

66. S. Leonce, "Off for a Soldier" (ca. 1863).

67. Corcoran, *Captivity of General Corcoran*, 45.

68. Ibid., 100.

69. John Mahon, "Corcoran's Ball!" (New York: H. De Marsan, 1863).

70. Eugene T. Johnston, "Corcoran's Irish Legion" (Boston: Horace Partridge, 1863).

71. Unknown Lyricist, "Glorious 69th."

72. Unknown Lyricist, "Pat Malloy" (Boston: Horace Partridge, ca. 1860).

73. Unknown Lyricist, "The Return of Pat Malloy" (Boston: Horace Partridge, ca. 1865).

CONCLUSION

1. Thomas Kean, "The Harp of Old Erin and Banner of Stars" (New York: H. De Marsan, 1861).

2. Edward Harry Kelly, "America, Ireland Loves You" (Kansas City: Edward Harry Kelly Publishing Co., 1917).

3. Thomas MacDonagh, "Marching Song of the Irish Volunteers," *Irish Review* 3, no. 34 (Dublin, 1913): 500–502.

4. Michael J. Fitzpatrick, "Irish Volunteers" (New York: Fitzpatrick Bros., 1917).

5. Halpine, "The Review: A Picture of Our Veterans," in *The Life and Adventures*, 218–19. For analysis of Union Army veteran sentiments, see Brian Matthew Jordan, *Marching Home: Union Veterans and Their Unending Civil War* (New York: W. W. Norton, 2015).

6. Halpine, "Song of the Soldiers," quoted by Samito, *Becoming American Under Fire*, 113.

7. Halpine, *New York Herald*, 20 November 1867, quoted by Samito, *Becoming American Under Fire*, 206.

8. Unknown Lyricist, "To the Glorious 69th!" (New York: H. De Marsan, 1861).

9. Mr. Mullaly, "Long Live the Sixty-Ninth" (New York: James Wrigley, 1861).

10. James G. Clark, "America to Ireland" (1868). General Philip Sheridan was born to Irish immigrant parents in Albany, New York, but his personal relationship to his ethnic roots as a second-generation American Irishman were more nuanced than his contemporaries. While at times the diaspora claimed him (and certainly have done so more in the decades and century following the Civil War than in the 1860s itself), he did not always play to these connections. Sheridan made infrequent appearances in American Civil War Irish songs.

11. Tony Pastor, "The Irish Volunteer, No. 3" (New York: James Wrigley, 1862). James A. Mulligan died from wounds received at the Second Battle of Kernstown, Virginia, in July 1864. Upon being shot, he was alleged to have urged his men: "lay me down and save the flag." Later that year, in tribute to the former 23rd Illinois "Irish Brigade" Regiment commander, Chicago-based George F. Root published a sentimental ballad under the title of Mulligan's dying expression. Although not mentioned in the piece directly, the second-generation Irish American Mulligan is the inspiring "dying hero" and "brave commander" this tangential Irish American Civil War song describes, who "fell . . . like the oak from mountain crag" uttering the words "'Lay me down and save the Flag'" George F. Root, "Lay Me Down and Save the Flag" (Chicago: Root & Cady, 1864).

12. "Mary of Montreal," "Written on Hearing the Death of General Corcoran," *Irish-American*, 30 January 1864.

13. Bernard Wayde, *Fighting Pat; Or, The Boys of the Irish Brigade*, in *The War Library: Original Stories of Adventure in the War of the Union* (New York: Novelist Publishing Co., 23 December 1882), 2.

14. See the most recent biographical work on Meagher's American life by Timothy Egan, *The Immortal Irishman: The Irish Revolutionary Who Became an American Hero* (New York: Houghton Mifflin Harcourt, 2016). Egan briefly mentions "The Escape of Meagher" (1852), but there is no discussion of American Civil War songs about the general in this biographical study.

15. Arthur Griffith, ed., *Meagher of the Sword: Speeches of Thomas Francis Meagher in Ireland, 1846–1848* (Dublin: M. H. Gill & Son, 1916).

16. Wayne Soini, *Porter's Secret: Fitz John Porter's Monument Decoded* (Portsmouth, NH: Jetty House, 2011), 40. Meagher's time as acting governor of Montana was brief: two years after the war, he was deemed to have drowned in the Missouri River at the waterfront settlement of Fort Benton, Montana, after he fell from a steamboat. The exact cause of death remains unknown—possible suggestions for Meagher's fate are that he went into the river deliberately, or accidentally, because of illness, intoxication, or even because of murder.

17. Corby, *Memoirs of Chaplain Life,* 187. For studies on American Civil War memory, commemoration, and anniversaries, see David W. Blight, *Race and Reunion: The Civil War in American Memory* (Cambridge: Harvard University Press, 2001); David W. Blight, *Beyond the Battlefield: Race, Memory, and the American Civil War* (Boston: University of Massachusetts Press, 2002); Robert J. Cook, *Civil War Memories: Contesting the Past in the United States Since 1865* (Baltimore: Johns Hopkins University Press, 2017); Caroline E. Janney, *Remembering the Civil War: Reunion and the Limits of Reconciliation* (Chapel Hill: University of North Carolina Press, 2013).

18. Corby, *Memoirs of Chaplain Life,* 193–94.

19. William Geoghegan, "The Irish Brigade at Gettysburg," quoted by Corby, *Memoirs of Chaplain Life,* 199.

20. William Collins, "In Memory of the Fallen Dead of the Irish Brigade," quoted by Corby, *Memoirs of Chaplain Life,* 196–98.

21. Unknown Lyricist, "Pat Murphy of Meagher's Brigade" (Boston: Horace Partridge, 1863).

22. Peter Welsh to Patrick Prendergast, 1 June 1863, in Welsh, *Irish Green and Union Blue,* 102.

23. Taoiseach Enda Kenny, "Friends of Ireland Luncheon" St. Patrick's Day Speech, White House, Washington, DC, 16 March 2017.

24. President John F. Kennedy, "Address Before the Irish Parliament," Dublin, Ireland, 28 June 1963. Kennedy's speech referenced Irish Brigade wartime history, particularly their heavy losses at Fredericksburg in 1862, Thomas Francis Meagher's leadership, and the history of other Irish American martial figures, such as Commodore John Barry in the American Revolution (the so-called father of the American Navy). The speech also talked about Ireland's global influence, and its poetic culture and history. The Irish Brigade flag still hangs in the Irish Parliament (despite calls to have it on permanent museum display).

25. Kenny, "Friends of Ireland Luncheon" speech.

26. President Bill Clinton, "Remarks to the Community in Dublin," College Green Dublin, Ireland, 1 December 1995. Clinton's comment on Irish global influence was a response to late twentieth-century impressions that "the world's global culture is becoming more American." The president's point was that American culture itself had Irish roots.

27. Lyons, *Brigadier General T. F. Meagher,* 97.

28. O'Riely, "The Irish Volunteers" (New York: James Wrigley, 1862).

29. Unknown Lyricist, "March of the New-York Volunteers" (New York: H. De Marsan, 1861).

BIBLIOGRAPHY

❧-❧-❧-❧-❧

REFERENCED INDIVIDUAL SONGS AND BALLAD POEMS

Numerous publications and versions of American Civil War ballads circulated in Union and Confederate society, printed as songsheets, broadsides, and in songster and musical scorebooks. Frequent publication of the same songs led to changes and additions to lyrics, creating more than one copy of an example. The most established versions of the Irish and general Civil War song examples referenced in the book are listed here.

Alexis. "Irish Brigade at Fredericksburg." New York: Lynch & Cole, January 1863.

Backus, Henry Sherman. "Irish Patriots of '98." New York: James Wrigley, ca.1860.

Barney, Corporal. "The Irish-American Army." New York: W. H. Murphy, ca. 1866.

Bennett, S. Fillmore. "The Irish Volunteer." Chicago: H. M. Higgins, 1862.

Bessie of Clifton, Long Island. "The Irish Brigade." New York: Lynch & Cole, July 1864.

Birch, Rev. E. P. "Yankee Doodle's Rise to Richmond." Richmond, VA: West & Johnson, 1862.

Boucicault, Dion, and E. H. House. "Wearing of the Green." Boston: Oliver Ditson; New York: Dodworth; Philadelphia: Johnson.

Brenan, Thomas. "A Ballad for the Young South." Richmond, VA: West & Johnson, 1862.

Brown, Thomas M. "Cead Mille Fealthe—A Hundred Thousand Welcomes." Boston: Oliver Ditson, June 1864.

Boylan, Kate M. "The Irish Dead on Fredericksburg Heights." New York: Lynch & Cole, 1863.

"By Himself." "Paddy the Loyal." Philadelphia: A. Winch, 1863.

C. M., Kate. "The Irish Brigade." Philadelphia: A. Winch, 1863.

Case, William. "The Fenian Blood-Hounds." Unknown Publisher, 1866.

Clark, James G. "America to Ireland." Unknown Publisher, 1868.

Collins, F. "Battle of Bull Run." New York: H. De Marsan and James Wrigley, 1861.

Collins, F. "The 69th Brigade." New York: James Wrigley, 1862.

Cross, John C. "Mother on the Brain." New York: H. De Marsan, 1864.

D. S. F. of East Brooklyn. "New War Song of the 69th Regiment." Boston: Horace Partridge, 1862.

Dix, John Ross. "Paddy's Lament." New York: Charles Magnus, 1864.

Donnelly, Thomas. "The New York Volunteer." Unknown Publisher, 1862.

Dunne, William. "The Father of All Songs." New York: H. De Marsan, 1864.

English, Joe. "The Irish Volunteer." New York: Dick & Fitzgerald, 1864.

Fay, M. "Irish Volunteers—Penn'a's Gallant 69th." Philadelphia: J. H. Johnson, 1863.

Ferris, William P. "Return of Gen. Corcoran, of the Glorious 69th." Boston: Horace Partridge, 1862.

Fitzpatrick, Michael. "Irish Volunteers." New York: Fitzpatrick Bros., 1917.

Fitzpatrick, P. J. "A Lamentation of the American War—Awful Battle at Vicksburg." Ireland: Unknown Publisher, 1863.

Flagg, Wilson. "The O'Lincon Family." Boston: Oliver Ditson, May 1862.

Geddes, J. L. "The Bonnie Flag with the Stripes and Stars." St. Louis: Balmer & Weber, 1863.

Gilmore, Patrick. "When Johnny Comes Marching Home." Boston: Henry Tolman & Co., 1863.

Hade, P. T. "Camp Song of the Chicago Irish Brigade." Chicago: Root & Cady, 1861.

Hade, P. T. "Camp Song of the Irish Brigade." Philadelphia: A. W. Auner, ca.1862.

Halpine, Charles Graham. "Sambo's Right to be Kilt". New York, 1863.

Hawkins, Col. W. S. "The Hero Without a Name." London: Spottiswoode & Co., 1865–66.

Higgins, Mary J. "To A Brother Fighting for the Union." New York: H. De Marsan, 1861.

Kean, Thomas. "The Harp of Old Erin and Banner of Stars". New York: H. De Marsan, 1861.

Kelly, Edward Harry. "America, Ireland Loves You". Kansas City: Edward Harry Kelly Publishing Co., 1917.

Johnston, Eugene T. "Corcoran's Irish Legion." Boston: Horace Partridge; New York: H. De Marsan, 1863.

Johnston, Eugene T. "The Drummer of Antietam." New York: H. De Marsan, 1862.

Johnston, Eugene T. "What Irishmen Have Done." New York: Charles Magnus, ca. 1866–70.

Johnston, Eugene T. "Who Will Care for Micky Now?" New York: James Wrigley, 1863.

Leonce, S. "Off for a Soldier." Unknown publisher, ca. 1863.

Lindsey, William H. "The Green Above the Red." New York: H. De Marsan, ca. 1860.

Lithgow, Mrs. Sinclair. "The Late Captain E. K. Butler." New York: Lynch & Cole, July 1864.

MacEvily, Thomas J. "War Song of the Irish Brigade." New York: Lynch & Cole, November 1861.

Mahon, John. "Corcoran's Ball." New York: H. De Marsan, 1863.

Mary of Montreal. "Written on Hearing the Death of Gen. Corcoran." New York: Lynch & Cole, January 1864.

McCann, Arthur. "Battle of Bull's Run." America: Unknown Publisher, 1861.

McCann, Arthur. "Irish Volunteer." Philadelphia: A. W. Auner, ca. 1862.

Macarthy, Harry. "The Bonnie Blue Flag." New Orleans: A. E. Blackmar & Bro., 1861–62.

Macarthy, Harry. "Our Country's Flag." New Orleans: A. F. Blackmar, 1867.

McCreery, John. "The American Star, National Song." Baltimore: F. D. Benteen, 1850.

McDermott, Hugh F. "The Irish Brigade." New York: Frank McElroy, 1863.

McFadden, Arthur. "Col. Owens' Gallant Irish Volunteers." Philadelphia: A. W. Auner, 1861.

Mullaly, Mr. "Long Live the Sixty-Ninth." New York: James Wrigley, 1861.

O'Neil, Kathleen. "No Irish Need Apply." Boston: Oliver Ditson; Philadelphia: Johnson and Lee & Walker, 1862.

O'Neil, Kathleen. "No Irish Need Apply." Ohio: S. Brainard, 1864.

O'Regan, Timothy B. "Save the Constitution." New York: James Wrigley, 1862.

O'Riely, Michael. "The Irish Volunteers." New York: H. De Marsan and James Wrigley, 1862.

Oulahan, Richard. "Corcoran's Irish Legion." New York: Lynch & Cole, November 1863.

Oulahan, Richard. "Corcoran! The Prisoner of War." New York: Lynch & Cole, September 1862.

Oulahan, Richard. "Corcoran's Zouaves." New York: Lynch & Cole, August 1863.

P. L. of Boston. "In Memoriam." New York: Lynch & Cole, November 1863.

Pastor, Tony. "The Irish Volunteer, No. 3." New York: H. De Marsan and James Wrigley, 1862.

Pastor, Tony. "Young America and Old Ireland." New York: H. De Marsan, 1862.

Poole, John F. "I Goes to Fight Mit Sigel." New York: H. De Marsan, 1861.

Poole, John F. "No Irish Need Apply." New York: H. De Marsan, 1862.

Poole, John F. "Pat's Opinion of the Stars and Stripes." Philadelphia: Dick & Fitzgerald, 1862.

Root, George F. "Lay Me Down and Save the Flag." Chicago: Root & Cady, 1864.

Root, George F. "On! On! On! The Boys Came Marching, Or, The Prisoner Free— Sequel to Tramp! Tramp! Tramp!" Boston: Horace Partridge, 1865.

Root, George F. "The Battle Cry of Freedom." Chicago: Root & Cady, 1862.

Root, George F. "Tramp! Tramp! Tramp! The Prisoner's Hope." Chicago: Root & Cady, 1863.

Ruth, Edmund, and John B. Stiegler. "The Irishman's Greeting to America." Boston: Oliver Ditson, 1853.

Sawyer, Charles Carroll. "Weeping Sad and Lonely, or When This Cruel War Is Over." Brooklyn, Sawyer & Thompson, 1863.

Sawyer, Charles Carroll. "Who Will Care For Mother Now?" Brooklyn: Sawyer & Thompson, 1863.

Smith, Robert. "We Will Have the Union Still." New York: James Wrigley, 1861.

Solus, Corporal Casey. "War Democratic View of McClellan's Nomination." New York: Lynch & Cole, October 1864.

Spear, Frank. "The New York Volunteer." New York: Dick and Fitzgerald, 1862.

Spear, Frank, and Sam Long. "The New York Volunteer." New York: He. De Marsan and James Wrigley, 1862.

Sterett, C. "A Reply to the Bonnie Blue Flag." New York: S. T. Gordon, 1862.

Sutherland, William. "What Irish Boys Can Do—Answer to 'No Irish Need Apply.'" New York: H. De Marsan; Philadelphia, A. W. Auner, 1863.

T. F. L. "The Irish for McClellan." New York: Lynch & Cole, October 1864.

Taylor, Bayard. "A Crimean Episode." Printed in Dwight's Journal of Music. Boston: Oliver Ditson, September 1861.

Taylor, Bayard. "Songs of the Camp." New York: Dick & Fitzgerald, 1862.

Tully, James. "The Gleam of Hope!" New York: James Wrigley, 1865.

Unknown Lyricist. "A Copy of Four Verses of Poetry Being Versus . . . Career of Brigadier General Corcoran." New York, April 1864.

Unknown Lyricist. "A New Song on the American War." Manchester: James Wrigley Jr., 1863.

Unknown Lyricist. "A New Song on the Last Battle Fought in America." Ireland: Unknown Publisher, 1862.

Unknown Lyricist. "Additional words to 'Bonnie Blue Flag' as sung by the Missourians during the war." Handwritten, ca. 1861.

Unknown Lyricist. "Col. Corcoran and the Prince of Wales." New York: James Wrigley, 1861.

Unknown Lyricist. "Comrades of the Cannon." Unknown Publisher, ca. 1863.

Unknown Lyricist. "Corporal Kelly." New York: Dick & Fitzgerald, 1862.

Unknown Lyricist. "Erin's Dixie." Vicksburg: H. C. Clarke, 1863.

Unknown Lyricist. "Escape of Meagher." Cork: Haly, 1852.

Unknown Lyricist. "Fenians Ever More." Boston: George D. Russell & Company, 1866.

Unknown Lyricist. "Free and Easy of Our Union!" Boston: Horace Partridge, 1861.

Unknown Lyricist. "Gay Is the Life of a Fighting America." New York: James Wrigley, ca. 1864.

Unknown Lyricist. "Glorious 69th." New York: James Wrigley, 1861.

Unknown Lyricist. "Glorious Old Flag, A Reply to the Bonnie Blue Flag." Philadelphia: Marsh, 1862)

Unknown Lyricist. "Grant to Washington Shall Go." Boston: Horace Partridge, 1869.

Unknown Lyricist. "Hurrah for the Union." New York: James Wrigley, 1861.

Unknown Lyricist. "Irish Brigade." Philadelphia: A. W. Auner, 1861–62.

Unknown Lyricist. "Irish Volunteer." Unknown Publisher, 1861.

Unknown Lyricist. "Kelly's Irish Brigade." Missouri: Unknown Publisher, 1861.

Unknown Lyricist. "March of the New-York Volunteers." New York: H. De Marsan, 1861.

Unknown Lyricist. "New Song on the Dreadful Engagement, and Tremendous Loss of Irish in America." Ireland: Unknown Publisher, 1862.

Unknown Lyricist. "No Irish Need Apply." Philadelphia: William A. Stephen, 1864.

Unknown Lyricist. "O'Toole & McFinnigan on the War." Boston: Horace Partridge, 1863.

Unknown Lyricist. "Our Country's Heroes." New York: H. De Marsan and James Wrigley, New York, 1864.

Unknown Lyricist. "Our Own Flag of Green." New York: James Wrigley, ca. 1860.

Unknown Lyricist. "Pat Malloy." Boston: Horace Partridge, ca. 1860.

Unknown Lyricist. "Pat Murphy of Meagher's Brigade." Boston: Horace Partridge and James Wrigley, New York, 1863.

Unknown Lyricist. "Pat Rooney and His Little Ones." New York: Lynch & Cole, May 1862.

Unknown Lyricist. "Return of Pat Malloy." New York: James Wrigley, ca. 1865.

Unknown Lyricist. "Reynolds' Letter on the American War!" Unknown Publisher, 1862.

Unknown Lyricist. "Song for the Irish Brigade." New Orleans: John Hopkins, 1861.

Unknown Lyricist. "St. Patrick's Day, No. 2." New York: James Wrigley, 1862.

Unknown Lyricist. "The Escape of Stephens, The Fenian Chief." New York: H. De Marsan, 1865.

Unknown Lyricist. "The Fenian Brigade!" Boston: Horace Partridge and New York: James Wrigley, 1862.

Unknown Lyricst, "The Flag with the Thirty Four Stars." Cincinnati: A. C. Peters & Bro., 1862.

Unknown Lyricist. "The Gallant 69th Regiment." Boston: Horace Partridge and New York: H. De Marsan, 1862.

Unknown Lyricist. "The Gallant Sons of Erin." New York: H. De Marsan, 1861.

Unknown Lyricist. "The Irish Brigade." Boston: Horace Partridge, January 1862.

Unknown Lyricist. "The Irish Brigade in America," also known as "The Soldier's Letter from America." Glasgow: James Lindsay, 1863.

Unknown Lyricist. "The Irish Picket." Boston: Horace Partridge, ca. 1862.

Unknown Lyricst. "The Irish Jaunting Car." London: H. Such, 1854.

Unknown Lyricist. "The Irish Jaunting Car." New York: Andrews, ca. 1854–55.

Unknown Lyricist. "The Irish Volunteers of 1860." Ireland, ca. 1860.

Unknown Lyricist. "The Sons of Erin's Isle." London: W. S. Fortey, ca. 1861.

Unknown Lyricist. "The Union Volunteer." New York: Dick & Fitzgerald, 1864.

Unknown Lyricist. "To the Glorious 69th!" New York: H. De Marsan, 1861.

Unknown Lyricist. "War Song of the New-York 69th Regiment." New York: H. De Marsan, 1861.

Unknown Lyricist. "War Song for the 79th Regiment". New York: James Wrigley, 1861.

Unknown Lyricist. "We'll Fight for Uncle Sam." New York: H. De Marsan, 1863.

Unknown Lyricist. "When This Cruel War Is Over, No. 2." Boston: Horace Partridge, 1863.

Unnamed Solider, Irish 1st Division, 2 Army Corp. "Oh, My Nora Creina Dear." New York: Lynch & Cole, September 1864.

Unnamed Soldier, 37th New York. "'Irish Rifles.' A Serenade in Camp." New York: Lynch & Cole, February 1862.

Vousden, Valentine. "The Irish Jaunting Car." Dublin, 1854.

Walsh, Thomas. "Our Brave Irish Champions—A New Song on the GREAT BATTLE FOUGHT IN AMERICA! On Sunday, 21st of July, 1861." Cork: Haly, 1861.

Wilder, Frank. "The Finnegins, Or Down to Eastport Town." Boston: Oliver Ditson, 1866.

Winner, Septimus. "Give Us Back Our Old Commander." Philadelphia: Winner & Co., 1862.

"Words and Music by an Irishman." "Corcoran to His Regiment, Or 'I Would Not Take Parole.'" Boston: Horace Partridge, 1861.

SONGSTERS AND SONGBOOKS

The Bonnie Blue Flag Song Book, Third Edition. Augusta: Blackmar & Bro., 1863.

The Camp-Fire Songster: A Collection of Popular, Patriotic, National, Pathetic, and Jolly Songs, Suited for the Camp or March, Containing a Number of Songs Never Before Printed. New York: Dick & Fitzgerald, 1862.

The Continental Songster: A Collection of New, Spirited, Patriotic Songs, For the Times. Philadelphia: A. Winch, 1863.

Crawford, Richard. *The Civil War Songbook: Complete Original Sheet Music for 37 Songs.* New York: Dover Publications, 1977.

Davis, Thomas. *The Spirit of the Nation.* Dublin, 1845.

Echoes from Dixie: A Collection of Songs Used in the South Prior to and During the War Between the States. Portsmouth: United Confederate Choirs of America, 1911.

Gems of the Emerald Isle: A Collection of Hornpipes, Reels, Jigs, &c., by P. W. Hughes. New York: R. A. Saalfield, 1867.

Harry Pell's Ebony Songster. New York: Dick & Fitzgerald, 1864.

Hopkins' New-Orleans 5 Cent Song-Book. New Orleans: John Hopkins, ca. 1861.

Hopkins' New-Orleans 5 Cent Song-Book. New Orleans: John Hopkins, 1861.

Lannigan's Ball Songster, Containing a Choice Collection of Irish Songs, Dutch Songs, Burlesque Speeches, Scraps of Fun, and Popular Comic Songs, Including the Famous Irish Comic Song of Lannigan's Ball, as Sung by Tony Pastor, J. C. Stewart, T. L. Donnelly, W. J. Florence, Fred May, and Other Comic Vocalists. New York: Dick & Fitzgerald, 1863.

Moore, Thomas. *Irish Melodies.* Multiple editions and publications from 1808.

Six Hundred and Seventeen Irish Songs and Ballads. New York: Wehman Bros., ca. 1890.

Songs of the South. Richmond, VA: J. W. Randolph, 1862.

Songs of the South. Richmond, VA: J. W. Randolph, 1863.

Songs of the South. Richmond, VA: J. W. Randolph, 1864.

Stephens' Fenian Songster: Containing all the Heart-Stirring and Patriotic Ballads and Songs, as sung at the meetings of the Fenian Brotherhood. New York: W. H. Murphy, 1866.

The Rebel Songster: Containing a Choice Collection of Sentimental, Patriotic and Comic Songs, Compiled by a Musical Gentleman of this City. Richmond, VA: Ayres & Wade, 1864.

The Southern Flag Song Book. Vicksburg and Augusta: H. C. Clarke, 1863.

The Southern Soldier's Prize Songster: Containing Material and Patriotic Pieces (Chiefly Original) Applicable to the Present War. Mobile: W. F. Wisley, 1864.

Tony Pastor's Irish Comic Songster. New York: Dick & Fitzgerald, ca. 1860s.

Virginia Songster. Richmond, VA: J. W. Randolph, 1863.

Walton, Martha A. *Walton's 132 Best Irish Songs.* Dublin: Fódhla Press, 1948.

Walton, Martha A. *Walton's Treasury of Irish Songs and Ballads.* Dublin: Fódhla Press, 1947.

Wright, Robert L. *Irish Emigrant Ballads and Songs.* Bowling Green, OH: Bowling Green Popular Press, 1975.

War Lyrics and Songs of the South. London: Spottiswoode & Co., 1866.

War Songs of the South. Richmond, VA: West & Johnson, 1862.

NEWSPAPERS AND PERIODICALS

Daily Dispatch (Richmond, VA)

Dwight's Journal of Music, vols. 13–24, May 1858–March 1865

Harper's New Monthly Magazine

Harper's Weekly

Irish-American, 1861–65. Also published and cataloged as *New York Irish American Weekly* and *Irish-American Weekly.*

Irish Republican (Chicago, IL)
National Era
New Orleans Daily Crescent
New York Herald
New York Times
Ottawa Free Trader (IL)
Winchester Daily Bulletin (TN)

PRINTED PRIMARY SOURCES

1860 Census Record Statistics of the United States. "Irish-born Populations in Major U.S. Cities, 1860." Washington, DC, 1866.

Burrill File, State Library of Massachusetts Special Collections. Massachusetts State House Flag Project Examination Report. Flag No. F100 Case D, Massachusetts Volunteer 21st Regiment Infantry banner. Boston, 1984.

Cavanagh, Michael. *Memoirs of General Thomas Francis Meagher: Comprising the Leading Events of his Career Chronologically Arranged, with Selections from his Speeches, Lectures and Miscellaneous Writings, Including Personal Reminiscences.* Worcester: The Messenger Press, 1892.

Clinton, William Jefferson. "Remarks to the Community in Dublin." Dublin, 1 December, 1995, via The American Presidency Project.

Common Pleas Court, Petitions for Naturalization Index—New York City/New York County Courts (1860). National Archives.

Conyngham, David Power. *The Irish Brigade and Its Campaigns: With Some Account of the Corcoran Legion, and Sketches of the Principal Officers.* New York: William McSorley & Co., 1867.

Corby, William. *Memoirs of Chaplain Life: Three Years Chaplin in the Famous Irish Brigade.* Chicago: La Monte, 1893.

Corcoran, Michael. *The Captivity of General Corcoran: The Only Authentic and Reliable Narrative of the Trials and Sufferings Endured, During his Twelve Months' Imprisonment in Richmond and Other Southern Cities, by Brigadier-General Michael Corcoran, the Hero of Bull Run.* Philadelphia: Barclay & Co., 1864.

Daly, Maria Lydig. *Diary of a Union Lady, 1861–1865.* Edited by Harold Earl Hammond. Lincoln: University of Nebraska Press, 2000.

Haines, Zenas T. *Letters from the Forty-Fourth Regiment M. V. M.: A Record of the Experience of a Nine Months' Regiment in the Department of North Carolina in 1862–1863.* Boston: The Herald Job Office, 1863.

Halpine, Charles Graham. *Baked Meats of the Funeral: A Collection of Essays, Poems,*

Speeches, Histories and Banquets, by Private Miles O'Reilly, Late of the 47th Regiment New York Volunteer Infantry, 10th Army Corps. New York: Carleton, 1866.

Halpine, Charles Graham. *Lyrics By The Letter H.* New York, J. C. Derby, 1854.

Halpine, Charles Graham. *The Life and Adventures, Songs, Services and Speeches of Private Miles O'Reilly [Pseud.], 47th Regiment, New York Volunteers, with Comic Illustrations by Mullen, from the Authentic Records of the "New York Herald."* New York: Carleton, 1864.

Hawes, Jesse. *Cahaba: A Story of Captive Boys in Blue.* New York: Burr Printing House, 1888.

Kenny, Enda. "Remarks With Prime Minister Enda Kenny of Ireland at the Congressional Friends of Ireland Luncheon." Washington, DC: 16 March, 2017, via The American Presidency Project.

Kennedy, John F. "Address before the Irish Parliament in Dublin, 28 June 1963", Dublin 1963, via John F. Kennedy Presidential Museum and Library (Boston).

Lyons, W. F. *Brigadier General T. F. Meagher; His Political and Military Career, With Selections from his Speeches and Writings.* Glasgow: Cameron and Ferguson, 1871.

McCarter, William. *My Life in the Irish Brigade: The Civil War Memoirs of Private William McCarter, 116th Pennsylvania Infantry.* Edited by Kevin E. O'Brien. Cambridge: Da Capo Press, 1996.

Meagher, Thomas Francis. *The Last Days of the 69th in Virginia, A Narrative in Three Parts.* New York: Lynch & Cole, 1861.

Rogers, William H. *The Great Civil War—William H. Rogers's Personal Experiences.* Boston: Bivouac, 1888.

Ryan, John. *Campaigning with the Irish Brigade: Pvt. John Ryan, 28th Massachusetts.* Edited by Sandy Barnard. Terre Haute: AST Press, 2001.

Wayde, Bernard. *Fighting Pat, Or the Boys of the Irish Brigade: The War Library, Original Stories of Adventure in the War for the Union.* New York: Novelist Publishing Co., 1882.

Welsh, Peter. *Irish Green and Union Blue: The Civil War Letters of Peter Welsh, Color Sergeant 28th Regiment Massachusetts Volunteers.* Edited Lawrence Frederick Kohl and Margaret Cassé Richard. New York: Fordham University, 1986.

MANUSCRIPT AND DIGITAL ARCHIVE COLLECTIONS

American Antiquarian Society (Worcester, MA).
    Isaiah Thomas Broadside Ballads Project: Verses in Vogue with the Vulgar, https://www.americanantiquarian.org/thomasballads/.

Bodleian Library, University of Oxford (Oxford, England).
    Broadside Ballads Online, http://ballads.bodleian.ox.ac.uk/collections.

Boston Athenaeum Library (Boston, MA). Cited in notes as BA.

    Crowley, Daniel. Letters to Cornelius Flynn (26 March 1863–17 May 1865).

British Library (London, England).

    Britain and the American Civil War online gallery resource (2013), http://www.bl
        .uk/onlinegallery/onlineex/uscivilwar/index.html.

Burrill File, State Library of Massachusetts Special Collections (Boston, MA).

    Massachusetts State House Flag Project Examination Report (1984).

Civil War Soldiers and Sailors Database System, National Park Services.

Duke University Libraries Digital Collections (Durham, NC).

    American Songsheets, http://library.duke.edu/digitalcollections/songsheets/.

Irish in the American Civil War, http://irishamericancivilwar.com.

Johns Hopkins University, Sheridan Libraries Special Collections (Baltimore, MD).

    Lester S. Levy Music Sheet Collection, http://levysheetmusic.mse.jhu.edu/.

Library Company of Philadelphia (Philadelphia, PA).

    Digital Collections, https://digital.librarycompany.org/.

Library of Congress (Washington, DC).

    Chronicling America: Historic American Newspapers.

National Archives (Washington, DC).

    Civil War Widows' Pensions. Cited in notes as CWWP.

National Library of Scotland (Edinburgh, Scotland).

    The Word on the Street Scottish Broadsides (1650–1910), http://digital.nls.uk/broad
        sides/.

New York Public Library, Special Collections (New York, NY).

    Charles P. Daly Papers and Letters (1839–92). Cited in notes as CPDPL.

New York University, Tamimnet Library and Robert F. Wagner Labor Archives, (New
    York, NY).

    Mick Moloney Irish-American Music and Popular Culture Irish Americana
        Collection.

Trinity College Dublin, Digital Collections (Dublin, Ireland).

    J. D. White Collection.

Vere Harmsworth Library (Oxford, England).

    Papers of William H. Seward.

Ward Irish Music Archives (Milwaukee, WI).

    Irish Sheet Music Archives Sheet Music Collections, http://irishsheetmusicarchives
        .com/sheet-music.htm.

SECONDARY SOURCES

Abel, E. Lawrence. "Harry Macarthy: The Bob Hope of the Confederacy." *Civil War Times* (2000): http://www.historynet.com/harry-macarthy-the-bob-hope-of-the-confederacy.htm.

———. *Singing the New Nation: How Music Shaped the Confederacy, 1861–1865.* Mechanicsburg: Stackpole Books, 2000.

Adams, James H. "The Negotiated Hibernian: Discourse on the Fenian in England and America." *American Nineteenth Century History* 11, no. 1 (2010): 47–77.

Almeida, Linda Dowling. *Irish Immigrants in New York City, 1945–1995.* Bloomington: Indiana University Press, 2001.

Anbinder, Tyler. *Five Points: The 19th Century New York City Neighborhood That Invented Tap Dance, Stole Elections, and Became the World's Most Notorious Slum.* New York: The Free Press, 2001.

———. "From Famine to Five Points: Lord Lansdowne's Irish Tenants Encounter North America's Most Notorious Slum." *American Historical Review* 107, no. 2 (2002): 351–87.

Anderson, Benedict. *Imagined Communities: Reflections on the Origin and Spread of Nationalism.* London: Verso, 2006.

Aspinwall, Bernard. "Irish Americans and American Nationality, 1848–66." In *Contemporary Irish Studies,* ed. Tom Gallagher and James O'Connell, 111, 130. Manchester: Manchester University Press, 1983.

Atkinson, David, and Steve Roud, eds. *Street Ballads in the Nineteenth-Century Britain, Ireland, and North America: The Interface Between Print and Oral Traditions.* London: Routledge, 2014.

Bailey, Candace. *Charleston Belles Abroad: The Music of Harriet Lowndes, Henrietta Aiken, and Louisa Rebecca McCord.* Columbia: University of South Carolina Press, 2019.

Barnard, Toby. *Brought to Book: Print in Ireland, 1680–1784.* Dublin: Four Courts Press, 2017.

Bateson, Catherine. "'For America's Bright Starry Banner': Expressions of Irish American Affiliation, Identity and National Loyalty in Civil War Songs." In *National and Transnational Challenges to the American Imaginary,* ed. Adina Ciugureanu, Edward Vlad, and Nicoleta Stanca, 27–38. Berlin: Peter Lang, 2018.

———. "'Forward For Our Homes!' Lyrical Expressions of Home Heard in Irish American Civil War Songs." *The Journal of History and Cultures.* Issue 9 (February 2019): 86–100.

Bayor, Ronald H., and Timothy J. Meagher, eds. *The New York Irish.* Baltimore: Johns Hopkins University Press, 1996.

Bean, Annemarie, James V. Hatch, and Brooks McNamara, eds. *Inside the Minstrel Mask: Readings in Nineteenth-Century Blackface Minstrelsy.* Middletown: Wesleyan University Press, 1996.

Belchem, John. "Nationalism, Republicanism and Exile: Irish Emigrants and the Revolution of 1848." *Past and Present* 146 (1995): 103–35.

———. "Republican Spirit and Military Science: The 'Irish Brigade' and Irish-American Nationalism in 1848." *Irish Historical Studies* 29, no. 113 (1994): 44–64.

Bernath, Michael T. *Confederate Minds: The Struggle For Intellectual Independence in the Civil War South.* Chapel Hill: University of North Carolina Press, 2010.

Bernstein, Iver. *The New York City Draft Riots: Their Significance for American Society and Politics in the Age of the Civil War.* New York: Oxford University Press, 1990.

Berthoff, Rowland. "Celtic Mist Over the South." *Journal of Southern History* 52, no. 4 (1986): 523–46.

Bielenberg, Andy, ed. *The Irish Diaspora.* New York: Longman, 2000.

Bilby, Joseph G. *The Irish Brigade in the Civil War: The 69th New York and Other Irish Regiments of the Army of the Potomac.* Cambridge: Da Capo Press, 1997.

Blessing, Patrick J. *The Irish in America: A Guide to the Literature and the Manuscript Collections.* Washington, DC: Catholic University of America Press, 1992.

Blight, David W. *Beyond the Battlefield: Race, Memory, and the American Civil War.* Boston: University of Massachusetts Press, 2002.

———. *Race and Reunion: The Civil War in American Memory.* Cambridge, MA: Harvard University Press, 2001.

Born, Georgina, and David Hesmondhalgh, eds. *Western Music and Its Others: Difference, Representation, and Appropriation in Music.* Berkeley: University of California Press, 2000.

Boyd, Steven R. *Patriotic Envelopes of the Civil War: The Iconography of Union and Confederate Covers.* Baton Rouge: Louisiana State University Press, 2010.

Breitenfeldt, Sara. *The Harp of Old Erin and Banner of Stars: Irish Music from the American Civil War.* Ward Irish Music Archive (Milwaukee), Lulu Press, 2011.

Brown, Thomas N. *Irish-American Nationalism, 1870–1890.* Philadelphia, PA: Lippincott, 1966.

Broyles, Michael. "Art Music from 1860 to 1920." In *The Cambridge History of American Music,* ed. David Nicholls, 214–54. Cambridge: Cambridge University Press, 1988.

———. "Immigrant, Folk, and Regional Musics in the Nineteenth Century." In *The Cambridge History of American Music,* ed. David Nicholls, 135–57. Cambridge: Cambridge University Press, 1988.

Brundage, David. *Irish Nationalists in America: The Politics of Exile, 1798–1998.* New York: Oxford University Press, 2016.

———. "Recent Directions in the History of Irish American Nationalism." *Journal of American Ethnic History* 28, no. 4 (2009): 82–89.

Burton, William L. *Melting Pot Soldiers: The Union Ethnic Regiments.* New York, NY: Fordham University Press, 1998.

———. "'Title Deed to America': Union Ethnic Regiments in the Civil War." *Proceedings of the American Philosophical Society* 124, no. 6 (1980): 455–63.

Campbell, Malcolm. *Ireland's New Worlds: Immigration, Politics and Society in the United States and Australia, 1815–1922.* Madison: University of Wisconsin Press, 2008.

Carroll, F. M. *American Opinion and the Irish Question, 1910–1923: A Study in Opinion and Policy.* Dublin: Gill & Macmillan, 1978.

Cash, W. J. *The Mind of the South.* New York, NY: Vintage Books, 1991.

Cline, Lawrence E. *Rebels on the Niagara: The Fenian Invasion of Canada, 1866.* New York: State University of New York Press, 2018.

Cockrell, Dale. "Nineteenth Century Popular Music." In *The Cambridge History of American Music,* ed. David Nicholls, 158–85. Cambridge: Cambridge University Press, 1998.

Coleman, Billy. "Confederate Music and the Politics of Treason and Disloyalty in the American Civil War." *Journal of Southern History* 86, no. 1 (2020): 75–116.

———. *Harnessing Harmony: Music, Power, and Politics in the United States, 1788–1865.* Chapel Hill: University of North Carolina Press, 2020.

———. "'The Music of a well tun'd State': *The Star Spangled Banner* and the Development of a Federalist Music Tradition." *Journal of the Early Republic* 35, no. 4 (2015): 599–629.

Cook, Robert J. *Civil War Memories: Contesting the Past in the United States Since 1865.* Baltimore, MD: Johns Hopkins University Press, 2017.

Corcoran, Michael. *For Which It Stands: An Anecdotal Biography of the American Flag.* New York: Simon & Schuster, 2002.

Cornelius, Steven H. *Music of the Civil War Era.* Westport, CT: Greenwood Press, 2004.

Craughwell, Thomas J. *The Greatest Brigade: How the Irish Brigade Cleared the Way to Victory in the American Civil War.* Beverly, MA: Fair Winds Press, 2011.

Cummings, Alex Sayf. *Democracy of Sound: Music Piracy and the Remaking of American Copyright in the Twentieth Century.* New York, NY: Oxford University Press, 2013.

Davis, James A. *Maryland, My Maryland: Music and Patriotism During the American Civil War.* Lincoln: University of Nebraska Press, 2019.

———. *Music Along the Rapidan: Civil War Soldiers, Music and Community During Winter Quarters, Virginia.* Lincoln: University of Nebraska Press, 2014.

———. "Music and Gallantry in Combat During the American Civil War." *American Music* 26, no. 2 (2010): 141–72.

Delaney, Enda. "Directions in Historiography: Our Island Story? Towards a Transnational History of Late Modern Ireland." *Irish Historical Studies* 148 (2011): 83–105.

———. "Migration and Diaspora." In *The Oxford Handbook of Modern Irish History*, edited by Alvin Jackson, 126–47. Oxford: Oxford University Press, 2014.

Delaney, Enda, and Donald M. MacRaild. "Irish Migration, Networks and Ethnic Identities Since 1750: An Introduction." *Immigrants & Minorities: Historical Studies in Ethnicity, Migration and Diaspora* 23, nos. 2–3 (2005): 127–42.

Demers, Joanna. *Steal This Music: How Intellectual Property Law Affects Musical Creativity*. Athens: University of Georgia Press, 2006.

Doyle, Don H. *The Cause of All Nations: An International History of the American Civil War*. New York, NY: Basic Books, 2015.

Drudy, P. J., ed. *The Irish in America: Emigration, Assimilation and Impact*. Cambridge: Cambridge University Press, 1985.

Duff, John B. *The Irish in the United States*. Belmont, CA: Wadsworth Publishing Company, 1971.

Egan, Timothy. *The Immortal Irishman: The Irish Revolutionary Who Became an American Hero*. New York, NY: Houghton Mifflin Harcourt 2016.

Erie, Steven P. *Rainbow's End: Irish-Americans and the Dilemmas of Urban Machine Policies, 1840–1985*. Berkeley: University of California Press, 1988.

Fallows, Marjorie R. *Irish Americans: Identity and Assimilation*. Hoboken, NJ: Prentice-Hall, 1979.

Fanning, Charles, ed. *New Perspectives on the Irish Diaspora*. Carbondale: Southern Illinois University Press, 2000.

Fenton, Laurence. "Charles Rowcroft, Irish-Americans, and the 'Recruitment Affair,' 1855–56." *The Historical Journal* 53, no. 4 (2010): 963–82.

Fitzgerald, Mark, and John O'Flynn, eds. *Music and Identity in Ireland and Beyond*. Farnham: Ashgate Publishing, 2014.

Fitzpatrick, David. "Irish Emigration in the Later Nineteenth Century." *Irish Historical Studies* 22 (1980): 126–43.

Fleischmann, Aloys. "Granny Wales, and the Mulberry Tree." *Isaiah Thomas Broadside Ballads Project:* http://www.americanantiquarian.org/thomasballads/items/show/120.

Foner, Eric. *The Fiery Trial: Abraham Lincoln and American Slavery*. New York: W. W. Norton & Company, 2010.

Foreman, Amanda. *A World on Fire: An Epic History of Two Nations Divided*. London: Penguin, 2011.

Fowke, Edith. "Canadian Variations of a Civil War Song." *Midwest Folklore* 13, no. 2 (1963): 101–4.

Fuller, Randall. *From Battlefields Rising: How the Civil War Transformed American Literature*. New York, NY: Oxford University Press, 2011.

Gallagher, Tom, and James O' Connell, eds. *Contemporary Irish Studies*. Manchester: Manchester University Press, 1983.

Garvey, Ellen Gruber. *Writing With Scissors: American Scrapbooks from the Civil War to the Harlem Renaissance.* New York: Oxford University Press, 2013.

Gebhardt, Nicholas. *Vaudeville Melodies: Popular Musicians and Mass Entertainment in American Culture, 1870–1929.* Chicago: University of Chicago Press, 2017.

Gleeson, David T. "Another 'Lost Cause': The Irish in the South Remember the Confederacy." *Southern Culture* (2011): 50–74.

———. "Ethnicity." In *A Companion to the U.S. Civil War,* edited by Aaron Sheehan-Dean, 763–78. Hoboken, NJ: Wiley-Blackwell, 2014.

———. "Irish Rebels, Southern Rebels: The Irish Confederates." In *Civil War Citizens: Race, Ethnicity, and Identity in America's Bloodiest Conflict,* edited by Susannah J. Ural, 133–57. New York: New York University Press, 2010.

———. "The Forgotten Nationalist: John Mitchel, Race, and Irish American Identity." *Reviews in American History* 38, no. 4 (2010): 658–63.

———. *The Green and the Gray: The Irish in the Confederate States of America.* Chapel Hill: University of North Carolina Press, 2013.

———. "'To Live and Die [for] Dixie': Irish Civilians and the Confederate States of America." *Irish Studies Review* 18, no. 2 (2010): 139–53.

Gleeson, David T., and Brendan J. Buttimer. "'We Are Irish Everywhere': Irish Immigrant Networks in Charleston, South Carolina, and Savannah, Georgia." *Immigrants & Minorities: Historical Studies in Ethnicity, Migration and Diaspora* 23, nos. 2–3 (2005): 183–205.

Gordon, Michael A. *The Orange Riots: Irish Political Violence in New York City, 1870 and 1871.* Ithaca, NY: Cornell University Press, 2009.

Grant, Alfred. *The American Civil War and the British Press.* Jefferson, NC: McFarland & Company, 2000.

Green, Nancy L. "Expatriation, Expatriates and Expats: The American Transformation of a Concept." *American Historical Review* 114, no. 2 (2009): 307–28.

Griffin, William D., ed. *The Irish in America, 550–1972: A Chronology and Fact Book.* Dobbs Ferry, NY: Oceana Publications, 1973.

Griffith, Arthur, ed. *Meagher of the Sword: Speeches of Thomas Francis Meagher in Ireland, 1846–1848.* Dublin: M. H. Gill & Son, 1916.

Grimes, Robert R. *How Shall We Sing in a Foreign Land? Music of Irish Catholic Immigrants in the Antebellum United States.* Notre Dame, IN: University of Notre Dame Press, 1996.

Hanchett, William. *Irish: Charles G. Halpine in Civil War America.* Syracuse, NY: Syracuse University Press, 1970.

Hannan, Leonie, and Sarah Longair, eds. *History through Material Culture.* Manchester: Manchester University Press, 2017.

Harris, Ruth-Ann M., and Sally K. Sommers Smith. "The Eagle and the Harp: The

Enterprising Byrne Brothers of County Monaghan." *Irish Studies Review* 18, no. 2 (2010): 173–83.

Harwell, Richard Barksdale. *Confederate Music.* Chapel Hill: University of North Carolina Press, 1950.

Heaps, Willard A., and Porter W. Heaps. *The Singing Sixties: The Spirit of Civil War Days Drawn from the Music of the Times.* Norman: University of Oklahoma Press, 1960.

Hendren, J. W. *A Study of Ballad Rhythm with Special Reference to Ballad Music.* New York: Gordian Press, 1966.

Herson, John. *Divergent Paths: Family Histories of Irish Emigrants in Britain, 1820–1920.* Manchester: Manchester University Press, 2015.

Hopkison, Michael A. "America and Ireland 1776–1976: The American Identity and the Irish Connection: Proceedings of the United States Bicentennial Conference of Cumann Merriman, Ennis, August 1976." *Journal of American Studies* 15, no. 2 (1981): 269–70.

Hunter, Jerry. *Sons of Arthur, Children of Lincoln: Welsh Writing from the American Civil War.* Cardiff: University of Wales Press, 2007.

Janney, Caroline E. *Remembering the Civil War: Reunion and the Limits of Reconciliation.* Chapel Hill: University of North Carolina Press, 2013.

Jensen, Richard. "'No Irish Need Apply': A Myth of Victimization." *Journal of Social History* 36, no. 2 (2002): 405–29.

Jones, Catherine. *Literature and Music in the Atlantic World, 1767–1867.* Edinburgh: Edinburgh University Press, 2014.

Jones, Martha S. *Birthright Citizens: A History of Race and Rights in Antebellum America.* Cambridge: Cambridge University Press, 2018.

Jordan, Brian Matthew. *Marching Home: Union Veterans and Their Unending Civil War.* New York, NY: W. W. Norton, 2015.

Kaskowitz, Sheryl. *God Bless America: The Surprising History of an Iconic Song.* New York, NY: Oxford University Press, 2013.

Kaufman, Will. *The Civil War in American Culture.* Edinburgh: Edinburgh University Press, 2006.

Keating, Ryan W. *Shades of Green: Irish Regiments, American Soldiers, and Local Communities in the Civil War Era.* New York, NY: Fordham University Press, 2017.

Kelley, Bruce C., and Mark A. Snell, eds. *Bugle Resounding: Musicians and Music of the Civil War Era.* Columbia: University of Missouri Press, 2004.

Kelly, Mary C. *The Shamrock and the Lily: The New York Irish and the Creation of a Transatlantic Identity, 1845–1921.* New York, NY: Peter Lang, 2007.

Kenny, Kevin. *The American Irish: A History.* Harlow: Longman, 2000.

———. "Diaspora and Comparison: The Global Irish as a Case Study." *Journal of American History* 90, no. 1 (2003): 134–62.

———. "'Freedom and Unity': Lincoln in Irish Political Discourse." In *The Global Lincoln,* edited by Richard Carwardine and Jay Sexton, 157–71. New York: Oxford University Press, 2011.

———, ed. *New Directions in Irish-American History.* Madison: University of Wisconsin Press, 2003.

———. "Twenty Years of Irish American Historiography." *Journal of American Ethnic History* 28, no. 4 (2009), 67–75.

Knight, David. "Thomas Francis Meagher: His Stonyhurst Years." *Decis: Journal of the Waterford Archaeological and Historical Society* 59 (2003): 41–52.

Kramer, Lawrence, ed. *Walt Whitman and Modern Music: War, Desire, and the Trials of Nationhood.* New York, NY: Garland Publishing, 2000.

Lee, J. J., and Marion R. Casey, eds. *Making the Irish American: History and Heritage of the Irish in the United States.* New York: New York University Press, 2006.

Lighter, Jonathan. *The Best Antiwar Song Ever Written.* Windsor: Loomis House Press, 2012.

Lohman, Laura. *Hail Columbia! American Music and Politics in the Early Nation.* New York: Oxford University Press, 2020.

Lott, Eric. *Love & Theft: Blackface Minstrelsy and the American Working Class.* New York: Oxford University Press, 2013.

Loughlin, James. "Allegiance and Illusion: Queen Victoria's Irish Visit of 1849." *History* 87, no. 288 (2002): 491–513.

MacDonagh, Thomas. "Marching Song of the Irish Volunteers." *The Irish Review (Dublin)* 3, no. 34 (1913): 500–502.

Mahar, William J. *Behind the Burnt Cork Mask: Early Blackface Minstrelsy and Antebellum American Popular Culture.* Champaign: University of Illinois Press, 1999.

McCaffrey, Lawrence J. *The Irish Diaspora in America.* Bloomington: Indiana University Press, 1976.

McCarthy, Cal. *Green, Blue and Grey: The Irish in the American Civil War.* Cork: The Collins Press, 2009.

McGarry, Stephen. *Irish Brigades Abroad: From the Wild Geese to the Napoleonic Wars.* Dublin: The History Press Ireland, 2013.

McGill, Meredith L. *American Literature and the Culture of Reprinting, 1834–1853.* Philadelphia: University of Pennsylvania Press, 2003.

McPherson, James M. *For Cause and Comrades: Why Men Fought in the Civil War.* New York: Oxford University Press, 1997.

McWhiney, Grady, and Perry D. Jamison. *Attack and Die: Civil War Military Tactics and the Southern Heritage.* Tuscaloosa: University of Alabama Press, 1982.

McWhirter, Christian. *Battle Hymns: The Power and Popularity of Music in the Civil War.* Chapel Hill: University of North Carolina Press, 2012.

———. "Music." In *A Companion to the U.S. Civil War*, edited by Aaron Sheehan-Dean, 1003–20. Hoboken, NJ: Wiley-Blackwell, 2014.

Meagher, Timothy J., ed. *From Paddy to Studs: Irish-American Communities in the Turn of the Century Era, 1880 to 1920*. New York, NY: Greenwood Press, 1986.

Miller, Kerby A. *Emigrants and Exiles: Ireland and the Irish Exodus to North America*. New York: Oxford University Press, 1985.

———. "Emigrants and Exiles: Irish Cultures and Irish Emigration to North America, 1790–1922." *Irish Historical Studies* 22, no. 86 (1980): 97–125.

———. *Ireland and Irish America: Culture, Class, and Transatlantic Migration*. Dublin: Field Day, 2008.

Miller, Kerby A., and Bruce D. Boling. "Golden Streets, Bitter Tears: The Image of America during the Era of Mass Migration." *Journal of American Ethnic History* 10 (1990–91): 16–35.

Miller, Kerby A., Arnold Schrier, Bruce D. Boling, and David N. Doyle, eds. *Irish Immigrants in the Land of Canaan: Letters and Memoirs from Colonial and Revolutionary America, 1675–1815*. New York: Oxford University Press, 2003.

Miller, Rebecca, S. "Irish Traditional Music in the United States." In *Making the Irish American: History and Heritage of the Irish in the United States*, ed. J. J. Lee and Marion R. Casey, 411–16. New York: New York University Press, 2006.

Milner, Dan. *The Unstoppable Irish: Songs and Integration of the New York Irish, 1783–1883*. Notre Dame, IN: University of Notre Dame Press, 2019.

Moloney, Mick. "Irish-American Popular Music." In *Making the Irish American: History and Heritage of the Irish in the United States*, ed. J. J. Lee and Marion R. Casey, 381–405. New York: New York University Press, 2006.

Monod, David. *Vaudeville and the Making of Modern Entertainment, 1890–1925*. Chapel Hill: University of North Carolina Press, 2020.

Moseley, Caroline. "Irrepressible Conflict: Differences between Northern and Southern Songs of the Civil War." *Journal of Popular Culture* 25, no. 2 (1991): 45–56.

Moser, David J., and Cheryl L. Slay. *Music Copyright in Law*. Boston, MA: Cengage Learning, 2012.

Moss, Kenneth. "St. Patrick's Day Celebrations and the Foundation of Irish-American Identity, 1845–1875." *Journal of Social History* 29, no. 1 (1995): 125–48.

Moulden, John. *Thousands Are Sailing: A Brief Song History of Irish Emigration*. Portrush: Ulstersongs, 1994.

Murphy, Angela F. "Daniel O'Connell and the 'American Eagle' in 1845: Slavery, Diplomacy, Nativism and the Collapse of America's First Irish Nationalist Movement." *Journal of American Ethnic History* 26, no. 2 (2007): 3–26.

National Museum of Ireland, Decorative Arts and History. *Soldiers and Chiefs: The Irish at Home and Abroad from 1550*. Dublin: History Ireland, 2007.

Nelson, Scott Reynolds. *Steel Drivin' Man: John Henry, the Untold Story of an American Legend.* New York: Oxford University Press, 2008.

Nettl, Bruno. *The Study of Ethnomusicology: Thirty-one Issues and Concepts.* Champaign: University of Illinois Press, 2005.

Nicholls, David, ed. *The Cambridge History of American Music.* Cambridge: Cambridge University Press, 1998.

Nie, Michael de. "A Medley Mob of Irish-American Plotters and Irish Dupes": The British Press and Transatlantic Fenianism." *Journal of British Studies* 40, no. 2 (2001): 213–40.

Nolan, Bobbie. "Language and Identity Among Irish Migrants in London, Philadelphia and San Francisco, 1850–1920." PhD diss., University of Edinburgh, 2020.

O'Boyle, Seán. *The Irish Song Tradition.* Dublin: Gilbert Dalton, 1976.

O'Brien, Gillian. *Blood Runs Green: The Murder That Transfixed Gilded Age Chicago.* Chicago, IL: University of Chicago Press, 2015.

O'Day, Alan. "Imagined Irish Communities: Networks of Social Communication of the Irish Diaspora in the United States and Britain in the Late Nineteenth and Early Twentieth Centuries." *Immigrants & Minorities: Historical Studies in Ethnicity, Migration and Diaspora* 23, nos. 2–3 (2005): 399–424.

O'Flaherty, Ronan, and Jacqui Hynes, eds. *Vinegar Hill: The Last Stand of the Wexford Rebels of 1798.* Dublin: Four Courts Press, 2021.

O'Hogain, Daithi. *The Hero in Irish Folklore.* Dublin: Gill and Macmillan, 1985.

Puleo, Stephen. *Voyage of Mercy: The USS Jamestown, The Irish Famine, and the Remarkable Story of America's First Humanitarian Mission.* New York, NY: St. Martin's Press, 2000.

Quinn, James. *Young Ireland and the Writing of Irish History.* Dublin: University College Dublin Press, 2015.

Quinn, John F. "The Rise and Fall of Repeal: Slavery and Irish Nationalism in Antebellum Philadelphia." *Pennsylvania Magazine of History and Biography* 130, no. 1 (2006): 45–78.

Ritchie, Fiona, and Doug Orr. *Wayfaring Strangers: The Musical Voyage from Scotland and Ulster to Appalachia.* Chapel Hill: University of North Carolina Press, 2014.

Saffle, Michael. "Across a Great Divide: Irish American Music and Musicians of the Civil War Era." In *Bugle Resounding: Musicians and Music of the Civil War Era,* ed. Bruce C. Kelley and Mark A. Snell, 169–201. Columbia: University of Missouri Press, 2004.

Samito, Christian G. *Becoming American Under Fire: Irish Americans, African Americans, and the Politics of Citizenship During the Civil War Era.* Ithaca, NY: Cornell University Press, 2009.

Schmidt, Jay. *Fort Warren: New England's Most Historic Civil War Site.* Amherst, MA: UBT Press, 2003.

Scroggins, Michael C. *The Scotch-Irish Influence on Country Music in the Carolinas: Border Ballads, Fiddle Tunes and Sacred Songs.* Cheltenham: The History Press, 2013.

Sheppard, W. Anthony. "Exoticism." In *Oxford Bibliography in Music,* ed. Kate van Orden. New York: Oxford University Press, 2016. https://www.oxfordbibliographies.com /view/document/obo-9780199757824/obo-9780199757824-0123.xml?rskey=mCBY94 &result=1&q=Exoticism#firstMatch.

Shields, Hugh. *Narrative Singing in Ireland: Lays, Ballads, Come-all-yes and Other Songs.* Dublin: Irish Academic Press, 1993.

Shiels, Damian. *The Forgotten Irish: Irish Emigrant Experiences in America.* Dublin: The History Press Ireland, 2016.

———. *The Irish in the American Civil War.* Dublin: The History Press Ireland, 2013.

Sim, David. *A Union Forever: The Irish Question and U.S. Foreign Relations in the Victorian Age.* Ithaca, NY: Cornell University Press, 2013.

Snay, Mitchel. *Fenians, Freedman, and Southern Whites: Race and Nationality in the Era of Reconstruction.* Baton Rouge: Louisiana State University Press, 2007.

Soini, Wayne. *Porter's Secret: Fitz John Porter's Monument Decoded.* Portsmouth, NH: Jetty House, 2011.

Sood, Arun. *Robert Burns and the United States of America: Poetry, Print, and Memory, 1786–1866.* London: Palgrave Macmillan, 2018.

Spann, Edward K. "Union Green: The Irish Community and the Civil War." In *The New York Irish,* ed. Ronald H. Bayor and Timothy J. Meagher, 193–209. Baltimore: Johns Hopkins University Press, 1996.

Stauffer, John, and Benjamin Soskis. *The Battle Hymn of the Republic: A Biography of the Song That Marches On.* New York: Oxford University Press, 2013.

Stevenson, Louise L. *The Victorian Homefront: American Thought and Culture, 1860–1880.* Ithaca, NY: Cornell University Press, 2001.

Stone, James H. "The Merchant and the Muse: Commercial Influences on American Popular Music Before the Civil War." *The Business History Review* 30, no. 1 (1956): 1–17.

———. "War Music and War Psychology in the Civil War." *Journal of Abnormal and Social Psychology* 36, no. 4 (1941): 543–60.

Taylor, Clare, ed. *Wales and the American Civil War.* Aberystwyth: William Reese Co., 1972.

Thompson, E. P. *Customs in Common: Studies in Traditional Popular Culture.* New York, NY: The New Press, 1993.

Tucker, Ann L. *Newest Born of Nations: European Nationalist Movements and the Making of the Confederacy.* Charlottesville: University of Virginia Press, 2020.

Tucker, Phillip Thomas. *Irish Confederates: The Civil War's Forgotten Soldiers.* Abilene, TX: McWhinney Foundation Press, 2006.

Tyrrel, Ian. *Transnational Nation: United States History in Global Perspective Since 1789.* Basingstoke: Palgrave Macmillan, 2007.

Ural, Susannah J. *The Harp and the Eagle: Irish-American Volunteers and the Union Army, 1861–1865.* New York: New York University Press, 2006.

———. "'Remember Your Country and Keep Up Its Credit': Irish Volunteers and the Union Army, 1861–1865." *Journal of Military History* 69, no. 2 (2005): 331–59.

———. "'Ye Sons of Green Erin Assemble': Northern Irish American Catholics and the Union War Effort, 1861–1865." In *Civil War Citizens: Race, Ethnicity, and Identity in America's Bloodiest Conflict,* edited by Susannah J. Ural, 99–132. New York: New York University Press, 2010.

Warfield, Derek. *Irish Songster of the American Civil War: Irish Songs, Ballads, Musical History and Lyrical and Poetic Legacy of the American Civil War.* Dublin: Derek Warfield, 1998.

Williams, Alfred M. "Folk-Songs of the Civil War." *Journal of American Folklore* 5, no. 19 (October–December 1892): 265–83.

Williams, Gavin, ed. *Hearing the Crimean War: Wartime Sound and the Unmaking of Sense.* New York: Oxford University Press, 2019.

Williams, William H. A. *'Twas Only an Irishman's Dream: The Image of Ireland and the Irish in American Popular Song Lyrics, 1800–1920.* Champaign: University of Illinois Press, 1996.

Wittke, Carl. *The Irish in America.* Baton Rouge: Louisiana State University Press, 1956.

Wylie, Paul R. *The Irish General, Thomas Francis Meagher.* Norman: University of Oklahoma Press, 2007.

Zimmermann, Georges-Denis. *Songs of Irish Rebellion: Political Street Ballads and Rebel Songs, 1780–1900.* Hatboro, PA: Folklore Associates, 1967.

INDEX

❋-❋-❋-❋